UNIVERSITY OF
WOLVERHAMPTON

The English Town, 1680–1840

THEMES IN BRITISH SOCIAL HISTORY

edited by John Stevenson

This series covers the important aspects of British social history from the Renaissance to the present day. Topics include education, poverty, health, religion, leisure, crime and popular protest, some of which are treated in more than one volume. The books are written for undergraduates, postgraduates and the general reader, and each volume combines a general approach to the subject with the primary research of the author.

Currently available:

THE ENGLISH FAMILY 1450–1700 *Ralph A. Houlbrooke*
POVERTY AND POLICY IN TUDOR AND STUART ENGLAND *Paul Slack*
CRIME IN EARLY MODERN ENGLAND 1550–1750 (Second Edition) *J. A. Sharpe*
POPULAR CULTURES IN ENGLAND 1550–1750 *Barry Reay*
GENDER IN ENGLISH SOCIETY, 1650–1850: The Emergence of Separate Spheres? *Robert Shoemaker*
THE ENGLISH TOWN 1680–1840: GOVERNMENT, SOCIETY AND CULTURE *Rosemary Sweet*
POPULAR DISTURBANCES IN ENGLAND 1700–1832 (Second Edition) *John Stevenson*
LITERATURE AND SOCIETY IN EIGHTEENTH-CENTURY ENGLAND *W. A. Speck*
CRIME AND SOCIETY IN ENGLAND 1750–1900 (Second Edition) *Clive Emsley*
THE LABOURING CLASSES IN EARLY INDUSTRIAL ENGLAND 1750–1850 *John Rule*
LAND AND SOCIETY IN ENGLAND 1750–1980 *G. E. Mingay*
SEX, POLITICS AND SOCIETY: The Regulation of Sexuality since 1800 (Second Edition) *Jeffrey Weeks*
THE WORKING CLASS IN BRITAIN 1850–1939 *John Benson*
THE RISE OF THE CONSUMER SOCIETY IN BRITAIN 1880–1980 *John Benson*
HEALTH AND SOCIETY IN TWENTIETH-CENTURY BRITAIN *Helen Jones*

The English Town, 1680–1840

Government, society and culture

ROSEMARY SWEET

Longman

Pearson Education Limited
Edinburgh Gate,
Harlow, Essex CM20 2JE,
United Kingdom
and Associated Companies throughout the world

*Published in the United States of America
by Pearson Education Inc., New York*

Visit us on the word wide web site at: http://www.awl-he.com

First published 1999

ISBN 0 582 317134 CSD
ISBN 0 582 317126 PPR

British Library Cataloguing in Publication Data

A catalogue record for this book is available from the British Library

Library of Congress Cataloging-in-Publication Data

Sweet, Rosemary.
The English town, 1680–1840 : government, society and culture /
Rosemary Sweet.
p.   cm. — (Themes in British social history)
Includes bibliographical references and index.
ISBN 0–582–31713–4 (csd). — ISBN 0–582–31712–6 (ppr)
1. Cities and towns—Great Britain—History.   2. Municipal
government—Great Britain—History.   I. Title.   II. Series.
HT133.S938   1999
307.76′0942—dc21   98–52960
                                                          CIP

Set by 35 in 10/12pt Baskerville
Produced by Addison Wesley Longman Singapore (Pte) Ltd.,
Printed in Singapore

Contents

List of Maps and Tables   vii
Author's Acknowledgements   ix
Publisher's Acknowledgements   xi
List of Abbreviations   xiii

1. *Introduction*   1

   Defining the Town   7
   Urban Demography   10
   Urban Typologies   14

2. *The Structures of Authority*   27

   Manorial Structures   28
   Parochial Structures   30
   Incorporated Bodies   33
   Trading Guilds   37
   Change through Legislation   42
   Statutory Bodies for Special Purposes   44
   The Consolidation of Oligarchy   56
   The Role of MPs   59
   Towns and the State   62
   After the Glorious Revolution   64

3. *Urban Administration*   75

   Regulating the Streets   76
   Street Lighting   81
   Urban Planning   84
   Water Supplies   86
   Clean Air and Pollution   88
   Law and Order: Riots and Disturbances   90
   Law and Order: Criminality   94
   Markets and Economic Regulation   98
   The Problem of the Poor   101
   Public Morality   104

Financing the Business of Government: Corporations   105
Local Rating Bodies   108
Personal Service and Public Duty   109

4. *The Divided Society*   115

The Franchise and Elections   117
Legal Challenges   122
Opposition and Conflict in Unincorporated Towns   123
Urban Radicalism   127
Radicalism: the Ways and Means   130

5. *Urban Government and the Movement for Reform*   141

Reform Renewal and Rationalisation   142
The Case for Reform   150
The Municipal Corporations Act of 1835   152

6. *Social Structure and Social Experience*   163

The Labouring Sort   164
The Middling Sort   179
Gentrification   191
Polarization and Politeness   198
Distinctions of Gender   203
Religion and Society in the Urban Community   207
Urban Dissent   211

7. *Urban Culture and the Urban Renaissance*   219

Perceptions of the Town   220
The Emergence of a Distinctive Urban Culture   228
Inns and Alehouses   231
The Assembly Rooms   234
Theatres   236
Musical Entertainments   238
Race Meetings   241
Walks, Gardens and Promenades   241
Literary Tastes and Literary Societies   243
Timing and Incidence of the Urban Renaissance   251

8. *Conclusion: Metropolitan Influence or
    Provincial Identity?*   257

Select Bibliography   267
Maps   273
Index   277

List of Maps and Tables

Maps

1   Distribution of urban settlements with over 2,500
    inhabitants in England and Wales in 1700   274

2   Distribution of urban settlements with over 2,500
    inhabitants in England and Wales in 1750   275

3   Distribution of urban settlements with over 2,500
    inhabitants in England and Wales in 1801   276

Tables

1   Urban population in thousands, *c.* 1670–1841   3–4

2   Number and size of urban settlements in England
    and Wales, 1700–1841   10

3a Population change in textile towns of East Anglia,
    southern England and the West Country   13

3b Population growth of the cotton towns, 1801–21   13

4   Patterns of employment, income, expenditure and
    residence, 1700–1840 (%)   165

Author's Acknowledgements

This book is the result of the frustration I felt as a research student at having to wade through the Webbs in order to make any progress towards understanding the workings of urban government in the eighteenth century. As will be clear to any reader, it is heavily indebted to their research, but it is, I hope, a little more user friendly. It was written whilst I was a junior research fellow at St John's College, Oxford and my biggest debt of gratitude, therefore, is to the fellows and the college, for providing the ideal surroundings, both intellectual and material, in which to undertake such a project. I would also like to thank the staff of the various libraries and record offices in which I worked, particularly those of the Bodleian Library, the Oxford History Faculty Library, St John' College Library, Brynmor Jones Library, University of Hull, Oxfordshire Archives, Southampton Record Office, Tyne and Wear Archive Service, West Devon Record Office and Winchester Record Office for their co-operation. John Stevenson was always a positive editorial force, and at Longman I met with a consistently friendly, helpful and efficient team. Both Paul Langford and Joanna Innes have always been unfailingly generous in their time, advice and encouragement, and this book would have been very much the worse but for them. I must also thank Hannah Barker and Alex Shepard who read and criticised the book in earlier incarnations, and Elaine Chalus for advice, support and frequent injections of good sense. Faramerz Dabhoiwala, Scott Mandelbrote, Michael Suarez, Tim Clayton, Perry Gauci, Jack Langton, Peter Borsay, David Eastwood, have all provided advice and information on numerous occasions. Finally, I must thank my family, who have already heard far more than they could ever want to know about eighteenth-century towns, for tolerating it all with patience and good humour.

Publisher's Acknowledgements

We are indebted to Oxford University Press for permission to reproduce the three maps from *The Impact of English Towns* by P. J. Corfield (1982).

List of Abbreviations

Archive Deposits
BCL   Bristol Central Library
Bodl.   Bodleian Library, Oxford
OCA   Oxford City Archives
PP   Parliamentary Papers
SDRO   South Devon Record Office
SRO   Somerset Record Office
TWAS   Tyne and Wear Archive Service

Journals and Periodicals
AmHR   *American Historical Review*
BIHR   *Bulletin of the Institute of Historical Research*
BJECS   *British Journal for Eighteenth-Century Studies*
EHR   *English Historical Review*
EcHR   *Economic History Review*
HJ   *Historical Journal*
JBS   *Journal of British Studies*
P&P   *Past and Present*
TDA   *Transactions of the Devonshire Association*
THSLC   *Transactions of the Historical Society of Lancashire and Cheshire*
TRHS   *Transactions of the Royal Historical Society*
VCH   *Victoria County History*

CHAPTER ONE

Introduction

Anyone who makes even a cursory examination of the historiography of eighteenth-century England over the last twenty years will be forcibly struck by how much of it is urban-based. Urban studies have transformed our understanding of the workings of eighteenth-century politics and society and the relationship between the metropolis and the provinces. Paul Langford's choice of title, *A Polite and Commercial People* (1989), for his volume covering the eighteenth century for the New Oxford History of England series, reflected the recent historiographical interest in urban society, and helped to ensure that issues surrounding the essentially *urban* polite and commercial society have remained to the fore in most subsequent scholarship. Some of the most fruitful recent research in eighteenth-century history, on the growth of the press and the public sphere, the rise of a consumer society, and the construction of class and gendered identities, has been carried out in a specifically urban context. The growth of urban society in the eighteenth century was demonstrably one of the most important elements in the dynamics of change which saw early modern England emerge from being a second-rate European power, essentially rural, under-industrialized, and with a system of 'confessional' politics, to being the leading world power with many recognisably modern attributes: an industrial, market-led economy; highly developed communications; and an increasingly secularised and liberal society. The study of towns and urban society, therefore, allows us access to many of the most important developments in eighteenth-century society. However, despite this fact, it is still relatively difficult to find any straightforward account of what it was like to live in a town, how towns functioned in terms of their government and administration, or

1

how they slotted into the larger structure of the nation state. The aim of this book is to provide an outline of the main characteristics of government and society in the English town over the long eighteenth century.

The period 1680–1840 arguably saw the English town undergo greater changes than in any preceding period, all of which were essentially the result of similarly unprecedented urban growth. The contrast between our two terminal points is, in many senses, remarkable. In 1680 the structure of government was still essentially that which had been inherited from the medieval period. By 1840, however, the groundwork for the modern town council, elected by a democratic, rate-paying franchise had been laid. Meanwhile, the balance of the nation's economy had shifted away from a primarily agricultural basis to a manufacturing one, and the proportion of the population living in towns had almost overtaken that of rural England. The country was well on the way to becoming a fully urbanized society, and the contrast between urban and rural society had deepened immeasurably. In the process, the structure of the urban system had been transformed. Town life was no longer synonymous with London; the metropolis lost the pre-eminence which it had enjoyed as economic and political arbiter at the beginning of the eighteenth century. Meanwhile, the ordering of the provincial towns underwent an extensive reshuffle. The old market towns of southern and eastern England fell down the ranks of the urban hierarchy and the balance of weight, in terms of population and political influence, had shifted towards the towns of the Midlands and the industrial north, which had become the engines of economic growth and the centres of extra-parliamentary activity.[1] Table 1, which lists the population by thousands in the largest English towns, from the late seventeenth century to the end of our period, illustrates the fluidity of the urban hierarchy. London dominates throughout, but towns like York or Colchester, which were pre-eminent at the start of our period, had sunk way down the rankings by 1841, while their place in the upper ranks was taken by urban upstarts such as Bradford or Bolton.

In the midst of flux and change, however, there were still continuities. A concentration on statistics and rankings masks the basic stability of the day-to-day experience of urban government and society. The first section of this book, chapters one and two, will establish how towns were governed – through what institutions and

1. Donald Read, *The English Provinces, c.1760–1960. A Study in Influence* (1964).

TABLE 1 *Urban population in thousands, c. 1670–1841*

c. 1670		c. 1700		c. 1750		1801		1821		1841	
London	475	London	575	London	675	London	959	London	1,600[7]	London	2,239
Norwich	20	Norwich	30	Bristol	50	Liverpool	83	Liverpool	138	Liverpool	286
Bristol	20	Bristol	21	Norwich	36	Manchester	75[1]	M'chester	126	M'chester	235
York	12	Newcastle	16	Newcastle	29	Birmingham	74	B'ham	102	B'ham	183
Newcastle	12	Exeter	14	Birmingham	24	Bristol	60	Bristol	85	Leeds	152
Colchester	9	York	12	Liverpool	22	Leeds	53	Sheffield	65	Bristol	124
Exeter	9	Gt. Yarmouth	10	Manchester	18	Sheffield	46	Leeds	63	Sheffield	111
Chester	8	Birmingham	8–9	Leeds	16	Plymouth	43[2]	Plymouth	55	Newcastle	90
Ipswich	8	Chester	}	Exeter	16	Newcastle	42[3]	Newcastle	54	Plymouth	70
Gt. Yarmouth	8	Colchester	}	Plymouth	15	Norwich	36	Norwich	50	Bradford	67
Plymouth	8	Ipswich	5–7	Chester	13	Portsmouth	33	Portsmouth	47	Hull	67
Worcester	8	Manchester	}	Coventry	13	Bath	33	Hull	45	Bath	63
Coventry	7	Plymouth	}	Nottingham	12	Hull	30	Bath	44	Norwich	62
Kings Lynn	7	Worcester	}	Sheffield	12	Nottingham	29	Nottingham	40	Stoke	54
Manchester	6	Bury St Ed.	}	York	11	Sunderland	26	Stoke	35	Leicester	53
Canterbury	6	Cambridge	}	Chatham	10	Stoke	23[4]	Bolton	32	Portsmouth	53
Leeds	6	Canterbury	}	Gt. Yarmouth	10	Chatham	23[5]	Sunderland	31	Salford	53
Birmingham	6	Chatham	}	Portsmouth	10	W'hampton	21[6]	Stockport	27	Nottingham	52
Cambridge	6	Coventry	}	Sunderland	10	Bolton	17	Bradford	26	Bolton	51
Hull	6	Gloucester	}	Worcester	10	Exeter	17	Preston	25	Preston	51
Salisbury	6	Hull	}			Leicester	17	Brighton	24	Stockport	50
Bury St Edmunds	5	Kings Lynn	}			Gt. Yarmouth	17	Exeter	23	Brighton	47
Leicester	5	Leeds	}			Stockport	17	Tynemouth	23	Oldham	43

TABLE 1   (*Cont'd*)

c. 1670		c. 1700	c. 1750	c. 1801		c. 1821		c. 1841	
Oxford	5	Leicester		York	16	Oldham	22	Sunderland	43
Shrewsbury	5	Liverpool		Coventry	16	York	22	W'hampton	36
Gloucester	5	Nottingham		Chester	16	Coventry	21	Derby	33
		Oxford		Shrewsbury	15	M'field	21	M'field	33
		Portsmouth } 5–7		Salford	14	Gt. Yarmouth	21	Coventry	31
		Salisbury				Chester	20	Exeter	31
		Shrewsbury				Shrewsbury	20	York	29
		Sunderland				Leiceseter	19	Halifax	28
		Tiverton				Dudley	18	Yarmouth	28
						Wigan	18	Worcester	27
						W'hampton	18	Wigan	26
						Derby	17	Tynemouth	25
						Halifax	17	S. Shields	23
						Ipswich	17	Shrewsbury	18
						S. Shields	17		
						Worcester	17		

Sources: E. A. Wrigley, *People, Cities and Wealth* (Cambridge, 1987), table 7.1, pp. 160–1; B. R. Mitchell and Phyllis Deane, *Abstract of British Historical Statistics* (Cambridge, 1962), pp. 24–6.

[1] Including Devonport.
[2] Including Gateshead.
[3] Stoke and Burslem.
[4] Including the Medway towns Chatham, Rochester and Gillingham.
[5] Including Wolverhampton, Willenhall, Bilston and Wednesfield.
[6] The 1821 and 1841 figures are for greater London.

Manchester and Salford are listed separately in this table, but many modern sources combine the two.

by which citizens. We will examine the record for efficiency and improvement and will consider the justification of some of the criticisms levied against them. Chapters three and four look more closely at the questions of politics and reform. Urban politics interacted very closely with parliamentary politics, given that the majority of the nation's MPs were returned by the parliamentary boroughs.[2] Reform was agitated at both a national and local level and there was considerable overlap in aims, rhetoric and personnel. Consequently, urban radicalism has generally been considered primarily in the context of parliamentary reform but, as chapter four will show, it was also a movement directed towards the reform of local government and was deeply rooted in local contests over power within the urban community. On paper, the decade of the 1830s brought about extensive change to the parliamentary franchise and the structure of incorporated boroughs, but we will look at these changes from the 'bottom up', which gives a very different perspective on reform, substantially modifying caricatures of corrupt and inefficient urban government. The third section, chapters five and six, will look in greater detail at the social structure of towns and the emergence of a distinctively urban, class-based society. Social or class identities can only be experienced through social interaction, and we will be looking at the occasions and contexts in which they were forged. We will discuss how the experience of government, urban improvement and political activity, discussed in the earlier chapters, contributed to the process and we will extend our view to encompass a broader range of urban cultural and social activity. Finally, we will develop the idea of what it actually meant to contemporaries to live in a town; what it was that attracted them to the urban lifestyle and, alternatively, what appalled them. London provoked the most powerful reactions, both positive and negative, and the influence of metropolitan culture and fashions upon provincial towns has always been emphasised. However, we will be challenging these assumptions, arguing instead in favour of a much stronger sense of provincial pride and urban identity.

This book covers a substantial and eventful period of history, and certain aspects of government and society must necessarily receive fuller treatment than others. The unreformed parliamentary system, and the movement for political reform in towns, has been the subject of a considerable amount of important research, which this book does not have the scope to cover. Similarly, the treatment

2. Until 1801, 405 of the nation's 558 MPs were returned by borough constituencies.

of the emergence of class identities, working class radicalism and popular disturbances offered here cannot do justice to the literature available on the subject. Much of the material in this book will deal with the business of government and administration in towns and the conduct of local politics. Despite the interest in the vitality of the unreformed electorate and the interaction between centre and locality, which has been evinced in so many recent political studies, there has been surprisingly little interest in the local context in which these political processes took place. It is remarkable that historians (and this study is no exception) are still so heavily indebted to the work of Sidney and Beatrice Webb, who carried out their research at the end of the last century.[3] The mechanics of urban government, the interaction of urban elites, and the attitudes and expectations of the governors and the governed require more study. Some of the ground in this book retraces that covered by Penelope Corfield in her pathbreaking study *The Impact of English Towns, 1700–1800* (1982), which was the first attempt to survey the political and cultural experience of eighteenth-century towns, rather than simply concentrating on economic and demographic features. Published nearly twenty years ago, it is still an immensely valuable introduction to the subject, but it has been a victim of its own success, in that by being so suggestive it has opened up many avenues of research which this volume, it is hoped, will go some way towards integrating. Its terminal point in 1800 is a logical one but, since so many studies of nineteenth-century towns take the Municipal Corporations Act of 1835 or the debates instigated by Edwin Chadwick in the 1830s on the health of the towns as their starting point, thereby locating themselves firmly in the Victorian era, there is something of a hiatus in the urban historiography of the early nineteenth century. By expanding the scope of this volume to 1840, it is hoped that something will be done to bridge this gap, and to highlight both the continuities and the extent of change which took place between the Georgian and the Victorian town. A similar hiatus afflicts the student of urban culture: Peter Borsay's admirable study of urban culture in the years 1660–1770 has informed all subsequent discussion of developments in the cultural life of towns, but when we look beyond 1770, and at towns which were less obviously cultural centres, the model of the 'urban renaissance' must be adapted and modified.

3. Sidney and Beatrice Webb, *English Local Government from the Revolution to the Municipal Corporations Act*, 9 vols. (1906–20).

Defining the Town

Late seventeenth-century England was not an urban society: in 1700 it has been estimated that over three-quarters of the population was rural, and of the 25 per cent inhabiting towns, one third to one half was concentrated in London. London, with a population of 575,000, far outstripped all the other contenders in the urban hierarchy – the next biggest town was Norwich at a little under 30,000, and the only other town with a population over 20,000 was Bristol.[4] By 1840, however, nearly 50 per cent of the population was living in towns, and one-third of the population was living in towns with a population in excess of 20,000.[5] Statistics such as these beg the question of what we mean by a town, and before we pursue a discussion of urban growth, we should establish a definition for what constituted urban status. Definitions of towns hinge on population, function (or economic role) and nucleation – that is, the extent to which a population was concentrated in one place, rather than strung out over a large and loosely populated area with no centre. Attempts to distinguish between village, town, borough or city, are not, in general, very helpful. Originally 'town' or 'tun' simply denoted any kind of settlement. By the eighteenth century it was more commonly used for larger centres, but nevertheless a settlement with a population of only 200 or 300 still might be termed a town by some observers. Similarly, 'city' did not necessarily denote greater size. Places which had historically acquired certain legal privileges were accorded the status of city, or borough, under a charter. However, even when they subsequently declined to a minimal size, they were still referred to as such. Romney Marsh in Kent, for example, was essentially a dispersed rural settlement, but because it had acquired a corporation it was theoretically a

---

4. Peter Borsay, *The English Urban Renaissance. Culture and Society in the Provincial Town, 1660–1770* (Oxford, 1989); P. J. Corfield, 'A provincial capital in the late seventeenth century: the case of Norwich', in Peter Clark and Paul Slack (eds), *Crisis and Order in English Towns, 1500–1700* (1972), pp. 263–70; Walter Minchinton, 'The Port of Bristol in the eighteenth century', in Patrick McGrath (ed.), *Bristol in the Eighteenth Century* (Newton Abbot, 1972), p. 128; Jack Langton, 'Urban growth and economic change from the seventeenth century to 1841', in Peter Clark (ed.), *Cambridge Urban History of Britain*, vol. 2 (Cambridge, forthcoming).

5. C. M. Law, 'The growth of urban population in England and Wales, 1801–1901', in *Transactions of the Institute of British Geographers*, 41 (1967), p. 130, table v; see also E. A. Wrigley, 'Urban growth and agricultural change: England and the continent in the early modern period', in E. A. Wrigley, *People, Cities and Wealth* (Cambridge, 1987), pp. 157–96.

borough.[6] Ely, being the site of a cathedral see, was a city, but with a population of only 3,400 in 1775, had little else in common with a city such as Norwich, which was a busy and dynamic manufacturing town, second only to London at the start of the century[7]. Meanwhile, Manchester, which was governed by the remnants of the rural manorial structure throughout the eighteenth century, could be referred to as a village, albeit a large one, not least by Daniel Defoe. Most historians have tended to decide on a minimum population figure from which to work, when discussing urban growth, but this can vary considerably. Penelope Corfield and C. M. Law selected 2,500 as their minimum figure, but it is important to remember that there were probably only about 70 towns of 2,500 or more in 1700, which suggests that this threshold might be too high.[8] Population figures are in themselves problematic, and evidence before the nineteenth-century census is sketchy and unreliable. Tax returns, bills of mortality and local censuses are used to try to arrive at reasonable estimates, but the vast number of imponderables – Dissenters whose births were not registered, seamen or soldiers away on service, the choice of multiplier for household size – mean that the plausible air of certainty, which a recital of population figures gives to statements, should always be greeted with a certain amount of scepticism.

A town cannot be defined simply in terms of its population; one must also take into account its function, role and structure. 'Urbanity' is not simply about levels of population. A settlement of 1,000 or less could qualify as a town because it was a centre of exchange and distribution, and because the economy was not primarily dependent upon agricultural production. The question of nucleation is also important, as it denotes the concentration of population and functions within a restricted area. This differentiates the town from more dispersed settlements and, in turn, it gives rise to distinctive social structures and social tensions. Peter Borsay, who adopted a rather more flexible approach than Corfield, including settlements of 500–1,000 in his discussion of urban culture, has identified around 700 small towns all over England, which serviced hinterlands of

6. Some of these problems of nomenclature are explored in Richard Lawton, 'Census data for urban areas', in Richard Lawton (ed.), *The Census and Social Structure* (1978), pp. 82–145.

7. Estimate for Ely taken from C. M. Law, 'Some notes on the urban population in the eighteenth century', *Local Historian*, x (1972), pp. 13–26.

8. P. J. Corfield, *The Impact of English Towns, 1700–1800* (Oxford, 1982), pp. 6–116; Law, 'Some notes on the urban population' and P. J. Corfield, 'Growth of urban population'.

between three to six miles, and represented the 'bedrock of the urban system'. It is important to remember that the cultural, social and economic role of *small towns* was of considerable influence until the end of our period – there is often a tendency to focus exclusively on the largest towns.[9] As we shall see, these places could support markets, inns, shops, theatres, book clubs – all of which can be seen as 'urban' features. In 1801 fourteen per cent of the population was still living in towns of between 2,000 and 20,000, and even in 1851, small towns and their rural hinterland accounted for 62 per cent of the population.[10] Consequently, more recent assessments of urban growth have generally followed Borsay, including towns under 1,000 in discussions of urbanization, given that most of these settlements did not cease to be 'urban' in a later period.[11] By 1840 some readjustments to the definition of urban status are needed. A population of 5,000, for example, would constitute a 'small' town by nineteenth-century standards, whereas in the seventeenth century this would have indicated a fairly major urban centre. The level of population needed to sustain a viable urban community had therefore changed. Tiny market towns could no longer compete with their larger and more successful neighbours, who increasingly benefitted from specialised industry and capital-heavy, mechanized forms of production. Nor could they offer the same range of services and goods, with the consequence that they were unable to retain their command over the custom of their hinterlands. As improved transport and communications facilitated travel between the greater urban centres, the smaller centres were often bypassed and some settlements underwent de–urbanization.[12] Whereas, in

9. Borsay, *The English Urban Renaissance, Culture and Society in the Provincial Town, 1660–1770* (Oxford, 1989), pp. 3–5; P. J. Corfield, 'Small towns, large implications. Social and cultural roles of small towns in eighteenth-century England and Wales', *British Journal for Eighteenth-Century Studies*, 10 (1987), pp. 125–38; For a discussion of the issues surrounding the historiography of the 'small town' see Peter Clark's introduction to Peter Clark (ed.), *Small Towns in Early Modern Europe* (Cambridge, 1995), pp. 1–21 and his article in the same volume, 'Small towns in England, 1550–1850: national and regional population trends', pp. 90–120; Michael Reed discusses their cultural importance in ibid., 'The cultural role of small towns in England 1600–1800' pp. 121–47.

10. J. D. Marshall, 'The rise and fall of the Cumbrian market town, 1660–1900', *Northern History*, xix (1983), p. 132; See also Law, 'Growth of urban population', p. 141, table xi.

11. Jack Langton, 'Urban growth and economic change from the seventeenth century to 1841', in Peter Clark (ed.), *Cambridge Urban History of Britain*, vol. 2 (Forthcoming).

12. J. D. Marshall, 'Rise and fall of the Cumbrian market town' and M. Noble, 'Growth and development in a regional urban system: the county towns of eastern Yorkshire', *Urban History Yearbook* (1987), p. 17.

TABLE 2   *Number and size of urban settlements in England and Wales,*
1700–1841

year	over 2,500	over 100,000	50–100,000	20–50,000	10–20,000	2,500–10,000
1700	68	1	0	2	4	61
1750	104	1	1	4	14	84
1801	253	1	4	12	32	204
1811	302	3	6	14	30	249
1821	352	4	8	22	36	282
1831	397	6	8	31	45	307
1841	450	7	13	35	64	331

Sources: P. J. Corfield, *The Impact of English Towns* (Oxford, 1982), table I, p. 8; and
C. M. Law, 'The Growth of Urban Population in England and Wales, 1801–1911',
Journal of Historical Geography (1967), table IX, p. 135.

1700, it has been estimated that there were around 700 towns under
5,000, by 1811, that number had dropped to 600. In 1801 25 per
cent of towns still had populations under 2,500, but this figure had
fallen to nine per cent by 1841. In contrast, as is shown in Table 2,
by the same date there were thirteen towns within the population
range 50,000–100,000, whereas 100 years earlier, London had been
the only one.

Urban Demography

Urban growth in the first half of the eighteenth century was slow:
there was probably only around a five to six per cent increase during
the period 1650–1750. Yet this was still unusual because the overall
population of England did little more than stagnate until the mid
1740s. In the wider European context, the population in towns
under around 40,000 increased merely in line with the general
population, if at all. The proportion of people living in towns with
populations over 10,000 in Europe remained constant between 1600
and 1800, whereas in England it rose fourfold. Professor Wrigley
estimates that 70 per cent of European urban growth during the
eighteenth century took place in England.[13] English urbanization
occurred earlier than elsewhere and produced an unusually integrated urban network, with a system weighted much more towards

13. Wrigley, 'Urban growth and agricultural change' in *People, Cities and Wealth*,
pp. 174–80. Wrigley built on arguments advanced by Jan de Vries in 'Patterns of
urbanization in pre-industrial Europe, 1500–1800', in H. Schmal (ed.), *Patterns of
European Urbanization since 1500* (London, 1981), pp. 77–109.

the middling rank of town.[14] This distinctive pattern of English urban growth has been attributed to a variety of causes.[15] Thanks to improvements in agriculture and transport, English towns had passed the stage when their expansion was limited by the inability of the hinterland to support an urban population over a certain level. Agricultural progress, in improved crop yields and more labour efficient techniques, augmented the food supply available to feed the non-agrarian population and released manpower from the land, enabling widespread and continuing migration to the towns to take place from the late seventeenth century onwards. Better transport by road, sea and canal cut the cost of travel and stimulated the growth of internal trade.[16] The peak of turnpike construction came between 1750–75 when 395 turnpike acts were passed. Canal mania caught hold of the nation somewhat later, with a preliminary flurry of 20 acts in the 1760s, to be followed by a much greater boom in the 1790s when 60 acts were passed.[17] These developments in transport were of crucial importance for conveying bulky commodities, such as coal, without which the population of London and other inland towns could not have been sustained. The gradual rate of increase in the earlier part of our period was largely due to the fact that rural population growth was very slow, but there were other limiting factors, such as the comparatively small size of the leisured classes who provided the demand for consumer goods and services. The most significant growth at this stage was in the ports, which were handling a much greater volume of trade – a manifestation of the knock on effect of the late seventeenth-century commercial revolution, which underpinned the prosperity of eighteenth-century England. Industrial and manufacturing expansion in the early eighteenth century had yet to make a significant impact on urban growth, but over the next two hundred years it was to become the most important factor, far outstripping growth provoked by increased consumer demand.

14. C. W. Chalkin, *The Provincial Towns of Georgian England. A Study of the Building Process, 1740–1820* (1974), p. 17; Jan De Vries, *European Urbanization* (1983).

15. Introductions to the demography of this period include: M. W. Flinn, *British Population Growth, 1700–1850* (1970); Roger Schofield, 'British population change, 1700–1871', in R. Floud and D. McCloskey (eds), *The Economic History of Britain since 1700*, 2nd edn (Cambridge, 1994), pp. 60–95; Martin Daunton, *Progress and Poverty. An Economic and Social History of Britain, 1700–1815* (Oxford, 1995), pp. 387–415.

16. J. A. Chartres, 'Road carrying in England in the seventeenth century: Myth and Reality', *EcHR*, xxx (1977), pp. 73–94.

17. E. Pawson, *Transport and Economy: The Turnpike Roads in Eighteenth-Century Britain* (1977), pp. 137–40; J. R. Ward, *The Finance of Canal Building in Eighteenth-Century England* (Oxford, 1974), p. 164.

After mid-century, population growth took off much more rapidly, reflected in both the increasing number of towns and the rising populations within them. The higher standard of living enjoyed by the nation at large during the previous half century had promoted higher fertility rates. This coincided with a decline in the plague and the virulence of the smallpox virus (which was also tempered by the use of inoculation, and latterly vaccinations), while the nineteenth-century scourges of tuberculosis, typhus and cholera had yet to become endemic. Overall, the population of England increased by around 50 per cent between 1750–1800. However, the most significant population increases took place in industrial and manufacturing areas and ports (which also supported related industries where there was a constant and ever increasing demand for labour), where growth was as much as 274 per cent.[18] Although some of the population increase was natural, the vast majority of urban growth was achieved by large-scale immigration from the surrounding hinterland. It has been estimated that nearly 60 per cent of urban growth in English towns, in the period 1776–1811, came from immigration.[19] From the late eighteenth century onwards the growth of Manchester and Liverpool, and the cotton towns of Lancashire, owed much to the number of Irish immigrants pouring across the Irish Channel.[20] As the urban population increased, this in turn created a greater demand for consumer goods and urban services, thereby generating more opportunities for expansion and employment. The balance in the distribution of urbanized areas shifted away from the south, which had formerly been the centre of the textile industries and trade, towards the Midlands and the north, as maps 1, 2 and 3 illustrate (see pages 274 to 276). The areas of greatest growth were the East Midlands (around Leicester and Nottingham), the Black Country (around Birmingham and Sheffield), the West Riding (around Leeds, Wakefield, Bradford and Halifax), the north west (around Liverpool and Manchester) and, in the nineteenth century, South Wales, around Swansea and the new town of Merthyr Tydfil. Common to all these areas was their proximity to the coalfields, which provided the fuel for manufacturing and industrial growth. East Anglia and the south west of England, which had formerly been the most heavily urbanized areas

18. Wrigley, *People, Cities and Wealth*, Table 7.3, p. 167.
19. J. G. Williamson, *Coping with City Growth during the Industrial Revolution* (Cambridge, 1990), p. 28.
20. R. Dennis, *English Industrial Cities of the Nineteenth Century* (Cambridge, 1984), p. 35, estimates that in 1841, 17% of Liverpool's population was Irish born.

TABLE 3A   *Population change in textile towns of East Anglia, southern England and the West Country*[4]

Colchester	1670 : *c.* 9,500	1801 : 11,520	1821 : 14,016
Canterbury	1676 : *c.* 7,500	1801 : 9,071	1821 : 12,745
Salisbury	1695 : 6,976	1801 : 7,668	1821 : 8,763
Worcester	1700 : *c.* 8,000–9,000	1801 : 11,352	1821 : 17,023
Shrewsbury	1750 : 13,328	1801 : 14,739	1821 : 19,602
Coventry	1694 : 6,714	1801 : 16,049	1821 : 21,242
	1748 : 12,117		

TABLE 3B   *Population growth of the cotton towns, 1801–21*

Town	Population in 1801	Population in 1821
Wigan	10,989	17,716
Bury	7,072	10,583
Oldham	12,024	21,662
Blackburn	11,980	21,940
Bolton	12,549	22,037
Preston	11,887	24,575
Stockport, Cheshire	14,850	21,726

Source: C. W. Chalklin, *The Provincial Towns of Georgian England. A Study of the Building Process, 1740–1820*, (1974) pp. 34–5.

of the country, underwent slow population growth and their towns slipped down the ranks of the urban hierarchy. A number of the former textile towns, such as Ipswich and Tiverton, actually experienced a measure of absolute decline. Their textile industries could no longer compete with those of the West Riding and Lancashire, where costs were lower. Table 2 demonstrates the contrast between the towns in the south of England, which underwent population increases of about 1–3,000 in the period 1801–21, while cotton towns in the north west, which were of a similar size in 1801, increased by 7–10,000 in the same period.[21]

By the end of our period, London was well on the way to becoming the giant urban sprawl which it is today – it was certainly the largest city in Europe. Villages, which had been quite distinct in 1700, had been incorporated into the conurbation, and the cities of London and Westminster had long since merged into the greater whole. Twelve seventeenth-century towns had become subsumed

21. Chalklin, *Provincial Towns of Georgian England*, pp. 32–54.

into London by 1801.[22] London combined the role of political and social capital, major entrepôt port, financial centre of Europe and it was also the location for finishing industries and the distribution of imported and manufactured goods. In the seventeenth century it had dwarfed all other towns, with a population of over 300,000, reaching over half a million in 1700. By 1801 it approached one million, and by 1841 it had almost doubled in size again. However, despite this very substantial growth, it was no longer so exceptional in terms of size, or in the problems that it faced. The contrast between the metropolis and the rest of the urban system had been blunted. Its proportionate share of the total urban population had shrunk, and its claim to represent the nation politically and economically was being challenged by the weight of wealth, population and influence embodied in the industrial and manufacturing towns. Cities, such as Manchester and Liverpool, now ranked amongst the commercial cities of Europe, alongside London. Provincial England had become a force to counterbalance that of the metropolis.

Urban Typologies

Population growth on this scale did not go unnoticed, and observers became much more precise in their use of language. Towns were differentiated in terms of their functional role, and in terms of their size. From the 1780s onwards commentators began to single out large towns, great cities, and populous cities as places which had specific characteristics and problems – many of which had formerly been identified only with London. After the first national census in 1801, it became possible to discuss the comparative size of towns with some degree of authority. Population assumed a correspondingly greater importance in the conceptualization of what constituted a 'town', as it was a (reasonably) certain and quantifiable characteristic, rather than using more nebulous concepts of legal status. The term 'city', which had previously indicated the presence of a cathedral see, was now conventionally used to refer to the largest urban settlements. Similarly, the 'village' became a more clearly defined construct. The village was what the town was not – the rural community, where traditional structures of authority and values still prevailed, as in the idealized vision of Goldsmith's *Deserted Village*.

22. Jack Langton, 'Urban growth and economic change', p. 12.

Contemporaries were also becoming more sophisticated in how they differentiated between different kinds of towns, on the basis of function or economic base. Broadly considered, there were four major categories into which the majority of towns fell, and which provide the basis of most functional typologies. These were the market and administrative centres, the port and dockyard towns, the manufacturing and industrial centres, and the spas and leisure towns.

The market towns represented the majority of the smaller towns and many larger ones. The term is something of a catch-all, covering many inland towns which were not primarily manufacturing or leisure centres. Overall they showed the slowest growth. They were generally characterized by a fairly diverse economic base, which serviced the needs of the surrounding hinterland, and one commonly finds that no more than fifteen per cent of the population were involved in any one trade. These towns benefitted from the growth of internal domestic trade, becoming 'inland entrepôts'.[23] Older towns on major trade routes found a new prosperity as thoroughfare centres, providing accommodation, and coaches and horses for travellers. Stamford, for example, was famous as a staging post on the Great North Road and renowned for the accommodation offered by its inns. The towns of Kent, in the shadow of London, prospered from the ceaseless volume of traffic plying the roads between the metropolis and the coast, transporting grain and other goods. Although many were small, their significance extended over a much larger region than their absolute size would suggest, as they provided services, entertainment, education and, most importantly, markets for the surrounding area. The very high ratio of inns and taverns to households suggests that there was constant traffic in and out of towns, with far more people 'using' them than is indicated by crude population figures. Sir Frederick Eden reported that the town of Hereford, with a population of 7,500 (a rather generous estimate) in the 1790s, had over 60 inns and alehouses, while in Ulverston in Cumbria, a town with no more than 1,000 households in 1829, there were at least 25 inns.[24] Despite the increase in specialist shops and retailing, the open market still underpinned the

---

23. Alan Everitt, 'The Banburys of England', *Urban History Yearbook* (1974), pp. 28–38; and Everitt, 'Country, county and town: patterns of regional evolution in England', in Peter Borsay (ed.), *The Eighteenth-Century Town, 1688–1820* (1990), pp. 83–115.
24. Sir Frederick Morton Eden, *The State of the Poor*, (ed.) A. G. L. Rogers (1928), p. 204; Marshall, 'Rise and fall of the Cumbrian market town', p. 174.

economy of exchange in England. It may seem surprising how many small market towns could co-exist within a restricted area, but we should remember that their market days were staggered across the week so that they did not compete with each other. In larger towns, markets would be held more frequently, often with set days for the sale of different commodities, such as fish or grain. Towns inevitably became associated with the particular produce which was favoured by the farmers of the hinterland. Farnham and Croydon, and other towns near London, were the centres for grain, reflecting the enormous scale of provisions demanded by the metropolis. Cirencester was renowned for its wool and Carlisle for the trade in cattle from Scotland. The importance of the market was reflected in the layout of the town: in a few older towns the stalls were simply ranged up and down the streets, but in general the market-place was the focal point and was dignified by a large market cross with ornate carving. The Bristol High Cross was decorated with a series of figures from the city's past, which served as a visual reminder of the city's history and rise to commercial prosperity. Many of these crosses were in fact removed during our period – gothic carving was not to everyone's taste and they blocked the thoroughfare. But the visual statement which they made, about the importance of the market and the town's economic might, was still embodied in the many market houses and Exchange buildings which were erected in their stead. Edifices, such as the cloth halls of Halifax and Leeds, or the Exchange buildings of Bristol and Liverpool, were among the most impressive structures of the provincial townscape. Local legislation was frequently obtained to improve and redevelop market-places, and between 1750 and 1850 over 100 acts, with provision for market improvement, were passed by Parliament.

All market towns acted as a focal point for the surrounding countryside, but the county towns were the administrative centres for a much larger region and, as such, had an influence which extended beyond their immediate economic hinterland. Almost all the business of county administration was carried out in the county or shire town – the meetings of the militia, land tax commissioners, charitable associations, turnpike trustees, and, most importantly, the holding of the Quarter Sessions and the Assizes all took place in the county town. In practice, the hierarchy of towns rarely conformed to a neat model of a provincial capital surrounded by a series of smaller country towns. There was often more than one such regional centre, especially in the larger counties, and the Assizes would alternate between the different towns. The East Riding, for example, had three additional centres – Beverley, Wakefield and Doncaster – as well as York, while in the North Riding, the sessions alternated between Thirsk, Stokesley, Helmsley, Gainsborough, Northallerton, Malton, Easingwold and Richmond.[25] These occasions attracted a large influx of visitors who attended not just for the administrative business, but the social occasions associated with it. For this very reason there was frequently considerable rivalry between towns as to which should host the Assizes. Twenty-six cities (including Wales) were also cathedral sees. Although the diocesan administrative machine was of less significance than the county system, the episcopal presence nevertheless gave additional status to the town, and attracted the kind of people whom contemporaries referred to as 'good company'. As Defoe commented upon Winchester, 'Here is no manufacture, no navigation; here is a great deal of good company; and a great deal of gentry being in the neighbourhood, it adds to the sociableness of the place. The clergy also here are, generally speaking, very rich and numerous.'[26] The custom of such genteel visitors became an important part of the urban economy of many of these county towns and, to a lesser extent, the market towns, and in this respect they shared much in common with spas and watering places (discussed below), which were devoted more exclusively to the pursuit of leisure.

The distinction between market town and our next category of manufacturing towns is a difficult one to draw. Indeed, Corfield has found that the term only became common usage in the second half of the century, although Daniel Defoe was typically prescient in using it to describe places such as Manchester and Macclesfield, or Tiverton and Taunton, in the 1720s.[27] Clearly all kinds of manufacturing towns would have a market, in addition to the manufactures, and many market towns were engaged in a range of small-scale manufactures – Witney was famous for its blankets and Woodstock for its steel and gloves. Categories must be determined by which element dominated the economy. Colchester had been an important textile manufacturing town in the seventeenth century, but although there was a small amount of textile production, which continued throughout the eighteenth century, it would not

25. C. W. Chalkin, *English Counties and Public Building, 1650–1830* (1998), p. 134.

26. Daniel Defoe, *A Tour through the whole Island of Great Britain*, (ed.) P. Rogers, Penguin edn (repr. 1986), p. 192; J. Gregory, 'Canterbury and the *Ancien Régime*: The Dean and Chapter, 1660–1828' in P. Collinson, M. Sparks and N. Ramsay (eds), *A History of Canterbury Cathedral* (1995), pp. 204–55.

27. Corfield, *Impact of English Towns*, p. 23.

be very helpful to categorize it as a textile manufacturing town alongside a centre of cloth production like Leeds. Its primary role had shifted from manufacturing to being a market town and social centre. From the second half of the century the manufacturing towns of England began to show some of the fastest urban growth. Birmingham more than doubled in size from around 23,000 in 1750 to 40,000 by 1770. By 1801 it had reached 71,000, and 183,000 by 1841. In 1750, Manchester's population (excluding Salford) was around 18,000, but by 1775 it had nearly doubled to 30,000. By 1801 it had grown to 75,000, and had reached 235,000 by 1841. Smaller towns were springing up too; centres like Bolton and Oldham, which had previously existed as scattered villages, were becoming major industrial centres, with populations of 12,549 and 12,024 respectively in 1801.[28] Around the Potteries in Staffordshire, dispersed populations became more densely concentrated, creating settlements, such as Burslem, which would qualify as towns in terms of population, but which were very deficient in the administrative and social infrastructure normally associated with urban centres. This was a new breed, which had little in common with the traditional market town and might more accurately be termed the 'industrial village'. After 1800, when the introduction of steam power led to far more factories being established in towns, rather than in the vicinity of rural water power, it is possible to add another sub-category – the factory town, immortalised in the caricature of Dickens's Coketown. Centres, such as Manchester or Preston, where a number of large industrialists employed huge work-forces in their factories, were very different in character from a town such as Birmingham or Sheffield, where the majority of the population were still operating within the workshop system, either independently or in small units of industrial production. Alexis de Tocqueville succinctly summarised the difference thus in 1835: 'At Manchester a few great capitalists, thousands of poor workmen and little middle class. At Birmingham, few large industries, many small industrialists.'[29]

The eighteenth-century domestic economy had already become well integrated, with a highly developed internal trade, and this enabled high levels of functional specialization to take place within individual towns. This trend towards the concentration of specific

28. Population figures from Law, 'Notes on Urban Population', pp. 22–6; B. R. Mitchell and Phyllis Deane, *Abstract of British Historical Statistics* (Cambridge, 1962), pp. 24–5 and Wrigley, *People, Cities and Wealth*, pp. 160–1.

29. Alexis de Tocqueville, *Journeys to England and Ireland*, (ed.) J. P. Mayer (New York, 1968), p. 93.

crafts in one region had been underway since the seventeenth century, or earlier in some areas.[30] The hinterland around the town would also be involved in the same form of production (it should be remembered that much industry and workshop production was still rurally based at this time). 'Craft regions' developed, specializing in particular products, for which the local town was not only a centre for processing and finishing, but was also the marketing and distribution point, and provided the financial services for the surrounding area. This specialization brought about advantages: it enabled much higher levels of skill to be reached and greater economies of scale to be implemented, through the division of labour. Nottingham and Leicester were famous for their hosiery, Coventry for silk ribbon weaving and watches, Northampton for shoes, and Sheffield for steel. There were a smaller number of towns which commanded an entire region as their hinterland. Birmingham dominated the Black Country and the manufacture of metalware. Manchester was the centre of the cotton spinning industry, but in addition it was the final destination for the cloth which had left Manchester in the form of spun cotton, which had been sent on to other urban centres in the hinterland, such as Preston, Oldham, and Blackburn, for weaving and dying, before returning back to Manchester for packaging and resale.

Ports and dockyards displayed similarly rapid growth, and, as we have seen, accounted for much of the urban population increase in the earlier part of our period. They were among the most densely populated towns in the country. England's manufacturing economy may have been about to take off into sustained economic growth, but manufacturing wealth did not begin to approach commercial wealth until the end of the century. London's overwhelming superiority as the major entrepôt was gradually eroded as provincial ports acquired more and more of the country's overseas trade, as well as the carrying trade. Liverpool was the most outstanding success story. From a population of around 5,100 in 1700 it had grown to 18,400 by mid-century. In 1801 its population stood at 82,000, and by 1821 it had topped the 100,000 mark at 119,000. Liverpool's success eclipsed that of Bristol, the other major west coast port, but not before the city had enjoyed a period of glory as second city of the realm: from around 20,000 in 1700 it had reached 55,000 by 1775, at which point it was already beginning to lose its pre-eminence in trade to its rival Liverpool, and it only managed to

---

30. Everitt, 'Country, county and town', p. 99.

grow to 61,000 by 1801.[31] Other ports showed similar, if less spec-
tacular growth. Whitehaven, Hull, Newcastle and ports all along the
north east, the south and the East Anglian coast all benefitted from
the increased volume in overseas trade and the carrying trade, even
if they did not undergo the same scale of expansion as Liverpool.
Wealth in the ports arose not just from the profits to be made from
commercial exchange, but because they were also the locations for
related industries – shipbuilding is the obvious example, but the
finishing and processing industries were also important, since it was
cheaper to process goods at the port before transporting them
elsewhere. Raw materials from the colonies acquired added value
by being processed before re-export to Europe. Bristol was notorious for the pall of smoke cast over it from its glass factories and its
sugar refineries, of which there were at least fifteen or sixteen by the
end of the century.[32] The demands of war were undoubtedly a major
stimulus to manufacturing production, but the impact of Britain's
success as a fiscal military state was most noticeable in the expansion of the royal naval dockyards.[33] Shipbuilding and servicing the
navy became a major source of employment, and the dockyard at
Portsmouth was one of the biggest industrial enterprises in the
country. Fears of invasion from France concentrated the attention
of the government upon the navy and the defence of the south
coast, with the result that Portsmouth and Plymouth had moved up
into the top rank of the urban hierarchy by 1801, with populations
of 33,226 and 40,000 respectively. In both these towns the naval
dockyard gave rise to what were effectively new towns, appendent
upon the old – Portsea and Dock (Devonport after 1824) – a development which was frequently the occasion of some tension with the
older community.

Ports did not all pursue the same business, of course – specialization in certain goods was as characteristic of ports as it was of manufacturing towns, and clear regional economies developed around
the major ports. Ports on the north sea coast traded with the
Baltic states and northern Europe. Hull serviced a large hinterland,
including the Yorkshire cloth industry and also the manufacturing
areas of Sheffield and the Midlands. Thanks to the opening up

31. Figures from Law, 'Notes on urban population', pp. 22–6 and Mitchell
and Deane, *British Historical Statistics*, p. 160. On the growth of Liverpool see e.g.,
F. E. Hyde, *Liverpool and the Mersey* (1971), pp. 1–43.

32. Minchinton, 'Port of Bristol', p. 133.

33. John Brewer, *The Sinews of Power. War, Money and the English State, 1688–1783*
(1989), pp. 34–42.

of the canals, a large part of her trade comprised the export of manufactured goods (cloth and metalware, joined by Staffordshire pottery in the late eighteenth century) and the import of raw materials, such as iron from Sweden, Norwegian timber for shipbuilding and other naval stores (notably tar, hemp and flax) from Russia, Prussia and the Baltic states. Liverpool's trade was dependent upon the colonies and Ireland to which the textiles of Lancashire, salt from Cheshire and a share of the products of the Potteries and the Black Country were exported.[34] Notoriously, the slave trade brought great wealth to the Liverpool merchants, but of more significance for the British economy were the imports of cotton which fed the textile manufactories. Bristol was the metropolis of an economy in the south west, servicing the west of England, Devon and Cornwall and South Wales. Imports were dominated by tobacco, indigo and sugar, and, to a lesser extent, slaves. The Bristol West India merchants, who controlled these trades, formed one of the most powerful of the commercial lobbying groups in the country. Smaller ports also had their specialisms. Poole's economy was dependent on the Newfoundland fishery, Great Yarmouth upon grain imports from the Baltic and the North Sea herring fishery. The coastal carrying trade was also an essential feature of the ports' economy. Bulky and heavy goods, notably coal, were far easier to transport by sea, and the Newcastle to London trade in coal provided much of the wealth of the Newcastle Hostmen ('hostmen' were the merchants who controlled the coal trade). Not all ports grew as quickly as Whitehaven on the Cumbrian coast which, from a base of a few hundred souls in the seventeenth century, grew to a population of around 16,000 by the mid-eighteenth century, on the success of the coal and tobacco trade, which put it among the top six English ports.[35] The picture was not entirely rosy, however. South coast and East Anglian ports, such as Sandwich, Southampton and Ipswich, struggled to keep their trade and even declined. Of all towns, ports were the most vulnerable to external factors over which they had little control. War-time restrictions on trade could fatally damage the wealth of a port: Whitehaven never recovered from its loss of the tobacco trade after the American War of Independence. Natural forces were even further beyond their control. Chester was supplanted by Liverpool as the Dee silted up, and York's trade suffered, in competition

34. Gordon Jackson, *Hull in the Eighteenth Century. A Study in Economic and Social History* (Oxford, 1972), pp. 10–25.
35. Sylvia Collier and Sarah Pearson, *Whitehaven, 1660–1800* (1991), p. 2.

with Hull, as the Ouse became unnavigable for vessels with a deeper draught.[36]

The final category is that of the 'leisure town'. These towns overlap to a certain extent with the regional centres and market towns, whose functions included the provision of social amenities, but they also number the 'purpose-built' spa towns and seaside resorts which were a phenomenon peculiar to the eighteenth century. Since most of these towns had previously been little more than villages, they did not have the same administrative infrastructure or regional role to play as the county town, and had a much narrower economic base. Spas and leisure towns characteristically revolved around a summer season, whereas in county towns the main influx of visitors tended to be during the winter (mirroring the London season) or for occasions such as the Assize Week. The origins of spa towns go back to the Elizabethan period, and nearly 40 different spas have been identified under the later Stuarts by Phyllis Hembry. Scientific and medical interest in the curative properties of different waters in the eighteenth century fuelled the expansion of spas and watering places, and lengthy treatises were published analysing the chemical composition of the local spring (the more sulphurous and nastier, the better) and discussing the relative merits of warm or cold waters, and the best time of day for taking them. As the vogue for taking the waters became entrenched in the lifestyle of the affluent, towns all over the country followed suit and tried to lay claim to medicinal waters – some with greater success than others. Hembry has calculated that 113 spas were founded between 1700 and 1815, although not all of these would have become urban centres – many spas remained essentially rural and very small.[37] Tunbridge Wells and Bath were two of the earliest success stories; both had originally begun as medicinal centres, where ailing valetudinarians sought a remedy for their diseases. Notable competitors in the second half of the century included Cheltenham, Malvern and Buxton.

As the fashionable world descended in increasing numbers to take the waters in these towns, the provision of entertainment, services and accommodation assumed a greater significance in the urban economy and, although spa towns still purported to offer cures for all manner of diseases, their chief attraction became the highly evolved social life, with its opportunities for conspicuous

36. Francis Drake, *Eboracum, or the History and Antiquities of the City of York* (1736), pp. 231–3.
37. Phyllis Hembry, *The English Spa Town, 1560–1815: A Social History* (1990).

consumption. Beau Nash, who came to Bath in 1707, did much to give the city its distinctive character and cachet by imposing strict routines and conventions governing social behaviour. Other resorts followed suit in employing a 'master of ceremonies', and attempting to enforce timetables and dress codes upon the company. The highly structured, and ultimately artificial, lifestyle became one of the defining features of the inland resort. The seaside resort became popular and fashionable somewhat later than the inland spa and never evolved quite the same rigidity of social conduct. Sea bathing was advocated at Scarborough as early as the 1730s, but Scarborough was also a spa, and the pump room, where the waters were taken, directly adjoined the beach, hence it was literally only a short move into the waters of the sea itself. Sea bathing took off more generally in the last quarter of the century, in the rather warmer waters of the south coast of England, and there were at least fifteen established coastal resorts by the turn of the century.[38] Margate was a popular destination in the 1770s but was later eclipsed by Weymouth and Melcombe Regis, under royal patronage. A number of declining port towns, such as Southampton and Hastings, took on a new lease of life as they reinvented themselves as seaside resorts. As early as 1751, the episcopal traveller, Bishop Pococke, observed of Margate that the economy had been transformed: 'For there is but little trade at this town, and if it had not of late been much frequented for bathing and drinking the salt waters they would have had very little commerce, except among themselves.'[39]

Most of these spa towns were to be found within striking distance of another great regional centre. Leisure towns were, in part, a product of the earlier success of urban development, as their economies were dependent on the nation's growing spending power, particularly that of the urban middling sort, and, as such, they were uniquely vulnerable to the vagaries of the fashionable world. The competition for custom between these towns was extremely fierce and increased the pressure for providing better facilities and investment in the urban fabric. Epsom, Tunbridge, and later Brighton and the other south coast resorts, owed their success to their proximity to the capital. Bath was further away, but was conveniently

---

38. Ibid., p. 304; see also John K. Walton, *The English Seaside Resort. A Social History, 1750–1914* (Leicester, 1983). On Margate see J. Whyman, 'A Hanoverian watering place: Margate before the railway', in Alan Everitt (ed.), *Perspectives in English Urban History* (1973), pp. 138–60.

39. J. J. Cartwright (ed.), *Dr. Pococke's Travels through England*, 2 vols. (Camden Society Publications, 1888–9), ii, p. 242.

placed for the metropolis of the west, Bristol. It was also one of the
earliest towns to apply for turnpike legislation, to improve access
to the town, acquiring its first act in 1707. Few towns acquired the
national status of Bath or Tunbridge Wells, but they still attracted
considerable custom from their regional hinterlands.[40] In the latter
part of the eighteenth century we find Blackpool and Southport
emerging as resorts to cater for rapidly expanding towns of Lancashire and the north east, while Harrogate and Knaresborough
joined Scarborough in competing for the custom of Yorkshire's
monied classes. The attempts of the Liverpool medical fraternity to
promote a valetudinarian image for their city were less successful
and, despite the reassurance of William Moss that the sulphurous
fumes from the copper works were actually antiseptic, they failed to
carry conviction, and the spa at Sion Hill, promoted in *An Essay on
Liverpool Spa Water* (1773) was never a great success. By contrast,
such was the popularity of resorts such as Bath or Brighton that
their rate of increase was comparable to, or even exceeded, that of
some of the northern manufacturing towns. By 1800, Bath was the
tenth biggest city in England, with a population of 33,000, having
grown from around 2,000 at the beginning of the century. Brighton's
population rose from 7,339 to 46,000 between 1801 and 1841, while
Cheltenham grew from around 3,000 in 1801 to 20,000 in a space
of 25 years.[41] These two towns took first and fourth place in the
table of urban growth rates (as opposed to absolute increase) for
the period 1800–41.[42]

  The economy of such towns was highly dependent upon providing
services to the wealthy, and this gave them a distinctive character.
There was a world of difference between the genteel society of the
leisure town, with its specialist shops, broad streets and organized
social life, and the smoke and grime of manufacturing towns,
which lagged far behind in the provision of cultural amenities and
urban improvement. In one sense, towns became more 'urban' in
this period, in that the features which distinguished urban from
rural society became more marked, but, concurrently, the question
of what characterized a town, and what 'urbanity' meant, becomes
far more complicated. Contemporary observers were fascinated by
the diversity of urban life and the variety of towns, and commented

---

40. Hembry, *The English Spa Town*, p. 114.
41. Sylvia McIntyre, 'Bath: the rise of a resort town', in Peter Clark (ed.), *Country
Towns in Pre-industrial England* (1981), p. 214; S. Farrant, *Georgian Brighton, 1740–
1820* (1980), p. 43; Gwen Hart, *A History of Cheltenham* (Leicester, 1965), p. 173.
42. Langton, 'Urban growth and economic change', p. 21.

endlessly upon their peculiar characteristics. Towns took great pride in their individuality and their distinctive identities and celebrated their difference in town guides and directories. The economic base of a town, which has been the underlying rationale for our typology so far, was essential in shaping this identity and culture, but it has to be taken into consideration alongside other variables, of which the structures of authority and government were of equal importance. The county town, with a highly complex corporate constitution, traditions of guilds and civic pageantry and a strongly pronounced civic identity, had little in common with the industrial villages of the Black Country or Lancashire, which had nothing to bind them together as an urban community beyond the overstretched structure of the parish or the manor. It is to these structural differences that we must now turn.

missed point – argue.

CHAPTER TWO

The Structures of Authority

> We often behold a pompous corporation, which sounds well in history, over something like a dirty village – This is a head without a body. The very reverse is our case – We are a body without a head.[1]

William Hutton's comment, quoted above, suggests that the corporation was the sole institutional form of urban government. However, as he himself went on to show in his history of Birmingham, there were plenty of other formal and informal structures through which power and authority could be exercised. The attempt to provide a definitive description of the structure of urban government is always frustrating; exception piles upon exception and the individual idiosyncrasies defy categorisation. As Bryan Keith Lucas acknowledges in *The Unreformed Local Government System*, there was in fact no system, and it is this fluidity and lack of structural formality which makes urban government such an elusive chimera to describe. For those who want a comprehensive account of the full range of variations, the Webb's study, *English Local Government*, still remains unsurpassed in its scope and detail.[2] Although to the late twentieth-century reader their interpretation appears heavily influenced by their socialist political agenda, their analysis of the different forms remains the best guide through the confusing complexities of local government. What follows below is a much briefer account of the basic structures which existed. We will examine in turn the different kinds of administrative bodies to be found in towns across England, beginning with the manor and the parish which were the

---

1. William Hutton, *A History of Birmingham* (Birmingham, 1781), p. 87.
2. Bryan Keith Lucas, *The Unreformed Local Government System* (1980); Sidney and Beatrice Webb, *English Local Government from the Revolution to the Municipal Corporations Act*, 9 vols. (1906–20).

oldest form of government. Then we will consider the corporations, permanent bodies established under a royal grant with responsibility for governing the town, and the trading guilds with which they were closely associated. The final category is that of the 'statutory bodies for special purposes' – bodies established by parliamentary statute during the eighteenth century, often to deal with specific problems. We must always remember that none of these structures were mutually exclusive, and nor were they immutable; urban government in this period was still very much an *ad hoc*, informal business. While we may talk of incorporated boroughs, manorial boroughs, parochial government and the authority of street commissioners, it is important always to bear in mind the plurality of institutions and forms which could co-exist, cooperate, or indeed compete, in any one town. The second section will therefore look at the way these bodies interacted within an urban community. The impulse to 'pigeon hole' and establish categories is of limited utility; it establishes artificial distinctions and obscures the fundamental similarities which existed between the different forms of government. We will see that underlying the differences in nomenclature and superficial organization there were important characteristics which were common to all. In the section which follows, therefore, we will attempt to establish what were the main variations in administrative structure, and the general principles which they shared in common. The 'structure' of government in any one town was the outcome of local needs and circumstances, rather than any overriding policy emanating from the centre. Our final section will therefore look at the changing relationship between urban government and the state, and the channels of communication between them.

Manorial Structures

Towns had, of course, originally evolved from rural communities, and the administrative structure of the manor and the parish was still present in every town to a greater or lesser extent, co-existing with other bodies which had been established subsequently. Many towns could boast the presence of an incorporated body which had superseded the earlier structures, but the division was not clear cut. In some towns the manorial courts (the court leet and the court baron) had become attenuated almost to the point of extinction, their functions having been taken over by the corporation or the parish, or the court of Quarter Sessions; in other towns the manorial courts were still the chief locus of administrative authority. In general, it was the court leet, as opposed to the court baron (which was traditionally purely concerned with the property of the lord of the manor), which proved the most durable of the manorial institutions. The court leet was comprised of a jury drawn from the inhabitant householders and was presided over by a chief officer. Depending on the degree of independence achieved from the original manorial lord (a measure of self-government had often been granted under a manorial charter), the townsmen had a greater or lesser say in the appointment of this officer and his subordinates.[3] The lord of the manor's nominal right of veto over office-holders was often the most tangible remnant of manorial authority in the borough, although he might still retain the right to certain rents and fees for the market. In many towns the role of the chief officer was very similar to that of the mayor in an incorporated town. He appointed certain officers who were responsible for ensuring that, for example, rubbish was not left on the streets or that bad meat was not exposed for sale in the market. These officers were supposed to note any instances of such offences being committed, and would present the culprits to the jury (made up of householders) at the court leet, which was held at least twice a year, if not more often. The leet jury would then impose a fine or amerciament (light punishment) upon the offender, on the assumption that this would deter him from committing such an offence again. There was no other means of enforcing the regulations. The system was one which operated best in a face-to-face environment where the principle of calling one another to account had some chance of success, and where the scale of 'nuisances' was sufficiently low that their prosecution did not become too time consuming a business. The manorial courts did not just persist in the smaller towns and villages, but provided the basis of government in many larger towns as well. In Manchester, for example, the Moseley family, as lords of the manor, still owned the rights of the market in the nineteenth century, and the court leet, along with the police commissioners, was responsible for the government of the town until it was incorporated in 1847. Similarly, the court leet retained an administrative role in Birmingham, another of the busiest and rapidly growing towns. The court leet in Lewes was far from defunct. Rather than going into decline, it had a resurgence when, in 1799 there was a

3. Marie Rowlands, 'Government and governors in four manorial boroughs in the West Midlands 1600–1700', *Journal of Regional and Local Studies*, 13 (1993), pp. 1–19.

movement within the town to revive the ancient constitutions of the borough.[4] Remnants of the court leet often continued alongside the corporations which displaced them, and can be traced in the names of the officers appointed by the corporation, such as ale-connors or haywards, and in the continued practice of summoning a leet jury for dealing with nuisances.

Parochial Structures

The only structure which was common to every town was the parish vestry. With the establishment of the poor laws in the sixteenth century the vestry had been made responsible for setting and collecting the rates, a local tax which was levied upon each household in the parish, and for administering these funds for the relief of the parish poor. Since then it had taken on other duties of day-to-day governance, some of which were essentially usurped from the court leet. During the eighteenth century Parliament imposed additional responsibilities upon the parish including the provision of fire engines, inspection of slaughter houses, and suppression of the sale of gin.[5] The parish officers included the surveyor of highways, the overseers of the poor and the constables. These offices, none of which carried a property qualification or had any salary, were appointed at the Quarter Sessions by the justices of the peace, while the church-wardens (generally responsible for managing parish funds and setting the poor rate) were usually elected at meetings of the vestry. By the start of our period the parish vestry had long since evolved into a unit of secular administration distinct from the spiritual cure of souls. As such, it was naturally particularly important in the smaller towns, which were at the bottom of the urban hierarchy, having never acquired the trappings of chartered rights, and where manorial influence was weak. Some vestries never extended their area of competence beyond setting the poor rates and electing parish officers, but others were more active. We find, for example, that it was still the main administrative structure in some of the rapidly growing industrial towns which sprang up during our period, such as Halifax or Oldham, where the sophistication of the administrative institutions failed to keep up with the rate of population growth. Here the parish was effectively the only body whose competence

4. V. Smith (ed.), *The Town Book of Lewes*, Sussex Record Society, 6 (1973), p. 104.
5. Sidney and Beatrice Webb, *The Parish and the County* (1906), p. 148.

extended across the town as a whole. Equally, in a burgeoning resort town such as Brighton, the vestry oversaw the town's growth and was an effective administrative body right into the early nineteenth century.[6]

The form of vestry government could vary greatly from place to place; there was no clear ruling on who was eligible to attend and to vote, and the conventions varied since there was no written constitution. Typically, a vestry was either 'open' or 'closed'. In its most open incarnations all residents of the parish could attend and vote at the vestry meeting, including women (confounding the commonly held assumption that eighteenth-century women were excluded from all aspects of public life). At a contested election for a churchwarden in East Looe in 1825, the corporation candidate led in a party of all the women and widows rated to the poor, who claimed their right to vote and duly elected their candidate – such occasions were unusual however.[7] Crowded meetings were not the most efficient form of government, particularly in urban parishes where very large numbers might be involved. In populous parishes a more compact, and by definition more oligarchic, executive body generally evolved, which was often termed the 'select vestry', comprising the priest, churchwardens, parish clerk and other leading members of the parish. Select vestries had existed in London parishes, for example, since the sixteenth century or earlier.[8] Meetings of the inhabitants at large would be held only once or twice a year, in order to elect churchwardens, audit accounts and to give sanction to decisions such as the raising of the militia; such occasions were often termed 'town meetings' rather than vestries, indicating the importance of the occasion as a forum for the opinion of the town, rather than its ecclesiastical significance. The select body, who would meet much more frequently, would levy parish rates at their discretion, and might take on responsibility for a wide range of duties. In provincial towns a similar situation had often arisen by default – whereby most of the questions of poor relief or highway maintenance were decided amongst an inner circle of churchwardens, parish clerk and possibly vicar in private meetings at a

6. J. A. Erredge, *The Ancient and Modern History of Brighton* (Brighton, 1867).

7. John Keast, *A History of East and West Looe* (1989), p. 73.

8. Ian Archer, *The Pursuit of Stability. Social relations in Elizabethan London* (Cambridge, 1991), pp. 69–71. By 1638, 59 out of 109 of the vestries within the city of London were select. However, Archer argues that this should not be seen simply as a move towards greater exclusivity, but was a response to a need for greater administrative efficiency.

local inn. More momentous decisions would be discussed in public meetings of the parish, called for the purpose, in the church. In 1818 and 1819 this move towards oligarchy was given legislative ratification under the Sturges Bourne Acts, which ruled that only those who had paid their poor rates were eligible to attend meetings, and provided for 'plural voting' according to property, so that those who were rated at a higher level had proportionately more votes than those rated at the minimum of £50 or less, up to a maximum of six votes. It also provided that the vestry thus assembled could elect a 'parish committee', effectively introducing government by select vestry. Under Hobhouse's Act of 1831 the legislation was altered again so that *all* ratepayers voted by ballot at annual elections, but the level set for ratepayers to qualify was so high as to exclude large numbers of the inhabitants in every parish to which it applied. Neither of these acts was compulsory in its application.

The influence which the vestry could yield was generally the greatest in unincorporated towns, but it is important to remember that the authority of even the most hegemonic corporations was not monolithic, and the parish vestry always represented considerable influence, if only on account of its responsibility for the management of poor relief. In the incorporated town of Leeds, the vestry proved a powerful body, due to its ability to levy rates, and the fact that it had assimilated the functions of the manorial great court, after the town had purchased the manorial rights over the borough in the seventeenth century. The corporation had prestige and authority, but a very restricted income, being poorly endowed with lands. Its ability to implement practical policies of improvement or welfare was therefore strictly circumscribed in comparison with that of the vestry, which had greater financial resources available to it from the poor rates. For most of the century the congruence of the Leeds civic elite, who were involved in attending the common council and the vestry, precluded any rupture in the administration of the town.[9] In Liverpool too, where the corporation was an efficient and dynamic body and the wealthiest outside London, the vestry was a crucial element in local administration and provided services complimentary to that of the corporation. Until 1780, the vestry clerk and the town clerk (the corporation officer) were one and the same person. The vestry was largely responsible for overseeing matters such as crime, poor relief, fire, public health and the upkeep of the streets, whereas the corporation concentrated on the management of trade, the corporation property and the development of the port and its commerce. The select vestry opposed moves by the corporation to introduce bills for 'improvement commissions' in the early nineteenth century, and to all intents and purposes the parish committee fulfilled a very similar role to that of street commissioners (discussed below) in other towns.[10] The best, or rather the most notorious, examples of government by parish vestry come from London, where all the variations of parochial government, from the 'clamorous proceedings and irregular behaviour of the great multitude' attending the vestries of Whitechapel, to the corruption of the closed vestry of St Martins in the Fields, to the enlightened rule of the patrician gentry in the select vestry of St George's Hanover Square, can be found. Again, rapid population growth beyond the bounds of the corporation of the City of London meant that semi-rural parishes had grown into densely populated urban communities, but without any additional institutions of government being superimposed. The select vestry of St Marylebone, established by act of Parliament in 1786, supervised the parochial paving, lighting and scavenging, employed its own police force and even retained a clerk in the House of Commons to keep it informed of matters which might effect the interests of the parish.[11]

Incorporated Bodies

It is the corporations which most people associate with the 'unreformed local government system', if only because it was the corporations which were the object of the 'reform' of local government in 1835. However, it is important not to let the incorporated towns steal centre stage in our view of eighteenth-century towns. In 1833 the Royal Commissioners identified a total of only 246 incorporated boroughs. Jack Langton's figures suggest that in the late seventeenth century there were over 900 towns in England and Wales, and around 1,100 by 1841.[12] Incorporated boroughs in our period, therefore, never constituted the majority of English towns,

10. H. Peet (ed.), *Liverpool Vestry Books 1681–1834*, 2 vols (Liverpool and London, 1912), i, pp. xc–xcii.
11. Quoted in Joseph Phipps, The Vestry Laid Open (1736), 11; F. H. W. Sheppard, *Local Government in St Marylebone. A Study of the Vestry and the Turnpike Trust, 1688–1835* (1958).
12. Jack Langton, 'Urban growth and economic change from the seventeenth century to 1841', in Peter Clark (ed.), *Cambridge Urban History of Britain*, vol. 2 (forthcoming), table 2.

and by 1835 they were no longer even representative of the upper ranks of the urban hierarchy. If anything, they were even more varied in constitution and in the scope of their activities than the parishes. For a town to be incorporated was a mark of status; it denoted the possession of special privileges, with respect to trade and government, which distinguished the town from its surrounding hinterland and its unincorporated neighbours. It was assumed to be a recognition, by the monarch granting the charter, of the importance of the town in a national context. The rights conferred by a charter varied in detail from town to town and had often been emended over the years. They generally included the right to hold courts, exemption from tolls within the town for freemen and freedom from similar levies throughout the kingdom. Incorporation also gave the town an identity at law, meaning that it could sue and be sued in the courts, which was of significance when contesting trading privileges or the right to tolls, for example. The following definition, taken from a contemporary legal treatise, illustrates the theoretical premise upon which corporate government was based, and the importance which the contemporaries attached to the legal status of incorporation.

> A CORPORATION then, or a body politic, or body incorporate, is a collection of many individuals united into one body, under a *special denomination*, having perpetual succession under an *artificial form*, and vested, by the policy of the law, with the capacity of acting, in several respects, as an *individual*, particularly of taking and granting property, of contracting obligations, and of suing and being sued, of enjoying privileges and immunities in *common*, and of exercising a variety of political rights, more or less extensive, according to the design of its institution, or the powers conferred upon it, either at the time of its creation, or at any subsequent period of its existence.[13]

The origins of corporate bodies were the subject of some debate and provided the stimulus for considerable antiquarian inquiry in the eighteenth century, (see chapter 5 below) as significant political implications were involved. Even today, the process by which the incorporated borough emerged remains far from unambiguous, and is further complicated by changes in terminology and the opacity of the defining charters.[14] Moreover many boroughs claimed their status and privileges as prescriptive rights, which long preceded

13. Steward Kyd, *A Treatise on the Law of Corporations*, 2 vols (1793), i, p. 1.
14. Susan Reynolds, *An Introduction to the History of English Medieval Boroughs* (Oxford, 1977).

any confirmatory charter or official incorporation. Many, but not all were parliamentary boroughs: before 1832 there were 158 municipal and parliamentary boroughs. Historians have generally followed the legal historian F. W. Maitland's view that the *corporation*, as opposed to the *borough* (which was originally a descriptive term) evolved as a body distinct from the 'community', in response to the need for some kind of permanent body to manage property or 'common land'; hence the 'corporation' was originally a kind of legal fiction, a body whose primary concern from the outset was the management of the corporate property, rather than administrative tasks.[15] Gradually, additional duties were acquired or assumed, and corporations merged with other bodies, such as the merchant guilds and the court leets. Its members naturally assumed a position of leadership within the urban community, but the extent to which the corporation was able to dominate government varied greatly from town to town.

The Webbs identified the crucial defining characteristic of corporations as the right to elect their own justices of the peace, as opposed to being under the jurisdiction of the county magistracy, but beyond this there was little else which was common to them all in terms of structure or functions. Even the judicial powers of the JPs varied considerably; in some towns they sat jointly with the county JPs, in others they had only a petty sessional jurisdiction, or they might have jurisdiction over all felonies. In seventeen English towns, which had been incorporated as counties in themselves, they had full criminal jurisdiction, extending even to capital punishment.[16] For all that the powers of corporations were laid down in the charter, these were ill-defined, and the older the charter, the less specific the terms tended to be. The constitutions of the individual corporations showed varying degrees of complexity and sophistication, in the attempt to balance the tendency to oligarchy amongst the wealthy elite, with at least an element of consent and popular involvement. By the eighteenth century the election procedure in towns such as Norwich or Newcastle had reached a level of tortuous intricacy. Again, the clearest summary of the varieties of form to be found is given by the Webbs, who in turn relied upon the Report of the Commission on Municipal Corporations in 1835.

15. F. W. Maitland, *Township and Borough* (Cambridge, 1898). See also James Tait, *The Medieval English Borough* (Manchester, 1936).

16. These were Bristol, Chester, Coventry, Gloucester, Lincoln, London, Norwich, Nottingham, York, Canterbury, Exeter, Hull, Lichfield, Newcastle, Poole, Southampton and Winchester.

Generalising very broadly, there were two kinds of corporation: those which were entirely confined to a select body, and those which had a more democratic element of freemen. All corporations were headed by a chief officer – the mayor or his equivalent, who would be assisted by a number of senior office-holders, often called the aldermen. Together they comprised a body called the common council, which in the case of the more select bodies comprised the entire corporation. The mayor, or his equivalent, was dignified with considerable importance in his public capacity as the representative of the town, and was expected to exercise leadership and exert his influence for the public good: 'therefore [he] is to be considered as the representative, and the center [sic] of the union of the town, upon all important and public occasions . . . to be upright, to be impartial, and to be worthy of his office, he should beware of using his weight in a public capacity, as an influence in any way whatever, except for the public good.'[17]

In some cases the common council was coterminous with the corporation itself, since the urban elite had successfully excluded the freemen from any participation in the administration of the town. In others, the common council formed an 'upper house', and there was a wider body comprised of the freemen as a whole, the number of which was indefinite, who might be involved, to a greater or lesser extent, in the government of the town. These towns often drew analogies between their own constitutions and that of Parliament, with the mayor representing the King, the aldermen the House of Lords and the freemen the Commons. The freemen might participate in civic elections, and in some towns had the right to assemble in common hall for deliberative purposes, but this did not mean that they were actively involved in the day-to-day running of the town. By the eighteenth century the electoral procedures had usually been effectively 'rigged' (either by excluding freeman participation entirely or limiting their choice of candidates to a short-list determined by the common council) to create what was effectively a self-selecting oligarchy (comparable to the closed parish vestry). In most cases the business of civic government rarely impinged upon the majority of inhabitants and it characteristically lay in the hands of this oligarchic group. In a few boroughs, such as Ipswich, there was theoretically much wider freeman involvement

---

17. William Roberts, *A Charge to the Grand Jury of the Court Leet for the Manor of Manchester*, reprinted in J. P. Earwaker (ed.), *Records of Manchester Court Leet*, ix (1889), p. 250. Roberts was actually referring to the office of portreeve, a manorial official, who occupied a position equivalent to that of mayor in other towns.

because there was no upper chamber in the corporation, and its affairs were supposedly managed by the whole corporation assembled in a guild meeting, but in practical terms power was nevertheless concentrated in the hands of a few. Uniquely, in Berwick, the assembled body of *all* the freemen constituted the common council of the town. Norwich represented the other extreme, in that there were two deliberative chambers which met, in addition to the freemen body as a whole: the aldermen's chamber and the common councilmen's chamber. This additional refinement gave added scope to political manoeuvring, but does not seem materially to have added to the efficacy of urban government.[18]

Trading Guilds

In a few corporations entry to the freedom of the city was based upon prior membership of one of the local guilds or companies.[19] In London, it was (and still is) necessary to take up membership of one of the livery companies before the freedom of the city could be assumed. Conversely, it was also the case that in a number of cities, such as Newcastle, it was impossible to become free of a company in order to trade without first taking up the freedom of the city. In many corporations, traces of the guild structure still existed in the meeting of all the freemen in Common Hall, or in the appointment and naming of officers. In Winchester it is clear that the corporation was the direct successor of the Guild Merchant, which had been the common assembly of the various trading guilds, but there was no universal direct line of descent between the governing body of the guilds and corporations. The annual meeting of the Court of Guild in Newcastle was given a new lease of life in the early nineteenth century when it was exploited as a base from which to challenge the authority of the common council.[20]

Originally the function of guilds had been to protect the trading interests of their members; they controlled admissions and apprenticeship (to prevent overcrowding), they oversaw prices and

---

18. Sidney and Beatrice Webb, *The Manor and the Borough* (1908), p. 721.

19. P. J. Corfield, *The Impact of English Towns* (Oxford, 1982), pp. 86–91. See also M. J. Walker, 'The Extent of the Guild Control in Trades in England 1660–1820', Cambridge Univ. Ph.D thesis (1985); and J. Barry, 'Bourgeois collectivism? Urban association and the middling sort', in J. Barry and C. Brooks (eds), *The Middling Sort of People. Culture, Society and Politics in England, 1550–1800* (1994).

20. Michael Cook, 'The last days of the unreformed corporation of Newcastle upon Tyne', *Archaeologia Aeliana*, 4th ser., xxxix (1961), pp. 207–28.

standards (to prevent fraud) and they might also regulate wages and conditions of work. Bye-laws would be issued to this effect, and officers appointed to enforce them. In the eighteenth century the prevailing trend in economic thought was in direct opposition to the basic principles of the guild economy. It rejected protectionist practices, and the system of trading monopolies and guilds were blamed for causing economic stagnation and decline. Not surprisingly, their economic role fell into gradual abeyance. The convivial element persisted longer, and there was a definite tendency for the guild to become a social and philanthropic institution. There was, however, considerable variation, both regionally and in terms of the type of trade effected, in the rate at which this took place. In Newcastle, the guilds seem to have reached a peak in membership in the early eighteenth century, and only began to show signs of serious decline in the latter period. However, incorporated crafts (which ranked lower in the hierarchy than the guilds) such as the keelmen (who loaded the coal onto the ships) maintained considerable vitality, as they functioned effectively as a form of early trade union, staging strikes and providing support for members.[21] In Oxford, the Taylor's Company was still trying to control the trade in the death throes of its existence in the 1780s and 90s, struggling against the competition from female mantua makers. The Cordwainers Company, in contrast, bowed out more gracefully, transforming itself into a dining society, with considerable social cachet. However, it is undeniable that the guilds, as urban institutions, were of far less consideration by the nineteenth century. Throughout the eighteenth century guild membership and freeman status underwent a steady diminution in importance. So much so in fact, that guilds were becoming subjects of historical and antiquarian curiosity in their own right.[22] Their place had been taken by friendly societies, workers' combinations and the earliest trade unions.

Unincorporated towns, like Birmingham, prided themselves on their freedom from antiquated customs and the restrictive practices of guilds, and claimed their prosperity was a direct result of their

21. Joyce Ellis, 'A dynamic society: social relations in Newcastle upon Tyne, 1660–1760', in Peter Clark (ed.), *The Transformation of English Provincial Towns 1600–1800* (1984), pp. 190–227. David Palliser notes that the guilds in York did not decline until well into the eighteenth century: 'The trade gilds of Tudor York', in Peter Clark and Paul Slack (eds), *Crisis and Order in English towns, 1500–1700* (1972), pp. 112, 116 n. 82.

22. Urban histories often devoted a considerable section to guilds and their history. See Rosemary Sweet, *The Writing of Urban Histories in Eighteenth-Century England* (Oxford, 1997), pp. 259–60.

open economies. William Hutton congratulated his fellow citizens upon the failed attempt to secure a charter of incorporation in 1716. Those who had sought incorporation, he claimed, had been 'dazzled with the splendour of a silver mace'. Had they succeeded, 'that amazing growth would have been crippled, which has since astonished the world, and those trades have been fettered which have proved the greatest benefit.'[23] It was certainly a commonplace in much contemporary literature that formerly prosperous cities such as York, Coventry, and Chester had declined due to their uncompetitive economies. Daniel Defoe, spokesman for free trade and commercial enterprise, may be awarded some of the blame for popularizing the idea that trade restrictions were incompatible with economic growth, through his widely read and highly influential *Tour through the whole Island of Great Britain.* He attacked the 'Pretence of Freedoms and Privileges' which he found at Bristol, and argued that but for 'Corporation-Tyranny' and freemen's rights the city 'would before now, have swell'd and encres'd in Buildings and Inhabitants, perhaps to double the Magnitude it was formerly of'.[24] However, from the twentieth-century perspective, such an explanation of economic decline appears overly simplistic. Not all incorporated boroughs showed the same symptoms; Liverpool flourished under the rule of a corporation, as did Newcastle, Plymouth, Portsmouth, Hull and Leicester and many other smaller towns. Even Bristol managed to achieve considerable prosperity, despite losing its position of second city. The mere fact that unincorporated towns like Manchester, Birmingham or Sheffield underwent dramatic expansion does not in itself indicate that this was due to their unincorporated status. Structural considerations, such as their proximity to coalfields and trading networks, were arguably of greater importance. Their failure to acquire a charter of incorporation should perhaps be seen simply as a reflection of the reluctance of eighteenth-century governments to issue new charters. In an earlier period, such prodigies of urban growth and prosperity would have been incorporated as a matter of course, as had the former urban leaders, Norwich and Exeter.[25]

As we have seen, the incorporated boroughs only constituted a minority of English towns, and even where they existed their competence was often limited, both by the extent of their jurisdictions

23. William Hutton, *A History of Birmingham*, 2nd edn (Birmingham, 1783), p. 326.
24. Daniel Defoe, *A Tour through the whole Island of Great Britain*, ed. P. Rogers, Penguin edn (repr. 1986), p. 362.
25. Corfield, *Impact of English Towns*, pp. 90–1.

and the powers which had been conferred upon them by charter. Some of these deficiencies could be supplemented, as we have already suggested, by the co-existence of parochial government and the manorial courts, but increasingly the process of urbanization posed challenges which could not be met within the existing structures. Two approaches evolved, through which the increasing burden of urban government could be met: the first was the increase in duties and authority exercised by the bench of justices of the peace and the Quarter Sessions; the second was the spread of statutory bodies for special purposes. The intensification of government, through justices of the peace, was an ongoing development which was common to both county and urban government.[26] Since the seventeenth century and earlier, there had been a trend in urban government towards concentrating administrative authority with the JPs.[27] The demands of central government for more vigilant policing of society and more information, especially during the French Revolutionary and Napoleonic Wars and the years following, meant that the Quarter Sessions and the bench became more formalised institutions, meeting with greater regularity and frequency, often displacing other older, private courts in the process.[28] It is important to bear in mind therefore that the changes which we see taking place in urban government were not unique to towns, but were one aspect of a gradual transformation in the way in which power was exercised at a local level throughout England, reflecting a *general* shift in attitude towards the duties and responsibilities inherent in local government as a whole.[29]

This elevation of the authority of the judicial bench had important implications for the way in which corporations evolved in incorporated towns. Magisterial authority undoubtedly bolstered the authority of the corporation and raised its profile, but at the

26. P. Styles, 'The development of county administration in the late eighteenth and early nineteenth centuries illustrated by the Records of the Warwickshire Court of Sessions, 1773–1837', *Dugdale Society Occasional Papers*, 4 (1937); E. Moir, *Local Government in Gloucestershire, 1775–1800*, Publications of the Bristol and Gloucestershire Archaeological Society, 8 (1969); D. Eastwood, *Governing Rural England. Tradition and Transformation in Local Government, 1780–1840* (Oxford, 1994).

27. S. and B. Webb, *Manor and the Borough*, pp. 389–94; and Peter Clark, 'The civic leaders of Gloucester, 1580–1800', in Peter Clark (ed.), *Transformation of English Provincial Towns*, p. 325.

28. Norma Landau, *The Justices of the Peace 1689–1760* (Berkeley, CA, 1984); Styles, 'The development of county administration.'

29. David Eastwood, *Government and Community in the English Provinces 1700–1870* (1997); Michael Braddick, 'State formation and social change in early modern England. A problem stated and approaches suggested', *Social History*, 16 (1991), pp. 1–17.

same time it exacerbated the oligarchic tendencies, and provoked the suspicions of those who wanted to see a higher degree of representative involvement. The overlap between the corporation and the bench was a useful one: it enabled cumbersome administrative machinery to be short-circuited. The mayor and aldermen could take decisions and exercise authority, in their capacity as magistrates, without having to go through the procedure of calling meetings of the freemen or common council. Oligarchy was consolidated as important and influential tasks, such as the granting of alehouse licences and the exercise of justice, were exercised by a self-selected and generally unaccountable body of men. This had created a situation, in most incorporated towns, whereby the effective governing body had become coterminous with the bench of magistrates, and there was clearly some confusion, in contemporary perceptions of local government, as to when leading citizens were acting in their capacity as corporation officials, and when they were acting as magistrates. The term chief magistrate, or magistrates, was very often used in preference to mayor and aldermen, indicating the higher priority accorded to their judicial role. As we shall see, many of the criticisms levelled against unreformed corporations in the latter part of our period were really directed against the members of the corporation in their capacity as magistrates, rather than as members of the corporation. The distinction was a nice one, and extremely difficult to uphold in practice and could cause tensions, as the distinction between the authority of an individual as a JP was easily confused with the authority which he exercised by virtue of his civic office. It is clear from the report of the Royal Commissioners that much of the alleged distrust and ill-feeling expressed towards the corporations arose from the judicial side of their duties, rather than reflecting upon the corporation as such. A particularly notorious case was the opprobrium which was cast upon the corporation of Bristol for the part which its aldermen, acting as justices, took in the suppression of the Bristol Riots in 1831.[30] It also subtly altered public perception of the role of the corporation in urban society, in that expectations of public service and accountability to the community became more pronounced, although at law, as many corporations argued in their defence, they were private bodies. This perceptual

---

30. G. Bush, *Bristol and its Municipal Government 1820–51*, Bristol Record Society, 29 (1976), p. 59. The Bristol aldermen were normally careful to draw a distinction between their public role as aldermen and their role as justices, especially with respect to the management of the police, which came under frequent criticism.

shift towards seeing corporations primarily as public bodies, was one of the factors creating a more hostile climate of opinion towards the unreformed system. There were some advantages to be gained by corporations too, however, in that the conscientious and diligent alderman, acting as justice of the peace, could reinforce the claims of the corporation to leadership within the community. Thus, the traditional structure of authority could draw additional strength, in parasitic fashion, from this extension of the judicial role.

The justices of the peace and the grand jury at Quarter Sessions were public bodies and ostensibly the servants of the state (as opposed to the private manorial courts or the semi-autonomous corporate bodies). As such they were the chief resource of the King, and in the latter part of our period, the Home Office, in the fight against crime, in regulating trade, preserving law and order, surveying the highways, inspecting gaols and overseeing the activities of the vestries and the administration of poor relief. In Plymouth, for a short period, the Quarter Sessions assumed responsibility for the lighting and cleansing of the streets. This solution to the problem was unusual and short lived. It was replaced by an improvement commission established by act of parliament. The local resort to parliamentary legislation, which the creation of such improvement commissioners represented, dominated the development of urban administration in our period and will be the focus of our next section.

Change through Legislation

Local legislative initiatives had been very infrequent prior to the eighteenth century. The relative infrequency with which Parliament met, and the short duration of its sessions, had inhibited its use in private bill legislation. More frequent and longer sessions made the process of piloting a private bill through Parliament much easier and more reliable.[31] This coincided with urban growth and greater urban prosperity, which created a situation in which urban authorities found that they needed new and more extensive powers to regulate and administer the urban environment more satisfactorily. Given that most charters had been granted long before it had been deemed necessary, or even desirable, to build pavements or introduce

31. Stuart Handley, 'Local legislative initiatives for economic and social development in Lancashire, 1689–1731', *Parliamentary History*, ix (1990), pp. 14–37.

oil lamps on a large scale, there was not much scope for extending the sphere of activity of the corporation. Some towns, where the corporation had maintained a leading role in the administration of the town, sought improvement acts to enhance the powers of the corporation. The corporation of Bristol acquired additional lighting, watching and paving powers as early as 1701 and various subsequent acts extended these and also their area of competence. Other corporations which exercised additional powers granted to them by statute included Bath, Exeter, Hull, Newcastle upon Tyne, York, Gloucester and Liverpool.[32] However, it was not always possible or expedient to increase the powers of the corporation in this way. Not all corporations exerted such an active role in administration, hence a local act to enhance their powers was not an obvious solution. In others, the local politics of the town meant that it would have been highly contentious to have granted additional powers to a closed body. Urban growth had created a situation in many towns where the jurisdiction of the old corporation failed to extend over large areas of the town, which were left unregulated. Bristol was unusual in acquiring an act of parliament in 1776 which brought the Hotwells, the fashionable spa in the suburbs, under its corporate jurisdiction. The solution which increasingly came to be preferred in the eighteenth century, was to establish a new body with statutory authority, whose competence extended over the town as a whole, and which had much greater powers of rating, borrowing money and compulsory purchase.[33] Significantly, improvement bills sometimes followed upon unsuccessful attempts to obtain or renew charters of incorporation. The town of Margate made an unsuccessful attempt in 1785 to acquire a charter of incorporation which would give them the authority to manage their own affairs, rather than being dependent upon Dover, and so resorted to a local act which established a body of improvement commissioners instead.[34] In general, the new bodies enjoyed much more extensive powers than even those corporate bodies which had acquired additional legislation.

32. The relevant acts are: Bristol, 11 and 12 Wm c. 23, 28 Geo II c. 32, 28 Geo III c. 65; Bath, 30 Geo II c. 65; Exeter, 1 Geo III c. 28; Hull, 2 Geo III c. 70; York, 3 Geo III c. 48; Newcastle upon Tyne, 26 Geo III c. 39; Doncaster, 43 Geo III c. 147; Gloucester, 1 and 2 Geo IV c. 22 and Liverpool, 26 Geo III c. 12 and 7 Geo IV c. 57.

33. The most detailed analysis of improvement acts, in terms of their constitutions and powers, is still to be found in F. H. Spencer, *Municipal Origins. An Account of Private Bill Legislation Relating to Local Government, 1740–1835* (1911).

34. Bryan Keith Lucas, *Parish Affairs. The Government of Kent under George III* (Kent County Council, 1986), p. 133.

Statutory Bodies for
Special Purposes

This was a phrase first coined by the Webbs, but it has proved a useful umbrella term to describe the huge variety of bodies created by local acts of parliament, with powers of borrowing or local taxation and the authority to undertake some aspect of urban government, or 'improvement'. They included turnpike trusts, canal companies, corporations of the poor, and improvement commissions. The earliest examples were the incorporated guardians of the poor, established to deal more effectively with the ever-present problem of poor relief within towns. The first of these outside London was established in Bristol in 1696, under legislation which enabled the various parishes to unite to build a workhouse for setting the poor to work. Thirteen other towns followed suit with similar incorporations between 1698 and 1712. These comprised elected boards of 'guardians' responsible for the centralised administration of poor relief through a workhouse, rather than leaving it to the individual parish. Bristol's corporation of the poor comprised a court of 60 guardians: the twelve wards of the city each elected four members and the remaining twelve were made up by the ex-officio representation of the mayor and corporation.[35] The effectiveness of these bodies in dealing with the problems of poverty and poor relief is, of course, open to question – what is important here is the precedent which was set for establishing a body accountable to ratepayers under an act of parliament. The creative potential inherent in this formula was to be fully realised in the eighteenth-century improvement commissions, and the first provincial improvement commission, established in Salisbury in 1737, was directly modelled upon such corporations of the poor. The Webbs estimated that over 200 towns outside London had established improvement commissions by 1835. By the end of our period there were only a handful of towns of any size which had not acquired at least one such act.[36] In addition, there was a proliferation of local legislation to enhance paving, lighting and watching powers, which

35. John Cary, *An Account of the Proceedings of the Corporation of Bristol in Execution of the Act of Parliament for the better Employing and Maintaining the Poor of that City* (1700).

36. The Webbs in *Statutory Bodies for Special Purposes* (1922), p. 242, noted that of the 40 towns with populations over 11,000 in 1831, only Leicester, Nottingham, Wenlock and Wigan had not been subject to improvement Acts.

either extended or confirmed the authority of existing bodies. The dynamism and impetus for change which critics found wanting in the corporations was more often channelled into the acquisition of local acts, which allowed for greater freedom of manoeuvre in undertaking new responsibilities; it was always easier to create new bodies than to reform old ones.

The characteristic 'improvement act' of the eighteenth century was the paving and lighting act. Its origins are easily traced back to the paving and cleansing acts passed for London streets during the reign of Charles II. In the years immediately following the Glorious Revolution the demand for local acts was still dominated by London and Westminster. It is really only after mid-century, with the end of the Seven Years War, that provincial towns really began to take advantage of the facility offered by Parliament. Larger towns led the way in the 1760s, and from the 1780s the pace of improvement steadily quickened. Another boom in improvement took place after the end of the Napoleonic Wars when we find a much more heterogeneous range of towns seeking legislation. There was a particularly marked peak around 1825–6, which coincided with the crest of the economic boom. Initially, most acts had been acquired by the older towns, many of which were incorporated. They were more common in trading towns with a considerable gentry and merchant presence, rather than industrial centres. By the nineteenth century, both the smaller market towns, such as Downham Market or St Neots, and the recent arrivals on the urban scene of the industrialising north and Midlands, were also seeking the benefits of an improved urban environment. Centres such as Burnley and Keighley, described in the acts as 'townships', 'parishes' or 'villages', were acquiring the features of urban society which would distinguish them from mere concentrations of population. The improvement commission often established an essential administrative structure for the town, which was otherwise unprovided for.

The regional distribution of improvement acts does not follow any clearly defined pattern. In general, improvement almost always followed upon connecting the town to the turnpike road system. The greater flow of traffic meant that new fashions and innovations could spread more quickly and, in practical terms, greater congestion in the streets and wear and tear on the roads made street improvement an urgent necessity. As the preamble to the Wolverhampton Improvement Act of 1777 put it, 'because a Navigable Canal has lately been made up to the said town, the number of carts and carriages used in carrying and conveying goods and merchandize is greatly increased'.[37] Urban one-upmanship meant that it was essential to keep up with neighbouring towns in the provision of urban amenities and a pleasant environment, if only to avoid losing out on valuable visiting trade and custom. It is also worth noting that the incidence of acts is not a foolproof means of charting the spread of improvement, since it was always possible to introduce improvement without seeking statutory authority for it, and there were many reasons why application for an act might be blocked. Ashford, for example, was repaved at a cost of £3,000 by levying a highway cess (rate) and through public subscription, without any need to turn to parliamentary legislation.[38] Leicester never acquired an improvement act during our period, but we should not deduce from this that the town was unlit, unpaved and uncleansed.

The improvement acts of the first half of the century tended to be framed as remedial measures, to rectify shortcomings, but as confidence in the potential of improvement increased, and as Parliament became more accustomed to the format of improvement bills, the petitions concentrated instead on outlining the benefits and greater convenience which would ensue. The rhetoric of 'improvement', refinement and civilization with which we associate eighteenth-century towns was predominantly a characteristic of the latter part of our period. Rather than seeking to limit the traffic through towns, which was causing congestion in the streets and destroying the surfaces, the later acts had clauses to widen the streets and lay down flagged pavements. Other features which became more common were measures for improving the water supply, the drainage and sewerage, and for lighting the town by gas. Gas was quick to catch on as it gave a better light and was ultimately cheaper to run. The first gas lighting was introduced to London in 1807 in Pall Mall, and the incorporation of the Gas Light and Coke Company followed in 1812. The peak in gas legislation lay from 1818–28 when 65 separate acts relating to the provision of gas in towns were passed, affecting over 50 different towns. Provisions for water supplies were also being made with greater frequency by the end of our period. Following the cholera epidemic of 1831, towns were, in retrospect, slow to implement large-scale programmes, but there was a marked upsurge in the number of acts specifically addressed

37. F. Mason, *Wolverhampton Town Commissioners, 1778–1848* (Wolverhampton Public Library, 1976), p. 1.

38. Keith Lucas, *Parish Affairs*, p. 139.

to the provision of water from 1833.[39] Both gas and water were often the subject of distinct acts, being put under the management of an individual company, in order to avoid either the corporation or the improvement commissioners from acquiring a monopoly over these essential services. One feature which was initially more prevalent in metropolitan improvement acts than those for provincial towns was the inclusion of provisions for watching the streets and providing for a more effectual police. In London, anxieties (real or imagined) about the rising crime rate ensured that this was one of the crucial reasons for seeking additional statutory powers. The inclusion of clauses for watching became much more common for provincial towns in the latter part of our period, particularly in industrial areas such as Lancashire, where the new cotton towns had little more than an inchoate structure of authority and no indigenous traditions of law enforcement. The acceleration of urban growth in the nineteenth century showed up the inadequacies of the traditional methods and highlighted the need to seek additional powers of watching and police.[40]

Improvement commissions displayed immense variety in their constitutions, comparable only to the minute variations in the composition and electoral procedure of the municipal corporations. Commissioners were selected on the basis of a property qualification, by co-option or election, or most rarely, constituted a whole class of ratepayers (those paying the paving and lighting rates were theoretically eligible to act as commissioners). There were basically four different modes of selection and most bodies employed some combination of two if not three of these. These were ex-officio membership, election, co-option and membership on the basis of a property qualification. Ex-officio membership almost always featured in corporate towns where it was important that the corporation should be represented, and generally comprised some variation on the mayor, aldermen and justices of the peace. This model was predictably less frequent in unincorporated towns, where there was no equivalent official body, but, where it did exist, one might find

39. For example, in 1834–5 there were 11 acts making specific provision for improving water supplies or setting up water companies in towns in England. In 1804–5 and 1824–5 there were 2 and none respectively.

40. Towns which had acquired police acts (as opposed to powers of watching) before 1835 were Bath (1793 and 1825), Birmingham (1812), Leeds (1815), Lincoln (1828), Plymouth (1824), Macclesfield (1814, 1825), Stockport (1826) and York (1825).

ex-officio manorial officials, MPs, resident JPs, and, especially in the years after 1800, local clergymen.[41] Co-option meant that the original membership was established by statute, and subsequent vacancies were filled by the selection of those who were already members. The size of these bodies ranged from fifteen in Stoney Stratford, to 258 in Durham, but most had a pool of 30 to 80 members. Candidates for co-option had to satisfy a property qualification (which again was subject to a wide degree of variation), laid down in the terms of the statute. The elective element was much less common in improvement commissions than in the poor law authorities, where, given that many of those of lower social status were involved in paying poor rates, it was more important and desirable (in view of the duties involved) to draw them into the administration. It has been calculated that between 1700 and 1835 100 acts, creating or modifying such bodies, reached the statute book via some elective element, whereas there were 230 which had absolutely no elective element at all and were predominantly co-optive in composition.[42]

By the early nineteenth century there was a clear trend towards including at least some elected element, and after 1835 most of the new bodies being established were predominantly elective. Elected bodies were potentially more democratic in composition, but the levels at which the property qualifications were set, as usual, confined membership to an urban elite. Even where a low property qualification produced a fairly wide franchise of those entitled to elect commissioners, the voters' choice of potential candidates was generally strictly circumscribed by much more rigorous property and/or residence qualifications for acting commissioners. Legislation, renewing improvement acts, often changed the original composition so that there was a stronger elected element, usually at the expense of the corporation ex-officio membership. Hence in Exeter, when amendments to the 1806 Improvement Act were being debated in 1809, it was demanded that not only should there be an elective element from amongst the ratepayers (which the 1810 legislation provided for) but that the aldermen/magistrates should absent themselves ex-officio from the new commission. In 1832 the

41. Spencer recorded only 3 instances where the corporate body appears to have been unrepresented in the ex-officio element, and significantly these all date from the end of our period: Leeds (1824), York (1825) and Dorchester (1835). He calculates that at least half the unincorporated towns had no ex-officio element at all. *Municipal Origins*, pp. 143, 145.

42. Ibid., p. 134.

Chamber's ex-officio membership was further reduced again from eight to six.[43] This pattern was repeated in unincorporated towns as well. Brighton acquired two improvement acts during our period. The first, granted in 1773, had appointed a body of 64 commissioners which was entirely co-opted, but the second, granted in 1810, after criticisms of their lack of accountability from the vestry, provided for the election of new commissioners by the town's ratepayers, who would also have access to the annual accounts.[44]

There was a fourth variation, found in some towns where the act defined a particular class of people, dependent on possession of property and occupancy, as the active body. This was the model adopted in 1792 in Manchester where anyone assessed on a £30 rental was eligible to take the oath of office as a commissioner. Considerable problems were caused in the 1820s when local politics became hotly contested, and all those eligible to attend were galvanized into doing so by the Whigs in order to oppose the measures of the dominant Tory elite. It was not unknown for meetings to attract over 800 commissioners. Proceedings degenerated into unruly disorder and government ground to a halt. When the act was renewed in 1828 it was stipulated that the commissioners should be elected by the ratepayers instead. There was a property qualification of £16 for the right to elect commissioners, and the commissioners themselves had to satisfy a property qualification of £28 (these levels were doubled for publicans).[45] There does not appear to be any kind of discernible pattern to the size and composition of these bodies; the outcome was the product of local interests, rivalries and traditions. We should also note that because statutory bodies were not subject to the Test and Corporation Acts, Dissenters, who were excluded from many (but not all) corporations, could be involved if they wished. In towns where it was felt that the corporation no longer represented the propertied, urban bourgeoisie, this kind of structure, which was based upon the principle of participation by the propertied, offered an important opportunity for those who were otherwise excluded from wielding influence and power.[46]

The existence of alternative bodies of administration provided the institutional framework within which local divisions and rivalries could be pursued. In some communities the polycentric distribution

43. Robert Newton, *Eighteenth-Century Exeter* (Newton Abbot, 1984), pp. 127–8, 162.
44. S. Farrant, *Georgian Brighton 1740–1820* (Brighton, 1980), pp. 52–3.
45. A. Redford, *The History of Local Government in Manchester*, 3 vols (1939), i, pp. 200–307.
46. Langford, *Public Life and the Propertied Englishman*, p. 221.

of power stimulated party conflict and deepened the divisions which existed between Whig and Tory, or high and low church. The politics of this will be discussed in a later chapter, but in this context we must note how the exclusion of one party from power could stimulate the establishment of an alternative structure, (although equally in some towns it is clear that it was necessary to overcome party strife first before anything requiring a measure of civic co-operation could be achieved).[47] It is striking that a number of the corporations of the poor, established in the 1690s in towns where the corporation was dominated by Anglican Tories, were initiated by Whigs and Dissenters who were otherwise excluded from participation (although it was certainly not the case that all corporations of the poor were bastions of dissenting Whiggery).[48] Similar circumstances lay behind the foundation of the Taunton Market House Trustees in 1769. This body was established largely by the dissenting community of merchants in Taunton, who were excluded from membership of the corporation by virtue of the Test and Corporation Acts, and who objected to the vast sums which were being spent on electoral bribery and to the subordination of the corporation to ministerial influence. In an exercise of professed public spirit, they and the independent MP, Sir Benjamin Hammet, devoted the money which would have been spent on elections towards obtaining an act for building a new market house, and carrying out other much needed improvements in Taunton. Relations between this body and the corporation were not always harmonious, as might be expected. On one occasion the minutes of the trustees recorded 'Ordered that a Bolt be fixed on the inside of the Door of the Back Parlour adjoining to the Guildhall, as Mr Cornelius refuses to deliver up the key belonging to the said Door, being directed to withhold it by several of the Corporation and ordered that the lock of the East Door of the Guildhall be taken off and 2 keys be made of it'.[49]

However, it should not be assumed that the establishment of an improvement commission always brought into administration a body of men who had previously been excluded; there was considerable variation from place to place, but very often the ex-officio common

47. Adrian Wilson, 'Conflict, consensus and charity: politics and the provincial voluntary hospitals in the eighteenth century', *EHR* (1996), pp. 599–619.
48. For example, Bristol (1696), Hull (1698), Colchester (1698), Exeter (1698).
49. SRO, D/B/ta 31/1/1 entry for 22 April 1774. See also Joshua Toulmin, *History of the Town of Taunton* (Taunton, 1791); and G. H. Kite and H. P. Palmer (eds), *Taunton: its History and its Market Trust* (Taunton, 1926).

council element provided the most active core. This was certainly the case in Bath, where the corporation had anyway been the moving force in acquiring the improvement act.[50] Moreover, since the majority were co-optive and even when elective hedged about with very significant property qualifications, the number of those eligible to participate was strictly circumscribed. In 1828, when the Manchester Police Commissioners obtained the amended legislation, out of a population of 140,000, there were only 8,000 who paid the police rate and less than 4,000 of these were eligible to act as commissioners.[51] The improvement commissioners could take on as exclusive and oligarchic a character as any corporation or select vestry. Thus, we find that popular feeling against the Cheltenham improvement commissioners was based upon exactly the same sentiments which opposed closed corporations in other towns; their lack of accountability, secrecy, exclusiveness and high-handedness. An attempt to increase their powers, to deal more adequately with the problem of police, was resisted at a public meeting, on the grounds that the unpopular manner in which the commissioners had exercised their powers offered no inducement to anyone to see them increased.[52]

We must now consider how these different forms of government fitted together and interacted. It is often suggested that urban government suffered from confusion arising from a conflict of jurisdictions, but this is not necessarily the right inference to draw. In some towns the corporation or vestry, and the improvement commission, could co-exist very happily and with little friction. The fact that there was often a substantial overlap in personnel, clearly eased matters greatly and could give an impressive unity and purpose to the government of the town. It is important to recognise the fluidity of the relationship which would allow, for example, the improvement commissioners in Wolverhampton, who also dominated the parish vestry, to bring the supervision of the highways under the purview of the commissioners, rather than the vestry, although there was no formal ratification of this in the legislation.[53] In Whitby, which was not a chartered borough, the burgesses, who had effectively ruled the town through the court leet, simply turned themselves into improvement commissioners under the act of 1764, and carried on as before, but with increased powers.[54] Local practice

---

50. R. S. Neale, *Bath: A Social History, 1680–1850* (1981), pp. 183–4.
51. Redford, *Local Government in Manchester*, i, pp. 311–12.
52. Gwen Hart, *History of Cheltenham* (Leicester, 1965), p. 311.
53. Mason, *Wolverhampton Town Commissioners*, p. 25.
54. Langford, *Public Life and the Propertied Englishman*, p. 227.

varied greatly, in some towns one finds a hard core of active citizens who were the leading figures in the corporation, the improvement commission, the guardians of the poor, the canal and turnpike trustees, and who led the way in philanthropic activities. In other towns, for example, Southampton, the statutory body was clearly a much more effective representation of the urban propertied than the closed corporation.[55] In incorporated towns, where there was ex-officio corporation membership, it was often the convention for the mayor to take the chair, and the corporation as a body would generally have subscribed towards the costs of acquiring the act. In this way the corporation could still assert its nominal right to leadership within the community, and, by awarding the freedom to public benefactors and servants of the community, or allowing other bodies to meet in the town hall, it could acquire more merit by association. This was important, given that in a number of cases the corporation had effectively handed over most of its responsibilities to the new body. In a number of towns, where the corporation was still a dynamic body, we find that the whole of the corporation was active in the new body.[56] There were only three towns, Leeds (1824), York (1825) and Dorchester (1834), where the corporation was awarded no kind of ex-officio membership. Authority was being redistributed within the community, and corporations found that their role had changed and their business was increasingly concerned only with the administration of their property and charities, regulating admissions to freedom and, in parliamentary boroughs, the exercise of political influence. The Royal Commissioners, investigating the corporation in 1835, did not fail to notice this restricted range of activity and the consequent concentration on political activity, but they interpreted it as a symptom of decay, rather than a redeployment of resources into channels where they could be used more effectively.

Jealousy and ill-feeling could easily arise, however, in any scheme which affected rights and property; improvement inevitably did, as we have already seen in the case of Taunton. Those involved had always to be sensitive to this possibility. In Chichester, the corporation found itself in a position of some embarrassment over proposals to obtain an improvement act in 1791. Their High Steward, the Duke of Richmond, was determined that the mayor and aldermen should be included ex officio, as they already represented the town

55. Ibid., p. 228.
56. Spencer, *Municipal Origins,* lists Liverpool (1762), Bath (1766), Plymouth (1772), Exeter (1810), Barnstaple (1811) and Dover (1830).

as a whole, rather than it being based solely upon a property qualification of £20 freehold. The corporation, however, did not share
his anxiety that their position in the community would be diminished, and begged that he would let them waive their claim, as
'they conceive that the Possession of it will be of little Utility to
them as a body,' and they feared that an insistence upon their right
to be included ex officio might jeopardize the success of a measure
in which 'they individually feel themselves much interested'.[57] A
motion on 7 February 1791 was made that 'in Order to avoid increasing the Animosities which are now too prevalent in this City such
Rights should be waived'. Animosities were not always so successfully averted. When the corporation of Liverpool were promoting
an improvement bill, which would have enabled a rate to be levied
for paving the streets in the 1790s, the vestry claimed that the legal
responsibility for the upkeep of the streets fell purely upon the
corporation, not the citizens, and pursued the matter to Quarter
Sessions. (The corporation was found to be responsible for the
ancient streets only.)[58] John Speed of Southampton was less tactful,
and waged a propaganda war against what eventually became the
1770 improvement act, on the grounds that it infringed upon the
rights and authority of the corporation.[59] It was not unusual for
corporations to express disapproval of proposals because they feared
that their rights and privileges might be curtailed, and to insist
upon the insertion of clauses safeguarding them in the bill. But
once these difficulties were overcome, there were few occasions of
prolonged friction. Where the corporation was an active administrative body, it was almost certain to be involved in the drawing up
of the bill, and where it had become little more than a committee
for managing the corporation estate, there was little chance that
there would be a conflict of authority.

Parliament was insistent upon due consultation with all the interests that would be affected, which in itself explains why contests over
authority tended to occur before, rather than after, the passage of
a bill. This was important because there was not always a consensus
as to the need for additional powers to be vested in a new or extant
authority, or the desirability of the proposed improvements: the
additional powers to levy a rate were particularly controversial. In

57. F. W. Steer (ed.), *Minute Book of the Common Council of Chichester, 1783–1826*,
Sussex Record Society, lxii (1963), pp. 28–9.
58. S. and B. Webb, *Statutory Bodies for Special Purposes*, pp. 304–5.
59. A. Temple Patterson, *A History of Southampton, 1700–1914*, 2 vols (Southampton,
1966), i, pp. 44–9.

many towns the improvement bills had to run a chequered course before they were finally ratified in Parliament, and a simple statement of successful or failed legislation belies the reality of conflict and dissension which divided the community before they were passed. Inherent conservatism and traditional mistrust of executive authority characterized English politics at all levels, and there were many who opposed improvement commissions, with their additional statutory powers of levying rates and compulsory purchase, on these very grounds. Opposition tended to be particularly strong from the less wealthy, who resisted any kind of additional taxation, and argued that such expenditure was unnecessary. Paul Langford has noted how, in towns with a large and vocal freeman electorate, improvement bills were acquired late, if at all: the freeman boroughs of Norwich and Bristol, for example, both acquired paving acts which set up a statutory body distinct from the corporation in 1806, although extensive improvements had been carried out prior to that under the auspices of their respective corporations.[60] Leicester, another freeman borough, as we have already noted, never had any improvement act at all. The correlation is not absolute, however; Oxford which also had a large and cohesive freemen electorate, for example, acquired a wide-ranging improvement act in 1771, for which no trace of freeman opposition has survived. Similarly, in unincorporated Manchester, the small shopkeepers and publicans fought a continual rearguard action throughout the early nineteenth century to obstruct any project, on the part of the Police Commissioners, which might lead to additional expenditure. Unscrupulous individuals, such as Gabriel Powell of Swansea, who opposed the proposed improvement scheme for Swansea for personal reasons, made significant mileage out of the natural reluctance of the ratepayer to surrender any additional sums, arguing that any improvements which were needed could be paid for out of the levy made upon household frontages, without going to the expense of an act of parliament.[61] William Hutton of Birmingham, prompted by self-interest, initially opposed the plans for improvement because it would have involved pulling down two of his properties. But once this problem was circumvented and the bill was put forward again, he gave it his full support and was one of the most active commissioners.[62]

60. Langford, *Public Life and the Propertied Englishman*, p. 249.

61. Rosemary Sweet, 'Stability and continuity: Swansea politics and reform, 1780–1820', *Welsh History Review*, 18 (1996), pp. 14–39.

62. William Hutton, *The Life of William Hutton* (1816), p. 111; on the street commissioners see C. Gill, 'Birmingham under the Street Commissioners, 1769–1851', *University of Birmingham Historical Journal*, i (1948), pp. 255–87.

It was often claimed, by those opposing improvement measures, that it was the responsibility of the corporation to effect such improvements out of its own resources. Those who did so, however, rarely had a full understanding of the reality of corporation finance; a result of the secrecy with which finances had traditionally been managed. In Southampton, it was protested that the spiralling costs of the poor rates were the consequence of the corporation off-loading its responsibilities onto the parish, which it was able to do because the ex-officio corporation element dominated the board of guardians. These suspicions were further fuelled by the defensive stance taken by some corporations, that the corporate revenues were the private property of the corporation, to be disposed of as the members saw fit.[63] A pamphleteer in Maidstone accused the Tory corporation of having reduced the corporation to beggary with their feasting so that 'we have been so very necessitous of late as not to be able to erect a *whipping post* without a subscription'.[64] In Macclesfield, where the corporation had been given the full powers of street commissioners, including that of levying a rate, its historian protested that the corporation enjoyed immense endowments but refused to devote them to the public good, making the inhabitants pay for all the improvements themselves.[65] Critics always overestimated the revenue at the disposal of corporations; in actual fact, by 1810 the Macclesfield corporation had accumulated a debt of £3,300, most of which had been spent on improving the supply of water to the silks mills, on which the industry of the town depended.[66] In practice, very few corporations had the financial elasticity to undertake grandiose projects. After all, when most of these bodies were incorporated, it could not have been envisaged that there would ever be cause for such a large call upon their finances, and the incorporating charter had often placed limits upon the amount of property which the corporation could hold. Those that attempted to take a leading role in schemes of improvement were likely to find themselves in severe debt as a result. The corporation of Bath was heavily involved in developing the town, and invested in extensive building programmes, which, despite the sale of land and a programme of retrenchment, burdened them with

63. A. Temple Patterson, *Radical Leicester. A History of Leicester, 1780–1850* (Leicester, 1953), p. 141.

64. *A Short Treatise on the Institution of Corporations and an Enquiry into the Bench of the Corporation of Maidstone* (Maidstone, 1786), p. 23.

65. John Corry, *The History of Macclesfield* (1817), p. 48.

66. C. Malmgreen, *Silk Town: Industry and Culture in Macclesfield 1750–1835* (Hull, 1985), p. 109.

a debt amounting to £55,863 in 1835. The Royal Commissioners
were shocked by the number of insolvent corporations which they
found in the course of their inquiry, but it is evident from their
report that much of this burden of debt was the outcome of investment in improvement (which may or may not have been well-
judged), rather than heedless extravagance or self-enrichment.

The Consolidation of Oligarchy

Although oligarchy had long existed in English towns, it is undeniable that over the eighteenth century it became more exclusive and
tightly controlled, even to the extent that in a number of towns
single individuals were able to establish a kind of tin pot dictatorship over the community, controlling not only the corporation but,
through the patronage at their disposal and the influence of the
aldermanic bench, over the town at large. Aristocratic patrons were
willingly compliant with such arrangements, adding the additional
weight of their patronage, as it rendered their own efforts to maintain their influence over a borough all the easier. With the corporation secured, it was possible for that influence to be extended over
other bodies – given the ex-officio representation of the corporation in bodies such as the improvement commissioners or guardians of the poor. The corporation often had the right of appointment
of churchwardens and even parish priests, which offered the additional possibility of dominating the vestry. John Mortlock achieved
this kind of ascendancy over the corporation at Cambridge. Having
been elected mayor, he changed the system of mayoral election
from that of the charter of 1568 to that of 1344, which enabled him
to manipulate the procedure in order to have what was effectively
absolute power over electing the mayor.[67] In Tiverton, Oliver Peard
and his family established an unassailable ascendancy over the town
during the middle of the century, with the connivance of Beavis
Wood, the town clerk, and political agent of the town's MP, Dudley
Ryder, who had put enormous amounts of patronage at Peard's
disposal by awarding him the office of commissioner for land tax.[68]

It was not always the mayor who dominated urban government
in this way. Even though it was possible for some families, such as

67. Helen Cam, ' "*Quo Warranto*" proceedings at Cambridge, 1780–1790', *Cambridge Historical Journal*, viii (1946), p. 155.
68. John Bourne (ed.), *Georgian Tiverton: The Political Memoranda of Beavis Wood*,
Devon and Cornwall Record Society, xxix (1986).

the Mortlocks, to monopolise officeholding within their families (between 1787 and 1809 Mortlock was mayor of Cambridge every other year, alternating with family members and dependants), the fact that the mayoralty was an annual appointment did operate as a check on personal hegemony to some extent.[69] However, the town clerk was in a different position, being a permanent appointment. In many towns, characters like Beavis Wood of Tiverton were clearly the prime motive force behind the corporation. In the *Report* of 1835 it was the town clerk who was often identified as the evil genius in corporations such as Leicester, as it was he who had the most detailed knowledge of what was going on and could act to encourage or inhibit abuse and corruption. Town clerks who acted as political agents, as Beavis Wood did for Dudley Ryder or William Elias Taunton of Oxford did for the Marlborough family, were vulnerable to accusations of increasing the political dependence of the borough, and making the corporation subservient to the interest of the patrons. In the short-term, however, it gave them added influence within the community and in the surrounding county. Moreover, as the town clerk was generally the leading solicitor in the town, and in that capacity was likely to hold other offices of importance, such as solicitor to the various statutory bodies for special purposes or clerk to the justices of the peace, his influence was exerted over a much wider area than simply that of corporate jurisdiction. Families like the Tauntons of Oxford, were able to exercise a near monopoly of the most important legal business in the city, and had their finger in every pie. Sir William Elias Taunton I, the agent of the Duke of Marlborough in the late eighteenth century, held the office of city solicitor and became town clerk in 1794. At this time he was also clerk of the peace, clerk to the market commissioners, clerk to the canal commissioners, and was himself a paving commissioner and a commissioner of sewers. In addition, he was steward to several of the colleges and in 1796 was elected steward to both the Mercers and Drapers Company and the Tailors and Cordwainers Company. He went on to acquire other positions of influence, becoming clerk to the Thames and Isis Navigation, clerk to the Oxfordshire Militia, and in 1806 was elected Recorder for the city. He died in 1825, but not before he had seen his sons become similarly established in the affairs of city, university and county. William Elias II, also a lawyer, succeeded his

---

69. Helen Cam, 'John Mortlock III, Master of the town of Cambridge', *Proceedings of the Cambridgeshire Antiquarian Society*, xl (1944), pp. 1–12.

father as Recorder in 1825. By then he had become a judge and
was less closely involved in Oxford affairs than his brothers Thomas
Henry, Daniel and George. The latter all became members of the
Common Council. Thomas Henry substituted for his father on many
occasions and held a similarly wide range of offices: clerk of the
peace, clerk to various turnpike trusts, steward to the incorporated companies and solicitor for several of the colleges. Daniel
followed the same tradition, but was less prominent than his brother,
and George, who broke the family tradition of law by entering the
church, consolidated the family's links between city and university,
being a fellow of Corpus Christi College. The Taunton ascendancy
could not last, however, and in 1825 when William Elias I died,
Thomas Henry was defeated in the election for town clerk when he
sought to replace his father.

As one would expect, this kind of personal rule was not unique
to the incorporated towns, and closed oligarchies existed in a variety of forms. Smaller towns were often very much under the influence of a single family, who held manorial rights and continued to
maintain a position of leadership within the town, as the Cholmley
family did in Whitby. Even in parochial government, that prototype
democracy, there was always the danger of the demagogue arising
to exercise a despotism. The activities of Joseph Merceron of Bethnal
Green were immortalised by the Webbs, who devoted pages to a
detailed picture of the dictatorship which he had established through
the open parish vestry. Merceron not only dominated the vestry,
but also the guardians of the poor, the watch committee and street
commissioners. He was treasurer of the parish funds and commissioner for levying the land, income and assessed taxes. In addition,
he was also a commissioner for sewers and a JP, which broadened
the scope of his authority even more, not least through the exercise
of the right to control beer shop licences and appoint overseers
of the poor.[70] The informality and fluidity of the structures of
power meant that even in the largest towns it was possible for one
individual to hold sway over huge areas of authority. By the end of
the eighteenth century, Manchester was governed by a combination of vestry, court leet, and police commissioners, and in 1815
an independent gas company was established. But this did not
prevent Thomas Fleming, the uncrowned king of Manchester, from
establishing a personal hegemony in the town from the 1790s
until 1819.

70. S. and B. Webb, *The Parish and the County*, pp. 79–90.

Fleming was clearly very capable in many areas and had a strong sense of public duty, but such accretions of power could never go uncontested for long; reaction always set in and the individuals in question often became highly unpopular. Fleming's rather cavalier manner of asserting ultimate executive authority left him vulnerable to charges of corruption and he was eventually forced to resign over his management of the police commissioners.[71] In an urban community, which was growing and expanding all the time, as most were by the later eighteenth century, it proved extremely hard to keep tight control over a society where there was high mobility and growth, and where there was always the potential for creating alternative networks of influence. Joseph Merceron's ascendancy came to an end when the rector of the parish led a revolt of the respectable inhabitants against him in the vestry. Oligarchies existed in a dialectical relationship with the rest of the community, and there was a recurrent cycle of consolidation and reaction.

The Role of MPs

One of the by-products of this torrent of local acts, which is less often discussed than the impact on the physical urban environment, is the effect on the relationship between borough and MP. The dramatic proliferation of local legislation and the greater frequency with which Parliament met, locked the MP and the urban constituency into a much more complex set of relationships and reciprocal obligations. The MP had to work harder on behalf of the borough: protecting its interests, promoting its bills and petitions and keeping the townspeople informed of other bills which might prove prejudicial to their interests. At the same time, such activity offered much more potential for the creation of an 'interest' and earning support, and the opportunity to play off different factions within a town, all of which were reliant on the crucial link with Westminster which the MP provided, and his potential for forwarding their own interests. The increasingly tortuous machinations of eighteenth-century politicians cannot be understood outside the context of urban improvement. Much has been made of the way in which patrons 'controlled' boroughs, and this paradigm has heavily determined the way in which the political history of the eighteenth century has been written. There has been a tendency in volumes such

71. Redford, *Local Government in Manchester*, i, pp. 241–3.

as *The History of Parliament*, to consider towns as uncomplicated pieces in an aristocratic game of chess, to be exchanged, lost and won and kept subservient to the political needs of the politicians at Westminster. It is not possible to discuss here the vitality and independence of the unreformed electorate and its voting patterns; these matters have been covered with great skill in a variety of recent studies, but it is important to consider the implications of the system for urban life in more general terms.[72]

Parliamentary patrons had to earn their control; they had to consult the interests of their constituencies, to court the electorate, to promote their concerns, to see the local bills through parliament, and protect them from adverse economic legislation; they had to subscribe to charities and subsidise the urban improvement schemes. Perry Gauci's study of Great Yarmouth in the early eighteenth century stands out amongst recent historiography as an account of the protracted lengths to which the Townshend family went to in order to secure its parliamentary ascendancy over the borough, from the years following the Glorious Revolution to the period of Walpolian 'stability'. There was an expectation that they should always promote the interests of the borough: in 1709, for example, Viscount Townshend was requested by the Yarmouth merchants to raise a list of trading grievances against the French, even while he was conducting European peace negotiations at the Hague.[73] Maintaining an interest in a seat was an expensive business, not simply because of the amount of money which was spent on wooing the voters at elections, but in terms of ongoing investment. Patrons were called upon to head every subscription, be it for charities, improvements or cultural pursuits, and cumulatively this could amount to considerable sums. In 1768 the Earl of Abingdon and Duke of Marlborough came to an arrangement with Oxford corporation to pay off their debts, which amounted to nearly £6,000; this was a particularly flagrant example of the way in which a corporation could manipulate the patron's desire to win a secure hold over a seat to their own advantage. Those of the Common Council, who were implicated in the deal, were briefly imprisoned and reprimanded by the House of Commons, and it acquired some notoriety as being the crucial surrender of independence to aristocratic patronage. But on the

72. The best example is Frank O'Gorman, *Voters, Patrons and Parties. The Unreformed Electorate of Hanoverian England, 1734–1832* (Oxford, 1989).

73. Perry Gauci, *Politics and Society in Great Yarmouth, 1660–1722* (Oxford, 1996), pp. 211–54. See also J. Triffit, 'Politics and the Urban Community: Parliamentary Boroughs in the Southwest, 1710–1730', Oxford Univ. D.Phil. thesis (1985).

other side of the coin, the corporation were released from a heavy
burden of debt, enjoying a period of renewed vigour until 1835, and
continued to exercise an important role in the life of the town.[74]
Their political subservience, if one chooses to call it that, was not
without advantages for the town as a whole. In the years after 1768,
we find the Marlboroughs providing fittings for the town hall,
regularly donating gifts of blankets and coals to the poor, subscribing to the Radcliffe Infirmary, the Holywell Music Rooms and
the various charitable and friendly societies. When Oxford rejected
the Blenheim candidate in 1812, the electorate were charged with
ingratitude, but similarly, MPs who declined to give their support
undermined the legitimacy of their position; it was part of their
expected role and unwritten contractual obligation which they entered
into when they were elected. MPs who neglected their interest
by failing to visit the borough, or to offer it their patronage,
did so at the risk of losing their seat. At the other end of our
period, in 1814, the independent John Lockhart jeopardised his
position in Oxford when his constituents read in the press that he
had spoken in favour of the bill for the non-importation of corn in
Parliament; reputedly over 4,000 inhabitants had signed a petition
against an alteration in the corn laws, and Lockhart's effigy was
burnt on Carfax, and he was 'much insulted in the street'.[75] Significantly, he was not returned at the next contested election in 1818.
Even in a rotten borough, such as Shaftesbury, which was regularly
bought and sold, the inhabitants objected to a completely unknown
candidate being foisted upon them in 1820, when the Earl of
Grosvenor bought out Earl Roseberry's interest in the borough.
The earl's electoral agent was forced to agree that in future more
deference and consultation was to be paid to the respectable voters,
while the earl consolidated his ascendancy by donating a new town
hall and market house in 1826.[76] The importance of such ongoing
investment to towns is highlighted in the comments of the Royal
Commissioners on the impact of the Great Reform Act of 1832.
They showed that since the fund of patronage had dried up, many
former rotten boroughs were in considerable financial trouble; the
corporations had no other source of revenue and towns which had
lived in blissful ignorance of the need for paving rates were now

74. Rosemary Sweet, 'Freemen and independence in English borough politics
c. 1770–1830', *P&P*, 161 (1998).
75. Bodl. MS Top. Oxon d. 247, p. 351, 3 June 1814.
76. *Swyer versus Rutter. A Plain Narration of Shastonian Occurrences, without comment*
(Shaftesbury, 1826–7).

having to look round for the finance among themselves. In Liskeard, it was noted that the school had collapsed since 1832, as it was no longer supported by the patron. The corporation, which had relied on having its annual deficit made up by aristocratic largesse, was now in debt and unable to carry out repairs to the roads or any other improvements.[77]

Towns and the State

We must now consider how the institutions of urban government related to government at the centre. What was the nature of the relationship between centre and locality, seen from the perspective of urban government? One way to approach this question is by focusing on the incorporated towns which, being dependent upon a royal grant of a charter, were bound to the King's government in a way that unincorporated towns were not. Although, as we have already argued, they are not representative of all towns, more general conclusions can be drawn from their experience. Our period is interesting because it spans two periods, during which the King's government intervened decisively to regulate the government of English towns, specifically the incorporated boroughs. In the first period, between 1682–7, 134 new charters were granted to English towns (the figure for the period 1660–81 was 85). In 1835, as a result of the inquiry of the Royal Commission, 178 corporations were remodelled on a uniform basis, ending their special privileges and idiosyncratic constitutions. The fact that this nineteenth-century remodelling provoked far less outcry suggests that significant changes had taken place in the relationship between the state and the localities, and in the attitude of urban authorities to central government.

Thomas Hobbes, writing in defence of the absolute power of the monarch in the seventeenth century, had identified corporations as a danger to national strength, they were 'many lesse commonwealths in the bowels of a greater, like worms in the entrails of a natural man'.[78] As strongholds of parliamentary power during the Civil War and after, many had certainly challenged royal authority, but the corporations of England had never enjoyed the independence of the continental city communes, and urban authorities had always looked to the centre for ratification and extension of their authority.

77. *Report of the Royal Commission on Municipal Corporations*, PP (1835), xxiii, pp. 527–9.
78. Thomas Hobbes, *Leviathan*, (ed.) C. MacPherson (1968), p. 375.

Royal policy towards the boroughs under the later Stuarts is part of the much bigger story of the Glorious Revolution, just as the reforms of 1835 cannot be divorced from the Great Reform Act of 1832. There is not space in this book to discuss the political context of these events in detail, however. In both instances it was the right of the parliamentary boroughs to return MPs, which made them the object of crown or government intervention.[79] The Stuarts' *quo warranto* proceedings challenged corporations to show by what authority they held their charter; the outcome was inevitably to demand that the corporation should surrender its charter to the King, in return for a new one. In 1683, the city of London had challenged the *quo warranto* proceedings at King's Bench, and had been defeated.[80] Thereafter, only a few corporations put up any resistance to the royal will. In Dunwich and Berwick, attempts were made to resist the *quo warranto* proceedings, and in Chester the freemen were called upon to oppose the surrender of the charter and their rights. But such defiance was to no avail. When the new charters were granted, they made provision for the King to nominate and remove members of the corporation at will – there was little that a corporation could do to influence the terms of the new charters, although some managed to acquire confirmation of additional rights or privileges in the process. Contrary to subsequent Whig historiography, this procedure did not provoke much resistance under Charles II, as he used these powers solely to undermine Whig or dissenting interests in the corporations, where the Corporation Act of 1660 had failed to prove effective. In many cases the impetus for such proceedings had come from the locality – from Tory gentry or factions within the corporation. Royal policies happened to coincide with the aspirations of Anglican Tories, who were struggling against dissenting Whigs for supremacy in urban politics.[81] James II, however, performed something of a U-turn in royal policy. His ambition to pack Parliament, to produce a body

79. There have been a number of important studies of the local politics of boroughs in the late Stuart period. See in particular the series of articles by Michael Mullett, 'The politics of Liverpool, 1660–1688', *THSLC*, 124 (1973), pp. 31–56; 'The internal politics of Bedford, 1660–1688', *Bedfordshire Historical Records Society*, 59 (1980), pp. 1–42; 'Conflict, politics and election in Lancashire, 1660–1688', *Northern History*, 19 (1983), pp. 61–86; ' "Men of Knowne Loyalty": the politics of the Lancashire borough of Clitheroe, 1660–1689', *Northern History*, 21 (1985), pp. 108–36.

80. Jennifer Levin, *The Charter Controversy in the City of London 1660–88 and its Consequences* (1969). King's Bench ruled that the corporation could forfeit its privileges by abuse or misappropriation of the trust.

81. R. E. Pickavance, 'The English Boroughs and the King's Government: a study of the Tory Reaction, 1681–5', Oxford Univ. D.Phil. thesis (1976).

amenable to easing the position of Catholics in the country, led him to appoint dissenters in many corporations, who he hoped would be likely to return MPs who would vote for repeal of the anti-catholic legislation. The charters which he granted included a clause which absolved the corporation members from having to taking oaths of allegiance or supremacy, or from taking communion. In sixteen cases, the parliamentary franchise was restricted to a narrower body – with the intention of making the electorate easier to manipulate. Whereas the policies of Charles had complemented those of the gentry and the Anglican establishment, James's open disregard for the established church placed the use of *quo warranto* in an entirely different light, and his invasion of chartered privileges and dismissal of office-holders was seen as another example of his contempt of property rights. In October of 1688, faced with the outright opposition of his subjects, who had issued an invitation to William of Orange, in a belated attempt at reconciliation, James II revoked all the charters granted since 1679, except in cases where the surrender of the charter had actually been enrolled.

After the Glorious Revolution

From the very beginning of the new reign the relationship between the crown and the boroughs was transformed. Fourteen charters were granted during the reign of William and Mary; the lowest number issued during any reign since King John.[82] Their successors granted even fewer. The Whig reformers, H. A. Merewether and A. J. Stephens, listed 46 new charters granted in the period 1690–1835. Statutes legislating for corporations in general were hardly more numerous; it would seem that Parliament remained reluctant to venture upon activity which might appear reminiscent of the arbitrary behaviour of James II. Whig plans to exclude from public office all those who had been associated with the surrender of the charters under the Stuarts came to nothing (not least because in many towns it would have eliminated the entire ruling class). There was considerably more state intervention in local government at the county level, of which the most obvious example was the purging of the commissioners of the peace.[83] Nothing comparable was

82. H. A. Merewether and A. J. Stephens, *The History of the Boroughs and Municipal Corporations of the United Kingdom*, 3 vols (London, 1835), iii, p. 1844.
83. Landau, *The Justices of the Peace*; D. Eastwood, *Government and Community in the English Provinces 1700–1870* (1997).

attempted with respect to towns. Apart from the City Elections Act of 1725, which limited the right of voting to the aldermanic council in the city of London (an attempt by Walpole's government to block a potential channel for the expression of opposition politics on the part of the common council), there were few measures introduced by the government affecting corporations, except for a handful of acts aimed at minimizing political conflict at civic and parliamentary elections.[84] Civic office was regarded as a form of property, and eighteenth-century governments were particularly wary of any kind of action which might be construed as interference in the property rights of Englishmen. The contrast between the eighteenth century and earlier periods has been seen as evidence of a lack of interest and lack of vision on the part of the state. In the eyes of nineteenth-century reformers it represented a culpable neglect which allowed the urban elites responsible for governing towns, to pursue their self-interested ends undisturbed by higher considerations of public service and accountability. It permitted the machinery of medieval administration to creak on, while it became increasingly unsuitable for coping with the requirements of a rapidly growing and industrialising society. Such charters as were granted in the eighteenth century emulated in form those of earlier periods, and did not show any accommodation to the progress of society.[85]

The evidence of legislation and charters is not, however, the best means of assessing the relationship between government and towns – we need to consider the changing political contexts as well. Charters were an expression of royal authority; after the Glorious Revolution the locus of the authority of the King had shifted to Parliament. Although the King could still grant charters, the elevation of parliamentary authority, as opposed to personal monarchy, naturally encouraged petitioners in the localities to seek parliamentary sanction for new powers (in the form of local legislation), rather than that of the King. Powers to erect a workhouse, for example, which might once have been granted in a new charter, would now be obtained through local legislation. Charters were not simply the expression of a creative policy towards urban government. Base financial motives had lain behind many of the earlier grants, and cash-strapped monarchs, such as King John, casting around for additional sources of revenue, seized upon the potential for raising

84. 11 Geo I c. 4, repealed in 1746; 19 Geo II c. 8; see also 3 Geo III c. 15, the Durham electoral qualification act and 10 Geo III c. 15, Grenville's election act.

85. *Report of the Royal Commission on Municipal Corporations*, PP (1835) xxiii, p. 17.

revenue offered by the granting of charters. Subsequently charters were continually sought by nervous civic leaders, in confirmation of rights, especially at the accession of a new monarch. Throughout the early modern period the crown had been manipulating the granting of charters for its own political, and latterly, parliamentary ends anticipating the wholesale intervention of later Stuarts.[86]

In the aftermath of the débâcle of the 1680s, no monarch or minister would have risked a similar policy in the eighteenth century, and confirmatory charters were rarely sought after the 1690s. Nor would any government have contemplated the political risks of creating additional parliamentary boroughs. The last town to receive such a privilege was Newark, incorporated as a parliamentary borough in 1676. Some corporations which had existed previously as parliamentary boroughs received their first charters of municipal incorporation,[87] and only Deal, incorporated in 1699, had enjoyed neither municipal nor parliamentary borough status prior to incorporation. A large proportion of the charters which were issued were done so with the specific aim of clearing up the legacy of confusion arising from the 1680s.[88] The situation was particularly complex in Bewdley, where a new charter was granted in 1708 replacing that of 1685, but not all the corporation recognised it, and 'for two years, in consequence of the Charters, Bewdley had two Corporations, and two Bailiffs who fulminated against each other like rival Popes'.[89] Only a few of the 40 odd charters granted during this period actually increased the powers available to the corporation. The other grounds upon which new charters were sought was the need to increase the number of justices of the peace. The principal justification offered by the inhabitants of Deal in their petition was the need for resident JPs and a court for dealing with problems of crime and law and order.[90] Throughout the rest of the century, when new charters were granted, they generally included an increase in the number of JPs amongst the provisions. One of the last charters to be granted before the Municipal Corporations

86. Peter Clark and Paul Slack, *English Towns in Transition 1500–1700* (Oxford, 1976), p. 126. See also Robin Tittler, 'The incorporation of boroughs', *History*, lxii (1977), pp. 24–42.

87. These were Fowey, Malmesbury, Eye, Wareham, Leominster and Bodmin.

88. Not all requests for new charters to overcome this problem were granted. Plymouth and Plympton both had their petitions for new charters in the 1690s turned down. S. Porter, *Exploring Urban History – Sources for Local Historians* (1990), p. 116.

89. John R. Burton, *History of Bewdley* (1883), pp. 44–5, quoted in S. and B. Webb, *Manor and the Borough*, p. 271 n.

90. Stephen Pritchard, *The History of Deal and of its Neighbourhood, from the Invasion of Britain . . . to the present time* (Deal, 1864).

Act, was to Preston in 1828, which had nearly tripled in size since the beginning of the century, and urgently needed an increase in the number of magistrates to cope with the rise in the volume of business.[91] There were important reasons for not seeking a new charter from the perspective of the localities also. It was an expensive business, and given that in many towns the authority of the corporation was not necessarily uncontested, and attempts to increase that authority might be looked upon with suspicion, such enterprises could well founder in opposition and expensive legal proceedings. The infrequency with which new charters was granted is in fact misleading; it was an option which was quite frequently discussed, but the legal cost involved effectively capped the number of applications. In early nineteenth-century Plymouth proposals for a new charter were drawn up on two separate occasions, and in 1826 matters went as far as a new charter being drafted, but it proved impossible to agree on the terms on which it was to be granted.[92]

There was, in fact, considerable coincidence in the aspirations of urban leadership and those in power at Westminster, in securing prosperity, stability and domestic security, which meant that, for example, government legislation would be implemented even if there was no institutionalised machinery in place for seeing that it was enforced. As Joanna Innes has remarked, 'Parliament cannot be classified in terms of any simple central/local dichotomy. It was an arena in which representatives of different levels of government met and collaborated'. The connection was strengthened in the process of the administration of justice; notably the Assizes were still an important occasion for creating a point of contact between centre, represented by High Court judges, and locality.[93] Research is making it increasingly clear that a simple opposition of interests does not do justice to the way in which the localities and, not least,

91. H. W. Clemesha, *A History of Preston in Amounderness* (Manchester, 1912), p. 231. Population in 1801 was 11,887 and in 1831, 33,112. Other examples of charters which made provision for additional justices included Leominster (1705), London (1741), Liverpool (1751), Bath (1763), Exeter (1769), Kidderminster (1827), Reading (1830).

92. On the second occasion it would seem that legal opinion advised it would be unwise, as the necessary investigations into the history of the corporation would give ground to those pressing for an extension of the franchise to include all inhabitant householders in the town. See also C. B. Welch, 'Municipal reform in Plymouth', *TDA*, xciv (1964), pp. 318–39; SDRO W 65, Plymouth Constitution Book, 1824–35, f. 28.

93. Joanna Innes, 'Parliament and the shaping of eighteenth-century English social policy', *TRHS*, 5th ser., xl (1990), pp. 63–92; and 'The domestic face of the military-fiscal state: government and society in eighteenth-century Britain', in *An Imperial State at War*, (ed.) L. Stone (1994), p. 107.

urban society, evolved in relation to the development of the state. Local identity and independence were powerful forces and could be mobilised to great effect – as we shall see in subsequent chapters – but while we acknowledge the reluctance of urban elites to countenance any diminution of their own authority and independence, we must also recognise their willingness to participate in a national framework, and to exploit the channels of communication which bound them to the centre. Recent studies of merchant communities in towns such as Bristol and Great Yarmouth have stressed how the merchants pursued their own interests in a national context and made full use of the resources available to them through Parliament.[94] Analyses of eighteenth-century legislation have shown both that eighteenth-century governments can be awarded a much more creditable record, and that localities and towns were increasingly turning to Parliament (rather than the crown) in order to increase or adapt their own powers or authority – as we have already seen in looking at local improvement acts.[95] As one writer commented in 1754, 'It is our peculiar felicity to live in an Age, in which the Ears of King and Parliament are open to all the Petitions and Remonstrances of the People, it must therefore be our own Faults, if any one Thing be wanting to compleat the Public Weal'.[96] Commercial and economic, cultural and social forces all had a powerful centripetal force.

It is difficult to talk in general terms of a parliamentary policy towards towns, in the way that the Webbs attempted. They suggested, for example, that Parliament preferred to endow new powers upon the statutory bodies for special purposes, rather than upon the corporations. But Parliament or the 'state' did not have such a specific policy; when it granted new powers it was in response to local request, and the constitution of statutory bodies resulted primarily from questions of local expediency and convenience, rather than specific policy. There are relatively few examples of corporations seeking additional powers and being denied; the preference for statutory bodies came from the local level, as opposed to Westminster. The similarity which can be traced between many of the

94. Gauci, *Politics and Society in Great Yarmouth*; David Sacks, *Bristol and the Atlantic Economy, 1450–1700* (Oxford, 1991).

95. Joanna Innes, 'The local acts of a national Parliament: Parliament's role in sanctioning local action in eighteenth-century Britain', *Parliamentary History* (1998), pp. 23–47. My thanks to Joanna Innes for allowing me to see a copy of this article before its publication.

96. John Spranger, *A Proposal or a Plan for an Act of Parliament for the better Paving, Lighting and Cleansing the Streets . . . of the City and Liberty of Westminster* (1754), preface.

statutory bodies reflects the fact that it was quicker and cheaper to adopt a formula which had been successful in other bills, rather than to begin each time with a *tabula rasa*. In so far as we can talk of a government policy, it was one which sought to protect the interests of the propertied by keeping a close eye on the levels of the property qualification in the acts, and by insisting on due consultation of the relevant interests. Failure to give sufficient publicity to proposals for improvement in the local press and public meetings would ensure the defeat of the bill. Legislation was passed in 1773–4 which demanded that adequate notice should be given through announcements posted on the church door and advertisements at the Quarter Sessions. After 1791, proposals had to be advertised in the press at least three times in the August and September preceding the parliamentary session in which the bill was to be presented.[97] There was also a well entrenched disposition to oppose monopoly and encourage anything which would promote competition, which became more significant in the early nineteenth century, when the supply of gas and water was coming under discussion. In most cases, the outcome was that water companies and gas companies were rarely subsidiaries of corporations or improvement commissions. Municipal regulation was, however, still in its infancy, even at the end of our period and the terms on which the gas and water companies were set up had little provision for ensuring minimum standards or regulation of profits.

At the level of day-to-day management of business, the chief point of contact between government, at the centre and in the locality, lay in the office of justice of the peace. JPs were expected to enforce parliamentary legislation where appropriate, and it was JPs and Lord Lieutenants who reported back to government with the results of inquiries and information, and later to the Home Office in times of disturbance. In the counties and unincorporated towns, the JPs represented a link in an administrative chain which bound the locality to the centre, in that the appointment of JPs lay in the hands of the Lord Lieutenant, who was in turn appointed by the crown (or the King's ministers). Incorporated towns, as we have seen, had acquired the right to appoint their own magistracy and had varying powers of criminal jurisdiction. This was a privilege which was highly prized, not only for the symbolic status it carried, but because of the independence which it offered from external influences. (It was this judicial independence and the potential for

97. Spencer, *Municipal Origins*, pp. 65–9.

exercising it in favour of dissenters in the late seventeenth century, which had worried the later Stuarts, and had encouraged them in their attempts to secure the appointment of office-holders sympathetic to their aims.) Any threat to the jurisdiction of the urban magistracy, on the part of either the government or the county, was regarded with deep suspicion. The attempt to end the jurisdictional autonomy of the Nottingham magistrates, by introducing county JPs in 1802, following violent election riots which they had allegedly failed to control, provoked feelings of outrage and indignation that local privileges and liberties should be so disregarded.

Originally JPs had been appointed for the performance of local government at the King's command. Following the Glorious Revolution, their role had become that of local government at the command of the King in Parliament, and by the end of the century JPs were essentially answerable to the Home Office under the Secretary of State. The Home Office had been constituted in 1782 as a department specifically responsible for domestic affairs. Most of the correspondence between the urban magistracy and the Secretary of State was preoccupied with questions of public order – from the point of view of government, the most important duty of the local authorities was to maintain the peace. In general, the interaction was co-operative and urban authorities saw the Home Office, not as an interfering agency to be resisted, but as a higher source of authority to be appealed to for advice or assistance on matters such as riots or prison reform. In 1833 the mayor of Plymouth was deputed to write to the Home Secretary on the state of the prisons in Plymouth 'with a view to obtain the opinion of his Majesty's Government as to the best course to be adopted by the Corporation'.[98] During the riots of 1826, the frequency with which local authorities appealed to the Home Office for military aid in maintaining law and order was regarded with some exasperation; one minister complained that 'they look to Government to remedy every evil – to give every assistance'.[99] However, friction could be a problem when government fears about security seemed to disregard local custom, or to threaten the traditional autonomy of the local magistracy. In the midst of war-induced anxiety about internal stability, the city authorities in Oxford were rebuked by Portland, the Home Secretary, in 1800, for their supposed failure to prevent an outbreak of food rioting

98. SDRO, W 64 Plymouth Constitution Book 1824–35, f. 74 resolution of 29 Jan. 1833.

99. Quoted in Stanley H. Palmer, *Police and Protest in England and Ireland 1780–1850* (Cambridge, 1988), p. 285.

in the city which had involved an attack on the gaol. In threatening to prosecute the mayor, the government was over-reacting to what was simply an attempt in the tradition of the 'moral economy' to have the Assize of Bread enforced.[100]

JPs continued to be lynchpins of local government, especially in rural areas, but by the end of our period the heyday of the urban JP had arguably passed. During the 1830s and 1840s, a very marked change had taken place with respect to the government's attitude towards urban administration. As one historian has put it, the era of lighting and watching had given way to the era of public health – local initiative was overshadowed by government directives.[101] In the mid-eighteenth century, as the possibilities of improvement by local legislation were just being adumbrated, it seemed that all that was necessary was to activate the requisite powers. As Joseph Hanway remarked in 1754, on the condition of Westminster streets, 'The laws already enacted are ineffectual; but it does not follow that all future laws, for the purpose now in question, will be the same'.[102] Such optimism could not last, and reformers became steadily more disillusioned with the futility of a system which was essentially reliant on the willingness of the public to cooperate, and had no coercive force or sanctions. It was the weakness of local authorities and their inability to implement ameliorative legislation which reformers identified as the main flaw in urban government as it had evolved in the early nineteenth century. The discretionary powers of magistrates and the petty prejudices of local oligarchies further vitiated the limitations of the system. By the 1830s, it was widely recognised that large towns posed special problems of public health and social order, and that the existing administrative machinery was ill-adapted to cope with the demands being made of it. From the late eighteenth century we can see the first fumblings towards general legislation in domestic matters, rather than simply a series of responses to individual cases in 'permissive legislation', such as Gilbert's Act of 1782. This act allowed parishes to unite, in order to establish a poor law union with a workhouse for administering poor relief more efficiently. Such acts were not compulsory – they merely

100. Wendy Thwaites, 'Oxford food riots: a community and its markets', in Adrian Randall and Andrew Charlesworth (eds), *Markets, Market Culture and Popular Protest in Eighteenth-Century Britain and Ireland* (Liverpool, 1996), pp. 137–62.

101. John Prest, *Liberty and Locality. Parliament, Permissive Legislation, and Ratepayers' Democracies in the Nineteenth Century* (Oxford, 1990), p. 25.

102. Joseph Hanway, *A Letter to John Spranger on his Excellent Proposal for Paving, Cleansing and Lighting the Streets of Westminster and the Parishes in Middlesex* (1754), p. 8.

created the possibility of setting up these new administrative areas, and its powers could not be activated until a majority of the rate-payers had voted for it. The formula of this kind of 'permissive legislation' was to be repeated with greater frequency in the nine-teenth century – for example, in Sturges Bourne's Select Vestry Act of 1819, under which a majority of two-thirds of the ratepayers had to vote to activate the legislation.[103] 'Model clauses' acts, such as the 1833 Lighting and Watching Act, made the whole procedure of obtaining such legislation much more routine and formulaic, and was intended to reduce the costs of local improvement acts (which averaged £1,627 in the 1830s), thereby enabling localities to cope with the problems of urbanisation at a less prohibitive cost. This 'legislative meccano', described by John Prest, was a first stage towards a more systematic regulatory approach to local government, albeit one which still respected the traditions of local autonomy.

    In the early nineteenth century, as government became better informed about the state of the nation through the inquiries of select committees and their reports, and the incremental gather-ing of statistical information, carried out under the auspices of a host of newly formed societies,[104] it became more feasible for polit-icians to develop an overall conception of the needs of the nation at large, and think in terms of a formulation of a general policy. Ideas of uniformity and rationalization accordingly became more prac-ticable and consequently desirable propositions. During the 1820s, this trend became particularly marked as, under Robert Peel, the Home Office began to realise its potential as a government depart-ment, and we see the enactment of what can justifiably be termed a programme of social legislation, with measures such as the Gaols Act (1823), and in 1834, the Poor Law Amendment Act and the Municipal Corporations Act (1835) – all of which provided for a greater measure of uniformity and accountability to government.[105] These changes were not the actions of an aggressive centralizing state

    103. See above, p. 32.
    104. Society for the Encouragement of Arts, Commerce and Manufacture founded in 1754 by William Shipley; provincial scientific, literary and philosophical societies; studies of political economy in county and urban histories; D. G. C. Allen, 'The Society of Arts and government 1754–1800', *Eighteenth-Century Studies*, 7 (1973–4); J. B. Harley, 'The Society of Arts and the surveys of English counties', *Journal of the Royal Society of Arts*, 112 (1963–4); D. G. C. Allen, *William Shipley, Founder of the Royal Society of Arts* (repr. 1979). For the 19th century, see Michael J. Cullen, *The Statistical Movement in Early Victorian Britain* (1975).
    105. A. P. Donagrodzki, 'The Home Office, 1822–1848', Oxford Univ. D.Phil. thesis (1973).

deliberately encroaching upon local autonomy. Rather, they arose from the recognition that the intractability of the problems which were being encountered, necessitated something more far-reaching and comprehensive than the piecemeal and *ad hoc* approach of local improvement acts administered by locally accountable bodies. Parliamentary sanction and direction was effectively being used to give greater force and powers of compulsion to reforming measures and bye-laws, which although well-intentioned had been rarely enforced. Perceptions of towns had changed too; large industrial towns seemed to pose a unique threat to the stability and well–being of society, and were therefore proper objects of legislative activity. From the 1830s, therefore, we see the beginning of a period of rationalization in the relationship between urban and central government, which epitomises a much more general shift towards greater state power and a more highly evolved bureaucracy, which was taking place in English political culture as a whole.[106] The links between the government and locality were becoming more tightly meshed, while the country was becoming more intensely governed.

106. Eastwood, *Government and Community*, esp. pp. 117–54.

CHAPTER THREE

Urban Administration

> It cannot but be felt and acknowledged by every man, that the glory
> of a City does not consist so much in the spaciousness of its streets,
> nor in the splendour of its palaces, as it does in the due regulation of
> its Inhabitants, and in the wholesomeness of its laws.[1]

Having looked at the structures of authority within towns, we will
now examine in more detail how urban authorities exercised their
power and performed the duties inherent in their various official
capacities. In the following chapter we will consider the process by
which towns were governed, looking at the contemporary expectations of urban government, the extent of its competence, the problems which had to be dealt with, and the ways and means available
to those managing them. It will become clear that, from a prag-
matic view of 'getting things done' and ensuring social harmony
and order, it is not helpful to attempt to draw anything more than
very general distinctions between the roles performed by corporations, as opposed to the parish, court leet or an improvement commission. As we have already seen, the balance of authority varied
from town to town. The court leet of one town would replicate the
functions of the corporation in another, whose role in the next
town would be mirrored by the improvement commissioners. Even
within one community there was always a fluidity of structure, so
that improvement commissioners might gradually supersede a corporation, or a parish supplant the court leet. In any town, whatever
the administrative structure, the streets still had to be paved, cleansed
and lighted, and rubbish still had to be removed. Markets always
needed to be regulated, law and order maintained, poor relief administered and the morality of society upheld. All these responsibilities

---

1. E. Sayer, *Observations on the police or civil government of Westminster* (1784), p. 48.

constituted a serious administrative burden and financial drain upon those in positions of authority. The second part of this chapter will focus on the different resources and strategies available, and examine the ethos of public service which underpinned the edifice of urban administration.

Regulating the Streets

The most visibly pressing administrative need in any town was to keep the streets clean. Left unregulated, streets could rapidly degenerate into a quagmire of mud and potholes, awash with liquid manure and the detritus of urban life. The upkeep of the streets was not merely a matter of convenience or aesthetics. Dirty, impassable streets acted as an impediment to trade and deterred visitors. The state of the streets had deeper implications for the urban body politic; contemporary thought compared the streets of a town to the arterial passages of the body. It was essential for the health of the body politic, therefore, that streets should be kept clear and to allow a free circulation of air. This contemporary description from the *Liverpool Vestry Books* gives an impression of the kind of problem which even a fairly efficient body could face:

> The streets are generally well cleaned by scavengers, who are regular and diligent in their duty; but in the execution of their business, while they remove one evil they never fail to create a greater. The soil, instead of being immediately carted away, as in London and other places, is raked into heaps about 12 ft. by 8, and two feet deep; these Cloacenian repositories are common in every part of the town, and remain eight or ten days, and sometimes longer before they are carted away, whereby passengers in a dark night, and often in the day, tread in them to the mid-leg, and children are sometimes nearly suffocated by falling into them. The exhalations in summer, by reason of these assemblages of soil being exposed many days to the sun, have a most pungent effect on the olfactory nerves of the passenger, nor are the inhabitants of those houses which are situated near them insensible of the pernicious effects of their effluvia on their health and constitution.[2]

The increase in the density of population and in the volume of traffic, which affected almost all eighteenth-century towns, greatly

2. Quoted in J. A. Picton, *Memorials of Liverpool, historical and topographical*, 2 vols (1873), i, pp. 255–6.

exacerbated the problem of regulation confronting the authorities. More people were passing through towns, and heavier vehicles with narrow metal wheels broke up the road surface more quickly. It has been calculated that in Hanoverian Northampton the inns of the town could provide stabling for 4–5,000 horses; convert that into productive capacity for manure and one begins to appreciate that the streets of most towns must have approximated a giant Augean stable.[3] Town centres were becoming much more crowded; there were notable suburban developments on the outskirts of many towns, but in the absence of a public transport system, the pressure was still to concentrate within the centre, resulting in what would now be termed 'urban infill', on a very large scale. Medieval and early modern towns had always included a substantial amount of open land used for market gardening and grazing livestock; early modern town plans bristle with trees and orchards. These open spaces were being built upon as never before. Meanwhile, patterns of life were slower to change: butchers still preferred to slaughter livestock in the open; pigs continued to run riot through the streets, cattle were still driven through the centre of the town for market and householders still emptied night soil into the streets at inopportune times. A more crowded environment rendered such practices increasingly objectionable, and the tolerance level of the 'public' for dirt, potholes and stench became lower. It is clear that in the course of urban improvement, expectations were changing. Whereas pigsties and broken pavements might not have seemed incongruous in the irregular and haphazard streets of a medieval city, in the refurbished environment of the eighteenth century they assumed the status of an eyesore. Cleanliness was literally next to godliness, as one correspondent to the *Bath Journal* made clear, in a letter complaining about the state of Avon Street where people were wont to 'ease nature' upon the pavement: 'Nastiness gradually produces sloth and debases and corrupts both the body and the mind.'[4] The link between the physical and moral corruption of the town was frequently made, and advances in medical knowledge made clear the connection between disease and filth. The ordure on the pavements and the stench from pigsties was not simply noxious to the senses, but accepted as a health hazard. The *History of Health and the Art of Preserving it* (1758), by James Mackenzie, had pointed

3. Alan Everitt, 'The English urban inn 1560–1760', in Everitt (ed.), *Perspectives in English Urban History* (1973), p. 102.
4. *Bath Journal*, 17 July 1777, letter from CIVIS, quoted in Trevor Fawcett (ed.), *Voices of Eighteenth-Century Bath. An Anthology* (Bath, 1995), p. 168.

out the dangers of insanitary dwellings and of burial grounds in populous areas, long before what we are accustomed to think of as the era of public health.

It did not prove easy to develop effective methods of dealing with these problems. Regulating such matters had always been one of the functions of urban government, and such nuisances were the bread and butter of the mayor's court or the court leet, and latterly the Quarter Sessions. Witnesses reported 'nuisances' when householders had broken the laws regulating the disposal of rubbish, or had failed to fulfil their obligations for cleaning the street at the court leet, and the offender was fined. There was no other means of retribution or enforcement. Not surprisingly, the responsibility of the householder to cleanse the pavement before his house, upheld by informal sanctions of the court leet, had long since proved inadequate. As a result, scavengers, forerunners of our modern dustmen, had been employed in most towns by the court leet, or the corporation, to clean the streets since the early modern period or earlier. The improvement commissions which were established in the eighteenth century did not introduce radically new means of managing the urban environment. They simply elaborated upon the system of bye-laws and fines which were intended to deter people from committing such offences, and continued to employ a scavenger to present offenders at the magistrate's court, much as had happened when it was the responsibility of the court leet. Active encouragement might be given to inhabitants to prosecute offenders – the Oxford Paving Commissioners allowed 2/6d from every fine, arising from a successful prosecution, to the individual who had reported it.[5] But prosecution was an expensive business and ultimately seldom worth the expense.

Improvement, or street commissioners and other similar agencies, had to make the choice between direct management of street cleaning, which allowed them to keep a tighter control over its performance but demanded more oversight from the commissioners, or contracting out, which left them with less overall control and always led to complaints that the scavengers were not fulfilling their contractual obligations. Most commissions seem to have alternated between both approaches; neither was wholly satisfactory. Attempts were often made to kill two birds with one stone by employing paupers from the workhouse to clean the streets. A number of paving commissioners adopted this plan between 1790 and 1830,

5. OCA R/6/2b, f. 50v, 9 Mar. 1772.

when the problem of finding employment for paupers was particularly acute, and paid the guardians of the poor a yearly sum for the labour of the workhouse inmates. In Oxford, for example, the guardians of the poor held a contract to sweep the streets for £130 pa for many years.[6] The contractor was then free to make whatever profits he could from the sale of manure and night soil – valuable products at a time when fertilisers were in their infancy. The potential of urban manure for agriculture was only highlighted in the second half of the eighteenth century, and was popularised by Arthur Young in his *Six Weeks Tour*.[7] Dust and ashes were also valuable commodities, being essential ingredients for the manufacture of bricks, which were in constant demand from the booming building industry. By the early nineteenth century, the commissioners of a parish such as St Marylebone were actually earning £2,350 pa from the sale of manure and dust. The scavenger of Plymouth had to appeal to the mayor for an alternative site for his dung heap because the one allocated to him by the bowling green was simply too vulnerable to theft.[8] Even in the 1840s, Edwin Chadwick's plans for reforming the nation's sewers included provision for covered pipes to carry off urban effluvia to fertilise outlying fields. One unfortunate side-effect of this rise in value was that it encouraged people to hoard the dung and dust in unsavoury heaps, constituting yet another health hazard.

An essential step in keeping the streets passable was to construct proper pavements and road surfaces to prevent them from being churned into quagmires, and to assist in drainage. Prior to the eighteenth century, 'paving' such as it was, consisted of sharp cobbles, laid so that they pointed upwards. These provided an extremely uncomfortable surface to walk upon, and were especially hazardous when rendered slippery by wet weather. A central gutter would run down the centre of the street, ostensibly to carry away all rubbish. This rudimentary system was replaced by flat, close fitting paving stones, with a raised pavement, edged with curb stones, and gutters at the side of the paved street. Paving was an extremely expensive undertaking, both in terms of raw materials and the labour involved. The streets had first to be surveyed, to ensure that

6. OCA R/6/2b, f. 51 commissioners' agreement to pay £130 pa. 27 Feb. 1833, the agreement was £900 for 3 years, R/5/6, p. 343.
7. Arthur Young, *A Six Weeks Tour through the Southern Counties of England and Wales* (1769).
8. SDRO, W 705, 20 June 1815; and S. and B. Webb, *Statutory Bodies for Special Purposes* (1922), pp. 315–43.

they were level and that the surface water could drain off. The paving stones, being so heavy, were very costly to transport and laying them evenly was a skilled job. In 1792 James Oakes surveyed the Guildhall Street in Bury St Edmunds and estimated that it would cost £100–£120 to pave just that street,[9] while the whole of Southampton was new paved in the 1770s for a total of £4,775 17s 10d. Once paved, the streets demanded ongoing investment to keep them in a state of reasonable repair. Heavy vehicles with narrow, iron-rimmed wheels broke up the surfaces, and burst water pipes necessitated taking up the paving for their repair. The contract for repairing the streets of Southampton for a year was £101 17s 4d.[10] Well paved streets and open vistas were the *sine qua non* of a civilized town and were immediately commented upon by visitors. It was, of course, only the main streets of the town which were subjected to this improvement. The poorer areas, away from the commercial centre, continued in their unpaved and insanitary state until the Victorians took action in the era of sanitary reform.

Streets also had to be regulated for obstructions, and what we would now think of as traffic offences. Gutters and drainpipes on houses were as primitive as the arrangements for carrying water off the streets. Without proper drainpipes rain-water was liable to cascade off roofs onto unwary passers-by, but care had also to be exercised that drainpipes did not project too far into the narrow streets. Shop signs were another hazard – Addison ridiculed their proliferation and the pretensions of their designs in the *Spectator*. But on a more practical level, they blocked the light from the streets lamps, and obstructed the passage of larger vehicles and the movement of air.[11] Given that in many towns, such as Bristol or Great Yarmouth, the medieval streets were too narrow to admit vehicles other than sledges or sedan chairs, this was a matter of some importance. Urban authorities were also accustomed to issuing numerous bye-laws regulating the use of the streets: pigs were not supposed to roam untended and were regularly impounded; driving too fast caused many accidents in city streets, and the speed of carriages was checked. Likewise, it was generally an offence to ride stallions through densely populated areas – for obvious reasons. Carriages

9. Jane Fiske (ed.), *The Oakes Diaries. Business, Politics and the Family in Bury St Edmunds, 1778–1827*, 2 vols, Suffolk Record Society, xxxii–xxxiii (1990–91), ii, p. 279.

10. Jan Stovold (ed.), *Minute Book of the Pavement Commissioners for Southampton, 1770–1789*, Southampton Record Series, xxxi (1990), p. 6.

11. Richard Steele and Joseph Addison, *Selections from the Tatler and the Spectator*, (ed.) Angus Ross, Penguin edn (repr. 1988), no. 28 'Street Signs', pp. 283–5.

and other vehicles which were parked blocking the street were subject to fines, and in some towns were even impounded (although there was no eighteenth-century equivalent to the wheel clamp). Our modern-day system of licensed cabs has its origins in eighteenth-century attempts to regulate sedan chairs and hackney carriages, by a system of licensing and a fixed table of charges and fees.

Street Lighting

Closely associated with the upkeep of the streets was the business of lighting; local acts were often referred to simply as lighting and paving, or lighting and watching acts. Lighting the streets before the eighteenth century had been a haphazard affair in most towns. Individual householders were generally expected to provide a lantern, lit by a candle, outside their house during the winter months, but otherwise moonlight offered the only means of illumination. In a few towns one or two lamps might be erected for a limited time in a central location, such as the market-place, at corporation or parish expense. The purpose of lighting was to promote law and order, therefore after dusk, when the city gates had been locked and the curfew called, there were few citizens on the streets, and there was in principle no need for any illumination. (The curfew was theoretically still imposed until the beginning of the eighteenth century, but never seems to have been enforced with much rigour.) By the end of the eighteenth century street lighting had become an essential feature of urban life and, like street cleaning, was no longer the responsibility of the individual householder. There was now far more going on in towns; more traffic, commerce and social activities, and people were going abroad after dark to an unprecedented extent. The contrast between the lights of the town and the darkness of the surrounding countryside became one of the defining features of urban life, and no celebration was complete without an illumination of the town, when the windows of every household and public building were lit up. Lighting was essential to avoid the hazards of the erratically cleaned streets, but it was the fear of assault, robbery and the rising crime wave which lay behind most of the protests against the Stygian darkness of the streets.[12]

12. Malcolm Falkus, 'Lighting in the dark ages of English economic history: town streets before the industrial revolution', in D. C. Coleman and A. H. John (eds), *Trade, Government and Economy in Pre-Industrial England* (1976), pp. 248–73.

Lighting, however, was also expensive, which in itself is sufficient to explain why it was not more widespread in towns at an earlier date. Oil street lamps, replacing the weak and unreliable light of candles, were first developed in London in the late seventeenth century, amidst the quickening pace of nocturnal social life. Joint stock companies were rapidly set up, which contracted to provide lighting with oil lamps for a specified number of hours. Provincial towns only followed suit slowly, under the auspices of the corporation or, more commonly, under the terms of an improvement act, which allowed for the levying of a lighting rate. Oil was the most expensive element but, in addition, lamp irons and glass lanterns had to be bought. The glass for the lanterns was expensive and easily broken; then as now the sound of breaking glass was both a gesture and an expression of alcohol induced exuberance, or defiance (breaking the street lights became a traditional element of the urban riot). Heavy penalties were inflicted upon those caught engaged upon the act, but the costs of repair rose effortlessly above the income from such fines. The annual cost of lighting a lamp in the 1770s was around 12–13s in most towns, depending on how long the lighting season was determined to last. In London, where lamps were lit all year round, the cost was about 25s.[13] All urban authorities drew up elaborate regulations to ensure maximum benefit for minimum outlay: lights were not lit during full moon or in the summer months; lamps, away from the main thoroughfares, would be extinguished earlier than those in the main area. The night-watchman was expected to check that the lamps were all burning satisfactorily, and to report any which were damaged or had been allowed to go out. The responsibility for lighting and servicing the lamps was generally contracted out, like the scavenging, and the contractors were always keen to cut costs by lighting up late, extinguishing early, and leaving other lamps unrepaired or unlit, creating a running sore of discontent among the ratepayers in most communities.

In the beginning of the nineteenth century gas lighting became a possibility, and by the 1820s its use was widespread. The first trial with gas lights was in London in 1807, and the Coke and Gas Light Company was incorporated in 1812. In Manchester, gas lights were introduced by the police commissioners in 1805 and 1807, although it was not until 1817 that a local act was acquired which formally gave the police commissioners the authority to manufacture gas.

13. Falkus, 'Lighting in the dark ages', p. 262.

Preston followed in 1815, as the first provincial town to be entirely lit in the new manner. Most of the larger industrial towns followed suit; by 1821 all towns over 50,000 had gas companies. By 1826, after another wave of gas acts peaking in 1822–3, almost all towns over 10,000 had also established gas companies. The introduction of gas lighting was far more comprehensive and swift than oil lamps – in itself illustrating what an important priority adequate street lighting had become in urban life.[14] Although desirable, the introduction of gas in place of oil was not entirely straightforward, in that it needed large-scale initial investment, and involved breaking up the pavements, paved at great expense, in order to lay down the pipes. There was considerable debate as to whether it was preferable for 'essentials' like gas, or water, to be supplied by a private company, which was seeking to make a profit, or a public body, such as an improvement commission or corporation, but with the risk of giving them a monopoly. Commissioners tried to occupy the moral high ground, claiming to represent only the interest of the public, and argued that profit motivated fat cat gas proprietors were defrauding their fellow townsmen by overcharging for the gas supplied, and supplying it in insufficient quantities, so that the lights were too dim and went out too early. Gas companies argued that private companies allowed competition in the market which would ensure higher quality and lower prices. These issues provided the context for considerable conflict in a number of towns in the 1820s and 30s; in Manchester it escalated to become the major issue dividing local politics in the 1820s.[15] Ultimately, of course, the issue had to be settled in Parliament, for whether gas was provided by public or private bodies, parliamentary sanction was needed. As we saw in the previous chapter, in so far as government had a policy, it would seem that there was a disposition towards encouraging competition, and a reluctance for monopoly. The situation in Manchester, where the police commissioners secured ownership of the gas works in the 1824 Gas Act, was unusual; few other commissions or corporations were given leave to establish or purchase a gas or water company, and the large income, which ownership made available to the Manchester authorities, was regarded with envy by other municipal bodies.[16]

14. M. E. Falkus, 'The British gas industry before 1850', *Economic History Review* (1969), pp. 494–508.

15. M. J. Turner, 'Gas, police and the struggle for mastery in Manchester in the eighteen-twenties', *Historical Research*, 67 (1994), pp. 301–17.

16. Ibid., p. 312.

Urban Planning

With the increasing pressure on space, and proliferation of building
in towns, urban authorities were forced into a much more *dirigiste*
stance on regulating buildings and enforcing standards of construction. Again, in some respects this was simply an amplification of a
traditional aspect of urban government; regulations about thatch,
drainpipes and projecting signs had always been imposed, albeit
somewhat ineffectually. The influence of eighteenth-century neo-
classicism, with its emphasis on order, symmetry, regularity and
balance, meant that it was no longer acceptable to have irregular
streets, with houses arranged haphazardly with crooked vistas, and
a miscellany of styles. There was also a practical dimension, in that
narrow streets were a considerable problem with the ever increasing
volume of traffic, but the aesthetics of the matter were crucial. Some
even went so far as to argue that it was a reflection on the state of
national morality, 'The refinement of taste in a nation never fails to
be accompanied by a suitable refinement of manners; and people
accustomed to behold order, decency, and elegance in public, soon
acquire that urbanity in private, which forms at once the excellence
and bond of society'.[17] It was the order and regularity of Bath which
was consistently singled out for the most favourable comment. The
American traveller, Jabez Fisher, wrote that it was 'the most beautiful
and elegant Town I have ever seen. Nothing can exceed the uniformity and neatness of these Buildings and being all of one kind of
Stone and that of a beautiful colour has a most happy effect'.[18]

The eighteenth century saw the first real building boom outside
the metropolis. Bow windows, projecting roofs, houses which were
out of line, drainpipes, or the lack of them, building materials
and even building styles, had to be subject to approval in order to
ensure a safe, commodious and aesthetically pleasing environment.
Building regulations were most rigidly defined in the growth of
London, where the precedent had been set in the 1667 Act for
Rebuilding After the Fire. Warwick and Northampton, in the late
seventeenth century, both lifted chunks verbatim from the London
Act, in the local acts which they acquired for similar post-fire re-
construction. The use of thatch was very commonly outlawed, as it

17. *Critical Observations on the Buildings and Improvements of London* (not dated),
p. 50.
18. K. Morgan (ed.), *An American Quaker in the British Isles. The Travel Journals of
Jabez Maude Fisher, 1775–79* (Oxford, 1992), p. 116.

presented such a fire hazard, and it is remarkable how the incidence of urban fires did diminish over the century. In the new suburban terraces and squares of the West End, structural requirements for foundations, external and party walls were laid down for four different 'rates' of houses, each with their appropriate level of ornamentation and decoration, in the 1774 Building Act. This was ostensibly in order to keep some kind of control over the cost cutting activities of speculative builders, but more immediately it meant that all the new developments were essentially similar in size and style, creating the ordered uniformity which is so characteristic of eighteenth-century cities.[19] It was not always necessary to seek statutory authority for enforcing building regulations; a common ploy, where the corporation owned and leased large amounts of property, was to bind the lessee to observe the relevant regulations in covenant clauses of the leases, clauses which became increasingly detailed over the century. Houses built in similar style opened up the possibility of creating larger architectural units of squares and terraces. In 1708, the first square outside London was begun in Bristol, setting the example for similar schemes in provincial towns across the country. Even older buildings could be brought into line with this new urban aesthetic by refronting them with a classical facade and introducing the requisite ornament and detail.

The possibility and desirability of a measure of urban planning, in order to avoid the 'confusion and deformity' which the architect John Gwynn complained of in London, soon became apparent. In *London and Westminster Improved* (1761) he deplored the lack of control exercised in the laying out and building of estates in the West End. Wholesale town planning and building regulation, however, could only be effectively implemented when a single individual owned all the property concerned and wanted to take an active interest. In most towns there were far too many property holders for a *dirigiste* system to be effectively imposed; even in a 'purpose-built' resort, such as Tunbridge Wells, plans foundered on a clash of conflicting property interests. The best example of urban planning is therefore to be found in the small town of Whitehaven on the north west coast, which achieved short-lived prosperity in the earlier eighteenth century, from the Atlantic trade with America and the coal industry of its hinterland. Sir John Lowther, the largest property holder, bought out all other interests, and he and his successors used their well-nigh absolute power to exercise strict

19. John Summerson, *Georgian London* (1978), pp. 125–6.

control over the development of the town, from a settlement of a few hundred in the seventeenth century, to a busy port of up to 16,000 by the 1760s.[20] In London, large landowners, such as the Grosvenor and Cavendish families in London, often took responsibility for the overall development of a specific area, such as Bloomsbury. They laid out the location of roads, drains and squares, and then leased the plots to builders on 99 year leases, which ensured a homogenous end product, but reduced the capital outlay.[21] In general, most corporations and improvement commissions did not go further than employing surveyors, who not only assessed the value of the property, but oversaw its development and drew up accurate surveys and plans. Hence, the 1821 Improvement Act in Cheltenham stipulated that all plans for new buildings and alterations should be submitted to the surveyor for inspection, who was empowered to enforce the regulations.[22]

Water Supplies

Nowadays, we are accustomed to associate a healthy environment with a pure water supply and an effective sewerage system, but in the eighteenth century the connection was far from axiomatic. The purpose of a sewer was to get rid of excess surface water, rather than deal with the effluvia of human society. Households were not actually connected to the sewers in the streets, indeed it was normally forbidden and special permission had to be sought. The provision of water, despite being one of the essentials of urban life, was still in its very rudimentary stages, and as with everything else, the responsibility for providing it was carried by a variety of different bodies from town to town. Corporations, such as Plymouth, York, Hull and Oxford, owned and managed the water works. In other towns they were leased out, and in London there had been a number of private water companies since the seventeenth century. The common pattern in the eighteenth century was to seek statutory powers to set up a water company, but they were subject to exactly the same kind of controversy, being 'public utilities', as the gas companies. Hence, in Oxford the corporation was reluctant to

20. J. V. Beckett, *Coal and Tobacco. The Lowthers and the Economic Development of West Cumberland 1660–1760* (Cambridge, 1981), pp. 180–200; Sylvia Collier and Sarah Pearson, *Whitehaven, 1660–1800* (1991).
21. Summerson, *Georgian London*, esp. pp. 98–112 and pp. 163–76.
22. Gwen Hart, *A History of Cheltenham* (Leicester, 1965), p. 299.

relinquish ultimate responsibility into private hands, although maintaining the water works was an extremely heavy drain upon their finances, and they acknowledged that the provision of water was a responsibility which they bore to the public. The corporation of Plymouth came under heavy criticism for the rates which it charged to those who had water piped to their house; it was argued that they were making it a source of private profit (which rather obscured the fact that the corporation intended to use the monies to defray the expenses of other public projects, such as the construction of the new hotel and theatre), whereas water was the 'exclusive right of the inhabitants' and should be 'unsusceptible of conversion to corporate property or being the subject of gains and profits'.[23] Similarly, the Manchester Police Commissioners opposed the creation of a joint stock company to manage the water works, because they would be committed only to their own private interest, and therefore decided to support a plan for a public service managed jointly by them and the churchwardens.[24]

Provisions for improving water supplies were patchy and infrequent until well into the nineteenth century. London was considerably in advance of the rest of the country in the extent of piped water available to households, and the use of steam power to pump water up to higher levels (a facility which was becoming increasingly necessary with the spread of water closets). Some rudimentary progress had been made in the late seventeenth century. Between 1670–1700 schemes or bills for improvements to the water supply were made in at least eight provincial towns, including the major centres York, Bristol, Norwich and Newcastle.[25] Although piped water reached more middling homes by the nineteenth century, few labouring families would have had access to it. The 'rental' for having water piped to one's house was 16s a year in Plymouth by 1822, presuming that the property was within reach of one of the main water pipes. This apparent neglect on the part of the authorities was not simply because people ignored the perils of a primitive water supply, but it was not an obvious necessity; water could be drawn from rivers and collected in rain-water cisterns without obvious

23. SDRO, W 564 complaints about the scarcity of water, unfoliated collection; W 65 Constitution Book 1824–35, f. 102.
24. A. Redford, *The History of Local Government in Manchester*, 3 vols (1939), i, p. 235.
25. Peter Borsay, 'The English Urban Renaissance: the development of provincial urban culture, 1680–1760', in Borsay (ed.), *The Eighteenth-Century Town, 1688–1820* (1990), p. 169.

risk to health, and the cost of introducing piped water, like piped gas, was considerable. The corporation of Plymouth spent over £7,000 on improvements to the water system in the 1820s, extending it, laying down cast iron pipes and fire plugs.[26] Arguably, the increase in water acts in the 1830s was due more to the newly available, cheap, cast iron pipes, which replaced the leaky wooden ones, than an enlightened sanitary policy. The perceived benefits of a sewerage system based upon the flow of water were only in their infancy, as civil engineers worked out the importance of gradient, water pressure and egg shaped pipes. Despite the proselytizing zeal with which Edwin Chadwick called for a circulatory sewerage system, based upon a continual flow of water, it was these structural factors, rather than a transformation in public awareness of the link between public hygiene and water born disease, which led to greater investment in water works and sewers.[27]

Clean Air and Pollution

The pollution of the rivers and the water supplies, due to inadequate sewers, was unarguably the major health hazard of towns in this period, but for contemporaries it was the pollution of the air which aroused greater concern. Open gutters, drains and heaps of manure of butchers' debris were regarded as urban nuisances, not only because they polluted the water supply, but because of their inconvenience and noxious fumes. John Spranger, advocating the removal or rubbish from the streets of Westminster, warned that, 'The Air of great and populous Cities must, at best, be bad; and nothing renders it more unsafe and destructive, than suffering putrid bodies of any kind to lie in it'.[28] The importance of clean air and the dangers to health posed by lack of ventilation and pollution had been recognised as a problem for rather longer than had the problems of insanitary living conditions and polluted water supplies. John Evelyn, diarist and Fellow of the Royal Society, published his famous tract *Fumifugium: or, The inconveniences of the aer and smoak of London dissipated* in 1661, decrying the noxious fumes of

26. SDRO, W 564 papers concerning the claims of inhabitants to water and lawsuits resulting, 1829–31.

27. Martin Daunton, *Progress and Poverty. An Economic and Social History of Britain, 1700–1850* (Oxford, 1995), pp. 225–6.

28. John Spranger, *A Proposal or a Plan . . . for the City and Liberty of Westminster* (1754), preface.

London, and advocating the planting of market gardens on the outskirts of the city to sweeten the air. Medical opinion blamed bad atmosphere for almost any ill. One of the arguments for broadening the narrow streets in medieval city centres was to improve the circulation of air, and open spaces within a town were jealously retained for their salubrious qualities. As middle class opinion became alarmed at the living conditions of the working classes in the 1820s, it was the lack of ventilation which was seized upon as the most serious health hazard in the back-to-back tenements and cellar dwellings of the great cities, although in our period little was done to remedy the situation. Visitors to towns such as Bristol, Birmingham, Liverpool and Swansea always commented adversely on the pall of smoke which hung over these places. Although the Liverpool doctor, William Moss, in his *Medical Survey of Liverpool*, proclaimed the antiseptic qualities of the effluvia of coal and sulphurous smoke, he was fighting a rearguard action.[29] More typical was the visitor to Bristol who deplored the 'great number of glass houses, whose high chimneys look like so many towers, and whose continual smoke not only darkens the city, but also conveys a very noxious effluvia to the inhabitants'.[30] The Manchester court leet and other bodies did take action against air pollution, fining offenders as with any other kind of 'nuisance' in the streets, but it was not until 1812 that Birmingham acquired the first Smoke Abatement Act.[31] Meanwhile, in 1804 the corporation of Liverpool successfully indicted the proprietors of the lime kilns adjacent to the infirmary, for the vast quantities of 'azotic gas' which were being generated, on the grounds that it was injurious to the health of the patients.[32] Legal action was taken in the 1820s in Swansea to reduce the emission of sulphurous smoke from the copper smelting industry, which was producing environmental blight. But one should note, in contrast, however, that it was 1837 before even the sketchiest provisions were made to improve the Swansea water supply, by building a reservoir. The quality of air was more pervasive than the quality of housing, and could not be ignored by moving into the more salubrious residential areas in the less crowded suburbs.

29. William Moss, *A Familiar Medical Survey of Liverpool: Addressed to the Inhabitants at Large* (Liverpool, 1784), pp. 30–45.
30. Nathaniel Spencer, *The Complete English Traveller: Or a New Survey and Description of England and Wales* (1771), p. 45.
31. Bryan Keith Lucas, 'Some influences affecting the development of sanitary legislation in England', *EcHR*, vi (1953–4), p. 95.
32. Thomas Troughton, *The History of Liverpool from the earliest authenticated period to the present time* (Liverpool, 1810).

Law and Order: Riots and Disturbances

'Police' in eighteenth, and indeed early nineteenth-century terminology, encompassed far more than crime prevention and detection. However, we will take the issue of police here in its narrower application of maintaining order and preventing crime. Crime, and the threat of disorder from mobs, assumed a higher prominence in urban life during our period than ever before. The maintenance of law and order was possibly the most important function of urban government; it was certainly the one which brought it into closest contact with the central authorities. It has already been suggested in chapter 2 that considerations of law and judicial authority were uppermost in spurring Charles II into the first phase of government intervention in the 1680s, and it is clear that mounting anxiety, in certain quarters, over the inability of urban authorities to maintain law and order in the face of political unrest, contributed to the reforms of 1835. Urban societies have always been highly volatile; the concentration of population, vulnerable to hardship and adverse economic conditions, coupled with an organized work-force, accustomed to cooperation, has ensured that the town, rather than the countryside, has always tended to be at the centre of disturbances. For all that Hanoverian England has acquired a popular image of somnolent stability, it was in fact a turbulent society, as historians of popular politics and the crowd have convincingly shown.[33] The Quarter Session records from London for the early eighteenth century, for example, show that outbreaks of violence in the capital were much more common than has commonly been supposed. London was unusual in the political sophistication of its work-force and the density of its population, and would therefore be expected to experience higher levels of urban protest. Similarly, most research on the crowd, or the 'mob', which was generally at the heart of these protests, has focused on London. The crowd was organized, even disciplined, and far from being made up of an unruly rabble, could include many of the more

33. John Bohstedt, *Riots and Community Politics in England and Wales 1790–1810* (Harvard, 1983); A. Charlesworth, *An Atlas of Rural Protest in England 1548–1900* (1983); H. T. Dickinson, *The Politics of the People in Eighteenth-Century Britain* (1994), ch. 4; Mark Harrison, *Crowds and History: Mass Phenomena in English Towns, 1790–1835* (Cambridge, 1988); G. Rudé, *Paris and London in the Eighteenth Century* (1970); R. Shoemaker, 'The London "Mob" in the early eighteenth century', *Journal of British Studies*, 26 (1987); J. Stevenson, *Popular Disturbances in England 1700–1832* (1992); E. P. Thompson, 'The moral economy of the English crowd in the eighteenth century', *P&P*, 50 (1971).

'respectable' members of the community.[34] But many other towns showed similar characteristics, although they still await the same kind of detailed study which Dr Shoemaker has carried out with respect to London.

The commonest form of unrest in urban society has always been the bread riot, provoked by rising prices and threats of scarcity. Although agricultural improvements meant that eighteenth-century England no longer faced subsistence crises, bread riots could still give serious cause for concern, notably during years of bad harvest and severe winters, such as 1709–10, 1739–40, 1756–7, 1766, 1781–3 and the 1790s. They were particularly common in ports or markets where there was a considerable traffic in grain, since, in times of high prices, the sight of grain being moved away was certain to fuel resentment and anger. Similarly, where there was a large population of non-agricultural labourers who were acutely vulnerable to the fluctuations in price, riots were always more frequent than in areas of more mixed economy, where the dependence was less absolute. Hence, an industrial town like Newcastle was often the focus of food riots by the pitmen and keelmen who worked in the mines and in the port. The bread riot was famously interpreted as part of a 'moral economy' by E. P. Thompson. Thompson saw the riot as a highly organized and complex activity which had very specific aims and a strong sense of its own legitimacy. By participating in a riot, the protesters intended to force those in authority to take action to redress a situation, arising from perceived malpractices in marketing or milling, which had led to an allegedly illegitimate increase in prices. Magistrates reacted by setting an Assize of Bread, to fix the price (bakers would subsequently be compensated for any losses made). Such action effectively legitimated the actions of the rioters by acknowledging the middlemen's profiteering, thereby increasing the likelihood of riot occurring again. In 1795, protests against the movement of grain, inspired by fears of dearth, were so widespread that the government, already nervous about any kind of mass activity in the wake of the French Revolution, took the unusual step of passing legislation against such demonstrations. Authorities often tried to pre-empt outbreaks of food rioting by taking preventative action. In the 1790s, JPs, and corporations in many towns, raised subscriptions in order to buy in grain and coal

34. Simon Renton, 'The moral economy of the English middling sort in the eighteenth century. The case of Norwich in 1766 and 1767', in Adrian Randall and Andrew Charlesworth (eds), *Markets, Market Culture and Popular Protest in Eighteenth-Century Britain and Ireland* (1996), pp. 115–36.

to sell at subsidised prices to the poor, during periods of hardship. In 1795, the corporation of Oxford donated 150 guineas for this purpose, and allowed the treasurer to advance up to £500 for the purchase of stocks of corn to be sold to the poor at a reduced price, and made the additional gesture of lobbying the city's MPs on the high price of corn. In 1800, tensions were still running so high that the mayor took the step of consulting with the local volunteer company about having troops ready for action, and issued a 7.00pm curfew. At the same time, 50 sacks of foreign wheat were bought in for the use of the city bakers, and the corporation undertook to indemnify the bakers for any losses they should make by selling bread below cost price, under the Assize of Bread.[35]

Historians have attempted to apply the same concept of the 'moral economy' to other kinds of disturbances which involved 'collective bargaining by riot', in order to restore a perceived status quo. Outbreaks of urban unrest, in the form of industrial protest or strike action and trade union activity, threatened order and social stability in many towns, and can be interpreted as attempts to force the magistrates to take action to regulate wages or fix prices in the same manner as a bread riot. Colchester was particularly badly affected by riots and demonstrations in 1715, when its cloth industry was severely affected by the embargo on trade caused by the War of the Spanish Succession. In Tiverton, weavers rioted recurrently in the earlier part of the century, especially in 1720, in protest against the merchants' import of Irish worsted. However, historians are not unanimous as to the extent to which the concept of the 'moral economy' can usefully be applied to the more assertive industrial disturbances, organized by trade union activity, which became more frequent from the late eighteenth century.[36]

Riots could also take the form of political protest at government measures, such as the imposition of taxation. The excise crisis of 1734, and the attempt to impose a cider excise in 1765, both provoked rioting in towns across the country. Similarly, the Jew Bill, a bid to naturalise Jewish immigrants, provided an opportunity for political opportunists to whip up xenophobia in a series of anti-government riots in the months leading up to the election of 1753. Political riots took on a new character in the age of radicalism,

---

35. OCA Corporation Minute Books, resolutions of 2 Jan., 8 July, 17 July and 30 Oct. 1795; 18 Sept. 1800. For the background to the riots see Wendy Thwaites, 'Oxford Riots: A Community and its Markets', in Randall and Charlesworth (eds), *Markets, Market Culture and Popular Protest*, pp. 137–62.

36. Bohstedt, *Riots and Community Politics in England and Wales*.

when socio-economic discontent threatened to combine with political activism. Urban demonstrations, like Peterloo in 1818, terrified
the authorities, who had always suspected that riots, ostensibly air-
ing socio-economic grievances, might really be the cover for political conspiracies to overturn the state.[37] If Walpole could detect the
seditious influence of Jacobitism in the Mother Gin Riots of 1736,
how much more dangerous to the constitution must the riots and
demonstrations of the era of radicalism have appeared? The full
flowering of political riots came in 1832, when cities such as Nottingham, Derby, and Bristol were hit by prolonged waves of demonstrations and destruction; those in Bristol escalated out of control,
causing extensive damage to property, and were only put down by
the introduction of military force.

Fears of violent rioters and social unrest gave the authorities
great cause for alarm, both at national and local level. Government
legislated to inhibit such occurrences, notably with the Riot Act of
1715. But there were also many additional acts for preventing combinations in trades (Stevenson calculates that over 40 had reached
the statute books before the General Combination Act of 1799),
and to minimise violence at elections.[38] It is hard to tell how far the
fears of disorder and damage to property were justified. Industrial
protests, particularly in the Luddite era, involved machine breaking, but this kind of destructive behaviour was focused sharply on
its target, and was not a case of wanton destruction. Notorious
outbursts, like the Gordon Riots, and the Church and King Riots
in Birmingham in 1792, were immensely destructive, but in most
instances the damage was usually along the lines of breaking windows or street lamps, lighting bonfires in the street and burning
figures in effigy. Mark Harrison's study of the crowd is an important
reminder that crowd activity was 'overwhelmingly non-violent in
character', and the descent into riot represented the breakdown of
the mechanisms of the consensual politics of the local community.[39]
It was for this reason perhaps that, throughout our period, urban
magistrates had little real power to deal with crowds which became
riotous. If their personal authority, in reading the Riot Act and the
threat of arrest, did not disperse a threatening crowd there was

---

37. Paul Langford, *The Excise Crisis: Society and Politics in the Age of Walpole* (Oxford,
1975); Perry Thomas, *Public Opinion, Propaganda, Politics in Eighteenth-Century England. A Study of the Jew Bill of 1753* (Harvard, 1964); Donald Read, *Peterloo: The
'Massacre' and its Background* (Manchester, 1969).
38. Stevenson, *Popular Disturbances*, pp. 167–8.
39. Harrison, *Crowds and History*, p. 316.

little else they could do, in the absence of police forces. If negotiations failed and violence escalated, it was possible to call in the army. This was a measure of last resort; it risked exacerbating tensions even further, with the possibility of fatalities (epitomised by the outrage provoked by the Peterloo 'massacre' when the yeomanry fired on the protesters, causing eleven deaths). By summoning the armed forces, the authorities were acknowledging their inability to maintain control, and allowing an external authority to intervene in their sphere of influence. Finally, the use of force was incontrovertibly linked in the popular imagination with arbitrary government; by calling upon armed strength, the authorities would have been calling into question the legitimation of their own right to rule.

Despite the fear of disorder, however, in some instances it is clear that the authorities turned a blind eye to mob activity, if not actively encouraging it, particularly when it suited their own political ends. Magistrates were notorious for ignoring the mobs who pelted Methodist ministers, for example, and at election times accusations and counter accusations were flung around in the pamphlet warfare as rival parties claimed that the other had been inciting the mob to violence. Elite manipulation was not an 'urban myth'; mobs and rioters could be used in waging the battles of a divided elite, particularly if a case was made that the interests of the freemen were somehow involved. But, as we suggested earlier, it would be wrong to suppose that the participants were without their own participatory logic. Popular protest could be a compelling form of argument, and therefore was predictably often caught up in internal contests over power and influence within the town, as well as being the expression of socio-economic discontent.

Law and Order: Criminality

Rioting was not a daily occurrence, of course, whereas the problems of petty crime and violence were. As we have seen, the most important reason for street lighting was as a deterrent against crime (although those who resented paying the lighting rates claimed that it made theft easier for the criminals). The problem had become increasingly acute in the eighteenth century, as intensive urbanization created a rapidly increasing and mobile population. By mid-century almost all towns had abandoned the curfew (the practice of locking the city gates at night), allowing for freer access in and out of the town. The very nature of urban life enlarged the potential for criminal activity, because there was more moveable property in shops, in houses and in people's pockets. For historians it is hard to tell whether crime actually rose in towns, or whether people became more sensitive to it and used the courts more, rather than settling matters informally. It is clear, however, that first in London and later in other towns, as they experienced more rapid growth, the traditional sanctions of the smaller urban community, which depended on personal acquaintance and face-to-face contact, could not operate effectively in an environment with high mobility and less social cohesion. The debate on crime and punishment, and the shift from exemplary to a deterrent-based mode of punishment, was extremely relevant to urban society – rural crime, by comparison, was far less of a problem and was rarely discussed.[40] The metropolis, being so much bigger than the provincial towns, suffered the problems first, and most acutely, but by the end of the eighteenth century anxiety about rising criminality, and how best to combat it, had become a cause which united those in positions of authority throughout the country.

Whether a town was incorporated or not does not appear to have made much difference to the practical enforcement of law and order or crime prevention. Most towns had no police force, in the modern sense, and relied on the efforts of a few constables, and the principles of 'watch and ward' inherited from the medieval era, for the preservation of law and order. A heavy reliance was placed upon the individual to instigate prosecution in cases of theft or personal violence and, just as in the machinery for regulating the urban environment through presentments made at court leet, there was no coercive power which could be brought to bear upon offenders. The constables, elected by the parish or the corporation, could only make presentments for public nuisances in the streets, and for minor disturbances such as a brawl between neighbours or the use of blasphemous language. The custom of watch and ward derived from the Statute of Winchester of 1285, which demanded that every householder, by turn, should be responsible for patrolling the neighbourhood and keeping watch at night. Very often, the obligation had been commuted for a cash payment, used to pay for the appointment of full-time watchmen. However, this system, which relied on the services of only a few watchmen, who, according to contemporary accounts were generally aged and infirm, was

40. J. M. Beattie, *Crime and the Courts in England, 1600–1800* (Oxford, 1986), esp. pp. 3–15, 520–638.

hardly satisfactory, and increasingly towns began to consider the idea of maintaining a permanent force from a rate, levied on the householders. This was often one of the elements of local acts, and explains why they were often known as lighting and watching acts. One of the first of these was procured by the vestry of St George's, Hanover Square, in 1734. Although the system of watching was essentially unchanged in practice, it appears that under the commissioners it was implemented much more effectively.[41] Constables and the watch have generally been derided, but recent research has suggested that they may actually have been more effective than commonly supposed. Professor Beattie comments that they were more active, more numerous, and more experienced by the end of the century than they would have been a hundred years earlier, and had contributed to a substantial improvement in the enforcement of order, especially in London.[42] He also suggests that watchmen were providing a more efficient service by the end of the century. Although the provision of a police force was retarded, one should not write off all the local piecemeal initiatives as insignificant, in many of the smaller to moderate sized towns, the *ad hoc* improvements wrought upon the watch system appear to have proved adequate. Certainly, in the reports of the Royal Commissioners they commented favourably upon the state of the police in a number of towns, and in many more it was deemed adequate.[43] Historians are in the problematical situation of relying for their information upon contemporary criticisms, from those who were pressing most forcefully the case for change, and therefore had an interest in presenting as black a picture as possible.

As in so many other areas, innovations were made first in London. The efforts of the Fielding Brothers (who established the original Bow Street Runners) in mid-century, and the work of Patrick Colquhoun, a stipendiary magistrate in the 1790s, in combating the criminality of the lower classes in the metropolis, tend to dominate the historiography of crime prevention in this period. Yet one should not assume metropolitan practices were slavishly adopted all over the country; in many areas there was considerable hostility to the idea of a police force, simply because it would be based upon the London model. After the Napoleonic Wars and the ensuing economic

41. J. T. Tobias, *Crime and the Police in England, 1700–1900* (1979). Elaine Reynolds, *Before the Bobbies. The Night Watch and Police Reform in Metropolitan London, 1720–1830* (1998), was published too late to improve the content of this section.

42. Beattie, *Crime and the Courts*, p. 71.

43. Congleton, Alnwick and Beverley were singled out for special mention.

depression, which heightened social discontent, there was a general shift towards more intensive policing in towns, particularly in the provision of a night watch. Some towns, like Manchester, acquired powers to levy a police rate in their improvement acts, and others at least had limited provision for watching included in them. The 1833 Lighting and Watching Act permitted vestries to levy a police tax, but the tiny scale of the parochial base of the scheme rendered it ineffectual. It was not until 1835 that there was any kind of general legislative provision concerning the policing of towns, which could compare with that for turnpikes, poor relief or even the maintenance of gaols. This is largely attributable to the deep-seated prejudice of the English against the idea of a police force, seeing it as the instrument of absolutism and an infringement of English liberties. The hostility came from both the rulers and the ruled; magistrates had no wish to see their autonomy undermined by the workings of a centralised police force, and the labouring sort feared it would be used as an instrument of repression. An act of 1829 created nine stipendiary high constables in Cheshire, who supervised a much larger number of petty constables, but this model was not replicated elsewhere. The lawlessness which broke out in Bristol, Derby and Nottingham, in the agitation before the Great Reform Act, alarmed the authorities at both local and national level, to the extent that the idea of a regular police force began to seem much more desirable in the 1830s. The magistrates in Coventry, for example, had gone so far as to write to Lord Melbourne in 1832, following the election riots, asking him to recommend someone whom they might appoint as chief constable after the manner of the metropolis.[44] The 1835 Act laid down the framework for a nation-wide police force, on the basis of the 1829 Metropolitan Police Act. Even so, the practice of policing appears to have continued more or less unchanged in many boroughs for some years after the act was passed. By 1837, only 93 of the 178 boroughs covered by the Municipal Reform Act had formed a police force, and by 1842 20 per cent still had not acted. Even when a police force was established, it was often composed of the constables, beadles and night-watchmen who had been responsible for keeping the peace before 1835. Practices, such as taking fees and part-time employment, persisted unofficially, despite being now forbidden, and few towns chose to adopt a large metropolitan style police force. Liverpool, with its numerous and potentially unruly population of

44. Evidence given to House of Lords, *Lords Journals*, lxvii (1835), p. 352.

Irish immigrants, had a police force of 590 men in 1838, for a population of 286,000 – an unusually generous provision at the time. Birmingham, by contrast, had only 30 day constables for a population of 183,000.[45]

Markets and Economic Regulation

The urban economy, just as much as the environment, occupied a significant part of urban administration. The essence of the eighteenth-century town lay in its role as a commercial centre for the exchange of goods. An assessment of the size and quality of the market was one of the first observations which visitors made when describing a town (although this tendency undoubtedly also reflects the influence of Defoe's *Tour* on eighteenth-century travel writing). The upkeep of the market-place was therefore a matter of the utmost concern for the town as a whole, and the provision of adequate marketing facilities and the regulation of trade was one of the most important responsibilities of the urban authorities. The local improvement acts were peppered with clauses for improving, building and moving the market-place, or erecting a market house. The increase in business being transacted in towns frequently meant that the traditional site had become too crowded, and there was also growing intolerance of inconveniences arising from market stalls and shambles blocking major thoroughfares. This meant that new sites for markets had to be found and new market halls erected. Even in 'leisure' towns, which depended upon providing services to the wealthy visitor, the market was still a crucial component of the urban economy. In Cheltenham, the market and its volume of trade grew so rapidly that four successive market houses had to be built within the space of a century.[46]

Whether the town was incorporated or not, if there was a market, there would also be a range of associated officials whose duty it was to see that tolls were collected, that livestock were not allowed to stray, to check on the quality of the meat and flour on sale, to enforce the Assize of Bread and to apprehend those guilty of forestalling (buying up provisions before they came to open market) or

45. Stanley Palmer, *Police and Protest in England and Ireland, 1780–1850* (Cambridge, 1988), p. 400.
46. Hart, *History of Cheltenham*, p. 182.

regrating (buying up provisions early on and then selling them at a profit later). In incorporated towns there had often been a special court for dealing with cases arising from the market, known as the pie poudre, but by 1835 the Royal Commissioners found that this had long since fallen into disuse in most places, and had generally been devolved to the more convenient forum of the Quarter Sessions. Although many of the trading regulations and sanctions were falling into abeyance, regionally the rate at which old practices gave way to an increasingly laissez-faire economy was extremely varied. In Oxford, for example, the mayor and vice chancellor continued to enforce the Assize of Bread at the market, until it was abolished in 1813, whereas elsewhere it had long since been abandoned. In many smaller towns market regulation continued to represent an important part of the mayor's duties, as in Penzance, where Henry Boase, who was mayor in 1816, recorded in his journal the daily routine of, 'Attending the market with constables and serjt. enforcing the regulations of standing and the new toll of 1d per basket on butter and salted fish'.[47] John Harris of Plymouth commented in wry amusement in 1807 that, 'Never since my recollection did any Mayor take that account of the market as did T. Eales Esq. I believe every market day he was there to see justice done to buyer and seller; in every respect he did credit to his office as Clerk to the Market'.[48] That Harris thought it worthy of comment, that the mayor was so active in this capacity, is in itself an indication of how far matters of market regulation had slipped down the mayoral scale of priorities in many towns.

On the same basis, in towns where trading restrictions were still strictly enforced, the corporation felt itself bound to uphold the rights of the freemen and their claims to exclusive trading privileges, although they themselves did not necessarily have an interest in such matters. As members of the corporate body, however, their claim to authority was predicated on protecting the rights and privileges given to the freemen in the governing charter. In Oxford, the administration of freemen admissions and overseeing the exercise of trade formed a major part of corporation business, and a standing committee was established in 1794 to deal solely with these matters. Pressure came from below, in the form of petitions to the common council, to take action against hawkers and peddlers and

---

47. George Boase, *Collectanea Cornubiensia: a Collection of Biographical and Topographical Notes relating to the County of Cornwall* (Truro, 1890), pt. 111, p. 1507.

48. SDRO, Acc 219 John Harris, 'An essay toward the history of Plymouth', vol. i, p. 53.

other traders who were undercutting the freemen of the city, without having taken out the freedom. In other towns, the admission of freemen was still a crucial matter of concern for the corporation, and represented a major part of their business, less because of the economic and trading implications, but because of the political rights associated with the freedom, and the fact that a substantial part of corporate income was derived from admission fees. In this respect, the regulation of freemen admissions had simply become another aspect of the administration of the corporation estate. In a few towns, such as Preston, where most of the 'police' functions had been taken over by the improvement commissioners or the Quarter Sessions, the corporation became little more than a property management committee, with nothing but leases granted, properties inspected, rentals, and freemen admissions to enliven the minute books.[49]

Corporate and guild regulation gradually crumbled before the inexorable advance of regulation by the market. But even when the older customary traditions had died out, the concept of the moral economy still palpably exerted its influence over people's expectations of public bodies: the outcry against Plymouth corporation, which had failed in its bounden duty to supply water to the inhabitants and was exploiting a fundamental necessity as a source of profit, was similar to the accusations levelled against those who hoarded grain to sell it at inflated prices in times of dearth. On the same basis, it may be argued that there was still considerable scope for leadership, on the part of the corporation, in the economic context, even if its paternalistic role in the 'moral economy' of the grain trade was disappearing. If corporations had sought to protect and promote the interests of the inhabitants by upholding their trading privileges in earlier times, in the eighteenth century, the same sentiments of duty to the community forced them along new avenues which led generally to Parliament. Many of the local acts passed in this period could have profound consequences for the local economies; the construction of turnpikes and canals could either attract new business to the town and decrease transport costs, or leave a former trading post stranded high and dry in the interstices of the new communications network. Legislation, giving powers to improve and construct docks and harbours, and to clear the silt from rivers and havens, were the essential building blocks

49. H. W. Clemesha, *A History of Preston in Amounderness* (Manchester, 1912), pp. 232–4.

for the expansion of ports such as Liverpool, Hull, Bristol and Whitehaven. In incorporated towns, this opened up a new sphere of action for corporations: they were expected to cultivate and negotiate with the local MP, to petition Parliament, and to initiate subscriptions and plans for improvement. Those which failed to exercise leadership in such matters inevitably came under criticism. Francis Drake, historian of York, took the opportunity in his history of the city to castigate the corporation for their neglect, which had led to the silting up of the Ouse and the diversion of trade to Hull.[50] The corporations of Hull and Liverpool, by contrast, instigated the construction and expansion of the port and dock facilities, which lay behind the prosperity and growth of both cities in the later eighteenth century. The claims to represent the economic interests, and to be safeguarding the prosperity of the town, were a crucial part of the rhetoric of legitimation for corporations across the country.

The Problem of the Poor

The paternalism of oligarchic government was also displayed in the philanthropy which was exercised on behalf of the urban poor. Eighteenth-century towns were the heirs of the 'godly cities' of the early modern period, when urban authorities, in towns such as Hull, Gloucester, Kings Lynn and Norwich, had implemented programmes of reform aimed at both the physical and moral improvement of the poor. Parishes and towns were bound to provide relief for the needy anyway, under the Elizabethan Poor Laws, but the tradition of the 'godly city', which was governed in the interests of the common weal, had become an important part of civic consciousness, and the expectation that the magistracy had a responsibility for both the physical and moral welfare of the poor was strongly influential throughout our period. *Godly* cities were no longer part of the urban rhetoric, and the common weal had an archaic ring, but the language of the common or the *public* good and *public* spirit was frequently resorted to in order to stimulate the authorities into action or to legitimate their acts.

The degree to which the urban magistracy were involved in the management of the poor varied from town to town. Under the

50. Francis Drake, *Eboracum: or the History and Antiquities of the City of York* (1736), pp. 229–33.

terms of the poor laws, each parish was responsible for the upkeep
of its own poor; using the poor rates agreed at vestry meetings to
administer pensions and outdoor relief, to apprentice poor children, to provide employment in the bridewell (if one existed), to
provide medical assistance, and less productively it was used in
litigation with other parishes over bastardy cases and the settlement
and removal of paupers. The role of the magistrates was to appoint
the overseers, to hear such cases as were brought before them, and
to hear appeals against the rates. As we saw in the last chapter, the
establishment of corporations of the poor, for a union of parishes
under the management of an elected body of guardians, following
the example set by Bristol in 1696, offered a potentially more efficient way of dealing with the problem of urban poverty, and removed
the responsibility for the administration of poor relief from the
magistrates and the vestry. By 1712, thirteen towns had followed
Bristol's example (nine of these had been 'godly cities' in the past).
Knatchbull's Act of 1723 allowed parishes to hire workhouses rather
than actually build them, and over 100 parishes (mainly urban) did
so in the next ten years. From the 1760s, there was another steady
stream of incorporations, as the pressures of war exacerbated anxiety
about poverty and rising poor rates. By 1834, another 40 towns had
acquired local acts for establishing incorporations of the poor.
The precise constitution of the incorporation of the poor varied
considerably from town to town, just as the improvement commissions did, with a similar mix of elected and ex-officio membership.
A particularly successful workhouse (in terms of cost effectiveness
for the ratepayers) flourished in Shrewsbury at the end of the
century, and was emulated in a number of other towns, after
Frederick Eden drew attention to its success in reducing the poor
rates from £4,605 3s 1½d to £2,992 12s pa. in *The State of the Poor*,
first published in 1797.[51] Workhouses were not, in general, the
panacea to the problem of poverty which the projectors had hoped;
few managed to break even, let alone subsidise the poor rates. They
were as vulnerable to mismanagement and corruption as any other
administrative body. Attendance at meetings of the guardians of
the poor proved as difficult to enforce as for corporations and
improvement commissions. Without constant oversight, the workhouses tended to be filled with the elderly, young children and the
infirm, rather than the able bodied who could perform useful labour,

51. Frederick Eden, *The State of the Poor*, (ed.) A. G. L. Rogers (1928), pp. 296–
301.

and appalling living conditions were all too common. Poor rates continued to rise steadily in most towns, provoking considerable discontent among the ratepayers. The overhaul of the system under the Poor Law Amendment Act of 1834 was hardly any more successful in providing a satisfactory solution, designed as it was to alleviate the problems of rural poverty, rather than those of the industrialised city.

However, the relief of the poor had never been entirely provided for out of the poor rates. Most towns had a range of charitable benefactions which provided endowments for almshouses, hospitals and schools, or left money for the relief of prisoners and debtors, provided interest free loans to tradesmen, or simply gave out annual doles of bread or money. The management of these was entrusted to either a body of trustees, the corporation or the vestry. The misappropriation of such funds was a standard complaint, and corporations in particular, who had abused their trust and failed to act in the best interests of the community, found their legitimacy was severely compromised. Opponents of the mayor and aldermen of Newark accused them of using funds intended for the 'common weal' of the town to support their own dignity and entertainment.[52] A parliamentary investigation, which was launched in 1782, to inquire into the extent of charitable provisions, led to some being recovered. A second investigation, in 1822, achieved far more in bringing abuses to light and in regularizing the way in which charitable accounts were kept. Charitable traditions were an important part of urban culture because they reinforced the sense of community and the public good, and embodied the ethos of the 'common weal'. Lists of charities and benefactions were often prominently displayed in public places, such as churches and town halls, or published in local histories and guides, as a reminder to fellow citizens of the traditions of which they were a part, and their own responsibility to the community. One local historian listed the charitable institutions of the city 'to the honor of the merchants, gentry, clergy, and opulent Citizens of Bristol, who know the way to their pockets, and have hearts and hands ready to compassionate the distressed, and to administer all necessary and suitable assistance'.[53] However, although bequests such as these could alleviate some distress, they could not provide a solution to the rising poor rates which faced every town.

52. Bernard Wilson, *A Discourse addressed to the Inhabitants of Newark against the Misapplication of Public Charities* (1768).
53. William Matthews, *The New History, Survey and Description of the City and Suburbs of Bristol* (Bristol, 1794), p. 88.

Increasingly, eighteenth and early nineteenth-century citizens looked to other means for providing the poor with assistance. Voluntary hospitals, public dispensaries and other charitable organizations provided one means of providing relief for the deserving poor in a controlled environment.[54] In the later eighteenth century the emphasis shifted to self-help societies and towards encouraging greater financial independence among the poor. The exploration of alternative means for the relief of the poor did not indicate that the urban magistracy was exonerated of its responsibilities. The mayor and aldermen were still expected to figure among the subscribers to charities and voluntary hospitals, and it fell upon the duty of the mayor to call the public meetings for raising subscriptions or distributing charitable relief. He would receive, in return, a vote of thanks for his public spirited action for his efforts on behalf of the poor.

Public Morality

Eighteenth-century towns were far from realizing the sacral civic community of the Protestant Reformation, but the question of poor relief was nevertheless closely allied to the issue of moral reform (only the deserving poor were worthy of relief, and rising poor rates were a reflection of the feckless immorality of the labouring sort). The expectation of leadership from the civic elite in such matters was deeply felt. At the beginning of the eighteenth century the mayor of Deal, Stephen Pritchard, attempted to use his authority as mayor to instigate a programme of moral reformation, single handed. He began his period of office by pinning up Queen Anne's proclamation to suppress vice and immorality in all public places. To all those who opposed the severity of his measures (closing tippling houses on Sundays, enforcing regulations against Sunday trading, whipping prostitutes, and placing seamen in the stocks for profane language) he replied that he was 'resolved on a reformation in Deal'.[55] Movements of moral reform swept through urban

54. Mary Fissel, *Patients, Power and the Poor in Eighteenth-Century Bristol* (1991); and Fissel, 'Charity universal? Institutions and moral reform in eighteenth-century Bristol', in Lee Davison, Tim Hitchcock, Tim Keirn and Robert Shoemaker (eds), *Stilling the Grumbling Hive. The Response to Social and Economic Problems in England, 1689–1750* (Stroud, 1992), pp. 121–44. See also Tim Hitchcock, 'Paupers and preachers: The SPCK and the parochial workhouse movement', ibid., pp. 145–66; and Donna Andrew, *Philanthropy and Police* (Princeton, 1989).

55. Quoted in S. and B. Webb, *The Manor and the Borough* (1908), p. 314.

society in periodic waves – Pritchard was a product of the late seventeenth-century movement for the Reformation of Manners, but at all times it was taken for granted that the magistracy had a responsibility for the moral welfare of the community.[56] This dimension to their authority was less explicitly articulated by the end of our period – it is doubtful whether Pritchard would have got away with denouncing his fellow citizens in morning service a hundred years later[57] – but it remained a powerful expectation. The mayor and corporation were expected to set an example in attending Church and in their public demeanour. Duties such as granting licenses to alehouses, regulating lodging houses or gaming tables, or punishing cases of bastardy, had obvious implications for the moral tone of the town. When allegations of corruption or impropriety were made against the civic elite, it reflected not simply a betrayal of their trust as leaders of the community, but a failure to set an example of upright and virtuous behaviour to those below them. Charitable relief, administered by the urban elite, was often conditional upon, or inseparable from, efforts at moral improvement, for the immorality of the poor was widely held to be in large part responsible for the degradation in which they found themselves. Poor relief could become an instrument of social control, as only the deserving poor, that is, those who conformed to the expectations of the elite, could benefit from it. One of the advantages of private charity over poor relief was that it allowed for much higher levels of discrimination to be used in selecting deserving recipients for relief.

Financing the Business of Government: Corporations

The ability of any institution to carry out the objects for which it was created is always circumscribed by the resources available to it, the greatest imponderable being money. The eighteenth century was

56. See e.g. Robert Shoemaker, 'Reforming the city: the reformation of manners campaign in London, 1690–1738', in Davison et al. (eds), *Stilling the Grumbling Hive*, pp. 99–120.

57. His diary records that, 'After prayers, when we came to sing psalms, being part of the 75th Psalm, and at particular verses, which were very appropriate to certain persons present, I stood up, spreading my hands, pointing round the Church to some whose ill lives I knew, as well as their conversations, which this Psalm most particularly hinted at'.

a particularly difficult time for most corporations, as their finances were generally extremely restricted. In many cases, their governing charter actually stipulated a limit to the value of the property which they might hold – a limit which was not adjusted to keep pace with inflation. The corporation of Taunton, for example, was not allowed to hold land to an annual value of more than £300. It is not to be wondered at that Taunton, and other similarly positioned corporations, were superseded by bodies with more impressive powers of raising revenue. Many parish vestries, by contrast, would have had a much higher income than the poorer corporations; especially as there was no statutory limit to the amounts which they could raise on the poor rates and the church rates. But having assumed leadership and responsibility for so long, corporations were expected to continue in the considerably amplified role demanded of them in eighteenth-century society, and when they failed to meet expectations they were heavily criticised.

The wealthiest corporations were generally in port towns where they had property rights over the harbour and could benefit from the upswing in trade by levying tolls. No corporation could match the success of the financial recovery staged by the city of London in the eighteenth century; in a process akin to the formation of the national debt, the corporation used the coal duties, which it was entitled to levy, to create a fund for paying off its debt, selling annuities and stock from the fund, and using it as security to raise other substantial loans for projects like the rebuilding of Newgate Gaol.[58] Liverpool, Hull, Bristol and Newcastle did enjoy very substantial incomes. Liverpool's revenues showed the most dramatic rate of increase. In 1704, the corporation received £255 from the town dues and £104 in rents. By 1829, the figures had risen to £22,000 and £23,000 respectively.[59] All these corporations expended large sums on developing the town's port facilities and investing in urban improvement. In inland towns, corporate wealth tended to be derived chiefly from land, generally let on very long leases, and was therefore far less elastic and vulnerable to inflation. The fines for renewal of leases on corporation property could be substantial, but the annual rentals were often derisory in comparison with the true value of the land. Sale of land was a possibility at the last resort, if the scale of the debt or the urgency of the situation

58. I. G. Doolittle, 'The Government of the City of London, 1694–1767', Oxford Univ. D.Phil. thesis (1979), p. 94.

59. J. Ramsey Muir and E. Platt, *A History of Municipal Government in Liverpool from the earliest times to the Municipal Reform Act of 1835* (Liverpool, 1906), p. 118.

demanded it, but it was a short-term solution as it eroded the capital wealth. Smaller sums were derived from market tolls, and fines paid on admission to the freedom. Corporations, such as Poole, preferred to resort to large-scale sale of freedoms to raise money, rather than levying a controversial rate. In 1764, 30 freedoms were sold at a cost of £25 each, in order to raise money for the building of the new guildhall.[60] The freemen of Plymouth did even better, raising over £3,300, by the sale of freedoms in the 1830s. It can be of little surprise that the Royal Commissioners found that most of the corporations were heavily encumbered with debt, with little hope of ever repaying it.

For all but the wealthiest corporations the bulk of their annual income went on day-to-day expenses, such as the upkeep of property, salaries and fees. Contrary to popular perception, the amount spent on feasting and entertaining was diminishing in most boroughs.[61] Mayoral salaries often showed a significant increase over the period, but in real terms there was rarely any gain, and by the late eighteenth century resolutions were being passed all over the country to diminish or abolish the salary, for reasons of economy. In very few towns could the mayor expect to make a profit out of office-holding. The largest single item in the 'running costs' was generally the legal expenses of the town clerk (whose office was permanent and salaried). In general, corporations could balance the books for ordinary expenditure. It was the extraordinary items which tended to tip the finances over into debt, whether it be the costs of protracted legal proceedings, or a sudden call for large-scale investment for rebuilding or improving the town. After 1835, the new town councils seldom found that they could make massive retrenchments. The sale of civic regalia, or the stocks of corporation port could raise some immediate cash and made a powerful symbolic gesture, but on the whole, the new town councils found that, if anything, their immediate resources were curtailed because of their loss of income from, for example, freeman admissions.[62]

60. D. F. Beamish, 'The Parliamentary and Municipal History of the Borough of Poole, Dorset, c.1740–1840', Southampton Univ. M.Phil. thesis (1982), p. 28.
61. E. J. Dawson, 'Finance and the Unreformed Borough; a critical appraisal of corporate finance, 1660–1835, with special reference to the Boroughs of Nottingham, York and Boston', Univ. of Hull Ph.D. thesis (1978), p. 639, shows the proportion spent on feasting in Boston dropped from 30% in 1741 to 4.96% in 1800.
62. The corporation of Preston raised £226 3s 7d from the sale of their wine stocks after 1835 (one of the aldermen, Sir Joseph Livsey, was the leader of the first temperance movement). Clemesha, *History of Preston*, p. 240. A different source quotes figure of £366 3s 6d, William Dobson and John Harland, *A History of Preston Guild* (Preston, 1862), p. 60.

Local Rating Bodies

From a purely practical perspective, the main reason for acquiring a local act was to secure adequate financial resources and jurisdiction over a more extensive area than that covered by the original corporation or a single parish, but that did not mean that improvement commissions were immune to the financial problems of corporations. Improvement acts always contained a provision for levying tolls or a town rate to pay for the undertakings, as well as authority to borrow money up to a specified sum. The 1771 Mileways Act allowed the Oxford commissioners to borrow up to £5,000 at four per cent interest, to levy tolls at St Clements gate into the city, and to raise a paving and lighting rate. Tolls were generally farmed out for a fixed sum, a practice which was relatively trouble free in administrative terms, but susceptible to the blight of inflation. However, rate collection was notoriously difficult; paving rates like poor rates were always in arrears, and commissioners (or parish officers) were often no better at keeping their accounts than the corporations. Financial scandal hit the Oxford commissioners within three years of their existence – at a meeting held on 1 February 1774 it was found that there was no clear idea of the state of the finances, and a committee had to be appointed to draw up a balance.[63] Opposition to local taxation was expressed by non-payment, and the higher the rate, the longer the list of defaulters. Prosecution for non-payment was always a possibility, but that in itself entailed expensive legal proceedings. Determining the optimum level was a matter of nice judgement and there was a general reluctance to set realistic levels of local taxation. Cash flow problems frequently halted proceedings, necessitating appeals for public subscriptions in order to bridge the financial gap. The initial improvement act in Birmingham, for example, allowed the commissioners to levy a rate of only 3s 9d and borrow up to £1,000, which was far too little to cover the costs involved. It took a very long time for public perceptions to change, and accept that local government was expensive, needing large amounts of finance, and that it could not all be managed by parsimonious book keeping. Improvement commissioners and corporations alike suffered from a lack of financial imagination upon the part of the ratepayers. This was a problem which continued to beset urban authorities well into the nineteenth century; the

63. Bodl. Gough Oxford 138, *An Attempt to state the Accounts of Receipts and Expenses relative to the Oxford Paving Act: with Remarks* (Oxford, 1774), p. 1.

reformers' arguments, that reluctance to pay arose from the unrepresentative and unaccountable character of urban government, clearly told only half the story.

Problems could also arise if the improvement legislation had been badly drafted, since this could limit the uses to which a rate could be put and the amounts which could be raised. The Wolverhampton Improvement Act failed to make it clear that the commissioners could levy a rate for maintaining the street, while fixing the limit on the lighting rates at a hopelessly unrealistic level. By 1831, almost nothing was being spent on the streets and two-thirds of the rates were going towards interest charges on loans.[64] Unless sanctioned in the act, a rate could not be applied to any improvement except that for which it was specifically intended. Corporations too suffered from this legal limitation; many were sued for wrongful application of their funds. The opponents of Southampton corporation's plans for using the revenues for improvements, seized eagerly upon such technicalities: the revenues of the town had been granted to maintain it as a fortified place – since that necessity no longer existed, it was argued that the revenues could not be applied to any other use not specified under the charter.[65] The rationale was to prevent extortion, but it was a powerful force for encouraging inertia and permitted flagrant obstructionism. The frequency with which acts to amend and explain appeared only a year after the original improvement legislation was passed, demonstrates the difficulties involved in drawing up effective legislation. The legal costs for these displays of legislative sagacity and for steering the bill through parliament were a measure of the skill involved. Messrs Walker and Morrell presented the Oxford paving commissioners with a bill of £1,027 for the 1771 Mileways Act.[66]

Personal Service and Public Duty

It has been argued that the work of street commissioners, however inefficient and defective, consolidated the view that there was some kind of communal responsibility for the upkeep of the urban environment; it was no longer the duty of the individual householder.[67] On the other hand, there was still a heavy emphasis on the responsibility

---

64. F. Mason, *Wolverhampton Town Commissioners, 1778–1848* (Wolverhampton Public Library, 1976), pp. 25–7.
65. *The Civil Wars of Southampton* (Southampton, 1794), pp. 9–10, 13.
66. OCA, R/6/2B, f. 1, Paving Commissioners Minutes, 23 April 1771.
67. P. J. Corfield, *The Impact of English Towns* (Oxford, 1982), pp. 177–8.

of the householder towards maintaining the upkeep of the streets by paying rates (effectively a commutation of his own service), and in keeping the pavement outside his house clean. Improvement acts continued to be based upon the assumption that the householder would be responsible for the repair and cleansing of the street or pavement outside his house, and fines were levied on those who failed in their duties.[68] Somewhat ironically, in many towns the paving commissioners also effectively contracted out, back to the householder: the process of paving could be accomplished more quickly, and with less trouble to the commissioners, if householders were encouraged to undertake the paving of the streets outside their buildings at their own expense, on the understanding that the commissioners would indemnify them as soon as funds allowed. This shift was a very gradual one and was far from complete by the end of our period. The contrast should not be drawn too sharply; it is by no means clear how effective the system of communal obligation was. One suspects it was more observed in the breach than the practice and that there was never such a hey-day of communal activity.

Despite the fact that an increasing amount of work was carried out by paid officials, by far the heaviest burdens fell upon the unpaid citizen, who performed services out of a sense of fellow obligation to his fellow citizens, whether as a member of the corporation, as a JP, as a guardian or overseer of the poor, or as an improvement commissioner. Public service was a duty inherent in membership of society. As the Gloucestershire JP, Sir George Onesipherous Paul reminded the grand jury in 1784, 'There exists no Freedom in this Country which acts against the general Good, except that of thinking ourselves dispensed from Public Duties'.[69] The ideal of public service was bound up with the notion of civic pride and status – only the leading citizens of known integrity and respectability were allowed to be suited to carry out civic office. Office, therefore, became a mark of status and prestige within the community and was, ideally, desirable in itself. Office-holders were men who 'from their good sense and respectability, derive their title to preside over the Town, and from their integrity, activity, and regard for its welfare, their title to officiate'.[70] Unpaid public service

68. B. Howard Cunnington, *Some Annals of the Borough of Devizes. Being a Series of Extracts from the Corporation Records, 1555–1791* (Devizes, 1925), pp. 166–96.

69. Sir George Onesipherous Paul, *Considerations on the Defects of Prisons and their Present System of Regulation* (1784), p. 83.

70. William Roberts, 'Charge to the grand jury of the court leet for the manor of Manchester', 1788 reprinted in *Records of Manchester Court Leet*, ix (1889), p. 252.

was held to be characteristically English, and an indication of English liberties. In the absence of a despotic state with a highly developed police force, the English cooperated with each other in pursuit of mutual welfare for 'the public Obligations of Individuals increase with the Degree of constitutional Liberty'.[71] Similarly, John Spranger warned that:

> This it is that gives us a certain Connection, a Regard to the public Good, which is unknown in most other Countries, and whilst we are duly touch'd with a Sense of our Duty to the Public, every Man in his Sphere will be ready and sollicitous to promote the common Emolument, of which he is always sure to share.[72]

Not only that, but it undoubtedly carried with it more or less legitimate forms of influence, whether it was in the granting of contracts, or access to an MP's ear. In most corporations there was also a strong feeling that civic office was the natural *quid pro quo* for the privileges attendant upon being a freeman of the city. This ethos underpinned the whole structure of urban administration. Undoubtedly it often fell short, and there was little which could be done to enforce it upon those who refused to recognise the obligation, beyond levying fines. It should be remembered that the fines levied by, for example, the corporation of London upon Dissenters and others who refused to take office, were not simply cash raising strategies, but an effort to distribute the burdens of the community fairly among its members.[73]

Powerful though the rhetoric of public service was, in reality there was increasing slippage between theory and practice. In many towns, it is clear that there were problems in attracting suitable individuals, both to take up office and to fulfil the ensuent duties, whether in the corporation, in the management of poor relief or in schemes of improvement and philanthropy. The reluctance of the rural landed gentry to perform their duties as JPs, in inspecting workhouses or administering the poor law, shows that the defects of unpaid public service were not limited to the urban environment. As the volume of work which JPs were expected to take responsibility for escalated, the number of those who declined to take office or were inactive, not surprisingly increased.[74] In the larger towns

---

71. Paul, *Considerations on the Defects of Prisons*, p. 83.

72. John Spranger, *A Proposal or a Plan for an Act of Parliament for the better Paving, Lighting and Cleansing the Streets, Lanes, Courts, Alleys. . . . of the City of Westminster* (1754), preface.

73. Doolittle, 'Government of the City of London', pp. 37–9.

74. David Eastwood, *Governing Rural England. Tradition and Transformation in Local Government, 1780–1840* (Oxford, 1994), pp. 78–80.

the problem was exacerbated by the declining numbers of resident householders who were eligible to take office and assume leadership. The urban elite were gradually moving out to the suburbs of the town, away from the noise, smell and overcrowding of the city centre, or even bought landed estates in the vicinity. Corporations fought a rear-guard action by passing bye–laws to ensure that membership of the aldermanic bench was conditional upon residency, but even the possession of a property in town did not ensure that the alderman in question would always live there. The financial drain could also be a serious disincentive to participation in civic life; it was generally considerably cheaper to pay the fine for not taking office, than to foot the bill for the various entertainments and salaries which the mayor was expected to pay for out of his own pocket, even when a mayoral allowance was made. Resolutions for an increase in mayoral salaries should not be seen as the equivalent of company directors voting themselves hefty pay rises, but as an acknowledgement of the rising cost of civic entertainment. Even in Bristol, where the mayor's salary reached a peak of £2,000 in the early 1800s, it was insufficient to fund the level of display and expenditure which the mayor was expected to provide, and the fine for refusal to serve, at £500, could be seen as the cheaper (and less onerous) option. Fourteen gentlemen, in 1810, were successively appointed as mayor, but paid the fine rather than take office.[75] The ruling oligarchy of a town was by no means always commensurate with the social and plutocratic elite, and this could create tensions. Many corporations were dominated by tradesmen, who regarded the social elite of urban gentry with suspicion, while considerations of social status reinforced the reluctance of the latter to take an active role in civic proceedings, because it would necessitate acting with their social inferiors. In Malmesbury, the Royal Commissioners found that the corporation consisted chiefly of uneducated labourers and tradesmen, and suggested that this was responsible for deterring 'respectable' persons from becoming involved in the town.[76]

Unincorporated bodies were often no better off. For several years after improvement acts had been obtained in Manchester and Wolverhampton, almost nothing happened, due to the apathy and inertia of the commissioners. As John Cross, steward of Manchester court leet, warned his audience in 1799, no matter what powers the legislature might bestow, they were all unavailing unless animated by the '*voluntary exertions*' of those to whom are committed the

---

75. J. Latimer, *Annals of Bristol in the Nineteenth Century* (Bristol, 1887), p. 37.
76. *Report of the Royal Commission on Municipal Corporations*, PP (1835), xxiii, p. 79.

management and direction of their powers'.[77] Characteristically, improvement commissioners started off with tremendous enthusiasm, holding regular meetings with a high level of attendance, but support would fall off once major decisions had been made, and the burden of day-to-day administration would be neglected or fall upon the shoulders of a faithful few. For all the commendable expressions of public spirit which introduced these acts, in practice the statutory bodies were seldom paragons of efficiency. The various minutes of improvement commissioners, across the country, suggest that the weaknesses of the corporations were paralleled in these improvement commissions; non-attendance, irregular book keeping and indifference. Even in a city like Birmingham it was rare for more than seven or eight, from the list of over 50 commissioners, to attend. In one year the first four out of five meetings had to be adjourned because they were inquorate, and there was always a considerable number who were dropped for not having attended a meeting for over a year.[78] In Plymouth, meetings were adjourned 20 times in a row in the 1790s.[79] When the Cheltenham commissioners sought renewal of their powers, in 1806, it was conditional upon the stricter keeping of accounts, and commissioners were enjoined that 'it is a duty of all Commissioners who take part in a debate on any question to attend meetings until the conclusion of the same and give their vote'.[80] There was a similar pattern of falling off in enthusiasm among turnpike trustees, guardians of the poor and other areas of public life, as one trustee remarked, 'I have known a turnpike meeting advertised from three weeks to three weeks for a year together, and never a competent number of justices or commissioners'.[81]

To a certain extent the non-performance of duties appears to have been a problem for whatever period of urban history one examines, and the 'flight from office' seems to have undermined the civic ethos of medieval towns as much as the eighteenth-century ones.[82] It is particularly hard to separate fact from fiction in the eighteenth

77. John Cross, 'Charge to the jury of the court leet, 1799' in *Records of Manchester Court Leet*, ix (1889), p. 257.

78. C. Gill, 'Birmingham under the Street Commissioners', *University of Birmingham Historical Journal*, 1 (1948), pp. 255–87.

79. SDRO 1621/A1 and A2, minutes of the commissioners for paving, lighting and watching.

80. Hart, *History of Cheltenham*, pp. 266–8.

81. Richard Burn, *Observations on the Bill intended to be offered to Parliament for the Better Relief and Employment of the Poor* (1776), p. 30.

82. See, for example, Jenny Kermode, 'Obvious observations on the foundation of oligarchies in late medieval English towns', in J. A. F. Thomson (ed.), *Towns and Townspeople in the Fifteenth Century* (Gloucester, 1988), pp. 87–106.

century, since so much of the critique of local government was based upon a comparison with an idealised notion of the past, and the fabricated ideal of the Anglo-Saxon constitution, which represented public service and virtue in its uncorrupted form. The ideal of voluntary service on the part of the civic community, did not disappear, it lived on (and still does), but it is questionable whether there was ever a time when all citizens participated equally in the government of the town, and performed their quota of civic service, as reformers fondly believed. The transition to salaried public service, and bureaucratic processes in many areas of administration, which was taking place over our period, highlighted even more acutely the shortcomings of the older tradition of unpaid service, and its anomalous position in a modernising urban society.

CHAPTER FOUR

The Divided Society

So far, we have considered the institutions of urban government, and the duties and responsibilities which they fulfilled, in order to maintain a well-ordered and stable environment. Contemporary descriptions and guides to eighteenth-century towns might tempt one to believe that under this governance they were utopian communities of industry, civility and philanthropy, living in harmonious co-existence and enjoying the profits of commerce, under the benign and beneficent rule of the urban elite. Attractive though this image was, no town lived up to such an ideal – a fact which our discussion so far must already have made clear. Dissension and conflict could and did occur at a variety of levels. As we saw in chapter 3 popular protest, in the form of bread riots and industrial disturbances, was endemic in urban society, and the labouring population was viewed by its social superiors as an unruly force, posing a permanent challenge to the social order. They were unschooled in the virtues of reason and restraint, and prone to displays of riotous behaviour and even violence. This was not the only form of disruption, however. Urban society was particularly prone to conflict, not just between employers and workers, or rulers and ruled; familial, religious and political divisions cut their own swathes through the wefts which bound urban society together. Religious sectarianism lived on in many towns, with intermittent inputs of additional animus from anti-Catholic or anti-Methodist agitation. Local and personal conflicts, over power and status within the community, and the clash of vested interests, combined with party politics and religious divisions to create a political culture which could be chronically unstable.

In this chapter we will be considering these divisions and tensions chiefly as they were manifested in party conflict and through the spread of urban radicalism. Political conflict was periodically fuelled by elections and the manipulation of parliamentary managers and patrons, but even on a day-to-day basis it spilled over into the social and philanthropic life of the town. As the movement for political reform became more widespread and its language more pervasive, we find specifically local grievances being articulated and expressed in terms of political reform and party principle. But this was a shift in degree rather than a fundamental change in the way in which the conflicts of urban society were conceptualized. The matrices, within which discontent and dissatisfaction with ruling elites had been expressed, had always had the potential to be aligned with the coordinates of party conflict. We will begin by looking at the question of disputed rights and privileges, and opposition to olig-archy in its specifically civic context, since it is important to remember that such conflicts were a characteristic feature of urban politics long before it became caught up in broader national move-ments. Throughout our period, the distribution of power within the community was regularly contested through civic elections and litigation. We will then look at how religious differences lay at the basis of many of the political divisions within towns, irrespective of whether they were incorporated or parliamentary boroughs or not. It will become clear that the presence of an oligarchic corpora-tion was far from being an essential ingredient for the creation of conflict within the urban community. We will then move on to look at how conflicts within the urban community related to the movement for parliamentary reform and the development of urban radicalism, giving particular attention to the issues within the local society which radicals exploited with regard to their broader agenda of parliamentary and government reform.

The difficulty in approaching this subject lies in distinguishing between the conflicts which arose from a difference of party polit-ics, religious sectarianism, or the distribution of power and inter-est within the urban society. A concentration on electoral history, and the type of study pioneered by Sir Lewis Namier and the *His-tory of Parliament* series, has tended to encourage an outlook which assesses urban politics as subsidiary to, and parasitic upon, West-minster politics, and which sidelines the urban agenda and its own internal coherence. Urban radicalism has generally been conceived simply in terms of opposition to political oligarchy, ignoring the ways in which it fed upon longer-standing local traditions and its implications for local struggles over status, power and influence within the community. More recently, there has been a move towards putting politics back into the local context. The 1680s have been particularly rich in local studies which have re-interpreted the Stuart interventions as being less the result of government policy than government responding to pressure from the localities, where interested parties saw the opportunity of 'using' government to further their own interests. The pressure for regulation, under Charles II, came from the Tory magistracy, who were disturbed by the ascendancy of the dissenting interest in their boroughs.[1] Similarly the work of John Brewer, Linda Colley, H. T. Dickinson, Frank O'Gorman, John Phillips, Nicholas Rogers and Kathleen Wilson has shown, from various perspectives, the strength and intensity of local politics, which made it a defining feature of urban life and enabled it to shape the national political culture.[2] We will be working within this historiographical framework to build up a picture of urban politics and radicalism, which is more firmly rooted in the local experience over the period of the long eighteenth century as a whole.

The Franchise and Elections

Domestic politics and parliamentary politics were, of course, inevitably intermingled, especially in the parliamentary boroughs which had the right to return MPs. It is therefore not surprising that the complex interconnection between the parliamentary franchise and other civic liberties is often overlooked, but this relationship is crucial to any interpretation of urban politics. The right to return an MP was granted in a charter with other privileges which defined the status and importance of the town. Any debate over the franchise always carried significant implications for the authority of the civic elite, since the terms determining the composition and constitution of the corporation were laid down in the same charter which specified who was eligible for the franchise. Any attempt to alter

1. R. E. Pickavance, 'The English Boroughs and the King's Government: a study of the Tory Reaction 1681–5', Oxford Univ. D.Phil. thesis (1976). See also ch. 2 above.

2. See, for example, John Brewer, *Popular Politics and Party Ideology at the Accession of George III* (Cambridge, 1976); Linda Colley, *In Defiance of Oligarchy: the Tory Party, 1714–1760* (Cambridge, 1982); H. T. Dickinson, *The Politics of the People in Eighteenth-Century Britain* (1994); Frank O'Gorman, *Voters, Patrons and Parties. The Unreformed Electorate of Hanoverian England, 1734–1832* (Oxford, 1989); John A. Phillips, *Electoral Behaviour in Unreformed England, 1761–1802* (Princeton, 1982); Nicholas Rogers, *Whigs and Cities. Popular Politics in the Age of Walpole and Pitt* (Oxford, 1989); Kathleen Wilson, *The Sense of the People. Politics, Culture and Imperialism in England, 1715–1785* (Cambridge, 1995).

this could be construed as an attack on the privileges and powers of the corporation. Similarly, since the franchise was often consequent upon acquiring the freedom of the city, its extension or restriction had a bearing on the economic and trading privileges in freeman boroughs. To question one privilege was to undermine the other. Granted, these issues were often subsumed in the rhetoric of liberty and free born Englishmen, but the fact that the franchise was regarded as a 'privilege', belonging to certain citizens and bound up with a nexus of other privileges, meant that it was easy to slide from the discussion of specifically urban chartered privileges to political rights more generally.

It is important to remember that opposition to oligarchy was nothing new in urban society. The imposition and consolidation of oligarchy, with which the Hanoverian era has been associated, developed from a trend which was already well established in the fifteenth century or earlier, whereby government became vested in a select body rather than the community at large.[3] The exclusion of the greater part of the burgesses from the business of government had provoked occasional protest, from the earliest periods of urban government, and as the Tudor and Stuart monarchs consolidated the process for their own political ends, the discontent generated surfaced in outbursts of urban unrest. Seventeenth-century Colchester saw recurrent conflict between the corporation and free burgesses, which culminated in the acquisition of a new charter in 1635. This seriously diminished the extent of popular participation in local government, by abolishing annual elections for all offices but that of the mayor.[4] The potential for conflict was exacerbated in the upheavals of the late seventeenth century when new charters were granted and old ones revoked, and confusion as to the precise status and composition of the governing bodies abounded.[5] This was particularly the case in boroughs where the participation of the freemen at large had not been fully excluded prior to the 1680s; conflicts arose between those who sought to take advantage of the possibility offered by a new charter to delimit the functions of civic government to an oligarchic elite, and those who wished to keep

3. Peter Clark and Paul Slack, *English Towns in Transition, 1500–1700* (Oxford, 1976), pp. 126–34.

4. John Walter, unpublished paper given in Oxford, 1997.

5. Pickavance, 'English Boroughs and the King's Government'; John Miller, 'The Crown and the borough charters in the reign of Charles II', *EHR*, c (1985), pp. 53–84; J. Levin, *The Charter Controversy in the City of London, 1660–88* (1969) illustrates the problems of legal status and interpretation in one particular borough.

the exercise of authority more open. Chester, for example, had a long tradition of opposition to oligarchy among its freemen, and parliamentary elections were consistently contested around local issues. It had endured acute constitutional confusion in the seventeenth century; the charter providing for freeman participation in civic elections was revoked by Charles II, but never officially surrendered. It was argued therefore that this, the charter of Henry VII, and not the Caroline one, was the one under which the town should be governed. The tradition of freeman involvement in the corporation, as well as the parliamentary franchise, was never forgotten. The rights of freemen in civic elections were raised time and again, in elections from the 1690s onwards, when the Whig candidate was repeatedly elected by the freemen as a champion of civic privileges, rather than for his Whig credentials.[6] The question of freeman participation in civic elections was raised in 1747 and was resurrected 1771, when the citizens asserted the popular right to elect a sheriff, which at that time was restricted to the votes of the common council alone. The charter of Henry VII was published in order to alert the citizens to their right to participate in the civic elections, while the corporation argued in response that, although the charter of Charles II was not ratified at the Glorious Revolution, customary practices, confirmed through a bye-law, should prevail over the grants of earlier charters. This ongoing resistance to oligarchy acquired political dimensions because it was through their influence over the common council that the aristocratic patrons of the borough, the Grosvenors, were able to secure the return of their candidates as MPs. The issue of freemen's rights became more controversial and prominent because they provided the rallying cry of the independents, opposing aristocratic influence in election campaigns such as that of 1784. But their importance in Chester went far deeper than simply the rejection of aristocratic borough-mongering.[7]

The right to vote in civic elections, which was being contested in Chester, similarly gave grounds for dispute in many towns, simply because practice had tended to vary over the years. Bye-laws had often been made to modify existing constitutions, and the legacy of Stuart intervention in the 1680s had simply added another layer of confusion. This has important implications for understanding the

---

6. Paul D. Halliday, 'Partisan Conflict and the Law in the English Borough Corporation', Chicago Univ. Ph.D. thesis (1993), p. 247.

7. J. Hemingway, *The History and Antiquities of Chester*, 2 vols (Chester, 1830), ii, pp. 246–7; Rosemary Sweet 'Freemen and Independence in English Borough Politics c. 1770–1830', *P & P* 161 (1998).

political tenor of eighteenth-century urban society. By calculating
the number of contested elections which took place in urban constituencies during the eighteenth century, historians came to the
conclusion that town politics descended into a state of torpor and
inactivity as England settled down into J. H. Plumb's era of 'political stability'. However, more recent research has shown that this
was far from being the case. Firstly, it should be remembered that
an election was simply the final outcome of protracted political
negotiations for local influence between rival parties in the town
and prospective MPs. Since elections were extremely expensive
undertakings and could be the occasion of considerable disorder,
causing damage to property and disruption to trade, there were
powerful reasons for avoiding going to the poll. More importantly,
as the experience of Chester has suggested, civic elections were
by no means always perfunctory non-events, and were often the
occasion of extremely high turn-outs.[8] They could be as fiercely
contested as parliamentary ones, if not more so, particularly as there
was often a greater degree of freeman participation. Political passions raged strongly in many towns, even while the MPs enjoyed
uninterrupted tenure of their seats. Not only were civic elections
annual rather than septennial events, but, given the range of elected
offices and the complexity of the electoral procedure in many boroughs, there was far more potential for electoral turbulence. In
Norwich, the divisions between Tories and Whigs dominated city
politics long after the Hanoverian accession brought political stability to Westminster. Conflict was further exacerbated by the dual
chamber system in the corporation, whereby a Whig common council could obstruct all the measures of the Tory aldermanic bench.[9]
Exploiting the connection between Toryism and Jacobitism, the
Whigs petitioned Parliament for an Election Act in 1723, which, by
forcing all resident adult males to take up their freedom, eventually
allowed the Whigs to secure a majority on the aldermanic bench.
This ascendancy did not last, and the Tories made good their ground
again, so the Whigs boycotted all meetings of the council for a
period of thirteen months, during which there were frequent outbreaks of mob violence and local government ground to a halt.
The Whigs petitioned for another election act (on the grounds of

8. John A. Phillips, 'Municipal politics in later eighteenth-century Maidstone', in
Eckart Hellmuth (ed.), *The Transformation of Political Culture. England and Germany in
the Late Eighteenth Century* (Oxford, 1990), pp. 185–203.
    9. D. O'Sullivan, 'Politics in Norwich, 1701–1835', Univ. of East Anglia M.Phil.
thesis (1975), pp. 67–100; Wilson, *Sense of the People*, pp. 385–8.

tackling corruption in local elections), which greatly reduced the possibility of participation by the freemen and gave the Whig aldermen a veto, thereby allowing the Whigs to regain the ascendancy for almost 50 years.[10] The pattern of conflict, based around civic elections, was repeated again in the decade of the 1790s, with the added stimulant of popular radicalism. In Exeter, civic elections tended to be occasions of popular license, attended by disorderly customs such as cock-fighting and bull-baiting. Like Norwich, large numbers of extra freemen were admitted just before elections took place, and bribing and treating were commonplace (proving a serious disruption to manufacturing production). Even the elections to the guardians of the poor were 'carry'd on, oftentimes, with more Noise and Party Fury than in some Places perhaps that of Representatives in Parliament'.[11] The mayoral election in Great Yarmouth was particularly violent, in 1733, involving even civic dignitaries in a fracas over the election of commoners: 'Mr Barry Love, the mayor's son would have drawn his sword but was hindered; notwithstanding that, the mayor took Mr Nathaniel Symonds by the nose, upon which he stroke [sic] Mr Love in the head with his cane'.[12] This kind of civic unrest was generally spasmodic rather than permanent; after a number of years, one party would gain the ascendancy in the corporation and use its power to pass bye-laws to entrench its position, as happened in Norwich. In the case of Maidstone, however, the conflict over civic elections was uninterrupted for much of the century. It first led to the complete breakdown of the corporation in the 1730s, with the dissolution of the corporation in 1740, and a new charter had to be secured in 1747. The party identified as 'Tories', who gained the ascendancy soon after, tried to exploit the loopholes in the wording, in order to pass bye-laws which would exclude the Whigs, by virtue of reducing the role of the commonality in elections. The issue of the rights of the commonality, with respect to civic and parliamentary elections, continued to dominate local politics into the 1830s.[13] It is hardly surprising that historians

10. For the terms of this act see Francis Blomefield, *The History of the City and County of Norwich* (1806), pp. 444–5.

11. Andrew Brice, *The Mobiad* (Exeter, 1770), p. 17. This was a humorous satire on the practice of 'mobbing' (i.e. encouraging excessive drunkenness and disorder) at Exeter elections, written by a local newspaper proprietor in the 1730s.

12. C. J. Palmer, *The Perlustration of Great Yarmouth, with Gorleston and Southtown*, 3 vols (Great Yarmouth, 1872–75), iii, p. 282.

13. *A Short Treatise on the Institution of Corporations and an Enquiry into the Conduct of the Bench of the Corporation of Maidstone* (Maidstone, 1786); William Robert James, *The Charters and other Documents relating to the King's Town of Maidstone* (1825).

of the unreformed electorate have found Maidstone to be a singu-
larly important borough for demonstrating the political sophistication of the people.[14]

Legal Challenges

One of the most noticeable aspects of the Maidstone case is the
frequent recourse which was had to King's Bench to obtain judge-
ments of *quo warranto* and *mandamus* against current members of
the corporation. This practice was by no means unique to Maidstone. The technique was first deployed in a systematic way by
Charles II and James II, who used the writ of *quo warranto* to question the authority of the governing charter of a borough, pre-
paratory to confiscating it. Townsmen were not slow to learn the
lesson of this exercise and in the years following 1688 it became a
favourite means for citizens to pursue their rivalries. The records of
King's Bench are filled with depositions against corporations, steadily
increasing throughout the eighteenth century. These records are
not so much evidence of the legitimacy of corporate rule being challenged *per se*, but rather bear witness to the continued divisions in
urban life, which provoked the legal proceedings in the first place.
They belie the assumption that, with the onset of Walpolian stability, the boroughs sank into a century of provincial torpor, bright-
ened by only the occasional electoral conflict. The rights of the
freemen did not have to be called into question, riots did not have
to be staged and civic elections did not even have to be contested,
in order to maintain intense levels of conflict. Power and influence
were contested through the ostensibly more civilized environment
of the court, rather than through resort to open violence. Divisions
within urban politics were in these cases often internal to the ruling
elite; in Scarborough there were scenes of family feuding which
necessitated a corporation order that no more than three members of each family could enter the corporation. The edifice of
the Venetian oligarchy was constructed upon deeply factious and
litigious foundations.[15]

14. For example, Phillips, *Electoral Behaviour in Unreformed England*; and Phillips, *The Great Reform Bill in the Boroughs: English Electoral Behaviour, 1818–41* (Oxford, 1992).
15. Halliday, 'Partisan Conflict and the Law'; S. McIntyre, 'The Scarborough Cor-poration quarrel, 1730–60', *Northern History*, xiv (1978), esp. p. 212; H. Cam, ' "*Quo Warranto*" proceedings at Cambridge, 1780–90', *Cambridge Historical Journal*, viii (1946), pp. 150–2.

One reason that the recourse to King's Bench became an increasingly attractive option was that, in the absence of royal or parliamentary intervention, it was effectively the only means of redress for those who were excluded from the corridors of power. At the same time the procedure was encouraged because legal writers and reformers were taking an increasingly rigid and definitive approach to corporations. William Blackstone had laid down what he held to be the five main characteristics of a corporation in his *Commentaries*, in 1765, and by the latter part of the eighteenth century a distinct corpus of corporation law was emerging under the aegis of the Lord Chancellor, Lord Mansfield, which by the nineteenth century had become a branch of study in its own right, and had spawned a number of commentaries, such as Kyd's *Treatise on the Law of Corporations* (1793) and Willcock's *The Law of Municipal Corporations* (1827). We might even identify a 'school' of lawyers and legal antiquarians who scrutinised the terms of urban charters in minute detail, to yield up precedents for the interpretation of the law. Unfortunately, the charters of incorporation or confirmation had not been granted with a view to clarifying matters for reformers in the future; not only was there endless room for dispute, but the charters were quite vague on points such as to whom the term 'burgenses' referred, simply because the rights of inhabitant householders at law had not been an issue when the original privileges were conferred.[16] The evidence was seldom conclusive.

Opposition and Conflict in Unincorporated Towns

There is a substantial amount of contemporary comment which suggests that non-parliamentary boroughs and unincorporated towns were perceived to be less politicised, and therefore less divided. Certainly the absence of pressure for parliamentary representation in Manchester, for most of the eighteenth century, owed much to the fact that the urban elite were persuaded that elections were disruptive, expensive and contrary to the town's commercial interests; interests which, at the time, were being adequately represented

16. Susan Reynolds, 'The history of the idea of incorporation or legal personality: a case of fallacious teleology' in *Ideas and Solidarities of the Medieval Laity* (Aldershot, 1995), p. 4.

in Parliament by sympathetic or interested MPs and the use of lobbying techniques. In 1788, it was still being argued that, 'This Town is happily freed from the feuds, the riots, and the tumults of Corporation Towns'.[17] Yet, although the parliamentary boroughs were more prone to conflict, it was far from being absent in other towns, even if they were not able to participate in general elections. The alignment of party groupings within a town can very often be traced back to religious differences. Almost all high churchmen identified with Tory policies as naturally as Dissenters and low churchmen upheld a Whig position. Many of the divisions in urban society were deeply rooted in sectarian differences, which could affect any urban community where there was a religious minority. The comment quoted above, referring to Manchester's supposed freedom from disturbance, was made precisely because it was feared that 'contracted prejudices' were threatening the promotion of the public welfare of the town. Manchester was in fact notoriously divided between high and low church parties for most of the first half of the century. By the beginning of the nineteenth century, divisions were emerging again between the dissenting manufacturers and the more established Tories, which continued to reflect the traditional religious tensions. The legacy of the seventeenth century and the Act of Toleration was that in many (but not all) towns Dissenters were excluded from public life. The Test and Corporation Acts theoretically prevented Dissenters, who were unwilling to compromise by practising occasional conformity, from office-holding, but the element of co-option and self-selection which existed in almost all bodies meant that not just corporations, but guardians of the poor, improvement commissioners and charitable trustees could become equally exclusive. Religion on its own was not enough to keep factionalism alive in towns, any more than it can be blamed for the outbreak of the Civil War – indeed the strength of civic consensus could often transcend religious divisions – but it was crucial in initiating and sustaining opposition.

Conflict, arising originally from religio-political differences, could be conducted through a wide variety of informal channels. It is never enough to look simply at the main administrative body, such as the corporation or court leet, to find evidence for the playing out of religious rivalries or contested politics. Even the ostensibly

---

17. William Roberts, 'A charge to the grand jury of the court leet for the manor of Manchester', *Records of the Manchester Court Leet*, ix (1889), p. 252.

neutral territory of philanthropy, the management of the poor and the charity school movement could become highly politicized ground, precisely because of their tendency to be established on a sectarian basis. We have already seen how many of the early poor law incorporations, such as Bristol and Exeter, emanated from dissenting circles in towns where the Anglicans dominated the corporation. Partisan sectarianism has been identified as the cause for the decline of charity schools and the movement for poor law incorporation after the 1720s.[18] Because they were generally dominated by high church Anglicans, these bodies were charged with being instruments for winning over Jacobite sympathisers. The opposition to parochial government in London was laid on similar foundations; biting criticisms of the management of select vestries in London, which were believed to be centres of Tory Jacobitism, came from the pen of Whig pamphleteers, such as Daniel Defoe.

Defoe's point may have been primarily political, but the kind of criticisms which he made, and the recommendations for better government which he offered, bear a striking similarity to the arguments associated with urban reformers towards the latter end of our period. Writing as Andrew Morton in *Parochial Tyranny*, he railed against the corruption and lack of accountability, the waste and extravagance and the betrayal of what was intended to be a public trust. The parish accounts were not available for public inspection, the vestry meeting was a farce. The business of the parish was decided by an inner clique, who feasted themselves at the expense of the respectable ratepaying householders. The parish charities had been swallowed up, the streets were uncleansed and unsafe and immorality flourished. He called for a vote in the parish meeting for every resident ratepayer, who would participate in regular monthly or quarterly meetings to regulate parish affairs. He advocated the appointment of a treasurer, who would be responsible for all the money collected under a reformed rating system, and a salaried clerk, who would keep the accounts, which would be made available for inspection by the parishioners at any time. The enforcement of law and order in the streets would be rendered more effective by the appointment of permanent salaried constables, rather than foisting the onerous duty on unwilling householders.

18. Craig Rose, 'London's charity schools, 1690–1730', *History Today*, xl (1990), pp. 17–23; and 'Evangelical philanthropy and Anglican revival. The charity schools of Augustan London, 1698–1740', *London Journal*, xvi (1991), pp. 35–66.

Finally, he called upon the government to send out commissioners to inspect all parochial charities and draw up an exact register of their nature, extent and intent.[19]

The reform of vestry government became a contentious issue again in the 1820s. The Sturges Bourne Acts of 1818 and 1819 were pieces of permissive legislation which allowed vestries to establish a 'closed' body. They had been welcomed by many who were suspicious of the unruly demagoguery of the open vestry, and feared for the interests of the propertied, but many others saw it as further evidence of the encroachment of oligarchy upon the rights of the people.[20] The rapid advance of notions of popular sovereignty made such exercises in oligarchy unacceptable, and in metropolitan radical circles there was mounting criticism. One pamphlet, published in 1828, prophesied that the 'nefarious and unconstitutional bodies' had become so intolerable that 'the day is not far distant when the system will burst like a whirlwind upon the heads of its abettors', and parishioners would be restored to the exercise and enjoyment of their rightful privileges. The rhetoric is very close to that levelled against unreformed corporations, and at one point the pamphlet referred to them as 'rotten boroughs' within the parish. Select vestries, corporations, and the co-opting improvement bodies, were all targeted as part of a system of government which was ill-adapted to the needs of early nineteenth-century society, and based upon premises fundamentally at odds with the rights of Englishmen, as they were understood by the radicals. But this pamphlet was also at great pains to remind its readers that the demands being made, and the criticism being voiced, were well rooted in precedent and were not the outbursts of dangerous innovatory reformers. The arguments put forward were, in fact, little more than a restatement of Defoe's *Parochial Tyranny*, given a nineteenth-century, post Sturges Bourne gloss. Rhetorical sleight of hand it certainly was, but pamphlets such as these serve as a reminder that the movement for urban reform has its own trajectory, and arose out of historical traditions which went back to the early eighteenth century or before. It was not simply a spin-off from, or dependent upon, the external influence of the movement for parliamentary reform, which for obvious reasons has always been accorded more attention.[21]

19. Andrew Morton [Daniel Defoe], *Parochial Tyranny; or the Housekeeper's Complaint against the insupportable exactions, and partial assessments of Select Vestries* (not dated).

20. See above, pp. 32, 72.   21. *Considerations on Select Vestries* (1828).

Urban Radicalism

Historians have tended to focus on periods of 'crisis' in the story of urban radicalism, ranging from the popular support for John Wilkes in the 1760s and 70s, to the Jacobin scares of the 1790s, the industrial unrest of the Peterloo era, and the widespread agitation and rioting in the years immediately preceding the Great Reform Act. There has been less interest in considering radicalism in the longer term, and in its relationship to the political experience of individual towns, rather than in the context of a wider movement for political reform, and the rise of extra-parliamentary politics. There are still great lacunae in our knowledge as to how radicalism was sustained and remained active in between specific crises or contested elections. In the discussion which follows, we will be sketching out some suggestions for filling in these gaps.

It should be stressed that 'radicalism' did not represent a neat package of political beliefs; radicals justified their position with reference to arguments ranging from natural rights liberalism, to Anglo-Saxon constitutionalism, from common law to religious millenarianism.[22] There was no common agenda to which all radicals subscribed, but there were certain key reforms which almost all demanded, and which become identifiable with a radical position in the years after 1780. These generally included one or more of the following points: the disenfranchising of rotten boroughs and the redistribution of seats, the extension of the franchise (an extreme minority demanded a universal franchise), the right to instruct representatives, and more frequent, if not annual, parliaments. These demands, and the language in which they were presented, differentiated the radical programme from the traditional anti-corruption agenda, which had been typical of the country party. Radicalism and reform also became more geographically widespread in this latter period. Prior to 1780, radical reform, such as it was, had been based chiefly in London, textile towns such as Norwich, and the cloth towns of the south west of England. But after 1790 it spread rapidly in the industrialising towns of the Midlands and the north, becoming particularly prominent in Sheffield, for example, where there had been no previous tradition of political activism.

The extra-parliamentary reform movement was naturally predominantly urban (hence the ease with which urban opposition or

---

22. H. T. Dickinson, *Liberty and Property. Political Ideology in Eighteenth-Century Britain* (1977); and Dickinson, *The Politics of the People*, pp. 221–54.

reform movements have been subsumed with parliamentary reform under the umbrella of urban radicalism). The majority of the clubs and societies were based in towns, often arising from traditional urban institutions, such as friendly societies, debating societies, or even meetings of the vestry. Urban activists led the way, in present-ing petitions to Parliament in support of reform, particularly after 1815, and in staging demonstrations, which reached their culmina-tion in the election riots preceding the passage of the Reform Bill of 1832. The reasons for the success of urban-based reform activity are obvious: the highly concentrated population and higher rates of literacy facilitated both the spread of a reformist programme and the organization of political protest. The question of political reform now held far greater implications for urban, as opposed to rural, populations. Whereas Christopher Wyvill's Association Movement (1779–84) had advocated the abolition of the rotten boroughs and the redistribution of seats, but had envisaged a higher degree of *county* representation, subsequent programmes of reform concentrated on the representation of urban areas, such as Man-chester, Leeds or Birmingham, rather than the counties.[23]

Furthermore, the distribution of the franchise within the par-liamentary boroughs was also under attack. Before 1832, the varia-tions in the nature of the franchise were as complex and numerous as those of the municipal institutions. There were six main types: these were householder (thirteen boroughs), which comprised all inhabitant householders not in receipt of poor rates – these were also known as pot-walloper franchises and could be extremely unruly (as in Taunton where two men were killed in the election riots of 1754); freeman franchise (91 boroughs), where all those who had taken up the freedom of the town could vote. These numbered some of the largest electorates, in cities such as Westminster, Bristol and Norwich. In scot-and-lot boroughs (of which there were 37), all those paying the rates were eligible, and in these too the elec-torate could be numerous. The franchise was more restricted in corporation boroughs (25), where it was limited to members of the corporation – these were some of the most easily managed boroughs. Finally, the 30 burgage boroughs were generally even safer, where the right to vote was attached to the tenancy of 'burgage' property – generally controlled by one aristocratic landlord. Universal man-hood suffrage was called for in more radical circles. But even those

---

23. John Cannon, *Parliamentary Reform 1660–1832* (1968); I. Christie, *Wilkes, Wyvill and Reform* (1962).

of a more conservative temper saw the advantage of re-allocating the franchise on more rational lines, based upon a property quali-fication, which would open up the close boroughs and eliminate the poorest (and therefore most easily corruptible) of the urban electorate. The size of the electorate ranged from the large freemen boroughs of Westminster, Bristol or Norwich, where there were sev-eral thousand potential voters, to the burgage and closed corpora-tion boroughs, where the votes of a handful of men, in the pocket of an aristocratic patron, decided the outcome, as was notoriously the case in the rotten boroughs of Cornwall.[24] The discrepancies and abuses in the boroughs provoked increasingly venomous attacks from the pens of reformers. Thomas Oldfield's *History of the Boroughs* (1792) provided a highly critical and extremely influential analysis of all the seats in the country, and the extent to which they were under aristocratic influence. It became commonplace to assume that the urban electorate was uniquely venal, and that boroughs were invariably under the influence of aristocratic interests – the urban freeman was perceived to be of much weaker moral fibre than the rural freeholder, when it came to resisting the temptation of bribery.

Oldfield had an axe to grind – his argument was that all char-tered boroughs represented a usurpation of the rights of the people – and his depiction of rampant venality and corruption needs to be moderated. But nevertheless, more recent estimates still suggest that up to three-quarters of the 432 borough seats were subject to some kind of magnate influence. Whether the Great Reform Act of 1832 was the landmark in parliamentary democracy, which it was once held to be, seems highly implausible in the light of revisionist scho-larship. But with respect to towns, the basis of the franchise was fundamentally altered and some of the vagaries of the representative system ironed out.[25] What it patently did not solve were the problems of electoral violence and the manipulation of voters. The pattern of urban politics in this respect remained essentially unchanged. The election scenes of Trollope's Palliser novels, or Eliot's *Felix Holt*, would have been easily recognizable to the pre-1832 generation as well.

Radicals saw the importance of translating their message into broader terms, which could appeal to grievances and did not arise out of a purely radical platform. We have already seen how the familiar objections against select vestries, which were being raised

24. For a more detailed analysis of the varieties of franchise in parliamentary boroughs, see e.g. John Brooke, *The House of Commons, 1754–90* (Oxford, 1968), pp. 1–81.

25. M. Brock, *The Great Reform Act* (1973).

in the early eighteenth century, were revived by the circle of metropolitan radicals in the 1820s. Radicals involved themselves in the
politics of day-to-day life in order to bring about the realization of
their aims at the local as well as the parliamentary level. The main
platform of the radical programme was indeed the reform of the
system of parliamentary representation, but obscured behind the
more extremist agitation was a range of reformist positions which
were generally more moderate in their stance. People supported
parliamentary reform for a variety of reasons; one of the foremost
of which was their perception of the state of local affairs, rather
than any commitment to ideological principles. Reformers had to
gather support by relating their message to local concerns. Hence,
the abuses of the unreformed parliamentary system were bracketed
with the 'oligarchy and corruption' of the corporations, and the
arguments for a broader electorate were presented as restoring to
the inhabitant householders a franchise, usurped by the corporation, which had been anciently theirs. Radicals were at the forefront of local campaigns, ranging from legal proceedings against
members of the corporation, to the investigation of charitable trusts,
or the abolition of tolls and exclusive trading rights, and were prominently involved in schemes to bring about more accountable and
useful local government.

Radicalism: the Ways and Means

Institutions, such as voluntary hospitals, friendly societies and public dispensaries, were established with increasing frequency in the
second half of the century, and prided themselves on their openness
and accountability, and the absence of the kind of self-interested
jobbery and monopolising tendencies, which were identified in the
traditional institutions of government. Organizations such as these
naturally involved the exercise of a certain amount of power and
influence within the community, and therefore had the potential
to become politicized bodies. Kathleen Wilson has demonstrated
that in Newcastle and Norwich reformers and radicals were often at
the forefront of these philanthropic associational activities, and they
then drew upon their experience of more democratic and accountable practices to sharpen their critique of oligarchy at higher levels.[26]

26. Kathleen Wilson, 'Urban culture and political activism in Hanoverian England:
The example of voluntary hospitals', in Hellmuth (ed.), *Transformation of Political
Culture*, pp. 165–84.

Naturally, one must not assume that all voluntary hospitals, public dispensaries and similar organizations were 'covers' for radical activism; there was a shared consensus on the importance of improving the physical and moral welfare of the labouring sort, which could draw upon a wide range of social and political affiliations. But because charitable and philanthropic schemes were relatively uncontroversial, their existence meant that urban radicalism could be assimilated within the political culture of a town, and was not permanently sidelined as unacceptable extremism.

The prominence of certain dissenting groups, in campaigns for parliamentary and urban reform, has often been commented upon. Some interpretations emphasise the dissenting experience of exclusion and the cultural heritage of opposition, which encouraged a disposition to criticism and political opposition. Others have stressed the theological imperative, particularly amongst the Unitarians, which drove them to oppose a system which compromised the freedom of the individual, in both religious and secular spheres. However, the extent to which religion was the overriding ideology informing the conduct of politics, is a different matter – and one which is not easy to determine. What is more easily verifiable is that dissent was an essential element in the development of urban radicalism – by the end of the eighteenth century Dissenters were at the forefront of movements in permanent opposition to the corporation in thirteen freemen boroughs identified by Frank O'Gorman.[27] In fact, in almost all boroughs except for Coventry and Nottingham Dissenters could be found in opposition to the corporation or other leading electoral interest. O'Gorman suggests that in 30 to 40 seats local politics was dominated by an Anglican-Dissenting divide. Recent work by James Bradley has highlighted the role of Dissenters in agitation against the American War and in organizing petitions, and he postulates a link between this kind of activity and the more fully documented activity of the radicals of the 1790s.[28] By the end of the century the movements for the repeal of the Test and Corporation Acts, and for Catholic emancipation, had ensured that political divisions were once again being construed in religious terms, with Dissenters prominent among the reformers, and Tories opposed to any measures which might undermine the alliance of church and state, upon which they believed the stability of the Revolution Settlement lay. The repeal of the Test and Corporation

27. A good analysis of the relation between religion and politics is offered in O'Gorman, *Voters, Patrons and Parties*, esp. pp. 359–67.
28. James Bradley, *Religion, Revolution and English Radicalism* (Cambridge, 1990).

Acts could not be divorced from the reform of the institutions of local and national government – the two went hand in hand. Divisions deepened in towns, such as Manchester and Leeds, where the increasing wealth of Dissenters derived from the growth of manufacturing industry had far outstripped their political influence in the community. Whig/dissenting interests were ranged more consistently against Tory/Anglican interests, intensifying the criticisms being levelled against the traditional structures – such as corporations and vestries – which were so frequently the preserve of the Anglican elite. Dissent could and did provide an extra dynamic to urban politics, but it should never be seen as synonymous with the movement for reform. The radical Dissenters represented but a small part of the dissenting community as a whole, the majority of whom frequently sided firmly with the *status quo*, and had no axe to grind for political change at a local or a national level.

The rather more tangible contribution of the provincial press to the politicization of the nation after 1760 has similarly long been recognised, and its role in promoting radical activities in towns offers no exception.[29] For obvious reasons, many provincial radicals were printers and newspaper editors, making use of their presses to disseminate a critical interpretation of government and the constitution, and to educate their fellow townsmen in their rights and privileges. Notable figures in the 1790s included Benjamin Flower of the *Cambridge Intelligencer*, Richard Phillips of the *Leicester Herald*, Joseph Gales of the *Sheffield Register*, Daniel Holt of the *Newark Herald* and Joseph Hewson of the *Tyne Mercury*.[30] There were, in addition, many others who produced short-lived news sheets, which proved unable to survive for long in the competitive world of the provincial press. We have radical printers to thank, in large part, for the much higher incidence of poll books and election ephemera from this period; elections presented the most opportune moment to appeal to the politically unaware and demonstrate the iniquities of the unreformed system. Contested elections provided the backdrop against which a whole variety of issues, generally locally specific,

29. Hannah Barker, 'Press, Politics and Reform, 1779–85', Oxford Univ. D.Phil. thesis (1994); Brewer, *Party Ideology and Popular Politics*; D. Read, *Press and People: Opinion in Three English Cities* (1961).

30. On Benjamin Flower's activities see Michael J. Murphy, *Cambridge Newspapers and Opinion, 1780–1850* (Cambridge, 1977). On Phillips see D. Fraser, 'The press in Leicester, c. 1790–1850', *Transactions of the Leicestershire Archaeological and History Society*, xlii (1966–7), pp. 53–75; A. Temple Patterson, *Radical Leicester. A History of Leicester, 1780–1850* (Leicester, 1954), pp. 63–79; M. J. Smith, 'Politics in Newark in the 1790s', *Transactions of the Thoroton Society*, lxxxiv (1980), pp. 59–67.

might be raised. Allegations concerning the past conduct of the corporation, claims for the rights of the freemen, calls for the restoration of traditional rights and privileges, or the publication of the charter, could be made in a context of political excitement in the squibs, ballads and addresses which proliferated in contested elections. These were often subsequently issued as a compilation, along with the poll books, and with a commentary on the history of the election. The contested election of 1803, in Nottingham, for example, which raised important issues of civic liberties and borough autonomy, gave rise to an octavo volume of over 360 pages in length.[31]

Radical printers did not confine their activities to elections, of course; it was a fundamental premise of radical activity that change could only be brought about if people were educated as to their rights and privileges, and in their responsibilities and duties as citizens. Public spirit imposed a duty to reveal abuse and corruption and lay bare the workings of oligarchy. There was a marked upsurge in the number of charters and urban histories which were published after 1780. This was due in part to a fashionable interest in antiquities and a response to the domestic tourist market, but there was also a substantial number which were published with the additional intention of arousing political awareness among the citizens, and demonstrating the perversion of the original charters which had given rise to oligarchy and aristocratic dependence.[32] The Charter of Poole was published in 1791 by a 'Friend to Liberty', with the simple admonition to its readers to 'Judge for Yourselves'. In 1825, William Robert James was rather more explicit when he invited the readers of *The Charters and other documents . . . of Maidstone* to ascertain from the documents what their real rights were and whether they enjoyed them, and called upon them to fight for their restitution. The printer of a copy of the Ludlow charter in 1821 undertook the project in order to illustrate the corporate rights of the commonalty, in whom the right of election was vested, and dedicated his publication to his subscribers, claiming to seek no reward but the knowledge that the publication 'might be instrumental in effecting a restoration of the rights and immunities of his fellow townsmen'. Another ploy was to draw attention to legal cases in which the corporation was challenged;

31. *Coke and Birch. The Paper War carried on at the Nottingham Election, 1803* (Nottingham, 1803).

32. Rosemary Sweet, *The Writing of Urban Histories in Eighteenth-Century England* (Oxford, 1997), pp. 187–235.

much mileage was made out of the dispute over the charter in Chester, for example, and the evidence brought before the judge at King's Bench was published *in extenso*. Investigations of charitable accounts and corporation finances were also a fruitful basis for radical investigations, and were a useful peg on which to hang other charges. Martin Dunsford's history of Tiverton, which contained much reforming rhetoric directed against both the corporation and the parliamentary system, was begun as an inquiry into the charitable benefactions which should have been available to the people of Tiverton. Joseph Clarke, formerly town clerk of Newcastle, published numerous pamphlets critical of the corporation, the most famous of which was *The Newcastle Freeman's Pocket Companion*, after witnessing the terrible conditions which prevailed at the Freemen's Hospital. This had led him into a more detailed investigation of the corporate finances, the uses to which they were put, and the spirit in which the terms of the charter were interpreted.[33] Even for those radicals who believed that specifically local issues were secondary to parliamentary affairs, they were still important because they served as a valuable introduction to the parliamentary reform, and, being closer to home, initially touched people more nearly and secured their interest, while issues of a more abstract nature often met with no response.

Opposition was most likely to well up when it was felt that corporation policy was operating against the interests of the freemen at large. The corporation of Warwick was condemned in 1737 for using surplus revenues for building a court-house, rather than devoting them to the good of the poor, as directed in the charter, and it led to a protracted suit in Chancery and an extensive reform of the corporation.[34] Similar allegations of misappropriation of charitable funds cropped up fairly frequently in many other towns, and the corporations in question were castigated for dereliction of duty and betraying the public trust. The commonest grounds for such disputes were over the management of corporation property and common lands, which existed for the benefit of the freemen at large. Disputes over grazing and encroachments often embittered

33. *The Whole Proceedings, in several informations in the nature of a Quo Warranto. . . . of the City of Chester* (Chester, 1791); *Copies of the Charters and Grants to the Town of Ludlow* (Ludlow, 1821); Martin Dunsford, *Historical Memoirs of the Town and Parish of Tiverton* (Exeter, 1790); Joseph Clarke, *The Newcastle Remembrancer and Freeman's Pocket Companion*, new edn, (Newcastle, 1817).

34. Joseph Parkes, *The Governing Charter of the Borough of Warwick* (1827); Philip Styles, 'The Corporation of Warwick, 1660–1835', *Transactions of the Warwickshire Archaeological Society*, lix (1935), pp. 9–123.

relations within a town; in Nottingham, the corporation were accused of having 'taken the best ground to the richest men and let the poor men have nothing'.[35] In the eighteenth century, as land values increased, and the pressure to enclose land for improvement and development intensified, the potential for a conflict of interests also increased. Divisions arose between those who wished to preserve the common rights and those who hoped to increase the overall rental value by enclosure. This highlighted problems arising from the unrepresentative nature of oligarchy; would a decision be made in the interests of the many or the few? It also raised the issue of accountability; if the rental were to increase, how would the revenues be disposed of? When proposals were made to enclose the Town Moor in Newcastle in 1769, the freemen opposed the measure on the grounds that it would destroy their common grazing rights. They would only agree to enclosure if the corporation made a legal undertaking to allocate the revenues to the maintenance of widows and orphans. The issue became quite a cause célèbre, and was caught up in the Wilkesite movement for reform in the early 1770s. The freemen's opposition to corporation oligarchy was equated with the Wilkesite struggle against ministerial tyranny and corruption.[36] In Bath, the lines of conflict were reversed: the freemen wished to see the common lands developed to maximize the overall rental value, whereas the common council members, for reasons of their own self-interest it was suspected, favoured leaving it undeveloped.[37]

Newcastle offers a particularly good illustration of how a conflict between freemen and corporation could rumble on, independently of developments in the movement for parliamentary reform. Discontent and disagreement did not disappear with the waning of John Wilkes' political star. The question of the management of the Town Moor continued to provoke ill-feeling, as did other matters, such as the corporation's neglect in failing to build a new bridge over the Tyne after the original had been destroyed in a flood. Newcastle joined in the Association Movement in 1779, and a Society for Constitutional Information was established in 1781, attracting many of those involved in the social and moral improvement of the town. When Matthew Ridley, MP and popular local figure, was elected mayor in 1780, he allowed the freemen access to the

35. Clark and Slack, *English Towns in Transition*, p. 133.
36. T. R. Knox, 'Popular politics and provincial radicalism in Newcastle upon Tyne, 1769', *Albion*, xi (1979), pp. 223–41.
37. Rowland Mainwaring, *Annals of Bath from 1800 to the Passing of the New Municipal Act* (Bath, 1838), p. 63.

corporation records in order that they might establish their rights and privileges. Although the radical agitation went off the boil for a period, there were still grounds for grievances which kept discontent simmering. The freemen's body, the Court of Guild, became increasingly assertive in the nineteenth century, leading to several confrontations with the common council in the 1820s, when it was demanded that the guild should be allowed to act as a democratic assembly, and the right of the mayor and common council to elect the new mayor was disputed. The freemen accused the common council of asserting absolute control over liberties and privileges, when they had simply been entrusted with the administration of laws and the conservation of rights. Their management of the conservancy of the river was said to have turned a public trust into a source of private emolument, whereby the money which should have been going to the improvement of the navigation had been channelled into private pockets.[38] Inquiries into the application of borough funds became more pressing; the system of leasing corporation land, the distribution of the charitable benefactions and other forms of patronage, the award of corporation contracts and the perquisites and fees enjoyed by corporation officers, came under close scrutiny. Radicals called for greater accountability, more openness in proceedings and an end to secrecy, and for the participation of the freemen at large in the deliberative and electoral process of the corporation. Eventually the guild submitted a plan for 'the better protection of the public revenue', by appointing a committee from its members which would 'control' the common council, and the radicals called for a revival of the Court of Guild as the only legitimate permanent body (reviving claims which had also been made in the 1770s).[39]

Feeling against Newcastle corporation was particularly strong, not just among the freemen, but in the town at large, because of the dues which were levied on shipping and the exemptions enjoyed by freemen. In common with many other port towns, it had long been argued in Newcastle that this system had actually driven trade away from the port. It had been argued that such sanctions were detrimental to the expansion of commerce since the seventeenth

38. *The Corporation Mirror* (Newcastle, 1829), pp. 4, 14–16.

39. *The Corporation Mirror*; Wilson, *Sense of the People*, pp. 352–6; P. Cadogan, *Early Radical Newcastle* (Durham, 1975); Michael Cook, 'The last days of the unreformed corporation of Newcastle upon Tyne', *Archaeologia Aeliana*, 4th ser., xxxix (1961), pp. 207–28; T. Knox, '"Bowes and Liberty": The Newcastle by-election of 1777', *Durham University Journal*, lxxxvii (1985), p. 150.

century and earlier, as they forced up prices, allowed monopolies and drove away custom.[40] John Collier's *Essay on Charters* (1777), and the reprints of a seventeenth-century anti-monopoly tract, *England's Grievance Discovered* (1786), were published in the wake of anti-corporation feeling, and expounded the case against the levying of tolls and against corporations with some force. The charge of neglecting port or harbour facilities, and other responsibilities essential for the economic well-being of the town as a whole, was arguably of even greater import than the management of corporation lands or charities, because it was an issue which concerned not just the freemen and the corporation, but the entire community free and non-free, and ultimately the prosperity of the nation as a whole. Not surprisingly, this issue featured prominently in the accusations levelled against corporations in the evidence presented to the Royal Commissioners. An essential part of this critique was the lack of accountability and the unrepresentative character of oligarchy, generally presented in terms of a perversion of the original terms of the charter. The corporation of Bristol came under particularly severe attack in the early nineteenth century, when there were fears that the business of the port was rapidly declining. Corporations were founded for the extension of business and commerce, but, it was argued, the corporation's refusal to reduce the level of the tolls was driving commerce away. They had been increased nine times since 1770. Had the sums so levied been laid out in improving the harbour, the critics argued that it might have been acceptable, but instead the tolls were 'wasted' on mayoral salaries, splendour and display while valuable trade was lost to other west coast ports with better harbour facilities.[41]

The payment of tolls was frequently contested at King's Bench, and defending the right to levy them proved a heavy drain on corporate finances. But corporations were in a no-win situation; they could not afford to relinquish them, but nor could they afford to defend them. The payment of tolls and dues touched the pocket, and therefore the sensibilities, of large numbers of people, and was therefore an obvious campaigning target and one which radicals consistently exploited. James Acland, a printer and radical agitator of the first order, cultivated the perennial opposition to corporation

40. R. Howell, *Monopoly on the Tyne, 1650–58. Papers relating to Ralph Gardner* (Society of Antiquaries of Newcastle upon Tyne, 1978).
41. *Twelve Letters on the Impediments which obstruct the Trade and Commerce of the City and Port of Bristol* (Bristol, 1823); G. Bush, *Bristol and its Municipal Government 1820–51*, Bristol Record Society, 29 (1976), pp. 45–8.

tolls in Bristol, and waged campaigns against the levying of harbour dues in the late 1820s. Having made himself *persona non grata* there, he shifted his attention to Hull, where he arrived in 1831 to begin a campaign against the fares levied by the corporation on the Humber ferry (already the subject of dispute since the 1790s).[42] On his arrival, he established a periodical, the *Hull Portfolio*, which called upon the people of Hull to stage a passengers' strike, and 'to maintain the unquestionable rights of the public – so long invaded by the Corporators of Hull, for the mere purpose of swelling that enormous income in which the great body of the burgesses have no participation'.[43] He skilfully used the issue to epitomise all that he held to be wrong with the old corporation, and to stir up suspicion and resentment among the inhabitants.

In 1835, the Royal Commissioners found a number of corporations heavily burdened with debt, chiefly as a result of legal costs incurred defending their rights to tolls. The radicals would have argued, of course, that objections were raised purely because of the lack of accountability; in a ratepayer franchise such tolls could be levied freely and the fault lay only in the system. With hindsight, this seems a rather utopian, if not disingenuous, view to take. The upsurge in cases towards the end of our period could equally be attributed to base cupidity and unwillingness to pay, coupled with an increasingly widespread realisation that the judges at King's Bench were sympathetic to such cases, and that there was a fair chance of success in challenging the payment of dues, rather than being a clear cut expression of dissatisfaction with corporate government. On a matter such as the levying of market tolls, the authorities in Manchester were just as open to attack as any incorporated town, and in 1786 the Committee for Asserting the Rights of Manchester was established in order to inquire into the tolls levied by the lord of the manor.[44] The structure of government was arguably less important than the natural reluctance of merchants and tradesmen to see their profits diminished; complaints would have been raised, and indeed were raised and still are raised, wherever and whenever tolls were levied.[45]

42. K. McMahon, 'James Acland and the Humber ferry monopolies', *Transport History*, 2 (1969), pp. 167–87.

43. *Hull Portfolio* (1831), p. 27.

44. A. Redford, *The History of Local Government in Manchester*, 3 vols (1939), ii, p. 191.

45. See, for example, Harriet Martineau, *Corporate Tradition and Natural Rights. Local Dues on Shipping. Issued by the Association to Obtain the Right Appropriation of the Liverpool Town Dues* (Liverpool and Manchester, 1857).

In this chapter we have looked at some of the grounds for conflict within towns, and the kind of issues which might divide the urban community. Urban radicalism was clearly an important factor in deepening some of these rifts, but we must also recognise that the form which radicalism took in towns was equally shaped by the indigenous political culture of the towns in which it took root, and the inevitable competition arising from a variety of vested interests. In the following chapter we will look at some of the responses to the critiques of urban government which we have broached here, while surveying more broadly the subject of reform in urban government.

CHAPTER FIVE

Urban Government and the Movement for Reform

William Cowper's damning lines on corporate government in his poem *The Task* have always been much quoted:

> Hence chartered boroughs are such public plagues
> And burghers, men immaculate perhaps
> In all their private functions, once combined
> Becomes a loathsome body, only fit
> For dissolution, hurtful to the main.[1]

Much of our discussion of radicalism and reform has been based upon corporations, and in particular those corporations which were also parliamentary boroughs, but this gives a rather misleading view of the nature and extent of the movement for reform within towns. Due to their high profile and easily recognisable form, corporations have become a kind of scapegoat for what later reformers and historians have seen as the deficiencies of eighteenth-century urban government. 'Corporation spirit' was singled out as the root cause of evil, and blamed for destroying the public virtue of even the most upright of private citizens. Decent and respectable men, when bound together in a corporation, would take part in transactions which they would consider disgraceful behaviour in a private gentleman.[2] Critics warned their readers against the insidious influence of corporation oligarchy which infected all that it became involved with, so that other bodies insidiously absorbed its evil system. This was mistaking cause and effect. If we look at late eighteenth-century Manchester, for example, the same litany of complaints which were levelled against corporations were laid at the door of the

---

1. William Cowper, *The Task*, Book IV, lines 671–5.
2. Thomas Johnson, *An Address to the Freemen of Lancaster on the subject of their Charter* (1817), p. 7.

vestry, court leet, and increasingly the more recently established
police commissioners.[3] Vestries, improvement commissions and
corporations were all the products of a society whose values and
assumptions, radical thought was now beginning to challenge on a
systematic basis, rather than in terms of individual abuses. Richard
Latimer, the radical journalist of the *Western Times*, described the
Exeter Improvement Commission as 'the best of the bad corporations with which the city is afflicted'.[4] The habits of government were
transferred from one body to another; hence the secrecy in meetings
and the reluctance to publish accounts afflicted the vestries and the
new statutory bodies as much as the corporations. But, by the same
token, the habits of better book keeping and financial efficiency
could also be transferred. The *ad hoc* reform of the structures of
early modern government applied equally to parish, manorial structures, corporations, and the special statutory bodies, all of which were
premised upon the same ideology.

In this chapter we will be considering the reform of urban government, in terms of internal renewal as well as the response to
pressure from radical reformers, and the measures imposed by
Parliament towards the end of our period in the Municipal Corporations Act. We will look at the obstacles which blocked reform
and the efforts which corporations, vestries and other informal
bodies made to implement procedural improvements, and introduce
greater efficiency and accountability in response to the increasingly
burdensome and complex demands being made. The spirit of reform
had already wrought far-reaching changes in government before
the legislation of 1835. However, we must also address the build up
of pressure for intervention by central government during the early
nineteenth century, and why it was thought necessary for Parliament
to embark on a large-scale remodelling of the corporate system,
rather than continuing with a laissez-faire approach.

Reform Renewal and Rationalisation

'Reform' does not invariably carry with it the implication of political opposition, although the alleged need for reform has always

---

3. John Cross, 'Charge to the jury of the court leet, 14 Oct. 1799', *Records of the Manchester Court Leet*, ix (1889), pp. 254–9; [Thomas Battye] *A Concise Exposition of the Tricks and Arts used in the collection of Easter Dues, with a list of items which compose this Divine Tax* (Manchester, 1800).
4. Robert Newton, *Eighteenth-Century Exeter* (Newton Abbot, 1984), p. 150.

been one of the primary legitimating claims of any opposition movement. Because the radicals were always more vocal, active and extreme, their interpretation has coloured our view of the unreformed
era disproportionately. It behove them, in the cause of parliamentary reform, to blacken the reputation of the select vestries and
the closed oligarchies, even if this was a distortion of the reality.
The pamphlets and squibs, which we rely on for our knowledge of
the internal dissentions of urban politics, mislead by magnifying the
extent of disaffection and by exaggerating and distorting the facts.
By their very nature they were violently partisan and were composed by radical agitators, such as James Acland, whose activities we
have already encountered, with the deliberate intention of stirring
up feeling against corporations and oligarchy. Acland's career took
him from London to France, Shaftesbury, Bristol, Stamford, and
Hull, after which he finally ended up in Bury St Edmunds. In each
town he collaborated with a printer to produce propaganda highly
critical of the state of municipal government. The distortions of the
opposition are hardly surprising, however, given that the 'secrecy'
of the proceedings of the common councils and other similar bodies
meant that information, with respect to income, expenditure, the
budget and the decision making process, was concealed from public scrutiny. This in itself has some validity as an indictment of their
mode of proceedings, but it does mean that we have to be careful
in accepting some of the estimates for corporation debts or their
financial resources.

All too often the corporation was upbraided for not applying
what were imagined to be its limitless resources upon projects of
improvement for the public good. Yet in reality, the fact that they
did indulge in a sumptuous feast of turtle and venison every year
did not necessarily indicate limitless funds, but rather a very finite
income of only a few hundred pounds or less, which could never
have gone far towards the kind of capital investment which was
being demanded of them. Some corporations, like Chippenham,
contributed their mite towards the good of the town, finding £100
to subscribe to the Lighting Act, from an income of only £227. Conversely, the members of the corporation of Great Dunmow clearly
felt that there was little worthwhile to be done with 20 guineas,
so indulged themselves in an annual feast.[5] Critics always greatly
overestimated the income at the disposal of the corporations, and
underestimated the drain of routine outgoings in maintaining

5. *Report of the Royal Commission on Municipal Corporations*, PP, (1835), xxiv, p. 1246
(Chippenham); xxvi, pp. 2215–16 (Great Dunmow).

buildings and paying salaries, and servicing debts. Granted, more could have been done to maximise the profitability of corporation property in many cases, but even so, as we have seen, the income was rarely comparable to the kind of income generated by paving rates, or available even to vestries under parish rates (as witnessed by the escalating sums raised in poor relief over the period). Common rights might also inhibit the realisation of the full value of large tracts of corporation property, as the corporation of Newcastle discovered when they attempted to obtain an enclosure bill for the Town Moor. Debt was not necessarily a sign of self-indulgent corporate profligacy: the corporation at Southampton, for example, was still burdened with a heavy debt in 1833, sustained in 1774 in building a new Audit House. The Commissioners expressed disapproval at the financial management of the corporation in Bury St Edmunds, who had spent over £1,000 on converting the theatre into a concert room, with an annual profit of only £20, leaving them with a debt of over £2,000, but they totally failed to appreciate that this conversion was part of a wider strategy for attracting more visitors to the town, on whose custom the local economy depended.[6] Equally, of course, we must not be too disingenuous in accepting the defensive rebuttals put forward by the bodies under attack in their own defence. In *The Civil Wars of Southampton* (a collection of pamphlets concerning local controversies from the 1790s), for example, we find not only the tirades of the outraged merchants and tradesmen against financial mismanagement and increases in corporation tolls, but the denials of the corporation party, and the 'statement' issued by the town clerk, Thomas Ridding, purporting to show that there had been no wrongful application of the corporation revenue. It is easy to detect 'creative accounting' and signs of being economical with the truth (as his critics were quick to point out).[7] We should always remember the circumstances under which such material was written – in moments of heated controversy, in an attempt to win over the sympathy of the readership.

There was in fact a general and widespread improvement in standards, procedure and efficiency, which was manifested not just in the more open and recently established statutory bodies, but also the most oligarchic vestries and corporations. Although there

6. *Report of the Royal Commission on Municipal Corporations*, PP (1835), xxiii, p. 889 (Southampton); xxvi, p. 2179 (Bury St Edmunds); Jane Fiske (ed.), *The Oakes Diaries. Business, Politics and the Family in Bury St Edmunds, 1778–1827*, Suffolk Record Society, xxxii (1990), pp. 157–8.

7. *The Civil Wars of Southampton* (Southampton, 1794), esp. pp. 17–20.

was still much in eighteenth-century administrative practices that we would classify as corrupt today, there was an identifiable shift towards a more 'modern' attitude to the conduct of public affairs. These changes were common to all areas of public life. The attention of historians has conventionally focused upon the measures for economical reform taking place in central government, but it is now increasingly recognised that the improvements in administrative performance, which become marked from the 1780s in the Commission for Public Accounts, for example, should be traced back to earlier efforts in the localities rather than vice versa.[8] The new improvement commissions, and equally the supposedly archaic structures of parish and corporation, were caught up in a changing culture which expected greater accountability and openness in proceedings, and which was increasingly hostile to jobbery and corruption. Meanwhile, procedures were becoming more complex and sophisticated, administration more bureaucratic and specialized, and the force of public opinion was steadily encroaching upon the administrative sphere of personal authority. It was these tensions which generated the force of the radical critique.

The most comprehensive study of the finances of unreformed local government, focusing on the cities of Nottingham, York and Boston, has presented us with a much more positive view of the financial rectitude of these bodies than was once supposed to be the case. Dawson argues that from the 1660s the management of the corporation estate in each town was not only 'sagacious and discriminating,' but, as the period progressed became even more 'well-advised'.[9] This is a pattern which may be traced in almost all towns – although clearly with varying impact. Greater efficiency was achieved by appointing salaried and permanent officials, rather than relying on voluntary unpaid service, improved techniques were introduced in accounting and auditing, and records were kept with much more care and precision. Property was surveyed by professional surveyors and leases granted to maximize revenue. In Hull, there was a major restructuring of the financial system around

8. J. Brewer, *The Sinews of Power. War, Money and the English State 1688–1783* (1988); and Paul Langford, *Public Life and the Propertied Englishman* (Oxford, 1991), p. 263; cf. also David Eastwood, *Governing Rural England. Tradition and Transformation in Local Government, 1780–1840* (Oxford, 1994). Eastwood examines reform in the context of county government, showing that reform of poor relief and prisons and other areas was adumbrated first at a local level.

9. E. J. Dawson, 'Finance and the Unreformed Borough: A Critical Appraisal of Corporate Finance, 1660–1835, with special reference to the Boroughs of Nottingham, York and Boston', Univ. of Hull Ph.D. thesis (1978), p. 98 and throughout.

mid-century, which appears to have improved substantially the accounting system, although it did make it less accountable to the freemen at large. Whereas, formerly, annually appointed chamberlains had handled much of the revenue (notably income from the corporation property), this was now taken over by the town's husband, a permanent salaried official, who was also responsible for the collection of tolls and dues. This rationalised the system and gave it continuity, without which forward financial planning and budgeting were extremely difficult. In addition, a sub-committee to oversee property rentals was appointed in 1767. These reforms certainly wrought their effect; the corporate income showed a steady increase from mid-century to c. £2,000 pa in 1770–1 and c. £6,000 pa in 1830–1. Significantly, Hull did not need to seek an improvement act with additional rating powers until 1810.[10]

Corporation minutes were peppered with resolutions to enforce fines for non-attendance and other offences, resolutions to prevent money being disposed of without the scrutiny of the governing body, or for the better keeping and auditing of accounts. The stringencies of war in the 1790s and early 1800s accelerated the shift towards more accountable and rigorous methods across the country, as inflation kicked in, poor rates soared, and trade stagnated under the blockade. Policies of retrenchment and financial reform were set in train; mayoral belts were tightened as salaries and entertainment allowances were cut, and great efforts were made to bring order and regularity to traditions of individualistic and *ad hoc* book keeping and accounting. It is easy to dismiss these as token gestures, paying lip service to reforming ideals. There was certainly a large amount of back-sliding, which might suggest that 'reform' did not amount to much, but there are equally plenty of examples where the minutes show a marked overall improvement in procedure.

These problems reflected the immaturity of the inherited structure of government, which was only in the first stages of 'bureaucratization'. Administrative reform was still heavily dependent upon the will and drive of individuals to sustain it. One person could have significant influence for good or evil. Where a town clerk, with a vested interest in the *status quo*, was resistant to change, there was little that could be altered. But, equally, when there was an individual, or group of individuals, determined to reinvigorate the corporation and to assert leadership, changes could be effected

10. *Victoria County History: East Riding*, ii (1969), pp. 195–8.

very rapidly. Gabriel Powell, town clerk of Swansea, had effectively blocked all schemes for improvement and development of the port, but once his era of 'personal rule' had ended with his death in 1789, the way was open for Charles Collins, a local surgeon and member of the common council, to instigate an extensive package of reform and improvement. Twenty-one meetings were held in the year after Powell's death, whereas prior to that they had averaged three or four a year.[11] Coventry, one of the most corrupt of eighteenth-century corporations, was transformed in the 1820s under the leadership of George Eld. The Royal Commissioners commented on the marked improvement in the affairs of the corporation since 1828, and in particular Eld's efforts in disentangling the accounts of the various charities and those of the corporation (a large number of benefactions had inexplicably gone astray during the eighteenth century).[12] Overall, they drew attention in their *Report* to administrative or procedural reforms, which had been implemented in nearly a third of the boroughs covered in the published version.

The model of decline needs to be substantially modified to give more recognition to the flexibility within the system. Most towns, especially the smaller ones, were actually far more effectively administered by the early nineteenth century than they had ever been before. The distinction between incorporated and unincorporated towns is ultimately an artificial one to draw, and is no prediction of the quality of government which a town was likely to have enjoyed. No large town managed to cope adequately with the challenges of urbanization, in the form of poverty, overcrowding and crime. But this apparent failure was not indicative of decline; rather it arose because the problems were unprecedented and no one had the understanding or the experience at that stage for implementing an effective strategy. For a long time a combination of individual initiative, public subscription and piecemeal reform had enabled a widespread demand for a thoroughgoing overhaul of the system to be postponed. It is easy to forget that where the pressures were less acute, there was an overall qualitative improvement in the urban environment, administered by a flexible partnership of corporations, vestries or improvement commissions.

11. Rosemary Sweet, 'Stability and continuity: Swansea politics and reform, 1780–1820', *Welsh History Review*, 18 (1996), pp. 14–39.

12. Peter Searby, 'Progress and the parish pump: local government in Coventry, 1820–60', *Transactions of Birmingham and Warwickshire Archaeological Society*, 88 (1976), pp. 49–60; *Report of the Royal Commission on Municipal Corporations*, PP (1835), xxv, p. 1838.

Rather than seeking explanations in terms of administrative decline, we should turn our attention to shifts in the public's expectations and perceptions of urban government. The duties and obligations of those in authority became defined with increasing clarity and rigour, and urban elites found themselves operating in a more critical and much more demanding environment. The publication of charters was one manifestation of a political culture keen to hold its office-holders to account for the performance of their duties. Provincial newspapers steadily increased their coverage of local affairs, reporting on meetings of the common council and the statutory bodies, and offering comments on the state of the streets or the management of the poor in their editorials. Most corporations, and even improvement commissions, were loth to admit reporters to their meetings, but came under increasing pressure to do so. The improvement commissioners of Exeter only agreed that their proceedings should be held in public under intense pressure in 1832.[13] Meanwhile, the corporation of Plymouth took the unusual step, in 1831, of passing a resolution to allow reporters to be admitted to the meetings of mayor and commonalty in Common Hall.[14] Some corporations had responded to these changes in the political climate and taken steps to publish accounts, and improvement commissioners were generally required to publish accounts under the terms of the improvement act (it was not always so easy to get access to these documents, however).[15] The public were becoming much better informed and were constantly being encouraged to be critical and to expect accountability. Not all towns were served by radical journalists, such as James Acland, who launched his barrages of criticism upon the incorporated bodies of Shaftesbury, Bristol and Hull, but even a modicum of reporting created a political culture in which the right of the public to information about, and participation in, the affairs of government was assumed, and in which those in authority were subjected to much more rigorous scrutiny. Similarly, the move towards pursuing internal disputes within the town by resort to King's Bench, which we

13. Newton, *Eighteenth-Century Exeter*, p. 162.
14. SDRO, W 65 Constitution Book 1824–35, f. 53, resolution of 24 June 1831. The *Wolverhampton Chronicle* was not allowed to report officially upon the meetings of the Town Commissioners until 1838. F. Mason, *Wolverhampton Town Commissioners, 1773–1848* (Wolverhampton Public Library, 1976), p. 1.
15. The Royal Commissioners mentioned 12 corporations where accounts could be inspected or where an abstract was published. These were Shrewsbury, Beverley, Newcastle, Plymouth, Deal, Bishop's Castle, Liverpool, Ipswich, Grantham, Great Grimsby and Norwich.

noted in the last chapter, necessitated a much closer definition of what civic office involved, and breaches of duty or lapses in procedure could no longer pass unnoticed. It is significant, but not surprising, that one of the provisions of the Municipal Corporations Act was to make it compulsory for corporations to publish the minutes of their proceedings and accounts annually.

What was tolerated in one age, in terms of public conduct, became unacceptable in another.[16] The perquisites of office, such as favourable leases for civic officers, granting contracts or even civic hospitality, had always been traditional means of rewarding those who undertook unpaid duties, and served as an incentive to others to take up administrative burdens. In corporations with limited resources, such strategies had been essential in securing the consent and cooperation of the inhabitants, particularly those qualified to take office. Feasting and ceremonial had traditionally made an important statement about the prestige of the town and its communal solidarity, and a meagre banquet or shabby robes and regalia diminished the status of the corporation in the eyes of the citizens and county society.[17] Such conventions were increasingly frowned upon by those who demanded that public life should be open and accountable. When Bristol corporation feasted the Duke of Wellington in 1819, it was loudly protested that, 'Only a body totally insensitive to the city's economic distress could indulge in strutting and feasting while having the effrontery to plead that it was too poor to effect improvements'.[18] A greater gulf was opening between what was acceptable in the actions of the private householder, and the conduct expected of him in his role in public life. A private individual was allowed to be swayed by prejudice or personal motives, but in his public capacity he was expected to behave in a completely disinterested manner. This was an issue which reflected a fundamental disagreement about the nature of corporate government. There were those who claimed that urban corporations, like trading companies, were private bodies and had no obligations according to their charter to the public at large, and that the corporation property belonged to its members to administer as they saw fit, whether it was for their personal gain, for political ends, or

16. Paul Langford, *Public Life and the Propertied Englishman* offers a sophisticated study of these shifts in attitude and expectations, in particular, pp. 207–87.

17. J. M. Triffit, 'Politics and the Urban Community. Parliamentary Boroughs in the South West of England 1710–30', Oxford Univ. D.Phil. thesis (1985).

18. J. Kington, *Thirty Letters on the Trade of Bristol* (Bristol, 1834), p. 38; John Latimer, *Annals of Bristol in the Nineteenth Century* (Bristol, 1887), p. 69 put the cost of entertaining the Duke at £925 17s.

even the good of the town. As the legal historian F. W. Maitland pointed out, the conviction amongst corporators that corporation property was morally theirs was fostered by Parliament's willingness to grant property and powers to other bodies such as the East India Company.[19] This defence was used by several corporations during the Royal Commissioners' inquiry of 1833–5. Many others, particularly those outside the corporation, argued that it was a body created purely for advancing the public good, and as such was obliged to be as open and accountable in its proceedings as possible, and that to advance private interest constituted an abuse of a public trust. As we have already seen, the trend towards subsuming corporate office within the authority of the bench emphasised the element of public responsibility. Critics laid great emphasis on the phrasing of the charters, in which the privileges and rights had been granted for the well-being of the inhabitants. As the historian of St Albans lamented 'it is much to be regretted that those interests do not appear to have been very materially consulted of late years'.[20]

The Case for Reform

The critique of corporations and oligarchy gained added cogency from the language of radicalism. The Lockean notion of government as a trust with a responsibility for good stewardship, was easily grafted onto civic traditions which taught that it was the duty of the corporation to uphold the common weal. Arguments for popular sovereignty were readily assimilated to the view that corporations derived their authority from the body of the freemen, and that the mayor and common council had usurped rights that had originally been granted to the resident freemen. Reformers insisted that representation and accountability would automatically resolve all difficulties, and that trade would automatically prosper when relieved of the punitive duties imposed by monopolising bodies. The author of the *Corporation Mirror* advised the mayor and burgesses of Newcastle to 'consider whether you can effect such a change in your constitution as will render you at all tolerable in the present state of society', and to return to the original intentions of the charter.

Radicals often presented reform in terms of renovating the existing framework and returning to the original intentions of the

19. F. W. Maitland, *Township and Borough* (Cambridge, 1898), p. 95.
20. Anon, *The History of Verulam and St Albans* (St Albans, 1815), p. 166.

charters. Like political reformers, rather than appealing to doctrines of natural rights (which the excesses of the French revolutionary era had rendered suspect, in the opinions of most respectable house-holders), they appealed to notions of an ancient Anglo-Saxon constitution. The Whigs had always countered the Tory view of history, that charters were the free gift of the monarch and that no rights existed independently of his volition, by claiming that the Normans had simply confirmed privileges which had been held since Anglo-Saxon times; the Stuarts had, it was argued, interfered with these privileges by attempting to restrict the full enjoyment of the franchise to a select body within the corporation.[21] During the eighteenth century the argument was extended in its scope of reference; it was not simply a question of rights which had been usurped since the incorporation of the borough, but the incorporation of the borough itself, and the concomitant usurpation of the rights of Englishmen which reformers began to attack. The radicals' view was that in the Saxon era there had been no incorporations, but that all towns had been boroughs and were governed by the ancient constitution of the court leet (which, as we have seen, still survived in some towns). All the resident householders, the burgesses, had participated in the government of the community and performed their obligation of civic service. The classic statement of this position came in H. A. Merewether and A. J. Stephens' *History of the Boroughs and Municipal Corporations* (1835), but preceding this publication were numerous local studies, often written by lawyers, which set out to prove, from a close analysis of the charters, the very same points; that boroughs had existed from the earliest times, and that burgesses were the free inhabitants of the borough who performed their duties, enjoyed privileges, paid scot and lot, and were sworn in at the court leet. Merewether himself had made a preliminary and influential statement of this position, with reference to the Cornish borough of West Looe in 1823. Similar arguments were advanced in boroughs as diverse as Huntingdon, Tiverton, Great Yarmouth and Warwick.[22] There was, of course, a strong political

21. See, for example, Robert Brady, *An Historical Treatise of Cities and Burghs or Boroughs* (new edn, 1777); See also R. J. Smith, *The Gothic Bequest: Medieval Constitutions in British Thought, 1688–1863* (Cambridge, 1983); and Philip Hicks, *Neo-classical History and English Culture from Clarendon to Hume* (1996), pp. 82–109.

22. Edward Griffith, *A Collection of Ancient Records, relating to the Borough of Huntingdon* (1827); [G. Coles], *Cursory Observations on the Charters granted to the Inhabitants of Tiverton in the County of Devon* (Tiverton, 1823); Anon, *On the Conduct of the Corporation of Great Yarmouth* (Yarmouth, 1825); Joseph Parkes, *The Governing Charter of the Borough of Warwick* (1827).

imperative here: to prove that the parliamentary franchise had also originally resided in all scot-and-lot payers (effectively all those contributing to the local rates), but we should also note the importance which was attached to restoring a more widespread involvement in local government, both as a means of counteracting the evils of oligarchy, and as a measure to improve the morality and civic spirit of the people at large. One of the motives of civic reform which is less frequently noticed was the expectation that the chance to participate actively in government would render the citizenry more responsible and virtuous. Francis Palgrave, one of the Royal Commissioners appointed to investigate corporation reform, was emphatic that the purpose of ancient municipal institutions had been 'to ameliorate the character and improve the condition of the lower orders', by bringing together master and men in the same organization.[23] Similarly, Merewether and Stephens concluded their introduction by calling for a revival of the court leet and ancient borough jurisdictions, claiming that eventually the people would be taught to govern themselves and in their capacity as burgesses, united in the cause of sound government, they would improve their social and moral condition and become better subjects.[24]

The Municipal Corporations Act of 1835

It is already beginning to become clear that there was no consensus as to what reforms were necessary in the corporations. At the most moderate end of the scale were those who wanted internal reform, who did not see the necessity of dismantling the system as a whole, and who can be identified with a long tradition of reform within urban government, which was based upon notions of the common good and public service. In most cases, it was held to be greatly preferable to improvise, on an *ad hoc* basis, rather than to risk inviting central intervention, which might upset not only the local balance of power but the balance of power within the constitution itself. More characteristic of a truly radical position was the view

23. Francis Palgrave, *Corporate Reform. Observations on the principles to be adopted in the establishment of new municipalities, the reform of ancient corporations and the cheap administration of justice* (1833), p. 4.
24. H. A Merewether and A. J. Stephens, *The History of the Boroughs and Municipal Corporations of the United Kingdom*, 3 vols (1835), i, p. lxvi.

that society had undergone such significant changes since corporations were first established, that they stood in need of far-reaching
structural change. As Acland put it, 'Other charters, more applicable to the wants of society, more conservative of the Rights of
the People, and more consistent with the enlightened spirit of the
age must be granted'.[25] At the most extreme level, Thomas Paine
had demanded the wholesale abolition of all chartered rights and
incorporation in *Rights of Man*, and this attitude was echoed in the
debates of 1835 when some parties advocated doing away with
corporations altogether.[26]

Reform eventually came in the Municipal Corporations Act of
1835, which rationalized the system of government in 178 urban
corporations. In part it was a tidying up exercise. The 1832 Great
Reform Act had highlighted the anomaly of a parliamentary franchise which was in no way coterminous with the municipal franchise. More importantly, it seemed to offer the Whigs the means
of ending Tory influence over the municipal boroughs and the
election of MPs, by opening up elections to the ruling bodies to
the propertied householders at large. *The Times* declared that, 'The
most active spring of election bribery and villainy everywhere is
known to be the Corporation system', and argued that without
corporation reform, parliamentary reform would be a dead letter.[27]
Lord John Russell, speaking on behalf of the bill for corporation
reform on 5 June 1835, asserted that the investigations of the
commissioners had proven that the municipal corporations had
employed their chartered powers 'in no manner for the good
government and well being of the boroughs – not that they might
be "well and quietly governed" to use the words of some of the
charters, but for the sole object of establishing an influence for the
election of members of this House'.[28] The Tory diarist Creevey,
considered it 'a much greater blow to Toryism than the Reform
Bill itself'.[29]

25. James Acland, *Hull Portfolio* (1831), p. 151.
26. Thomas Paine, *Rights of Man*, (ed.) Mark Philp (Oxford, 1995), pp. 274–5;
Hansard Parliamentary Debates, 3rd ser., vol. xxix (1835), p. 668.
27. *The Times*, 25 June 1833, quoted in G. B. A. M. Finlayson, 'The Municipal Corporations Act.1835', Oxford Univ. B. Litt. thesis (1959), p. x.
28. 'Speech of the Right Hon. Lord John Russell, delivered in the House of Commons, 5th June, on Corporation Reform, with a Bill to provide for the Regulation
of Municipal Corporations in England and Wales' (1835), p. 9.
29. Quoted in Bryan Keith Lucas, *The English Local Government Franchise. A Short
History* (Oxford, 1952), p. 55.

   Benthamite utilitarianism – the doctrine of the greatest good for the greatest number – which had recently acquired considerable influence in Whig circles, provided the intellectual framework for reform, as it had also for the reform of the Poor Law in 1834. The Benthamites were firmly opposed to the unreformed system, on the grounds that it was inherently and unashamedly oligarchic and inefficient. Their understanding of town government was that it should exist only for the benefit of the people, whereas the corporations, it was held, consistently put their own self-interest before the common good. It was believed that an open and democratic franchise would create an accountable and effective body, which would derive its strength from the trust and cooperation of the rate-paying householders. In retrospect, their faith in the triumph of public spirit through democratic forms seems overly optimistic. A Select Committee was entrusted with inquiring into the problem in 1833, but it soon became apparent that the task was of far too great a magnitude to be dealt with in this way, and the investigation into the state of the municipal corporations of England and Wales was entrusted to a Royal Commission of Inquiry. This was composed of 20 commissioners, the majority of which were lawyers, led by the MP for Huddersfield, John Blackburne, and Joseph Parkes, a noted Benthamite lawyer and reformer, who had already carried out an extensive and highly critical investigation into the conduct of the corporation of his home town Warwick.[30] The commissioners were manifestly *not* an impartial body. Most of them were firmly committed to the abolition of the system as it stood, and were therefore predisposed to be receptive to adverse criticism of the corporations they visited. There was a widespread feeling at the time that the corporations were being prejudged. Over the next two years the commissioners toured England and Wales, visiting 285 towns, of which 246 were identified as having corporations. The published report covered 186 boroughs in England and Wales. This investigation was not of the same ilk as the *quo warranto* proceedings of the seventeenth century, and did not produce the same kind of controversy. Although, there were suggestions that the commission was unconstitutional and illegal, on the grounds that it was set up by royal as opposed to parliamentary authority, there was little in the way of organized resistance. The corporation of Norwich made an attempt to coordinate a policy of non cooperation, but failed to summon up a vigorous response. Most corporations

---

30. Parkes, *Governing Charter of Borough of Warwick.*

saw the writing on the wall and cooperated with the commissioners. Only five (Corfe Castle, Dover, Lichfield, Maidstone and Romsey) declined to give any information, and four more refused to allow access to their accounts (Arundel, Hull, Leicester and Rochester) on the rather specious grounds that it would be a violation of public trust if they were to allow their records to be produced.

It was widely accepted, not least in many of the corporations, that some measure of reform was desirable – indeed, as we have seen, reform had been underway for a number of years in a significant proportion of the boroughs affected. The individual reports for each borough were for the most part detailed, and sometimes surprisingly appreciative of the merits of the bodies which they visited, and the efforts which had already been made towards internal reform, although equally there is clear evidence of prejudice against them. However, this comparatively balanced approach was lost in the Summary of the *Report*, which was hurriedly drawn up at the end of 1835 for presentation to the House of Commons. It presented a distorted interpretation of what the commissioners had found. Individual abuses were highlighted and seemingly made to apply across the board. Extravagance, embezzlement and political corruption appeared to be endemic. The introduction came to this damning conclusion, 'They exist, in the general majority of instances, for no purposes of general utility'. They neither possessed nor deserved the respect of the inhabitants and were in need of a thorough reform.[31] Unfortunately for the reputation of the unreformed corporations, this hastily drawn up summary exercised a far-reaching influence over their posthumous image.

When the bill came before Parliament, it passed comparatively smoothly through the House of Commons, where, to the reformers' surprise, few objections had been raised. Even the opposition leader, Robert Peel, agreed that something had to be done to render urban government more effective. It faced much more intense criticism in the upper house, where attention shifted from the functional performance of the corporations, which had been the crucial factor in the debates in the Commons, to their constitutional importance. The Lords saw the corporations as an essential part of the fabric of the constitution, which had recently received such a heavy battering in the Great Reform Act, and were fully aware of the political implications of the manoeuvres. Lord Lyndhurst declared that, 'The Corporations of England, the Church, and the hereditary Peerage,

31. *Report of the Royal Commission on Municipal Corporations*, PP (1835), xxiii, p. xli.

stood as barriers between the throne on the one side and the Democracy on the other – a check to the arbitrary power of the Prerogative – a check to the licence of Democracy'.[32] They questioned the legality of the Commission which had proceeded without parliamentary sanction. They argued that property rights could not be invaded without adequate proof, which the *Report* failed to give. They objected that the proposed bill represented an invasion upon the rights and prerogatives of each town, and they feared that the new town councils would introduce an undesirable and dangerous element of democracy into the constitution.

As one would expect, the corporations which were affected did not accept the measures proposed with unalloyed enthusiasm, and full use was made of the opportunity to petition the House of Lords against the perceived injustices of the bill. Opposition was strongest in freeman boroughs, where the freemen stood to lose substantial privileges – rights to charities, common land, and most importantly the franchise. The bill was attacked for arbitrarily invading the inherited rights and privileges of freemen, for whom such rights represented an important form of property. If these inherited rights could be abolished, what other privileges were safe? The House of Lords might find the privileges of the peers done away with on similar grounds of political expediency, the church and the universities could be the next to be undone. Parliamentary authority was usurping the powers of the crown, and threatening to destabilize the balance of the constitution. The bill was also opposed on the grounds that it was a purely political measure, and would not lead to improvement in municipal government or benefit the public good in any way. Opponents objected to the imposition of a uniform measure across the board, and were quick to point out that in many corporations the commissioners had found little to criticise, or had even expressed positive approval. While individual abuses were acknowledged to exist, it was argued that in many of the corporations to be affected by the legislation, the problems identified in the *Report* were irrelevant, and it was therefore wholly unfitting to interfere. Alternative paths for reform could be followed; individual charters could have been surrendered and regranted with amended constitutions, remedying specific abuses, but this possibility was ignored for a general measure which had the political advantage of ending Tory domination of the corporations, and thereby shoring up the Whigs' electoral position. Hence, it was party

32. *Hansard Parliamentary Debates,* 3rd ser., vol. xix (1835), p. 1387.

political considerations as much as ideological principles which led the government along the path of centralization and uniformity.[33]

The actual terms of the act did not produce a great shake-up in the structure of government. The municipal boundaries were redrawn, bringing the areas of suburban growth under corporate jurisdiction for the first time. Replacing the closed oligarchies was a town council directly elected on a rate-payer franchise of house-holders who had been resident for three years. The government's commitment to the elective franchise was thereby demonstrated, but given that only ratepayers qualified, it was still only the proper-tied who were represented, and, in effect, the municipal franchise differed little from the £10 householder franchise for the election of MPs.[34] The special status of freemen was abolished, but the privil-eges and rights were continued during the lifetime of the existing freemen. The councillors, who had to meet a property qualifica-tion, were elected for three years at a time, and went out of office on a triennial basis. Aldermen were elected for a period of six years by the councillors, and the mayor was similarly indirectly elected. These provisions represented something of a compromise. The Lords, fearing the implications of the bill for the electoral pro-spects of toryism had introduced a number of 'wrecking amend-ments', which were intended either to sink the bill entirely, or at least to safeguard the privileges and property of corporations and freemen. The property qualification for councillors, the division of towns over 6,000 into wards, and the inclusion of indirectly elected aldermen were all the result of the Lords' intervention.

The Webbs welcomed the reform of 1835 as a milestone on the road towards centralised control, and imposing a uniform standard and accountability to some higher authority. But even in the nine-teenth century, it was clear that whatever else may have changed, the act had done little to solve the structural problems which had burdened the unreformed bodies, let alone urban government more generally. The act itself affected only a minority of the total urban population. It is easy to forget that it affected only a few of the larger English towns: only one-seventh of the population now lived in incorporated towns. The corporation of London was left untouched, and of the unincorporated towns, which by the 1830s accounted for many of the larger cities, only Manchester and

33. Ibid., vol. xxviii, pp. 831–2, 1005, 1070, 1101; vol. xxix, pp. 738–40, 743, 753, 1385–7; vol. xxx, pp. 351, 355. On the political background to the bill see G. B. A. M. Finlayson, 'The politics of municipal reform in 1835', *EHR*, lxxi (1966), pp. 673–92.
34. Keith Lucas, *The English Local Government Franchise*, pp. 63, 67.

Birmingham availed themselves of the opportunity to take up incorporation before 1840, in 1837 and 1838 respectively. When we look at the towns affected by reform in the immediate aftermath of 1835, the tangible change in the practice of government is not remarkable. The provisions of the act were very sketchy as to how the new town councils should actually exercise their powers. In terms of achieving centralization, rationalization and freeing local government from the political battleground, the act was far from successful. In general, the socio-economic composition of the new town councils was very similar to that of the old corporations; the towns continued to be run by the middling urban elite. In terms of personnel, there was often a significant changeover, especially in the larger industrial towns, where the newly rich manufacturers, who were often also Dissenters, had previously been excluded from the predominantly Tory and Anglican corporations. Some towns saw an almost complete reversal with the Whig/Liberal interest seizing control, as in Liverpool where there were 43 Liberal councillors to five Tories, or Coventry, where the Liberals outnumbered the Tories by 32 to four (24 of these Liberals being Dissenters).[35] The new town councils of Hull and Leicester reacted harshly against their predecessors, vilifying their reputation and selling off the corporation plate and insignia, as well as the accumulated port supplies. However, this was not a universal pattern: in many towns, such as Plymouth and Oxford, the transition was much smoother, and a significant number of the old council were re-elected.[36] More importantly, there was very little change in the exercise of government itself, beyond the fact that corporations were now elective and could levy rates. Office-holding was still unpaid, and still conferred considerable honour and status upon the individual, legitimizing social leadership. It continued to be the preserve of the propertied; the qualification for councillors stood at £1,000, or property to the value £30 pa – sufficient to exclude all of the less substantial of the middling sort. Nor were the improvement commissions immediately displaced.

The power of these commissions was, in theory, transferred to the new councils, but it was left to the individual bodies to activate

---

35. Derek Fraser, *Power and Authority in the Victorian City* (Oxford, 1979), p. 26; Searsby, 'Progress and the parish pump', p. 55.

36. In Oxford, of the 32 members of the old common council who stood as candidates for election in 1835, 19 were re-elected, and all the new aldermen had been former common council men. *VCH Oxfordshire* (1979), iv, p. 288; C. E. Welch, 'Municipal reform in Plymouth', (*TDA*, xciv 1966), p. 337.

them. In a number of towns the commissions continued to exercise greater power than the corporation, and Parliament continued to pass local legislation, conferring special powers on individual statutory bodies.[37] Although the act gave the new town councils authority to raise police forces, the responsibility for activating these powers remained with local initiative – and many towns preferred not to incur the expense. The ability of central government to make any effective change in local government was strictly limited to the degree of support which they could command for their policies among those in authority. Where their vision of reformed municipal government was not shared the changes were very muted. The Home Office could request quarterly returns on crime statistics, for example, but the extent to which it could enforce their return, or hold any local authority accountable was strictly limited. Similar observations have been made with respect to the implementation of the new poor law by the local guardians: many places were, in practice, virtually exempt from its operation, despite the visits of assistant commissioners.[38] While local authorities maintained the freedom to dispose of their revenues as they saw fit (within reason), the government's ability to lay down policy was circumscribed. In 1848, it was claimed that powers of draining, cleansing and paving had been vested in only 29 town councils, in 66 they were divided between the council and improvement commissioners, in 30 they were vested in the improvement commissioners alone, and there were still 62 towns where no such powers were exercised at all.[39] It was only later in the 1840s and 50s that government began to expand its executive side with respect to dealing with the problems of urbanization, as seen in the establishment of bodies such as the Central Board of Health. Apart from the short-term political gain of ending the Tory ascendancy within the corporations, the main achievement of municipal reform was to clear up some of the anomalies of corporate constitutions, to establish the elective principle more firmly, and to create a more direct correspondence between civic office and urban wealth.

The reformers' optimistic belief that popularly elected bodies would be free of partisan politics and self-interest was rapidly

37. In Stamford neither the unreformed corporation nor the new town council exercised much influence or authority. By the 1840s most of the responsibility for the town's amenities had passed to the improvement commissioners instead. A. Rogers, *The Book of Stamford* (Buckingham, 1983), p. 94.

38. A. Temple Patterson, *A History of Southampton, 1700–1914*, Southampton Record Series, xi (1966), p. 175.

39. Finlayson, 'The Municipal Corporations Act, 1835', p. 255.

shattered. The new town councils often found themselves in an even worse financial position than their predecessors. Towns like Oxford, which had derived a regular income from admission fees and the sale of freedom, suddenly lost this source of revenue. In Lincoln, the old corporation had exercised its right to do as it wished with the corporation property and had sold it off, before handing over to the new body, while in Scarborough, the property was hurriedly let out to the corporation members on long, and very favourable, leases. Other corporations resisted such temptations, but nevertheless the transition to paying regular salaries, rather than relying on fees, made the business of government much more expensive for the new town council.[40] Even if the handover was amicable, the new body had still to manage the inherited debts of the old. Although they had rating powers, the deep antipathy displayed by householders to any form of additional taxation meant that increasing rates was never an easy option. Rates were still levied on property rather than any kind of income based assessment; hence, much of the commercial wealth being generated by companies and businesses went untapped.

Far from freeing local government from party rancour or manipulation for political ends, the 1835 legislation often led to even more intensified party conflict, as control of the corporation was now contested at regular rather than erratic intervals. The division of towns into wards, each electing its own councillors to represent them, increased the tendency towards social segregation and heightened the potential for conflict between different districts with divergent interests. Finances were still closely bound up with political manoeuvrings, and the financial policy of rival groups was the crucial issue upon which they sought to gain the support of the inhabitants. In Congleton, the corporation was contested between the cheap, Liberal party, who were against increasing rates and expenditure, and the 'dear' Tory party, who were in favour of increased public expenditure.[41] In Leeds, by contrast, the Tories took up the position of the cheap party. Having lost their position on the corporation to the Dissenters and Whigs they juggled the accounts to show how much less costly local government had been under their aegis before the 'day parades of dandy policemen' had caused the rates to soar (the new uniformed police

40. K. J. Atton, 'Municipal and Parliamentary Politics in Ipswich, 1818–47', Univ. of London, Ph.D. thesis (1979), pp. 138–9.
41. W. H. Semper, 'Local government and politics since 1700', in W. B. Stephens (ed.), *The History of Congleton* (Manchester, 1970), p. 94.

force).[42] Even with a democratically elected town council, oligarchy could still prevail. Since aldermen were elected for six years by the council itself, it was possible for one party to retain overall influence long after it had lost a majority among the town councillors. This was what happened in Bath, where the Liberals retained their dominance over town government for most of the nineteenth century, due to their success in nominating the aldermen at their original victory in 1835.[43] It was indeed still possible for one individual to establish a personal hegemony, as in the days of the unreformed system. John Wilson, who was town clerk of Congleton from 1851–56 and 1867–94, was known as the King of Congleton. Familiar complaints about corporate inertia were also uttered. The new town council in Stamford rapidly became as ineffectual as the old corporation – administrative energies were channelled through the improvement commission established in 1841 instead.[44] 1835 had done nothing to assuage the political and sectarian divisions within the urban community; it had simply opened up the corporation to being regularly contested. As Derek Fraser has observed of the Victorian town, 'Politics for Victorians, unlike ourselves, began not at Westminster but at their own front gates'. From an eighteenth-century perspective one might feel inclined to comment 'plus ça change', but it does confirm that the reforms of 1835 did nothing to liberate urban government from political conflict.[45] There was, however, an important shift in the attitude of central government to the administration of the country in the localities. Parliament had asserted its authority not just to abolish rights which had been granted by the crown, but also to lay down rules and standards for the government of towns. The immediate impact of 1835 was limited, but it closed the door on one era of urban government, and opened the door to another in which the directives of the state would have a greater role to play.

42. Derek Fraser, *Urban Politics in Victorian England. The Structure of Politics in Victorian Cities* (1979), p. 127.
43. Graham Davis and Penny Bonsall (eds), *Bath. A New History* (Keele, 1996), pp. 127–8.
44. J. M. Lee, 'Stamford and the Cecils: A Study in Political Control, 1700–1885', Oxford Univ. B. Litt. thesis (1951); pp. 188–90, See also Semper, *Local Government in Congleton*, p. 104.
45. Fraser, *Urban Politics*, p. 9.

CHAPTER SIX

Social Structure and Social Experience

Diversity was the keynote to urban society: diversity of occupation and social status, diversity of economy, diversity of religious and political affiliation. The mobility and instability of urban society accentuated these tendencies. There was continual immigration to towns, not just to London and the major provincial towns, but over the urban hierarchy as a whole, as people were drawn by the opportunities for employment, or the prospect of more generous poor relief. Instability was inherent in the social structure; long established family dynasties were the characteristic of rural, not urban society, and there was a high turnover in urban elites. Higher mortality rates contributed to the transience of family fortunes, as did the vagaries of commercial enterprises. Extended credit networks meant that indebtedness was inherent in all business life, and bankruptcy was a perpetual threat which hung over all trading concerns. The road from rags to riches could be easily reversed. Represented within urban society were the uttermost extremes of rich and poor. The possibility of making one's fortune and rising up the social ladder, in the style of Dick Whittington, was an important and enduring element in the urban mythology. But the numbers who achieved such success were few, and the descent could be equally precipitous as moralists were eager to point out. Between the two polarities lay infinite gradations of wealth and status. The complexities of organizing the hierarchies was one of continual interest to contemporaries – the harder it became to distinguish social rank with certainty, the more important it was to do so. Twentieth-century historians are not much better off, but we will discuss below some of the more important features of the three major divisions of urban society: the labouring sort, the middling sort, and the better sort or gentry. We will look at their working patterns, lifestyles and cultural pursuits, and the evidence for the emergence of a class-based society in this period. In the second part of this chapter we will consider other variables in the composition of society, in particular the difference made by gender and the role played by religion and the churches in urban life. Urban society depended upon collaborative action and a sense of common identity for its effectual functioning, a goal made all the harder to achieve by the socio-economic, religious/political and gender differences inherent in all communities.

The Labouring Sort

We shall find them all jumbled together as the 'lower orders', the most skilled and the most prudent workmen, with the most ignorant and imprudent labourers and paupers, though the difference if great indeed, and indeed in many cases will scarce admit of comparison.[1]

It is estimated that around 70 per cent of the urban population fell into the category of labouring classes. The labouring classes, the lower orders, the poorer sort were often discussed and treated as an undifferentiated mass by their social superiors, but as Francis Place, one of the most literate of their representatives, pointed out in the extract quoted above, they were far from being a homogeneous whole. Place began writing his autobiography in 1823, looking back on a working life beginning in the 1790s, but what he said held true of the century as a whole. The skilled artisans were the highest wage earners of the manual labourers. Printers, cutlers, cabinet makers, blacksmiths, wheelwrights, and practitioners of new crafts, such as fine cotton weavers, iron puddlers and engineers, were all capable of earning a substantial wage and might even employ journeymen. Occupation aside, there was often little else to mark them off from the tradesmen hovering at the lower end of the middling sort, and they could earn substantially more, but the manual element to their labour set them apart. The skilled element of the work-force probably comprised around fifteen per cent, but their wages were frequently 50–100 per cent higher than those at the unskilled end of the labour market. According to the petitions against the Orders in Council, presented by the Birmingham Chamber of Commerce in 1812, skilled workers were commonly earning

1. Quoted in John Rule, *The Labouring Classes in Early Industrial England* (1986), p. 35.

up to £3.00 a week.[2] Unskilled common weavers might receive very little at all in wages, in comparison with a technically proficient framework knitter, for example, but their occupation or 'craft' was still definitely one up from being common labourers, who occupied the lowest position among the labouring sort. These were generally casual workers paid by the day for tasks such as breaking stones, mending roads, coal heaving, or dockers or builders. When Sir Frederick Eden made his inquiries on the state of the poor in the 1790s, he found that most such labourers were being paid around 9s a week.[3] Porters, sailors, hawkers and peddlers were similarly eking out a precarious existence at the bottom of society, being paid a matter of sixpence or less by the day. Labouring women were even worse off, and were almost invariably paid as unskilled labour, whatever the job.[4]

Nationally, patterns of employment changed significantly over the century, as the proportion of the labouring population employed in agriculture steadily lost ground to the manufacturing and trading sectors.

TABLE 4   *Patterns of employment, income, expenditure and residence, 1700–1840* (%)

	1700	1760	1800	1840
Male employment in agriculture	61.2	52.8	40.8	28.6
Male employment in industry	18.5	23.8	29.5	47.3
Income from agriculture	37.4	37.5	36.1	24.9
Income from industry	20.0	20.0	19.8	31.5
Consumption/income	92.8	73.6	76.3	80.1
Investment/income	4.0	6.8	8.5	10.8
Exports/income	8.4	14.6	15.7	14.3
Urban population	17.0	21.0	33.9	48.3

Source: from Nick Crafts, 'The industrial revolution', in Roderick Floud and Donald McCloskey (eds), *The Economic History of Britain since 1700*, 2 vols, 2nd edn (Cambridge, 1994), i, p. 45.

2. Eric Hopkins, *The Rise of the Manufacturing Town. Birmingham and the Industrial Revolution* (Stroud, 1998), p. 151.
3. Sir Frederick Eden, *The State of the Poor*, (ed.) A. G. L. Rogers (1928).
4. Rule, *The Labouring Classes*, pp. 35–40; see also his, *The Experience of Labour in Eighteenth-Century Industry* (1981). On women's labour see Bridget Hill, *Women, Work and Sexual Politics* (Oxford, 1989); Pamela Sharpe, *Adapting to Capitalism. Working Women in the English Economy, 1700–1850* (1996); Deborah Valenze, *The First Industrial Women* (Oxford, 1995).

Although mining, iron smelting and much textile manufacture were essentially rural rather than urban industries, manufacturing growth within towns was nevertheless remarkable, as the expansion of Birmingham, Manchester and the towns of the Midlands and Yorkshire demonstrates. By 1840, an increasing proportion of the population was labouring in factory conditions, although this shift was far from universal. It had become marked only comparatively recently and in a restricted number of towns. The breakthrough in the textile industry had come with the invention of the power loom in 1820. This had ended the golden age of hand loom weavers, who had continued to work in the home long after the mechanization of spinning had taken place, with the invention of the Spinning Jenny and Arkwright's Mule, patented in 1764 and 1771 respectively. Cotton and silk production had been factory-based rather longer, but their overall importance in the economy was still significantly less than that of woollen cloth production. The metallurgical industries, with which Birmingham and Sheffield were associated, continued to be based upon the workshop throughout our period. Both towns were renowned for being centres of small, independent artisans, without the gentry element or merchant plutocracy of other towns, a fact which was much commented upon by contemporary visitors.[5] This pattern precluded neither a high degree of specialization and division of labour, nor technological innovation, but the putting-out system perpetuated the outward form of the domestic workshop without necessitating the centralization of all production in the factory.

In the medieval and early modern periods, the workshop mode of production had allowed for a progression up the hierarchy from being first taken on as an apprentice, to working as a journeyman. There was also, theoretically, the possibility that any apprentice might end up as a master craftsman, with his own workshop, and apprentices and journeymen working under him, just as befell the industrious apprentice, Goodchild, in Hogarth's highly moralist series, *Industry and Idleness*, engraved in 1747. The myth was still trundled out in manuals of advice or moral guidance, as an inducement to industry and obedience, but the prospect that 'by serving an Apprenticeship of seven Years, a Youth may become free of this great City, and many hope one day to be exalted to the Mayoralty;

5. For example Alexis de Tocqueville, *Journeys to England and Ireland*, (ed.) J. P. Mayer (New York, 1968), p. 93. '... at Birmingham the workers work in their own houses or in little workshops in company with the master himself.'

since we have had many Instances of Men from the lowest Circumstances of Life who have arrived at and filled that Chair with Honour and Reputation', had very weak foundations in truth.[6] The reality was that in most large-scale industries, whether they were textile or metallurgical, the economies of production and the division of labour meant that the possibilities of rising above the position of journeyman were being steadily blocked off. The introduction of more mechanized production led to the 'deskilling' of labour in some industries, with a consequent fall in the wages paid, and in the number of the labouring sort who were self-employed. The system of apprenticeship itself was disintegrating; shortages of labour, especially in London, meant that apprentices were unlikely to complete their indenture, or else would opt for wage labour from the start.[7] Apprenticeship was most commonly found at the bottom of the scale, as a means of coping with the children of the parish poor (who were notoriously apprenticed to factories in the cotton towns of the early nineteenth century), or to the more prestigious crafts and trades, such as goldsmiths or merchants, where the premium could be as high as £400. In London the self-employed constituted only five to six per cent of the workers by 1800, and this was the centre of independent craftsmen. The whole mechanism of guild regulations was being broken down. Apprenticeship was effectively abolished in 1814, with the repeal of the Statute of Artificers, while in the meantime, the wage dependent factory workforce was becoming more widespread.[8]

The growth of manufacturing and industry fuelled the expansion of towns and absorbed the population increase in the labour market, but it was not the only source of employment for the poor. By 1840, 47.3 per cent of the male population was employed in industry (having taken over from agriculture as the chief form of employment), but up to 1811, service, rather than industry, was the chief source of new jobs in urban areas.[9] The rise in the number of

6. R. Campbell, *The London Tradesman* (1747), p. 303. It is interesting that both this and *Industry and Idleness* were published in the same year. This was probably the latest point in the century at which such assumptions could have been expressed with so much confidence.

7. The chronology of the decline of apprenticeship and its regional variations is extremely confused, but see K. D. M. Snell, *Annals of the Labouring Poor: Social Change and Agrarian England, 1660–1900* (Cambridge, 1985), esp. pp. 228–32.

8. J. R. Kellett, 'The breakdown of gild and corporation control over the handicraft and retail trade in London', *EcHR*, x (1958), pp. 381–94.

9. Nick Crafts, 'The industrial revolution', in Roderick Floud and Donald McCloskey (eds), *The Economic History of Britain since 1700*, 2 vols, 2nd edn (Cambridge, 1994), i, p. 45; Jeffrey Williamson, 'Coping with city growth', ibid., p. 341.

middling households greatly increased the demand for domestic servants. It was a mark of status for those newly risen above the level of the labouring sort to employ a person, usually a girl, for the performance of household tasks. Domestic service was a characteristically urban form of employment, and it was responsible for attracting large numbers of migrants, particularly women, to London and other towns every year. The reformer, Jonas Hanway, put the number of migrants at 5,000 pa in the 1770s. More recently, Bridget Hill has not found grounds to query this, and she suggests that a contemporary estimate of 910,000 employed in service (of which 800,000 were women) was probably quite accurate.[10] At 13.4 per cent of the population, it does not rank with agriculture or textiles as a source of employment in national terms, but this belies its importance for urban women, who found employment in service far more frequently than men. Service was not an easy option. By far the majority of servants were employed in small households, with only one or two servants, rather than in the grander establishments which employed a retinue of retainers. Very heavy demands were made upon their labour, and the remuneration was slight. Board and lodging were provided, but the income over and above that was as little as £5 a year, and out of this, servants were expected to provide their own tea. Servants were also entitled to perquisites or 'vails' – proposals to abolish these provoked footmen riots on a number of occasions. As usual, female servants were paid considerably less than men and were unlikely to be able to put by much in the way of savings, which might enable them to 'better' themselves.

What difference did the changes imposed by urban industrialization make upon the lives of the labouring sort in towns? It has been argued that the industrial work-force lost a sense community and of corporate identity, but this has proved difficult to substantiate. The corporate identity which workers had enjoyed, through membership of a guild, was clearly receding in importance for most crafts, and indeed, had never existed in many others. But there was still the sense of belonging, and of an inherited skill inherent in any craft, which a handloom weaver was able to pass down to his son, for example. Skilled trades had their 'customs of the craft', based around rituals of acceptance and sanctions against those who broke rank in any way. Solidarity was maintained outside the workplace through drinking and other recreational activities and proximity of

10. Bridget Hill, *Servants. English Domestics in the Eighteenth Century* (Oxford, 1996), pp. 4–7.

habitation. The attempts of workers in the early nineteenth century to revive and extend the Elizabethan restrictions surrounding employment arose not only because they feared losing their jobs to machines, but because they recognized the threat to their values and their way of life.[11] Group identity was also reinforced through collective action and membership of the trade combinations and early trade unions, which were more active than has often been supposed. It is estimated that there were at least 333 strikes in England between 1717 and 1800. The number of anti-combination laws on the statute books and the complaints of employers are in themselves proof of the capacity to cause disruption. The early historians of trade unionism, who depicted the eighteenth-century movement as an ephemeral and rudimentary affair, were employing anachronistic definitions which demanded evidence of continuous association. Historians are now much more willing to give credit to the power of collective strike action in artisan trades, and the concomitant importance of association in working class culture.[12]

The origins of trade union organization have also been traced back to the opportunities for association among the labouring sort, which were offered by the friendly societies and box clubs. These operated primarily as mutual insurance societies; a subscription fee was charged which was used to build up a fund to assist members in sickness, old age and death and to provide the means for conviviality on occasion. As such, they had been in existence on a small scale in some areas prior even to the eighteenth century (Defoe's 'Essay on Friendly Societies' was published in 1697), but they saw a tremendous growth in the latter part of the eighteenth century and beyond. The societies expanded most rapidly in the early nineteenth century, especially in the northern industrial areas, where there was the greatest degree of economic growth and change. According to a parliamentary report of 1803, there were 9,672 friendly societies in England, with a total of 704,350 members (which was approximately eight per cent of the resident population).[13] Nearly half the adult male population was said to belong to one by mid-century.[14] Some of these variants of self-help were looked upon with suspicion, as employers feared the independence which organization and self-help might encourage; workers combinations in industrially advanced areas, such as Newcastle, or in the textile

11. Rule, *Experience of Labour*, pp. 109, 114–17.
12. Rule, *Labouring Classes in Early Industrial England*, pp. 255–65.
13. Patrick Colquhoun, *A Treatise on Indigence* (1806), p. 115.
14. P. H. J. H. Gosden, *The Friendly Societies in England 1815–75* (1969).

towns of the south west, were notorious for their proclivity to 'combine' in the kind of strike action which we have noted above. When the keelmen of Newcastle wanted to establish their own hospital, through voluntary deductions from their pay, their employers, who belonged to the corporation, sought to establish their own control over it to prevent the money from being used to support a strike.[15] Their suspicions may not have been unfounded; Francis Place records that when he began employment as a breeches maker, he was told that the benefit club (equivalent to a friendly society), which he had just joined, was actually intended as a fund for supporting the members in a strike for wages – it was a woefully inadequate one, however, as he went on to relate.[16] Other employers and ratepayers encouraged the friendly societies as a means of inculcating the principles of thrift and self-help among the working classes, and therefore diminishing the likelihood of their becoming a burden on the poor rates. Their main anxiety, therefore, was to discourage the aspect of conviviality, and break the traditional association with a local tavern or alehouse, which threatened to undermine the functional purpose of the societies. Many of the lesser middling sort joined these societies also, as it was important to provide for unforeseen hardship for themselves and their families. The mutual support and access to credit which such societies provided, was crucial in securing financial and economic independence, and offered a safety-net of protection from debt.

Industrial change has often been associated with the rise of large-scale manufacture and factory discipline, which had important repercussions on the structure of the working day.[17] Rather than working purely by piece rates, payment was strictly dependent on the hours of labour put in. Clocks were installed, time-sheets introduced and factory bells rung. In many factories the working day was set at thirteen hours, *after* deductions for meals and breaks, and in some cotton spinning mills an eighteen hour day was enforced. This changed the patterns of work and leisure and the forms of popular recreation. Long working hours were far from being a novelty; a survey of tailors in 1747 suggested that a fourteen hour day was nothing out of the ordinary, but the freedom with

15. Joyce Ellis, 'A dynamic society: social relations in Newcastle upon Tyne 1660–1760', in Peter Clark (ed.), *The Transformation of English Provincial Towns, 1600–1800* (1984), p. 211.

16. G. Wallas, *The Life of Francis Place, 1771–1854* (1898), p. 6.

17. The classic statement on this subject is E. P. Thompson's essay 'Time, work-discipline and industrial capitalism', in Thompson, *Customs in Common* (1993), pp. 352–403.

which workers disposed of their time became far more circumscribed.[18] The new time discipline made it impossible for artisans to observe Saint Monday (traditionally workers had taken the first day of the week off to recover from the excesses of the weekend), or to allow their labour to pile up towards the end of the week, although it took considerable time for this practice to die out completely.[19] The alehouse would have appeared to have lost some of its centrality in working class culture by the nineteenth century, and if Francis Place is to be believed, the coffee house, in London at least, became more important as a focal point for the labouring community as the level of drinking fell.[20] The number of holidays and festivals, inherited from the agrarian calendar, which had punctuated the year, was likewise whittled down to avoid wastage of labour; a shift which was also encouraged by middle class fears about disorder and revelry.[21] However, as Eric Hopkins has reminded us in his study of Birmingham, the time discipline of the factory regime was far from universal. 'Industrialization' did not always take the form of the factory regime, and in Birmingham was manifested by increased efficiency and specialization within traditional modes of production. Manufacture was still centred in small workshops and the pattern of labour changed very little, if at all, between 1760 and 1840. The observation of St Monday continued unimpaired, in Birmingham at least, until well into the nineteenth century. Fairs and wakes (originally a church festival), interrupted the working week for days at a time, and excessively long working days do not appear to have been the norm. Employers still found that an entire week could effectively be lost through the inebriation of their employees incapacitating them for work.[22] Valiant though the efforts of the middle classes may have been to eliminate the drunken propensities of the labouring sort, and to introduce more rational forms of recreation, their success was always limited – both in Birmingham and other towns, and the subculture of cock-fighting, animal baiting and the gin shop continued to offend the sensibilities of an improving middle class.

Employment throughout our period was highly seasonal, in both town and countryside, and acutely vulnerable to variations in the

18. Rule, *Labouring Classes*, pp. 132–3.
19. Douglas E. Reid, 'The decline of St Monday, 1776–1867', *P&P*, 71 (1976), pp. 76–101.
20. Peter Clark, *The English Alehouse. A Social History 1200–1830* (1983), pp. 308–9.
21. Rule, *Labouring Classes*, pp. 217–18.
22. Hopkins, *Rise of the Manufacturing Town*, pp. 40–61,102–17, 151–72.

economic cycle, triggered by variables such as war or harvest failure. Building and other outdoor trades were always scaled down in the winter months, if not rendered impossible by the weather. In ports, the severe winter conditions and adverse winds put a halt to sea-borne trade and shipbuilding. Nation-wide thousands might be laid off work. A slump in demand could result in an immediate cut in wages or a laying off of hands. Employment also fluctuated with the 'season'. In London there was always a slack period, when the 'company' left town in the period after Christmas, before their return later in the spring, and in the summer after the end of July. In the 'leisure' towns and coastal resorts, the season came rather later (Bath unusually had both a winter and summer season, which lasted nearly eight months), but there were similarly always slack periods before and after. Employment opportunities were always bleakest in winter, when there were fewer hours of daylight, when the weather was worse, and when the economy was at its most sluggish. At the same time, the need for fuel was at its greatest, while the cost of coal and bread were inflated by scarcity and difficulty in procuring basic necessities. Even with the construction of canals, supplies could not be ensured for inland towns when the waterways froze up for months on end. It is no surprise that poor relief expenditure peaked during the winter months. Living standards between 1750–1820 showed little improvement, although of course there were short-term fluctuations, such as the 1790s, when the real value of wages clearly fell considerably. There was also a significant variation between the different trades. In Nottingham, in the period 1780–1820, the standard of living for the lace makers undoubtedly rose to unprecedented heights, as the best bobbin net machine-workers could earn up to £5 or even £10 a week. Their framework knitting brethren, however, whose prosperity had peaked rather earlier, were struggling to get by on around 12s a week.[23]

For those who were unable to find employment, or were prevented from supporting themselves, there was, in theory, always the safety-net of poor relief. The English prided themselves that in their country there was no need for the poor to starve to death, because assistance for the needy was always available from the parish. There was a strong life-cyclical pattern in those seeking poor relief. Families with small children, with many mouths to feed and only one full-time labourer, were often in need of support, as were the elderly who could not be maintained by their families. In between these two vulnerable periods in the life-cycle, individuals could support themselves and even contribute to the poor rates. The preference was to distribute outdoor relief. It was easier to administer than the alternative, running a workhouse, and recipients generally preferred to receive a handout in their own homes, rather than be confined in a workhouse and put to work.[24] Relief might take the form of a cash dole, provision in kind, or assistance with rent. Periodically, alarm would be expressed at the spiralling poor rates. The 1770s and 1790s were periods of particularly intense debate, which ultimately led to the Royal Commission of 1832 and the Poor Law Amendment Act of 1834. The usual response was to establish a workhouse, or reinvigorate and reform an existing one. Workhouses were supposed to be a more cost-efficient alternative, although they rarely turned out so in practice.[25] As Anne Digby has commented upon the Norwich workhouse of the 1780s, lax administration had converted it 'into little more than a comfortable lodging house'.[26] Paupers were receiving three beef dinners a week, with eighteen ounces of meat. This was considerably more than the soldier's allowance, or what an agricultural labourer would receive, but nevertheless, residence within the workhouse entailed a considerable loss of personal freedom. Although it was intended that these institutions should be self-supporting, from the labour of the inmates, who would learn skills and self-discipline through industrious employment, matters seldom worked out in this way, because such a regime demanded a very high level of supervision and organization on the part of the master of the workhouse and the guardians of the poor. Where labour was performed it often provoked the

24. For a case study of the various strategies for dealing with poor relief employed in one area, see G. W. Oxley, 'The permanent poor in south-west Lancashire under the old poor law', in J. R. Harris (ed.), *Liverpool and Merseyside* (1969), pp. 16–49. On workhouses, see, for example, Tim Hitchcock, 'Paupers and preachers: the SPCK and the parochial workhouse movement', in Lee Davison, Tim Keirn, Tim Hitchcock and Robert Shoemaker (eds), *Stilling the Grumbling Hive. The Response to Social and Economic Problems in England, 1689–1750* (Stroud, 1992), pp. 145–66.

25. Joanna Innes, 'The "mixed economy of welfare" in early modern England: assessments of the options from Hale to Malthus (c. 1683–1803)', in Martin Daunton (ed.), *Charity, Self-Interest and Welfare in the English Past* (1996), pp. 139–80.

26. A. Digby, *Pauper Palaces* (1978), p. 46; Isaac Wood, *Some Account of the Shrewsbury House of Industry* (Shrewsbury, 1791). The regime in the Manchester Workhouse is described in G. B. Hindle, *Provision for the Relief of the Poor in Manchester, 1754–1836* (Manchester, 1975), Ch. 4.

resentment of other employees, who saw their own businesses being undercut by the industry of the workhouse inmates. Occasionally, an energetic individual, such as Isaac Wood of Shrewsbury, would temporarily turn a workhouse around into a profitable enterprise, but more often the inmates were under-employed, and lived in considerable squalor. The accusations of 'filth, wretchedness and indecency' which were heaped upon the management of the Norwich workhouse in 1826 were far from unusual, and had their parallels in many other towns. Cash doles, on the other hand, were believed to encourage idleness if not administered with sufficient discretion, and it was far harder to keep a limit on the amounts being distributed by the overseers, and in periods of crisis expenditure could soar.

Those who were 'on the parish' represented another of the gradations within the labouring sort, albeit one which was mutable, reflecting changes in the life-cycle and opportunities for employment. Life at subsistence level was an 'economy of makeshifts'. Many of those who were in receipt of relief on a longer term basis had no regular occupation, and could not benefit from the occupational identity which was inherent in a skilled craft, or the associated opportunities for forging ties through the workplace or friendly society. Life for those at the very bottom of the pile would have been rootless and dislocated. The polite veneer of philanthropy covered up drunkenness, sexual exploitation, endemic disease and malnutrition; a miserable and brutal existence which one can begin to sense from the harsh reality of the scenes of low life depicted by Hogarth in engravings such as *A Harlot's Progress* (1731), *Gin Lane* (1751) or the *Four Stages of Cruelty* (1751).[27] The safety-nets of poor relief or friendly societies should not delude us into ignoring the hardship, deprivation and abuse which would have been part of the normal way of life for a significant proportion of the urban population.

It is notoriously difficult to generalize about standards of living, chiefly because we have so little information for the eighteenth century. By contrast, in the nineteenth century, information from the parliamentary inquiries and statistical surveys abounds, and from the 1830s we have a very detailed picture of the living conditions endured by the nineteenth-century working class, with graphic descriptions penned by zealous reformers, such as Dr Kay of Manchester:

27. M. Dorothy George, *London Life in the Eighteenth Century* (repr. 1992) offers one of the best accounts of the realities of life among the labouring sort in the metropolis.

What little furniture is found in them is of the rudest and most common sort, and very often in fragments – one or two rush-bottomed
chairs, a deal table, a few stools, broken earthenware, such as dishes,
tea-cups etc. etc., one or more tin kettles and cans, a few knives and
forks; no fender; a bedstead or not, as the case may happen to be;
blankets and sheets in the strict meaning of the words unknown –
their place often being made up of sacking, a heap of flocks, or a
bundle of straw, supplying the want of a proper bedstead and feather
bed; and these cooped into a single room, which serves as a place for
all domestic and household occupations.[28]

How far this description may be said to have differed from conditions prevailing in towns in earlier periods is of course impossible to establish, but we may be certain that the progress of urban
improvement and civilized society, upon which the eighteenth
century prided itself, would have had little bearing upon the lives
of the urban poor. Indeed, living conditions were probably considerably worse in urban areas than rural; what attracted the migrant
population, and which towns relied upon to sustain their population growth, was the prospect of higher wages and employment.
The changes in agriculture, identified with an 'agricultural revolution', served to release labour from the land, and also produced
higher crop yields to feed the growing population; rural under-
employment encouraged the move towards the towns.[29] Historians have calculated the 'premium', which was necessary to attract
workers to cities and compensate for the decline in the quality of
life, by contrasting the difference in the wage rates between urban
and rural areas. In the north, where there were greater problems of
overcrowding and hygiene in the towns, the wages were between
twelve to 30 per cent higher than in the countryside, whereas in the
south the difference was between eight and 20 per cent.[30]

Spiralling population put great pressure on space, and drove
the rental value of property upwards inexorably. Families were
crammed into smaller areas, often highly unfit for habitation. The
problems were most acute in the textile and manufacturing towns
such as Leeds, Liverpool, Nottingham, Manchester and Preston, where
developers sought to maximise space for housing the poor with the
construction of the back-to-back terrace. These were houses built

28. *Westminster Review,* ix (1833), p. 387, quoting from Philip Kay's *Moral and Physical Condition of the Working Classes in Manchester* (1833).
29. Comparatively little work has been done on migration to towns in the eighteenth
century, although see Peter Clark, 'Migration in England during the late seventeenth
and early eighteenth centuries', *P&P,* 83 (1979), pp. 57–90.
30. Williamson, 'Coping with city growth', p. 352.

with no through-ventilation, around an enclosed courtyard, again with a very limited opening to the air. Generally, there would be only one privy per courtyard, serving around 20 people, with no other means of sewage disposal, nor provision for clean water. When the first cholera epidemic struck in 1832, it was in these courtyard dwellings that it wrought the most damage. In Nottingham, where the boom in the cotton industry had spurred particularly rapid growth, the Board of Health, set up to deal with the cholera epidemic, established that out of over 11,000 houses standing in the town, between 7,000 and 8,000 had been constructed as back-to-back dwellings, with no means of through-ventilation and with shared conveniences.[31] In Liverpool and Manchester an even more unhealthy environment was to be found in the cellar dwellings, which had achieved notoriety long before the miasma of cholera had drawn the public's attention to the offensiveness of back-to-backs. Cellar dwellings were exactly what their names suggest. Entire families would live in one room, which was dark, poorly ventilated, and often awash with stagnant water. Some were deliberately built as accommodation, but as housing pressures increased, particularly following upon the influx of Irish immigrants to Liverpool from the late eighteenth century onwards, more and more cellars of ordinary houses were being sublet. By 1790 it was estimated that in Liverpool they housed about one eighth of the population.[32]

The extent of the problem did not really become marked until the 1820s and 30s, when the fastest period of population growth had taken place, and the threat of cholera precipitated the authorities into taking some remedial action. But in Manchester and Liverpool, which had undergone precocious growth before the end of the eighteenth century, the appalling living conditions of the labouring poor were already being commented upon. John Aikin, Dissenter, doctor and topographical writer, warned that 'the closeness with which the poor are crowded in offensive, dark, damp and incommodious habitations [is] a too fertile source of disease'. At around the same time, a Liverpool physician, Dr Currie, was blaming the dampness and polluted atmosphere of the crowded cellars for the spiralling number of deaths from typhus within the parish.[33]

31. Chapman, 'Working-class housing in Nottingham', p. 152.
32. J. H. Treble, 'Liverpool working-class housing 1801–51', in Chapman (ed.), *History of Working-Class Housing*, p. 168. See also I. Taylor, 'The Court and cellar dwelling: the eighteenth-century origins of the Liverpool Slum', *THSLC* (1970), pp. 1–43.
33. John Aikin, *A Description of the Country from thirty to forty miles around Manchester* (1795), p. 192; Charles Creighton, *A History of Epidemics in Britain*, 2 vols (1965), ii, p. 141.

But for the most part, observers simply commented smugly on the great improvement to the appearance of the town, brought about by pulling down slums, without appreciating the need to provide alternative accommodation as a replacement. Currie's contemporary, William Moss, even attempted to argue a case for the salubrity of cellar dwellings, on the grounds that they did not permit the intermingling of noxious fumes. 'Being detached, a cellar can neither receive nor communicate anything infectious in the manner that necessarily happens in the inhabited rooms of a house that all communicate by one common staircase.'[34] Ignorance was a major problem, but so too were vested interests; those who had owned slum property would be at risk of losing their monopoly on cheap property if alternative or better accommodation was constructed. An improvement bill in Liverpool, which proposed to close down all occupied cellars in 1802, was defeated by the property owners who stood to lose out on rent.[35] James Butterworth, author of a history of Manchester published in 1822, suggested that his readers should take a walk through the poverty and misery to be found in the back streets of the city, as it would provide them with a valuable and chastening experience.[36] But most visitors preferred to follow the conventional town guides, which took them through only the town centres and prosperous residential areas, where the efforts of the improvement commissioners had at least had some effect.

Disease spread the more rapidly because of the lower levels of immunity among the labouring population and the poorer diet, which left them less able to withstand infection. The situation was further exacerbated by the high levels of immigration, which accounted for an estimated 60 per cent of city growth between 1776 and 1811.[37] Large numbers of unskilled and malnourished labourers poured into Lancashire from Ireland in the early nineteenth century, flooding the manual labour market and inhabiting the cellar dwellings and the lodging houses of the most deprived areas. These newcomers to the urban environment were more susceptible to disease, hence the mortality rates among the immigrant population were always higher.[38] London was the only city to show an overall

34. William Moss, *A Familiar Medical Survey of Liverpool* (1784), pp. 41–2, quoted in Treble, 'Working-class housing in Liverpool', p. 167.

35. B. D. White, *A History of the Corporation of Liverpool, 1835–1914* (Liverpool, 1951), p. 33.

36. James Butterworth, *The Antiquities of the Town and a Complete History of the Trade of Manchester* (Manchester, 1822), p. 78.

37. Williamson, 'Coping with city growth', p. 337.

38. A. Sharlin, 'Burial seasonality and causes of death in London, 1670–1819', *P&P*, 79 (1978), pp. 126–38.

decline in the crude death rate in this period, and it is argued that the reason for this is that the area from which its immigrants were recruited was restricted, as it had to compete with other provincial towns. Consequently, within that catchment area, a pattern of immunity similar to that of the metropolis had developed.[39] The virulence of the seventeenth-century killer, the plague, diminished in our period, but that of smallpox had increased, and was followed by a rise in the incidence of typhus, consumption (TB) and measles. The improvements in life expectancy, from which the upper classes demonstrably benefited in this period, were much less marked among the working population, upon whom the smallpox vaccination, for example, would have had little impact.[40] Typhus was becoming increasingly common in the manufacturing towns. Here, where the problems were most acute, physicians, such as Thomas Percival, John Ferriar, and other members of the Manchester Literary and Philosophical Society, had made the connection between insanitary living conditions, poor health, and the need for public action. But their proposals were shelved for the most part by the Police Commissioners, who were unwilling to engage in such expensive and interventionist activity.[41] The Board of Health, which they managed to set up in 1796, fell far short of their original vision and the only part of their suggestions to be implemented was the Fever Hospital, established 1796. The wave of panic among urban authorities, created by the cholera epidemic of 1832, meant that medical opinion was at last able to channel public anxiety into constructive activity. It was another ten years, however, before Edwin Chadwick made his 'Report on the Sanitary Condition of the Labouring Population of England and Wales', by which time the scale of the problem had grown to such an extent that public opinion was acutely aware of the need for remedial action. The 1840s certainly represented a watershed for the improvement of sanitation, in terms of public debate and government response, but the problem had long been recognised and precedents outlined, if not fully implemented from the late eighteenth century.[42] As with so much

---

39. Leonard Schwarz, *London in the Age of Industrialisation* (Cambridge, 1992), p. 151.

40. Peter H. Lindert, 'Unequal living standards', in Floud and McCloskey (eds), *Economic History of Britain*, pp. 361–4.

41. Thomas Percival, *Observations on the State of Population in Manchester* (1789); John Ferriar, *Medical Histories and Reflections* (Warrington, 1792).

42. Creighton, *History of Epidemics*; Ferriar, *Medical Histories and Reflections*; B. Keith Lucas, 'Some influences affecting the development of sanitary legislation in England', *EcHR*, vi (1953–4), pp. 290–6. But see also the response, E. P. Hennock, 'Urban sanitary reform a generation before Chadwick?', *EcHR*, x (1958), pp. 113–19.

of nineteenth-century legislation, the origins can be traced back to localised precedents at the provincial level.

The Middling Sort

Villages have since sprung up into immense cities; great manufactures have spread over wastes and mountains; ease, comfort and leisure, have introduced, among the middling orders of society, their natural companions, curiosity, intelligence, boldness, and activity of mind. A much greater proportion of the collective knowledge and wealth of the nation has thus fallen to their lot.[43]

The success and achievements of the urban 'middling sort', celebrated here by the radical Whig peer, Lord John Russell, has continued to fascinate twentieth-century historians, charting the emergence of middle-class culture and identity in eighteenth-century towns. Its size, standard of living, values, morals, habits and behaviour have all been subjected to scrutiny. The real challenge to the political power of the aristocratic ruling elite, from the towns, did not come until the nineteenth century. But the wealth, confidence and assertiveness of the nineteenth-century bourgeoisie was heralded in the culture of the eighteenth-century polite and commercial citizen, who began to encroach in a significant fashion upon the gulf which divided the rich and poor. 'Class', however, is a term which should be used with discretion. Eighteenth-century society does not lend itself to being described in terms of class interests. The appearance of a middle *class* consciousness, based upon the possession of a common culture and shared values, only begins to become a tangible reality in the late eighteenth and early nineteenth centuries. The preference in the eighteenth century was to talk in terms of the middling sort, ranks, interests or classes.[44]

Who are we talking about when we refer to the middling sort? It is difficult to define with any degree of accuracy, especially as contemporaries themselves could come to no agreement as to who the middling sort were. They were not even exclusively urban; a yeoman farmer, for example, would definitely have been ranked as middling. Typically, the middling sort were buyers and sellers and

43. 'Speech of Lord John Russell in the House of Commons on the 14th Dec. 1819, for transferring the Elective Franchise from Corrupt Boroughs to Unrepresented Great Towns' repr. in *Edinburgh Review*, xxxiii (1820), p. 378.
44. P. J. Corfield, 'Class by name and number in eighteenth-century Britain', *History*, 72 (1987), pp. 38–61.

providers of services – quite literally the 'middle-men'. Modern principles of social classification, on the basis of socio-economic criteria,
were alien to the eighteenth-century mind, hence the historian must
employ a considerable degree of flexibility. At the very bottom of
the scale in the early eighteenth century, 'middling' is generally
understood to include those who had an income of at least £50
a year. With the impact of inflation and a rising cost of living, a
lower bench mark of £80 seems more suitable, certainly for the
metropolis. The outside upper limit was probably around £2,000,
but for the bulk of the middling sort their income would have been
between £150 to £200.[45] Bearing these figures in mind it is possible
to estimate that the middling sort would have comprised about 20
to 25 per cent of the population in most towns. By contrast, it has
been estimated that in London the upper classes constituted two to
three per cent of the population.[46] But these boundaries cannot be
rigidly adhered to; retail and wholesale shopkeepers, skilled craftsmen, merchants, and manufacturers, could find their income
fluctuating considerably from year to year, and many shopkeepers
and chandlers, for example, would have been considerably poorer
than skilled artisans working in the textile industries. We must be
equally open-minded about determining the upper limits, where
the wealthiest and most upwardly mobile middling sort began to
acquire genteel status and merge with the social elite. We cannot
rely simply on income levels here, it was also a question of occupation, lifestyle and upbringing. Many middling merchants may have
had more disposable income than lesser gentry, but they lacked the
same social status, derived from birth and 'breeding'.

Within the middling sort, there were, of course, subtle gradations too; wholesale shopkeepers, such as mercers, drapers and
hosiers, were of higher status than the retail shopkeepers, and among
the shopkeepers, the dealers in the luxury finished goods, such as
china or silverware, occupied a position above those who dealt in
foodstuffs and other basic goods. What we consider now as the
'professions', that is, occupations such as lawyers, surveyors and
physicians, were above the shopkeepers and generally on a par with
the merchant elite (who often moved into banking). It was easier
for professionals, such as lawyers and clergy, to mix with the county
gentry, but within the professional class itself there was a wide gulf

45. Schwarz, *London in the age of Industrialisation*, p. 54; for the earlier part of this
period see also Peter Earle, *The Making of the English Middle Class* (1989), pp. 3–16;
and Margaret Hunt, *The Middling Sort. Commerce, Gender and the Family, 1680–1780*
(Berkeley and Los Angeles CA, 1996), pp. 15–18.
46. George Rudé, *Hanoverian London* (1971), p. 58.

between the impoverished curate and the holder of a rich living, or the country attorney and the successful London barrister. The emergence of the 'professions' as an urban elite, was a distinctively eighteenth-century phenomenon.[47] This is clearly illustrated in the changing composition of the governing bodies of many of the incorporated towns, particularly those where the traditional trades gradually ceased to play such an important role in the economy, as in Exeter or Oxford. In 1770, there were fifteen grocers, three attorneys and no bankers on the common council of Oxford, which numbered around one hundred members. By 1830, there were ten attorneys and at least seven gentlemen with banking interests, while the number of straightforward grocers (as opposed to dealers in more specialised goods) had dropped to two.[48] In Exeter, the chamber of 24, which had once been the preserve of the cloth merchants, had become dominated by the medical interest; five members were doctors or surgeons in 1831.[49] Shopkeeping too was an eighteenth-century development, especially for the smaller provincial towns. Because of improved communications and the development of a carrier trade, the shopkeeper gradually displaced travelling merchants and fairs.[50] Furthermore, the growth of a consumer market and increasing technological expertise opened up new areas of craftsmanship and retailing for the middling sort. Robert Campbell's *The London Tradesman*, published in 1747, listed no less than 72 different occupations or trades to which parents might apprentice their sons, many of which were further subdivided. The occupation of goldsmith, for example, included the subdivisions of jeweller, snuff box maker, tweezer and tweezer case maker, silver turner, burnisher and metal guilder, chaser, refiner and gold finder. Town directories, which became common among provincial towns from the 1770s, offer an immediate sense of the steady proliferation of specialist trades and professional services.[51] Clearly, the larger the town, the wider the range of services which could be supported, and in London, or towns such as Bath, where the economy was dependent upon the extravagance of the visitors, the representation of luxury

47. P. J. Corfield, *Power and the Professions in Britain, 1700–1850* (1995).

48. OCA, Common Council Minute Books; *Bailey's Western and Midland Directory* (1784); *Universal British Directory* (1790–8); *Pigot's New Commercial Directory* (1823–4).

49. Robert Newton, *Eighteenth-Century Exeter* (Exeter, 1984), p. 142.

50. Hoh-Cheung and Lorna H. Mui, *Shops and Shopkeeping in Eighteenth Century England* (1989), p. 27.

51. Ian Mitchell, 'The expansion of urban retailing 1700–1815', in Clark (ed.), *Transformation of English Provincial Towns*, pp. 259–83; P. J. Corfield with Serena Kelly, 'Giving directions to the town: the early town directories', *Urban History Yearbook*, xi (1984), pp. 23–34.

goods and services was the highest. It is estimated that around 20 per cent of London shops were providing luxury goods and services during the eighteenth century, whereas in the country as a whole the figure was eight per cent.[52]

As business depended on buying and selling, the middling sort placed a high value on literacy and numeracy. It was literacy which, as Margaret Hunt points out, could make the difference between life as a journeymen or rising up the ranks to be an independent householder. Middling demand led to an enormous expansion in educational provision in this period, which was concentrated in the towns. Newspapers carried hundreds of advertisements for private schools, 'commercial academies' and specialist writing and mathematical schools, where boys would learn vocational subjects, such as book keeping, the use of globes and modern languages, rather than the recondite classical education undergone by the children of the aristocracy. Traditional urban grammar schools found themselves forced to adapt their curriculum, based as it was on Latin and Greek, in order to compete in this changing educational market. Girls did not share in this educational programme, but that is not to say that their education was entirely neglected. Literacy and basic numeracy were essential prerequisites in managing a household, or assisting a spouse in business (and many widows took over their husbands businesses after their death), quite apart from the additional polish and politeness of social skills, such as music and dancing, which were becoming increasingly important as markers of social status and refinement.[53]

Estimates put the usual middling household somewhere between four and seven people – this was slightly higher than the equivalent figure for the labouring sort, for whom higher mortality meant fewer children, and who would not have been in a position to employ any servants. The family, or the household, was the essential unit of middling life. Businesses were generally conducted as family enterprises. Wives and children, especially sons, were expected to assist in the running of the business, and apprentices and journeymen were conventionally treated as part of the family household. The actual shop, warehouse or workshop was located below or adjacent to the family living quarters; even banks were located

52. Mitchell, 'Expansion of Urban Retailing', p. 60.

53. Richard S. Tompson, *Classics or Charity? The Dilemma of the Eighteenth-Century Grammar School* (Manchester, 1971). On girls' education see Susan Skedd, 'Women teachers and the expansion of girls' schooling in England, c. 1760–1820', in Hannah Barker and Elaine Chalus (eds), *Gender in Eighteenth-Century England* (1997), pp. 101–25.

within the home. Whereas among the labouring sort entire families were often crammed into one or two rooms, the middling sort would generally inhabit their own house, or at least several rooms within a house. Peter Earle found that most of the families which he studied in London leased rather than owned their properties.[54] Comparable studies have still to be carried out for other parts of the country, but an impressionistic survey suggests that house ownership had yet to become the defining mark of middle class aspirations, as it is today. The size of the house would clearly vary according to the disposable income of the family, but typically the more prosperous middling sort lived in the kind of terrace which still survives in many towns. These houses might be several storeys high, with two or three rooms on each floor, and usually included a yard at the back with outhouses and possibly stabling.[55]

Most middling families would have spent the greater part of their income upon food and clothes. Luxury goods and 'consumer durables' accounted for a much less significant, albeit growing part of their expenditure. Low levels of taxation and inflation coupled with economic growth engendered a society with unprecedented amounts of disposable income. It is estimated that by 1780 around twenty to twenty-five per cent of the population could afford an average household expenditure of £30 pa on manufactured goods and commercial services.[56] The middling sort represented the most rapidly growing part of the consumer market and were using newly acquired wealth to purchase the clothes, clocks, books, patent medicines and other commodities of the consumer revolution. The home became the display cabinet for silverware or pewter, glass, china, mahogany furniture and wall papers. The amount of time and money invested in the 'domestic sphere' and its upkeep was dramatically increased, reflecting the primary importance of home and family in middling values. Hence it is that the middling sort has been associated with the 'birth of a consumer society'.[57] Whereas amongst

54. Earle, *Making of the English Middle Class*, pp. 206–9.
55. In Edinburgh and Glasgow the usual size of a tenement among the middling sort was 4 to 5 rooms plus a kitchen: Stana Nenadic, 'Middle-rank consumers and domestic culture in Edinburgh and Glasgow, 1720–1840', *P&P*, 145 (1994), p. 140. Nenadic suggests that households in England were of a similar size.
56. Mui, *Shops and Shopkeeping*, p. 13.
57. N. McKendrick, J. Brewer and J. H. Plumb (eds), *The Birth of a Consumer Society: The Commercialization of Eighteenth-Century England* (1983). For modifications of this interpretation see B. Fine and E. Leopold, *The World of Consumption* (1993), pp. 121–37 and Grant McCracken, *Culture and Consumption* (Bloomington and Indianapolis: Indiana, 1988), esp. pp. 3–30. A recent overview is offered in the collection of essays edited by John Brewer and Roy Porter, *Consumption and the World of Goods* (1993).

the labouring sort the home, such as it was, was overcrowded, forcing socialization and recreation out into the street or the alehouse,
amongst the middling sort, much more recreational and sociable
activity was done within the home, often based around the consumption of food and drink. Contemporary diaries make it clear
that social visiting was an extremely important part of the middling
lifestyle and the huge expansion in the amount of crockery and
china (especially for tea drinking), pewter-ware and other items for
the preparation and consumption of food bears witness to the
importance of the sharing of food and drink in such companion-
ship. Supper, taken in the evening, was a simpler meal than dinner,
and was the frequent focus of sociability, as was the increasingly
popular custom of taking tea. The multiple course dinner served in
the evening, which became popular amongst aristocratic and metropolitan circles towards the end of our period, was never associated
with the lifestyle of the middling sort.

One interpretation of the rise of consumerism argues that it
was stimulated in an urban environment, by the zeal for emulation
of social superiors, who lived in much greater proximity to those
below them than in country areas.[58] However, recent research on
consumption, in both urban and rural areas, using probate inventories, has suggested that the urban middling sort were not necessarily more consumer-minded than their rural counterparts. What
was more important was the ease of access to consumer goods, so
that in an area like the north east, where there was frequent trade
with London, on account of the traffic in coal, consumer behaviour
was much more advanced than in the towns of Hampshire, for
example.[59] Lorna Weatherill found that there was little difference
in the consumption patterns of the rural and urban middling sort,
but that the shopkeepers and professionals were more likely to
invest their money in goods than were the lesser gentry, which
suggests a limit to the extent to which social emulation can be
applied as an explanation. The extent of a second-hand market in
goods and clothing, which Nenadic has uncovered in Scottish towns,
also runs against a simple model of consumption driven by fashion
and social climbing. Other factors, such as social differentiation,

---

58. H. J. Perkin, 'The social causes of the British industrial revolution', *TRHS*,
xviii (1968), pp. 123–43.

59. Lorna Weatherill, *Consumer Behaviour and Material Culture in Britain 1660–
1760*, 2nd edn, (1996). Nenadic's article 'Middle-rank consumers and domestic
culture' was based upon Scottish inventories, but her arguments against social emulation as the sole factor in consumption are of much wider application.

functional utility, family tradition and emotional investment, must be taken into account as motives for consumption. Consumer behaviour must also be seen in the context of changes in production, particularly in the textile industry, and the impact which this had on the availability and price of goods.[60] More immediate influences upon patterns of consumption were derived from advertising. Advertisements, tradesmen's cards and marketing gimmicks, made their appearance in the pages of the press and in the shop windows; eye-catching 'puffs', special offers, competitions, free gifts, and price ticketing, all encouraged the novice consumer to participate in the rapidly expanding world of goods.[61]

In many ways, the culture of the middling sort was an essentially domestic one, bound up with the family and the household, and there was also a very strong associational element to it. Clubs, societies and associations proliferated in eighteenth-century towns, with a membership which was predominantly drawn from the middling sort. In addition to the basic opportunities for social intercourse, which membership of a society offered, a considerable proportion of urban life was organized through voluntary associational activity. Charitable relief was administered through Societies for Bettering the Condition of the Poor (first established in 1796), and medical assistance was made available through hospitals and public dispensaries, run by voluntary societies. Urban improvement was promoted through discussions at literary and philosophical societies, which might offer a prize for the scheme most conducive to the public good.[62] The projects proposed might then be realised by an improvement commission, made up predominantly of the middling sort. Cultural amenities, such as libraries, concerts and theatres were organized through subscription societies. Crime and immorality were countered by 'vice societies' for the prosecution of felons, and charity schools provided education for the poor in the principles of Christian morality.[63] At the most informal end of the scale

60. On the textile industry and consumption see Beverley Lemire, *Fashion's Favourite. The cotton trade and the consumer in Britain, 1600–1800* (Oxford, 1992), esp. pp. 77–114.

61. Neil McKendrick, 'The Consumer Revolution of eighteenth-century Britain', in McKendrick, Brewer and Plumb (eds), *Birth of a Consumer Society*, pp. 9–33.

62. The infirmary in Newcastle (founded 1751) was the result of a contest between members of a private literary society to see who could come up with the plan most beneficial to the community. John Brand, *The History and Antiquities of the Town and County of the Town of Newcastle upon Tyne*, 2 vols (London, 1789), i, p. 413.

63. Joanna Innes, 'Politics and morals: the reformation of manners movement in later eighteenth-century England', in Eckhart Hellmuth (ed.), *The Transformation of Political Culture* (Oxford, 1990), pp. 57–118.

were societies, effectively little more than drinking or dining clubs, which simply met regularly at a certain tavern or inn for an evening of good fellowship. At the other end of the spectrum was the more formalized structure of national networks of societies, such as the freemasonic lodges. Under the patronage of members of the royal family and the aristocracy, these spread rapidly through the towns of provincial England from the 1720s onwards, attracting large numbers of respectable urban men. Freemasons were far removed from the rather esoteric image which they enjoy today; characteristically they were identified with schemes of philanthropy and the public good, processed in civic festivals, and were prominently placed on the list of subscribers to public improvement, rather than participating in mysterious and exclusive rituals.

However, it is important to bear in mind that 'collective' behaviour had always been a part of urban life, and we should be wary of over-emphasising the element of novelty, for fear of losing sight of continuities. In many ways, the clubs and societies which we associate with the eighteenth century were extensions of traditional forms of urban activity. Guilds and trading companies had always been more than regulatory economic bodies, drawing their members together in social and philanthropic activities. Their charters stressed the importance of fostering love, unity and Christian charity and upholding honesty.[64] Broader economic and demographic trends undermined their ability to retain their hold on the economic life of towns, but the social and philanthropic side to their activities continued in many of the older incorporated towns, such as Oxford and Coventry, where guilds held annual dinners and administered charitable relief until well into the nineteenth century. We must remember too, that the absolute decline in guild membership did not set in until the 1790s, and the rate of decline in apprenticeship admissions varied considerably, with respect to town and occupation. Membership of the corporation and the body of freemen, had exerted a similar unifying bond on the diverse elements of urban society. Although there was a tendency for corporations to become more oligarchic and exclusive, withdrawing from the population at large, there is no need to assume that the civic ideal lost its relevance for a collective identity. Evidence, ranging from urban histories to election propaganda, suggests that civic feeling, which focused on the corporation and the charters, still carried considerable emotive

64. Christopher Brooks, 'Apprenticeship, social mobility and the middling sort, 1550–1800', in Jonathan Barry and Christopher Brooks (eds), *The Middling Sort of People. Culture, Society and Politics in England, 1550–1800* (1994), p. 76.

force in many towns.[65] In many respects, the freemasonic lodges, which became integrated into the fabric of urban life so rapidly, occupied the place in society which had previously been occupied by the guilds, and like guilds their membership provided 'a means by which social barriers could be crossed without undermining the social order'.[66]

Political arithmeticians, from Gregory King to Patrick Colqhoun, devised schemes by which to categorise the immense diversity of urban society and to estimate its wealth, but none of these formulations embraced a tripartite, class-based division of society.[67] Contemporary commentators did not analyze society in terms of income brackets, but in terms of characteristics, virtues or vices. Urban apologists asserted the claims of the middle rank of society to virtue and industry, qualities which underpinned the commercial and landed wealth of the nation. Likewise, critical observers dismissed the middling sort as mean and avaricious, or as inveterate social climbers. But, above all, middling society aspired to be nothing, if not polite. The 'polite and commercial people' of eighteenth-century England numbered among them the landed elite, but also those whom twentieth-century historians would commonly identify as belonging to the 'middling sort'.[68] 'Politeness' was more than the observation of common courtesy, as it is now; it embodied an entire social code and expectations of behaviour. Urbanity, ease of sociability, and good taste were all inherent in politeness. As theorists from Hume to Smith argued, its rise was inherently linked to that of commerce, which 'softens and polishes the manners of men'; manners, which during the preceding feudal era, had been violent, aggressive and intemperate.[69] It was therefore particularly appropriate to the urban context, where the conduct of commerce demanded the observation of civility and courtesy. Partisan behaviour, which spilled over into the sphere of 'polite' society, was deeply regrettable. Rival assemblies, literary societies or charities were a sign of a

65. Rosemary Sweet, *The Writing of Urban Histories in Eighteenth-Century England* (Oxford, 1997). See also 'Freemen and independence in English borough politics c. 1770–1830', *P&P*, 161 (1998).

66. John Money, *Experience and Identity: Birmingham and the West Midlands, 1760–1800* (Manchester, 1977), p. 138.

67. Corfield, 'Class by name and number in eighteenth-century Britain'. For attempts to update these tables, see P. H. Lindert and J. G. Williams, 'Revising England's social tables, 1688–1812', *Explorations in Economic History*, 19 (1982), pp. 395–408.

68. Professor Langford took the phrase from William Blackstone, *Commentaries on the Laws of England* (1765–9), iii, p. 326.

69. William Robertson, *History of the Reign of the Emperor Charles V*, 4 vols (Edinburgh, 1819), i, p. 97.

divided community, in which the pursuit of narrow party ends had taken precedence over the common good and civilized ideals. Many societies, therefore, drew up regulations which explicitly excluded all those using profane language, gambling or drunkenness, and specified instead philanthropy, fellowship and learning on an inter-denominational basis. They offered a forum for social intercourse, free from political or sectarian divisions, and encouraged values of moderation and public spirit. Since it was a contemporary common-place that politeness was the outcome of civilized social exchange and conversation, the club or society was both an indication of the degree of refinement already achieved, and offered the appropriate environment for further smoothing the rough edges of urban life.

Attempts to extrapolate the existence of class identity in the eighteenth century are therefore somewhat anachronistic. Yet, in the nineteenth century it is plausible to argue that the transition from middling sort to middle class had been made, largely within the context of urban society. The experience of association, and voluntary activity on a non-partisan basis, was arguably an essential ingredient in the process; it brought the middling sort together in common activity, breaking down the occupational boundaries, and bridging the gulf between merchant and manufacturer, shopkeeper and lawyer, offering them the chance to articulate their values and establish a sense of common interest. Voluntary societies, whether for cultural or philanthropic purposes, such as those studied by Professor Morris in Leeds in the first few decades of the nineteenth century, could provide the necessary foundations for the creation of a sense of class identity, and overcome the obstacles posed by sectarian and political divisions.[70]

On a more practical level, running a voluntary hospital or a char-ity gave those involved an experience of the exercise of authority. They had the opportunity to participate in public life, comparatively unfettered by bonds of deference and oligarchy, and the chance to implement and develop principles of accountability, equal vot-ing and more open and efficient government – principles which are now generally deemed characteristically middle class. There were important political implications to this; when the standards of administration practised in the voluntary institutions were com-pared against those of, for example, the unreformed corporation,

70. This argument is best developed with reference to the middle class in Leeds by R. J. Morris, *Class, Sect and Party: The Making of the British Middle Class, Leeds, 1820–1850* (Manchester, 1990).

the latter was inevitably found wanting. The regularized accounting procedures, the openness of meetings and the potential egalitarianism of the organization contrasted unfavourably with the chaotic finances, secrecy and oligarchy of unreformed bodies. The experience of association contributed to the shift in public opinion, which became less tolerant of a system based upon oligarchy, unpaid service, and patronage. It reinforced the sense of independence, which was so characteristic of middling values and which was the driving force behind the movements for parliamentary reform, and sharpened the critique of those who were in opposition – as we saw in chapter five. As Kathleen Wilson has argued, these societies fostered a 'participatory mode of citizenship', and encouraged the articulation of ideas, which challenged elite leadership and the established model of parliamentary politics. The Birmingham Book Club was prominent in petitioning in support of parliamentary reform throughout the West Midlands, while in Newcastle almost all of the town's leading political radicals had been involved in the running of the voluntary hospital. The management of the infirmary was upheld, in pointed contrast to what was perceived as the oligarchic and self-interested character of government, at corporation and parliamentary level.[71]

In many accounts of the emergence of the middle class, the culture and values of the Dissenters feature prominently.[72] Their traditions of personal religion, which stressed the responsibility of the individual, both for his own salvation and his prosperity in this world, voluntarism and a greater propensity to question the established authorities of church and state, have been linked with the 'middle class' virtues of thrift, industry, independence, opposition to privilege and the rise of 'possessive individualism'. Dissent created supra-local allegiances between members of the same denomination, foreshadowing the national identity of class, whereas the strength of the Anglican parish was as a focal point for the local community. Because of their exclusion from civic office, on account of the Test and Corporation acts, Dissenters were often at the

71. Kathleen Wilson, 'Urban culture and political activism in Hanoverian England: the example of voluntary hospitals', in Hellmuth (ed.), *Transformation of Political Culture*, pp. 165–84; and see also Wilson, *The Sense of the People: Politics, Culture and Imperialism, 1715–85* (Cambridge, 1995) pp. 63–83; Money, *Experience and Identity*, p. 107.

72. See in particular John Brewer, *Party Ideology and Popular Politics at the Accession of George III* (Cambridge, 1976); 'Commercialization and politics', in McKendrick, Brewer and Plumb, *Birth of a Consumer Society*; and Earle, *Making of the English Middle Class*.

forefront in oppositional urban politics, particularly in the movements for improvement, reform and philanthropy, as they sought
to exploit other avenues of power. It would, however, be absurdly
reductionist to assume that thrift and personal morality, or even
opposition, were the monopoly of Dissenters, or that such qualities
were the only defining features in the emergence of a middle class
identity. The continued importance of civic and religious solidarities in the middling culture of eighteenth-century Bristol has been
skilfully described by Jonathan Barry, and as we have already seen,
the ideology of the family continued to provide an important basis
upon which the values of the middling sort were formed.[73]

However, it is undeniable that by the late eighteenth century the
bonds of guild, church, and community, which had united early
modern society, were becoming increasingly loose. In the new towns
of the industrial north and Midlands, such traditions had never
effectively existed. The conceptual power of the common weal,
which underlay the civic ideal, became less compelling in the more
pluralistic and socially stratified society. By the passage of the Great
Reform Act in 1832, the middle classes had achieved a level of
consciousness and organization which could not have been fore-
seen in the eighteenth century. Growing prosperity and swelling
numbers brought greater confidence. It was also now unavoidably
apparent that urban interests diverged from those of the landed
classes. The debate over the repeal of the Corn Laws, in the 1820s,
is often taken to indicate a crucial turning point, when the manufacturers and industrialists realised that they could no longer assume
an indentity of interest with the predominantly landed MPs who
were representing them in Parliament. Of rather longer standing
was the recognition of the labouring sort as an entirely separate
class – a class which could be threatening and subversive, as in the
protests of the Luddite era and Peterloo. A class whose poverty
necessitated an ever increasing burden of local taxation, and which
needed the directive energies of the middle class for its education
and moral improvement. By the 1830s, the urban middle class was
acknowledged as the engine of commercial and industrial growth,
leading the way in philanthropy and in the observance of morality,
and fully aware of the importance of its contribution to the nation's
prosperity and continued expansion.

73. Jonathan Barry, 'Bourgeois collectivism? Urban association and the middling
sort', in Barry and Brooks (eds), *The Middling Sort of People*, pp. 84–112. See also his
introduction, pp. 1–27.

Gentrification

Nottingham begins to be much frequented by gentlemen, some who retire to it from their country-houses, others who have left off trade, and many gentlemen of the neighbourhood have houses here for winter.[74]

Middle class culture, whenever it emerged, was defined in opposition to both the culture of the working classes and the aristocracy. Outside London, the aristocracy seldom played an active role in urban life, beyond the honorific functions of heading subscriptions, bestowing charity and promoting their candidate's campaign at a contested election. Their life was divided between the country house and the London season. It is far harder to generalise about the influence of the gentry in urban life and culture, however. The issue is further complicated by the historical profession's invention of the rather anomalous category of 'pseudo-gentry' or 'town gentry' in this period. The pseudo-gentry comprised not just gentlemen who had abandoned rural society for the town, but also the elite of the professional and mercantile classes, who had withdrawn from business to adopt the lifestyle of the gentleman, and mixed with county society, while continuing to reside in town. Had Bishop Pococke, quoted above, been aware of the term, he would have surely commented that Nottingham was becoming full of pseudo-gentry. John Brewer describes a typical example, John Marsh, a solicitor, who came into an inheritance, and tiring of the insularity and expense of country living, bought a townhouse in Chichester in 1787, where he lived for the rest of his life, becoming heavily involved in charitable works and the musical life of the town.[75] It has been estimated that by the second half of the eighteenth century these pseudo-gentry accounted for nearly four per cent of the population of county towns, and in some towns, with a stronger 'leisure' element, might account for up to fourteen per cent.[76] But estimates such as these should be used with caution. 'Pseudo-gentry' is a modern term which contemporaries would not have used, and deciding which groups it included is hazardous. It also implies an identification with gentry, rather than urban values which cannot necessarily be substantiated.

74. J. J. Cartwright (ed.), *Dr Pocock's Travels through England*, 2 vols (Camden Society Publications, 1888–9), i, p. 168.

75. John Brewer, *The Pleasures of the Imagination. English Culture in the Eighteenth Century* (1997), p. 536.

76. Peter Borsay, *The English Urban Renaissance, 1660–1770* (Oxford, 1989), p. 204.

It has been forcefully argued that in seventeenth-century post-Restoration society, there was a 'crisis' in the towns as they recovered from the destruction and disruption of the years of Civil War. During this period, local gentry took the opportunity to assert or extend their influence over the towns.[77] They took advantage of the 1661 Corporation Act, which allowed county JPs to intervene in civic government, particularly in enforcing religious conformity. The intervention of Charles II in borough charters, rather than being part of an absolutist programme of centralization, was often initiated by local Tory gentry, who wanted to disempower the dissenting elite in towns, and who instigated the *quo warranto* proceedings themselves. Gentry and nobility sought election as High Stewards and Recorders, they stood as MPs, and they infiltrated the corporation and the magistracy. But we must remember that their motives for doing so were primarily political. Considerable doubt is now being expressed as to the extent to which the gentry and nobility really succeeded in pulling the strings of urban politics, and asserting themselves in urban life. There is an important difference between becoming involved in urban politics and being able to determine the outcome. Clearly, a case can be made for their influence in some towns, such as Leeds, where the leading merchants and the county gentry had practised intermarriage for generations,[78] or in the tiny rotten boroughs of the south west, which were financially dependent upon noble patronage. But equally, in other towns there is no sign that gentry influence in urban government and politics became significantly more extensive in this period. On the contrary it was resisted, as in Nottingham, where gentry efforts to invade the corporation were countered with the assertion that 'we never have any Gentlemen here among us'.[79]

The gentry presence in towns certainly became more noticeable (and had been becoming so since the sixteenth century at least), and was frequently commented upon by travellers in the early part of the eighteenth century. Their presence in town was not just in order to assure themselves of gaining a parliamentary seat. They

77. Peter Clark and Paul Slack, *English Towns in Transition, 1500–1700* (Oxford, 1976).

78. R. G. Wilson, *The Merchant Community of Leeds, 1700–1830* (Manchester, 1971), pp. 16, 220–33.

79. J. M. Triffit, 'Politics and the Urban Community: Parliamentary Boroughs in the South West of England, 1710–30', Oxford Univ. D.Phil. thesis (1986); D. Gray, *Nottingham through 500 years* (Nottingham, 1960), p. 103, quoted in M. Mullett, 'Popular culture and popular politics: some regional case studies' in C. Jones (ed.), *Britain in the First Age of Party* (1987), p. 137.

came to towns because the urban environment had become more attractive, offering a variety of entertainments and services. County towns were the administrative centres for a range of county meetings, such as the militia, turnpike trusts, and the land tax commissions. The town was a financial centre where they could arrange loans and mortgages, and increasingly, with the advent of provincial banking, invest their money. It was the source of an increasingly wide range of consumer goods and luxuries, and was the prime marriage market. The cost of living was often much lower in towns, and many travellers commented upon the number of gentry residing in places such as Lewes or Warwick on account of the cheapness of provisions. An increasing number of younger sons were being apprenticed to merchants and provided with a career. John Aikin described how country gentlemen began to apprentice their sons to the newly wealthy merchants of Manchester, during the reign of George I. (Many, he claimed, could not stand the life and fled, or else resorted to the taverns and drunken oblivion because of the lack of entertainment on offer.)[80] Gentry families became enmeshed in the commercial networks of London, and began investing in enterprises such as the East India Company. (This should remind us of the reciprocal influence which a commercial urban culture exercised upon the gentry who visited the towns.)[81] Nor should we forget that the county town at least was a pivotal point in the wider county community – town and country had never been hermetically sealed communities, and towns were always at their busiest when the penetration of rural society was at its highest at markets or festivals, or occasions such as the Assizes or parliamentary elections when the whole of county society would be drawn to the county town.[82]

It is often assumed that the gentry dominated urban culture, introducing new fashions from London, leading the way in creating a society which sought to emulate that of the metropolis, and which lost sight of its earlier civic traditions. Urban and county elites united in pursuit of harmony and rational amusement, and led the way in the flowering of urban culture which has been dubbed the

80. Aikin, *A Description of the Country from thirty to forty miles around Manchester*, pp. 183–4.
81. Susan E. Whyman, 'Land and trade revisited: the case of John Verney, London merchant and baronet', *London Journal*, 22 (1997), pp. 16–32.
82. The interpenetration of town and 'country' is explored by Alan Everitt, in 'Country, county and town: patterns of regional evolution in England', in Peter Borsay (ed.), *The Eighteenth-Century Town, 1688–1800* (1990), pp. 83–115.

'urban renaissance'.[83] In towns where there was a high proportion of 'pseudo-gentry' this was particularly true; in the smaller county and cathedral cities and the 'leisure towns', whose economies were largely dependent upon providing service, the gentrification of urban culture was most palpable.[84] Bury St Edmunds was just such a town, whose 'chief trade' was described by Defoe as 'depending on the gentry who live there, or near it'. Astute corporations noted the attractions of bowling greens, tree-lined promenades and greater cleanliness for ladies and gentlemen, and gave their encouragement to such improvements in order to attract more visitors, who would bring business and employment to the town. The rapidity with which the luxury trades expanded in a town such as Shrewsbury is an indication of its popularity as a 'leisure town' among the gentry, but also of the inventiveness and adaptability of the town's trade and craft sector, in responding to and exploiting the market. However, we should not rule out the notion that the townsmen themselves had an interest in these 'leisure' facilities, and welcomed the improvements to the environment in their own right. The strength of indigenous traditions, coupled with urban pride and independence, meant that any gentry influence was mediated and adapted to the local circumstances.[85] Towns should not be seen as the passive recipients of imported gentility.

It must be appreciated, however, that the influence of landed wealth was far less significant in towns with their own substantial mercantile plutocracies, such as Norwich or Bristol. As other towns increased in prosperity and grew in population, the cultural clout of the gentry suffered competition. By the end of the eighteenth century, the middling sort actually represented greater spending power than the aristocracy. William Hutton, the historian of Birmingham, had little time for the contribution of the gentry to urban life: 'Gentlemen, as well as buttons, have been stamped here; but like them, when finished, are moved off'. The distinctiveness of urban middling culture became progressively more marked as their collective wealth increased. As we have seen, research on patterns

83. Roy Porter, 'Science, provincial culture and public opinion in enlightenment England', in Borsay (ed.), *The Eighteenth-Century Town*, pp. 243–67; Borsay, *Urban Renaissance*.

84. Angus McInnes, 'The emergence of a leisure town: Shrewsbury 1660–1760', *P&P*, 120 (1988), pp. 53–87. See also the debate with Borsay ibid., pp. 189–202.

85. Peter Borsay, 'The London connection: cultural diffusion and the eighteenth-century provincial town', *London Journal*, 19 (1994), pp. 21–35; K. Grady, *The Georgian Public Buildings of Leeds and the West Riding*, Thoresby Society, lxii (1989), pp. 96–102; Sweet, *Writing of Urban Histories*, pp. 236–75.

of consumption has exploded the theory that the purchase of consumer goods by the middling sorts was driven chiefly by the desire to emulate the gentry.[86] In many cases, integration into an elite or metropolitan lifestyle was actively resisted by members of the middling sort, particularly in a newly emergent town, such as the textile town of Bradford, where there was no tradition of gentry influence.[87] Inhabitants of Bristol, it was said, preferred the 'social endearment of fireside pleasures' to the dissipation of public amusements, of the kind to be found in London.[88] Even if it is true that the middle classes were following the gentry and the aristocracy, with similar patterns of consumption and social life, unless they can be shown to have been self-consciously imitating the lifestyle of those above them, can it really be termed 'emulation'?

If the cultural dominance of the gentry had limitations, their influence in government was even more circumscribed. Names of county gentlemen often featured in corporations, on improvement commissions or as governors of hospitals, but the reality was that their presence was seldom felt. When the minutes of these bodies are examined, the regular attendees carrying out business and making decisions, were predominantly the resident middling sort. The names of the landed gentry added a touch of social prestige and distinction, and their support could be crucial should assistance in parliament or the courts be required, but in day-to-day administration the names were an irrelevance. Granted, the appearance of the suffixes Gent. and Esq. against the names of corporation members and other leading figures in the urban community became far more widespread over the century. But this was less an indication of gentrification in sociological terms than a mark of the very success of the middling sort, who appropriated the terms in recognition of their own growing prosperity and self-confidence. They also wanted to distinguish themselves from the less successful middling sort – as William Richard, the historian of Kings Lynn, commented rather caustically, 'All the leading Families of this Town are in fact *tradesmen*; yet even these are very capriciously and superciliously distinguished into *Gentlemen and Tradesmen*'.[89]

86. Weatherill, *Consumer Behaviour*, pp. 194–6; Beverly Lemire, *Dress, Culture and Commerce. The English Clothing Trade before the Factory* (1997), pp. 122–4; Fine and Leopold, *The World of Consumption*.

87. T. Koditschek, *Class Formation and Urban Industrial Society: Bradford, 1750–1850* (Cambridge, 1990).

88. J. Corry and J. Evans, *The History of Bristol, Civil and Ecclesiastical*, 2 vols (Bristol, 1816), ii, p. 371.

89. William Richard, *The History of Lynn*, 2 vols (1812) ii, p. 1168.

In the latter part of the eighteenth century, we find that in many corporations, the gentry element, if it existed, actually diminished.[90] The fact that in many cases corporations became more oligarchic and less representative of the town, did not mean that they were falling under gentry influence, on the contrary, it generally indicated the success of a particular interest within the town in dominating the government. The corporations of Newcastle and Bristol were both notoriously exclusive and dominated by wealthy merchants, but although their wealth might equal that of the landed gentry and they might intermarry with them, their origins and interests were indisputably bound up with the town. Towns as diverse as Oxford and Scarborough, saw a declining gentry element in the corporation, and selling the freedom of the city to the gentry became a less attractive means of raising finance. The force of oligarchy in Bath meant that the residential social elite never participated in the affairs of civic government. Even in 1800, the corporation numbered only three members who presumed to style themselves Esq. Improvement commissions or turnpike trusts might offer an alternative opportunity for members of the gentry to exercise influence, but, in the case of Bath, where the corporation was a powerful and active body in the development and administration of the town, their freedom of action was circumscribed.[91] By the end of the century the gentry were on the retreat; towns which had once been known as centres of gentility, such as Preston or even the small county town of Beverley, were now firmly 'middle class', with a growing industrial population.[92] John Courtney of Beverley, a member of the 'urban gentry', recorded the disgust he felt when, at a meeting of the Assembly Rooms to discuss holding a ball, other townsmen present voted against inviting the country gentlemen. Courtney resigned from the committee in protest, and predicted it would be a 'shabby ball'. Four days later he noted that it was the older inhabitants who had wanted the country gentlemen to be included.[93] The new blood in the town had no interest in keeping up the ties. In 1835, the Royal Commissioners found that the gentry dominated corporations only in towns where there was not sufficient wealth among the inhabitants to resist their influence.

90. S. McIntyre, 'The Scarborough Corporation quarrel, 1730–60', *Northern History*, xiv (1978), pp. 208–26.

91. Graham Davis and Penny Bonsall, *Bath. A New History* (Keele, 1996), p. 38.

92. *VCH East Riding*, vi (1989), p. 135.

93. University of Hull, Brynmor Jones Library, MS Diary of John Courtney Esq., entries for 26 and 30 March 1789.

There is evidence to suggest that the polite world of the urban renaissance, which drew together the elites of town and county, was beginning to pass away in many towns by the end of the century. The historian of Kendal noted in 1832, that the gentry were no longer interested in attending the annual venison feast or the book club.[94] Fewer advertisements for assemblies, balls and other social events were appearing in the provincial press, and the annual races were abandoned in some towns due to a lack of contending horses.[95] Improvements in communications and travel meant that it was easier to travel to London, and the role of county towns, in providing cultural entertainment, suffered in comparison. At the same time, in the rapidly growing manufacturing and industrial towns, the urban elite differed significantly from the professionals and pseudo-gentry of county towns. They were self-made men, who had acquired their wealth through manufacturing. They were often from dissenting backgrounds, and politically at odds with the established Anglican order. Leeds was one town where the manufacturers had traditionally enjoyed a close relationship with the surrounding gentry, but in the latter part of the eighteenth century, their ascendancy began to be challenged by rival families, who had entered the elite from a Whig dissenting, rather than Tory Anglican background. These merchants and manufacturers had no such ties, and the culture of the middle class in Leeds, in the early nineteenth century, drew further and further away from that of the landed elite.[96] Manchester manufacturers had a reputation for cultural philistinism – 'A thorough Manchester man sees more beauty in rows of red brick than he would in groves and "alleys green" than he would in the songs of the lark or the nightingale'[97] – a charge which was naturally refuted, but notwithstanding, it was symptomatic of the cultural gulf between traditional landed gentry and the new urban elites. By the late eighteenth century not only were the gentry being challenged as consumers, but their influence was being questioned more generally, not just on political grounds, but more covertly, in the cultural sphere, as the proponents of urban culture became more self-conscious and self-confident in their own values. Cultural

---

94. Cornelius Nicholson, *The Annals of Kendal* (Kendal, 1832), p. 218.

95. J. Jefferson Looney, 'Cultural life in the provinces: Leeds and York, 1720–1820', in A. C. Beier, D. Cannadine and J. M. Rosenheim (eds), *The First Modern Society: Essays in English History in Honour of Laurence Stone* (Cambridge, 1989), pp. 483–512.

96. R. G. Wilson, *Gentlemen Merchants of Leeds*; Morris, *Class Sect and Party*.

97. *Gimcrackiana: or Fugitive Pieces on Manchester Men and Manners Ten Years Ago* (Manchester, 1833), p. 159.

institutions, such as the Royal Manchester Institution for Art, established and controlled by the middle class manufacturers to encourage native art, showed that artistic patronage was no longer the natural preserve of the aristocracy.[98]

Polarization and Politeness

Whatever the verdict on the influence of the gentry upon urban life, it is indisputable that there were certainly far more opportunities for the middling sort to mix with the gentry in a social context, and to join with them as participants in the consumer revolution. Indeed, the increase in intercourse created a crisis of anxiety in many circles over the difficulties in preserving social distinctions. Urban life offered unprecedented chances for those with no money or of base social origins to pass themselves off as of superior class. *The Way to be Rich and Respectable* (1775) gave guidance to its readers on how to live like a gentleman with limited means – showing both how the niceties of social gradations were expressed through the minutiae of outward display and deportment, and how this in turn could be exploited to make a life lived on £200 pa appear like that of a gentleman on £400. The huge volume of literature produced in this period, defining genteel behaviour and warning against the dangers of social mobility, is an index of the levels of anxiety reached. As Matthew Bramble complained in Smollett's novel *Humphry Clinker,* 'The gayest places of public entertainment are filled with fashionable figures; which, upon inquiry, will be found to be journeymen taylors, serving-men, and abigails, disguised like their betters'.[99] If we lay aside the question of participation by deception, there were aspects of polite culture which even someone on the very fringes of the middling sort, with a wage of £40–£60 pa, could engage in. Novels could be purchased albeit second-hand for one shilling or less, while prints and woodcuts were less than six pence, and newspapers and periodicals could be read in the numerous coffee houses for the price of a drink. Seats at the theatre could be bought for as little as three pence, and the gardens of Vauxhall were not beyond even a servant's wages.

98. John Seed, '"Commerce and the Liberal Arts": the political economy of art in Manchester, 1775–1860', in John Seed and J. Wolff (eds), *The Commerce of Capital: Art, Power and the Nineteenth-Century Middle Class* (Manchester, 1988), p. 67.
99. Tobias Smollett, *Humphry Clinker,* (ed.) Angus Ross, Penguin edn (repr. 1988), p. 119.

But conversely, as Matthew Bramble's comments would lead one to expect, there were still many ways in which the demarcation lines could be drawn. If one social barrier was broken down, another could soon be erected in its place. The commonest form of exercising social exclusivity was of course through a prohibitive pricing policy. The entrance fee of one guinea, plus the additional annual subscription of a further guinea, for the Bristol Library Society, in 1773, rising to four guineas in 1798, automatically excluded large numbers of the middling sort.[100] In other societies, entrance was balloted for, or was by invitation only, and a rigorous screening took place. Theatres were attended by people from across the social spectrum, but within the theatre there was a complex hierarchy in the seating arrangements, enforced by the grading of ticket prices. The 'company', the wealthy patrons of the play, were seated far removed from the rowdier areas comprising the cheapest standing tickets, while the nobility were literally the most socially elevated in the boxes. In effect, there were several social worlds within one playhouse. The same pattern repeated itself in the grandstand at the race-courses, and even at the assembly room. Many towns held separate assemblies for the tradesmen and gentlemen to obviate the need for painful occasions of social mixing, and in spa towns servants and tradesmen were excluded from mixing with 'the company' at all times. The success of conduct and etiquette books, in laying down the norms of behaviour for a strictly stratified society, is a reflection of both the inherent social mobility of urban society and the widespread consensus as to the importance placed on preserving social distinctions.[101]

In an influential interpretation of urban culture in this period, Peter Borsay encapsulated this shift towards a more socially differentiated society, through a study of urban rituals.[102] He identified three different types; the popular, the civic and the elite. The popular comprised the more licentious celebrations or festivals, anniversaries and the traditional entertainments of cock fighting, bull baiting and the riotous proceedings at wakes and fairs. The civic rituals had originally been communal events on civic occasions, such as the installation of the new mayor, which drew upon the citizens at large in processions and communal feasting. Elite rituals

100. Paul Kaufman, *Borrowings from the Bristol Library, 1773–84: A Unique Record of Reading Vogues* (Charlottesville, 1960).

101. Marjorie Morgan, *Manners, Morals and Class in England, 1774–1858* (1994).

102. Peter Borsay, '"All the Town's a Stage": Urban ritual and ceremony, 1660–1800', in Clark (ed.), *Transformation of English Provincial Towns*, pp. 228–56.

were of more recent origin and comprised those activities which involved the gentry and the urban elites in polite entertainment, but from which those below were excluded. Borsay argues that the civic aspect became less important and withdrew upon itself, losing its communal aspect. Civic feasts metamorphosed into private dinners for the corporation behind closed doors, and the pageantry of civic festivals was curtailed on the grounds of economy and social order. Popular culture, meanwhile, flourished. It lost some of its rural components and became informed by a higher degree of literacy and more deliberate organization. At the same time, it became increasingly marginalized, regarded with disdain by those who were participating in the polite recreations of elite activity.[103] Much of popular culture was centred traditionally upon the alehouse which, apart from being a necessary source of alcohol, was the focal point for all kinds of social activity, and provided services such as loans, acting as pawnbrokers or labour exchange. The middling sort, however, tended to withdraw their patronage to the more decorous inns and taverns, and magistrates attempted to curb the consumption of alcohol by the labouring sort, by reducing the number of licenses issued to alehouses. Bull baiting was suppressed by civic authorities, anxious about the possible threat to public order posed by such outbreaks of barbaric licence, and displaying humanitarian concern for the fate of the innocent bull.[104]

The spread of prosperous suburbs on the edges of towns, offers another indication of this shift towards social differentiation; whereas, in earlier times craftsmen and merchants traders had lived 'above the shop' in the centre of the town, it became customary to move away from the crowded city centre and the noise and the filth into the genteel environs of the suburban villa. Early in the eighteenth century, Henry Bourne, a Newcastle curate, noted, of some former merchant houses in the Close, that, 'Of late years these Houses have been forsaken, and the wealthier Inhabitants have chosen the higher part of the Town'.[105] There was a clear trend for the city centre to become the habitation of the poor, and therefore it became even less desirable as a place to live in. The chronology by which these changes occurred varied from town to

103. C. Phythian Adams, 'Milk and Soot: the changing vocabulary of a popular ritual in Stuart and Hanoverian London', D. Fraser and A. Sutcliffe (eds), *The Pursuit of Urban History* (1983).
104. K. V. Thomas, *Man and the Natural World. Changing Attitudes in England, 1500–1800* Penguin edn (1984), pp. 159–60, 185–8.
105. Henry Bourne, *The History of Newcastle upon Tyne* (Newcastle, 1736), p. 126.

town, but it is clear that a much sharper sense of the divisions within society was emerging; a change which was not noticed without regret by contemporaries, who nostalgically cherished the ideal of a unified community. Antiquaries began to record the local festivals and rituals, such as Hock Tide or Shrove Tuesday. Henry Bourne published the first study of this kind, *Antiquitates Vulgares* in 1725, but it achieved much wider popularity, and attracted far many more imitators, when another Novocastrian, John Brand, published a greatly enlarged version, *Observations on Popular Antiquities* (1777). Studies such as these were infused with a nostalgia for a lost golden age of a community united in the common weal. Ahistorical though their interpretations may appear today, they show that contemporaries too were aware of a greater social fragmentation in urban society. As John Throsby wrote, of bygone customs in Leicester, they were 'a scene, upon the whole of joy, the governing and the governed in the habits of freedom, enjoying together an innocent and recreating amusement, seeming to unite them in bonds of friendship rather than to embitter their days with discord and disunities'.[106]

The cultural boundaries between the labouring sort and those above them, from the midding sort up, were being drawn with greater precision and rigidity. Social interaction between the poor and their betters increasingly took place in the context of situations which put the poor in a position of dependence or subordination. As the distributors of charity and poor relief, visitors to the workhouse or as governors of the infirmary, the social elites could distance themselves from the poor and exercise their control and authority over them. If the middling sort were sober, moral and industrious, and the aristocracy privileged, extravagant and immoral, the labouring sort were regarded with suspicion for their supposed idleness and propensity to violence. The poor had fewer of the refinements of civilization, and were therefore more easily ruled by vulgar passion rather than reason and sentiment. They posed a permanent threat to property and to the social order. Poor rates hit the middling sort hardest, falling most heavily on urban dwellers. Therefore any behaviour which seemed likely to increase the burden of parochial taxation was regarded with deep suspicion. The success of the friendly society movement and the provident savings banks, from the latter part of the eighteenth century onwards, owed much to the support of middle class philanthropists. They actively

106. John Throsby, *The History and Antiquities of the Town of Leicester* (Leicester, 1791), p. 166.

concerned themselves with their promotion, as a means of reducing the numbers dependent on poor relief, and of encouraging what they deemed to be desirable forms of behaviour among the recipients.[107] Moralists condemned the supposed profligacy of the urban poor, who spent their wages on gin or at the alehouse, or who frittered their money on tea and sugar rather than saving it against need. John Clayton warned the poor of Manchester that they had brought their misery upon themselves with their feckless idleness, wasting their wages on luxuries and staying in bed all morning during the winter rather than getting out to work.[108]

The rural poor, by contrast, were not exposed to the same temptations, and were generally discussed as 'deserving'. The poor always comprised the majority of the population, and could therefore challenge those in authority through sheer force of numbers. In a town, where there was so much property tied up in moveable goods and buildings, this was of considerable significance; it was well known what destruction a mob could wreak when out of control. The Sacheverell riots of 1709, the Gordon Riots of 1780, and Church and King riots of the 1790s, were the most notorious and extreme examples of a kind of rioting which was endemic in urban society, and which struck fear into the hearts of eighteenth-century townsmen. Any behaviour, on the part of the lower orders, which seemed likely to lead to riotous behaviour was therefore inherently dangerous. This was one reason why traditional activities, such as bull baiting and cock fighting, were steadily banished from the urban environment. Even an event such as a celebratory illumination of the town, when lights were placed in all the windows, could be potentially explosive; not only because of the increased risk of fire, but because the enthusiasm of the lower orders might lead them to stone the windows of anyone who had failed to signify their approbation in the appropriate manner. Control of the lower orders was therefore an underlying theme in all the moral reform programmes directed at improving the labouring sort, and in the enactment of bye-laws prohibiting any kind of activity which might be considered to encourage riotous behaviour. The paranoia of the authorities steadily increased, with the rise of working class radicalism and popular movements from the late eighteenth century. By the early nineteenth century the urban work-force, spawned by the growth of

107. P. H. J. H. Gosden, *Self-Help. Voluntary Associations in Nineteenth-Century Britain* (1973), pp. 1–34.

108. John Clayton, *Friendly Advice to the Poor, written and published at the request of the late and present officers of the town of Manchester* (Manchester, 1755), pp. 5, 29, 35–6.

factory production in towns such as Manchester, inspired fear among many commentators; in 1836 it was observed that:

> Manufacturers naturally condense a vast population within a narrow circuit; they afford every facility for secret cabal and co-operative union among the work people; they communicate intelligence and energy to the vulgar mind; they supply, in their liberal wages, the pecuniary sinews of contention should a spirit of revolt become general; and the ample means of inflaming their passions and depraving their appetites, by sensual indulgences of the lowest kind.[109]

The newly grown industrial towns of the nineteenth century created an urban society which departed radically from anything which had gone before in many ways, but perhaps the most significant was the transformation of substantial elements of urban society into a bipartite system of employer and employee, a society in which the socio-economic divisions which we have been discussing would have been felt at their most acute. Society may have become more generally polite, but there were definite limits to how far down the social scale politeness could penetrate. The polarization of society, therefore, was perhaps inherent in the spread of politeness.

Distinctions of Gender

As we have seen, urban society became more clearly stratified along class lines, and the culture of the labouring and middling sort diverged more markedly. Socio-economic divisions were inherent in the structure of urban society, but they were modified by other factors, the most obvious of which was gender. In the following section we will look more closely at the position of women in towns, and the advantages and disadvantages which urban living posed for women, as opposed to men. Much of the foregoing discussion was broadly applicable to the experiences of both men and women, but many of the generalizations made above, and in other accounts of urban society, implicitly ignore women. It is therefore a valuable exercise to consider more precisely how women fared in the urban context, both in the workplace and in leisured pursuits, and the difference that considerations of gender made in the urban environment.

---

109. Quoted in P. Gaskell, *Artisans and Machinery: the Moral and Physical Condition of the Manufacturing Population considered with reference to Mechanical Substitutes for Human Labour* (1836), p. vi.

Historians have found that there was a significant demographic expansion of the female population, producing a predominance of women, particularly in large towns. Bath's population was 61 per cent female, and only Oxford (populated by celibate dons and male undergraduates) in the 1801 census, actually had a male majority. At least part of the explanation for this imbalance may reside with the attractions of the urban lifestyle for women. Contemporaries certainly blamed women for succumbing more easily to the attractions of town, and enticing their professedly unwilling husbands there, to engage in a round of expense, frivolity and luxury. Women's supposedly weaker faculties of reason and heightened emotional susceptibility made them uniquely vulnerable to the glittering allure of the city and urban luxury. Satirists and moralists warned that life in the town offered women the chance to escape the confines of patriarchal authority, and many lines were penned warning husbands of the dangers of bringing their wives to town. Characters such as Lady Booby in Fielding's *Joseph Andrews*, or Mr Pinchwife's young bride in Wycherly's *The Country Wife*, embodied these anxieties all too well. Evidence of this kind should not be taken too seriously, for it was deeply rooted in a long literary tradition. However, the attractions of urban living, specifically for women, do deserve to be taken more seriously. Some historiography has suggested that the role of middling women, in particular, became more restricted in this period, and that they were increasingly confined to the home in the domestic sphere, while being excluded from a male 'public sphere'.[110] Whatever the merits of this interpretation for a later period, it is clearly deeply problematic when applied to the long eighteenth century.[111] Women had active social lives, which they described at length to each other in letters and diaries, clearly showing them participating in a 'public sphere' alongside men. In towns, women were able to go out shopping, attend concerts, the theatre, assemblies, card evenings, take walks in the public gardens and squares, and visit circulating libraries. It has been suggested that middling women would have spent even less time in the home than their husbands because they were absent for much of the day,

110. Leonore Davidoff and Catherine Hall, *Family Fortunes: Men and Women of the English Middle Class, 1780–1850* (1987).

111. A. J. Vickery, 'Golden Age to Separate Spheres? A review of the categories and chronology of English women's history', *HJ*, xxxvi (1993). Vickery develops her arguments at greater length and with fuller contextualization in *The Gentleman's Daughter. Women's Lives in Georgian England* (1998); see also Hannah Barker and Elaine Chalus, *Gender in Eighteenth-Century England. Roles, Representations and Responsibilities* (1997), pp. 1–27.

shopping and running errands.[112] Unaccompanied women after dark might be frowned upon, but together, or in the company of a servant, women were able to venture forth 'on the town' and enjoy novelty and entertainment outside the home with a greater freedom than they would be allowed in the Victorian era.[113] The contrast would have been particularly marked for those women from the upper classes, accustomed to spending at least part of the year on the country estate, where the range of activities available to them was strictly limited. Notions of feminine propriety excluded them from much of rural public life, and left them with a very limited range of activities and diversions. Single women and widows were able to live independently on limited means with far greater ease in the town than in the country, often combining together in 'spinster clusters' to share expenses and chores. The West End of London in the later eighteenth century was dominated by aristocratic ladies of leisure – droves of dowagers and unmarried women were pensioned off by their families to live an inoffensive life in the safety of London Society. Beyond the idiosyncratic world of the *beau monde*, women might be excluded from the majority of coffee houses and the homo-social world of the tavern or the club, but, in turn, the circulating library was acknowledged to be an essentially feminine preserve, and they too were able to establish their own clubs and societies and ran their own charities, particularly concerning themselves with lying-in charities and friendly societies for women.[114]

Lower down the social scale, female migrants were attracted to towns by employment opportunities. More commercialized techniques of agricultural production had led to women being squeezed out of the agrarian labour force, and more specialized manufacturing processes excluded those who had no skilled training. Better opportunities were available in the town, where domestic service offered the prospect of employment for even the unskilled, and where pay exceeded that which could be earned in the country districts.[115] We have already noted that a higher proportion of

112. Margaret Hunt, 'Wife beating, domesticity, and women's independence in eighteenth-century London', *Gender and History*, 4 (1992), p. 12.

113. These arguments are developed at much greater length in Joyce Ellis, '"On the Town". Women in Augustan England 1688–1820', *History Today* (Dec. 1995), pp. 20–7.

114. Vickery, *The Gentleman's Daughter*, pp. 250–77.

115. Robert B. Shoemaker, *Gender in English Society, 1650–1850* (1998), ch. 5 offers the most up to date survey on women and work, and an excellent review of the recent historiography. The opportunities available to women in towns clearly has implications for the debate over the emergence of 'separate spheres'.

domestic servants were female than male; during the eighteenth century there was a gradual feminization of domestic service so that by the nineteenth century it had become an almost exclusively female occupation. By 1840, in York, nearly three-quarters of all female employment was in domestic service.[116] In large households, women might be employed alongside men; the preponderance of women came from the increasing number of small middling households who could afford to employ only one servant, and whose origins were probably little different from those whom they employed. For such families, the attraction of cheap, unskilled female labour was obvious, especially given the increased amount of housework which was created by a greater degree of domestic comfort and furnishings.

Domestic service was not the only occupation open to women, and moreover, those who were over 35 years old were unlikely to find employment in service. They were more likely to be found in the clothing trade, doing sewing, laundry or cleaning.[117] Women from middling families might be apprenticed to mantua makers or milliners, but for many labouring women the only option took the form of what was effectively sweated labour, producing the ready-made clothing which became one of the principal commodities of the consumer revolution. Wages were pitifully low, as employers exploited the fact that women were beyond the protection of guild regulation; a fact which also gave employers more flexibility in introducing new labouring practices. Arguably, it was the plentiful supply of cheap female labour, rather than technological innovation, which facilitated the increased production of the early industrial revolution.[118] The numbers involved can never be accurately assessed, as in most cases work was put out in the home, and records do not survive. Similarly, suggestive hints indicate the extensive involvement of women in the second-hand clothing trade, particularly as pawnbrokers.[119] Employment prospects for women were certainly better in towns, but it was nevertheless a vulnerable lifestyle not least for servants. It was rare to spend more than one or two years in the same household. Servants were poorly paid, with little chance to accumulate savings, and were acutely vulnerable, being

116. Alan Armstrong, *Stability and Change in an English Country Town* (1974), p. 29, quoted in Hill, *Servants*, p. 15.

117. Shoemaker, *Gender in English Society*, p. 178.

118. Maxine Berg, 'What difference did women's work make to the industrial revolution?', *History Workshop Journal*, 35 (1993), pp. 22–44.

119. Beverly Lemire, *Dress, Culture and Commerce. The English Clothing Trade before the Factory, 1660–1800* (Manchester, 1997).

young and single, and without the protection of friends or family. They were defenceless against the sexual advances of their employers and were easily dismissed. Finding alternative employment was not always straightforward, and for many the slide into prostitution and petty crime could hardly be avoided.

Prostitution was a peculiarly urban vice, and one which caused contemporaries considerable alarm, not least because of the alarming spread of venereal disease. The fate of the innocent country wench who arrived in London and fell into the hands of a procuress, whose story Hogarth told in the *Harlot's Progress,* reflected society's anxiety about the immorality of city life. But it also bears witness to the precariousness of the position of the unprotected female in a large town. As Henry Mayhew recognised in the nineteenth century, the high level of prostitution was due to 'the low rate of wages that the female classes of this great city [London] receive, in return for the most arduous and wearisome labour'.[120] Any woman who dressed gaudily, and walked the streets alone at dusk or later, was liable to be apprehended on suspicion of streetwalking. Magistrates and constables could exercise considerable discretion in their powers of arrest and detainment – and were not always above suspicion in their implementation. The University Proctors in Oxford, who exercised similar powers in the interests of safeguarding the morals of the undergraduates, were notorious for apprehending innocent women and abusing their rights of breaking and entry (which allowed them to enter any property in which they suspected there might be prostitutes, even against the wishes of the house holder). Courtesans and upper class prostitutes might do extremely well in their profession, but for most street walkers it was a life of misery and degradation.

Religion and Society in the Urban Community

From our examination of government and politics in the preceding chapters it has already become clear that religious issues were fundamental to many of the political and social divisions which fractured urban society. There is an irony here, in that traditionally the church was supposed to be the focal point in the community, bringing together all believers in the expression of brotherly love and

120. Quoted in Shoemaker, *Gender in English Society*, p. 76.

unity. In this section we will be looking at how religious forms and ideals affected urban life. At the beginning of our period, it was still plausible to argue that religion was primarily an expression of corporate identity, rather than simply a matter of personal belief. By the nineteenth century, this attitude had been substantially modified, but still retained considerable force, in that one's religious affiliation was still one of the most important factors in shaping social and political identities. Religious and secular authority was mutually complementary; the one upheld the other. The alliance of church and state was fully realised in the urban equivalent of 'squarsons', such as Samuel Williamson, vicar of Congleton 1785–1831 and mayor on two occasions, or Vaughan Thomas, rector of a hamlet just outside Oxford, but also extremely active in local government within the city, and chairman of the Board of Health during the cholera epidemic of 1832. In the early eighteenth century, the Protestant ideal of the godly magistracy still had considerable bearing upon the corporations of many towns, where the common council was virtually coterminous with the vestry, the mayor signed the vestry minutes, and the most important events of the civic year were enacted in the church.[121] The civic calendar was undoubtedly becoming secularized, but the church service or sermon was still an integral part of most celebratory or commemorative occasions. The swearing in of the new mayor was solemnized by a service which all the members of the corporation attended in their ceremonial robes and civic regalia, making a statement of their authority and standing within the community, and the church was deeply implicated in upholding this established order. Infirmaries, hospitals and schools all profited from annual charity sermons given for their benefit. Few public institutions could be opened, and few national anniversaries marked, without the ringing of church bells or a service of thanksgiving in the presence of the civic dignitaries.

However, the meeting of church and state in one building could be fraught with difficulties. Since the Reformation, in many urban parishes the civic elite had held the right of appointment to benefices and lectureships, providing yet more opportunities for the pursuit of political conflicts through the institutions of the church. High and low church divisions within a corporation would be highlighted over the appointment to a benefice. Once appointed, it was easy for the incumbent to fall out with his patrons. The vicar of

121. W. M. Jacob, 'Church and borough: King's Lynn, 1700–1750', in W. M. Jacob and Nigel Yates (eds), *Crown and Mitre: Religion and Society in Northern Europe since the Reformation* (Woodbridge, 1993), pp. 63–80.

Congleton was engaged in a long drawn out quar
tion during the 1770s; he accused them of enc
and undermining his authority, while they acc
too much for burial fees and refusing to visit
this, were mutual suspicions over churchm
ate extent of the respective spheres of the
the jealousy between the cathedral chapter and co
unseemly quarrels over precedence. The cathedral clergy cha
the right of the corporation to have the sword of state carried
before them in processions in the cathedral. Eventually the corporation went to the lengths of building their own private chapel
where their secular authority, embodied by the sword, could be
asserted uncontested.[123] This confrontation epitomises the extent
to which the church occupied not just a role of spiritual leadership,
but had extensive claims to secular jurisdiction which left it deeply
implicated in the political and administrative life of the town.

The Anglican parish was not just a communion of believers, but
a 'unit of obligation' and often the most coherent organization in
the town. Although, in administrative terms, the urban parish was
generally less important than its rural counterpart, every parish was
locked into networks of power and influence within the community
by virtue of the powers inherent in the vestry. The power to levy
rates, to dispose of benefactions, and to manage church property
could become politically significant – even conducting marriages
and services of baptism could acquire political overtones, in that
the individual thereby acquired his settlement in that parish. In a
pot-walloper franchise, where all inhabitants not in receipt of poor
relief were eligible for the vote, the issue of who was 'on the parish'
could be of crucial significance. Many petitions of 'undue return'
were made after elections, on the basis of allegations that votes had
been cast by people 'on the parish'. Clergymen, when resident, were
generally figures of some standing in the community. Urban parishes
tended to attract the more highly educated and ambitious priests,
as there was more to offer in terms of career advancement and
alternative sources of income, such as teaching or medicine – many
urban appointments were attached to the mastership of a grammar
school, for example, with the opportunity of taking additional private pupils. Such men, who commanded respect by virtue of their

122. W. B. Stephens, Robert W. Dunning, Joan P. Alcock and M. W. Greenslade,
'Religion in Congleton', in W. B. Stephens (ed.), *The History of Congleton* (Manchester, 1970), p. 217.
123. J. Latimer, *Annals of Bristol in the Eighteenth Century* (Bristol, 1893), p. 126.

education and their social status, exercised considerable influ-
over their parishioners through the medium of the pulpit,
d many, like Dean Tucker of Bristol, engaged freely in pamphlet
warfare and political debate. In view of this, magistrates were, not
surprisingly, often unwilling to leave the management of parish
affairs in the hands of the vicar. Vestry and minister could easily
become caught up in the politics of urban society, in an age when
divisions between high and low church parties, or Anglicans and
Dissenters, were of primary importance in determining political
affiliations. John Triffitt's analysis of such confrontations, which
were being waged between local government and church-based
groups in the southwest of England, can be paralleled in towns
across the country, throughout our period. In early eighteenth-
century Plymouth, factionalism within the corporation was played
out as rivalry between the different parishes, with the ascendant
party among the councillors effectively hounding the obdurate
curate of the parish into 'opposition'. They claimed that 'the
leaders and better sort of them confess they do Not go there out
of Devotion, but purely to Create and keep up a faction'.[124] We
need only to look at the end of the eighteenth century and the nineteenth century to see how this tradition was perpetuated in radical
opposition to corporations and oligarchy. The vestry, or as it was
increasingly termed, 'the public meeting' was crucial in organizing
opposition movements in many towns, whether it was a matter of
blocking an improvement act or petitioning for parliamentary
reform.[125]

It would, however, be wrong to focus exclusively on the tensions
within urban society, which were created by religious pluralism and
the friction between church and state. The parish church was still
a crucial focal point for the community, although clearly, as the
sophistication of urban society progressed, it was faced with far more
competition than in earlier periods. In crudely materialistic terms,
if we look at the money invested in public building, the church
attracted more money than any other category. In a study of twelve
towns in the West Riding, it was found that of the £1.25 million
spent on public buildings between 1700–1840, 42 per cent was
spent on building or renovating churches. Between 1700–1800 over

124. John Triffitt, 'Believing and belonging. Church behaviour in Plymouth and
Dartmouth, 1710–1730', in S. Wright (ed.), *Parish, Church and People. Local Studies in
Lay Religion, 1350–1750* (Hutchinson, 1988), p. 190.
125. E. S. Chalk, 'Tiverton letters and papers, 1724–1843', *Notes and Queries*, 170
(1936), p. 93; Anthony Howe, *The Cotton Masters, 1830–60* (Oxford, 1984), p. 136.

130 churches were built, or substantially reconstructed, in provincial towns outside London. Most cost at least £3,000, but some, such as All Saints in Newcastle, cost as much as £27,000.[126] Most of this money came from local sources – loans raised on the credit of church rates, and through public subscription, with some wealthy individuals subscribing upwards of £100. Church building attracted even more investment in the early nineteenth century, as awareness of the need to provide for the urban masses was heightened by evangelical activities. The 1818 Church Building Act provided a fund of £1 million and an additional £500,000 in 1824. By offering subsidies, it did much to facilitate the building of new churches in industrial areas where there was no other provision, but the burden of finance still lay on local initiative. In Oxford during the 1820s, one church, St Clement's, was built entirely anew, and extensive repairs and alterations were being carried out upon six others, while in Sheffield, where there was a real dearth in parochial provision, six churches were erected during this period. As the influence of puritanical asceticism, reacting against catholic baroque excesses in the matter of church furnishings, died down, numerous churches were equipped with organs and organists. New peals of bells were installed and stained glass windows were acquired – and almost always financed through private gifts or public subscription. The church clearly had a considerable command upon the allegiance of its parishioners, for such sums to be forthcoming, when there were many other calls upon their philanthropy, not to mention the other opportunities for investment and conspicuous display. Amidst so much that was new in urban society, the church still continued to operate as an important focus for the community and centre for middling sort activity.

Urban Dissent

The identity between church and borough was symbolically brought to an end when the Municipal Corporations Act destroyed the hegemony of the Anglican corporations. Mounting pressure came from Dissenters, who found themselves still excluded from the avenues of municipal authority, even after the repeal of the Test and Corporation Acts in 1828, and this contributed to the decision to overhaul the

126. C. W. Chalkin, 'The financing of church building in the provincial towns of eighteenth-century England', in Clark (ed.), *Transformation of English Provincial Towns*, p. 285.

unreformed system. Municipal authority now derived its legitimacy by virtue of being freely elected by the inhabitant ratepayers, under a constitution sanctioned by parliamentary legislation, rather than drawing on the ideals of the godly magistracy. But even before the legislation of 1835 finally dismantled the institutional structure, there were few, if any, towns where the Church of England had retained its supremacy unchallenged. Even in Oxford, where the university was the seat of high church Anglicanism, there was always a dissenting congregation, albeit a small one. In early nineteenth-century Westmoreland, for example, one fifth of all Dissenters in the county of Cumberland were concentrated within the town of Kendal (with a population of just over 11,000 in 1831), representing nine different denominations, in addition to the church of England; Quakers, Unitarians, Inghamites, Independents, Roman Catholics, Glassites, Wesleyan Methodists, Scotch Seceders and Primitive Methodist.[127]

The Dissenters had emerged as a much more palpable presence in English towns following the Toleration Act in 1689, which allowed them to practise openly in licensed meeting houses. This gave rise to Anglican fears of an increase in Nonconformity, which, coupled with the spread of low church latitudinarianism under the Whig ascendancy, had provoked the cry of 'Church in Danger' among those of the high church party. In fact, the numbers of Dissenters seem to have declined in most towns during the first part of the eighteenth century. The falling-off was particularly marked among the upper reaches of urban society – by the second half of the eighteenth century dissent had become more characteristic of the lesser middling sort. In the later eighteenth century, however, the numbers of Dissenters began once more to increase. Not among the Presbyterians and the Unitarians, but amongst the Congregationalists, the Baptists and the Methodists. Although Wesley had insisted that the Methodist church was within the Anglican establishment, after his death in 1791, all pretence at maintaining this fiction was abandoned, and the Methodist church was recognised as a separate institution. Its remarkable expansion in the years following must therefore be chalked up to the success of Nonconformity rather than Anglicanism. The ability of Methodists to move in to those urban areas where the provisions of the Anglican church were weakest, in centres such as Bristol or Newcastle, offered a profound challenge to Anglican complacency. By the time of the

127. Nicholson, *Annals of Kendal*, p. 133; J. D. Marshall and Carol A. Dyhouse, 'Social transition in Kendal and Westmoreland', *Northern History* (1976), pp. 127–57.

1851 religious census, it was found that, whereas the overall population had risen by fifteen per cent since 1801, the Nonconformist
congregations had increased by 97 per cent. This increase did not
take place exclusively among the urban population, however. In
fact, a comparison of the distribution of dissent in 1715 and 1851,
indicates very little change with respect to the proportion of Nonconformists in towns, although the relative distribution between
the different denominations had changed. The biggest increase in
new dissent in the early nineteenth century had not been in towns
at all, but had taken place in rural areas and industrializing villages
such as South Wales and in the townships of Lancashire.[128] Old
dissent was still characteristically urban, but the spread of the
Baptists, Congregationalists and above all methodism had ended
the traditional relationship between towns and nonconformity. Most
explanations for the attraction of methodism and nonconformity
to the working classes and specifically urban populations, have concentrated upon sociological factors – the need for the element of
'belonging' and social structure, which these movements offered
amidst the anomie and social dislocation of urban life. Alternatively,
the emphasis is placed upon the appeal of a religion which offered
spiritual independence and autonomy in a strictly deferential and
hierarchical society. Hence, the adoption of methodism, or Nonconformity could be construed as an act of political defiance, and a
rejection of the authority of the governing elite, whose religion was
that of the Anglican church. Psychological explanations have also
been forthcoming; E. P. Thompson famously identified the 'chiliasm
of despair', which enabled Methodist revivalism to reap the benefits
of the defeat of radicalism and protest in the 1790s.[129]

Ultimately, the fundamental inability of the Anglican church to
provide for the populations of urbanizing areas was the structural
premise on which all these interpretations must rest. It is clear that
the inflexibility of the parochial structure was an important contributory factor in determining the relative success or failure of the
Anglican church in retaining the allegiance of the urban population. In the nineteenth century, the structure was still pretty much
what it had been in the Middle Ages; Norfolk had 731 parishes,
over 50 of which were in Norwich alone, whereas in the entire
county of Lancashire there were merely 70. Given that it was necessary to go through the time and expense of acquiring an act of

128. Michael Watts, *The Dissenters*, 2 vols (Oxford, 1995), ii.
129. For an introduction to these issues see David Hempton, *Methodism and Politics in British Society, 1750–1850* (Stanford CA, 1984), pp. 75–7.

parliament before a new parish could even be established, it is hardly surprising that the spontaneity of the nonconformist tradition of setting up a chapel or meeting house wherever there was need, was considerably more successful in the harvesting of men's souls. As the mayor of Liverpool explained in a letter to the Home Office in 1792, in which he sought assistance in constructing parish churches for the industrial townships of Lancashire, 'in all these places [there] are nothing but Methodist and other meeting houses, and as the people in the country are in general disposed to go to some place of worship on the Sunday, they go there because there is no other'.[130] Establishing a new parish or dividing an old one involved considerable expense and, as usual, ran up against the barrier of vested interests when incumbents objected to seeing their surplice fees and incomes halved. Nor were there enough clergy to serve in the parishes – graduates of Oxford and Cambridge were apparently more likely to feel a vocation to serve in the south rather than north of the Trent. In Rochdale, in 1818, there were 89 nonconformist preachers and clergy, holding 66 services a week, whereas the Church of England could field only five clergymen to hold six services, distributed between three churches. The problem was not simply an absence of churches; there was a serious shortage of space within the church. Pews were property to be bought, leased, or sold, and pew rents were an important source of income – however, they took up almost all the space in the nave, leaving little room for free seating for the poor. It was calculated that in Sheffield, which had a population of over 60,000 poor in 1821, there were less than 300 free seats in the parish church. In the 80 parishes in London, only one-ninth of the population could be accommodated. However, even the flexibility and dynamism of revivalist Nonconformity failed to meet the challenge of those areas which the Anglican church had conspicuously failed to provide for. Churchgoing was never a universal practice, and although we do not have the benefit of a religious census for our period, it is clear that in many urban areas the rates of both church and chapel attendance could be as low as 12 per cent among the labouring sort in the early nineteenth century.[131] The poorest parishes in the largest towns proved to be as impervious to the evangelizing efforts of Nonconformists as they had been to the Anglican ministry.

The success of dissent among the working population meant that in many areas the religious divisions of church or chapel came to

130. Quoted in Watts, *The Dissenters*, ii, p. 123.
131. Hopkins, *Rise of the Manufacturing Town*, p. 162.

reflect the social division of employer and employed. However, this was far from being universally the case, and, as we have already seen, there were powerful and influential dissenting interests amongst the elites in many towns. Nonconformity was not an insuperable barrier to office-holding. By practising occasional conformity, it was possible to combine a career in public life while continuing to remain outside the Anglican communion. A number of corporations included Dissenters among their number, and a few were effectively dominated by the dissenting interest for years at a time. In Bridport in the 1770s, it was reported that an 'anti-Test' was in operation, whereby no one was admitted to the corporation unless a Dissenter.[132] Nineteen out of 57 active members of the corporation in Poole were Dissenters in 1740–1, and Dissenters continued to be admitted until the 1770s. Sixty-six of Nottingham's mayors were Presbyterian in the eighteenth century, and Dissenters filled the mayoralty for a number of years in Bristol, Coventry, Norwich and Bridgewater. Indeed, so many of the magistracy were Dissenters in Bridgewater, that when the Presbyterian meeting house was rebuilt in the 1780s, a long pew for the use of the corporation was specifically provided.[133] It was predominantly Presbyterians who took advantage of practising occasional conformity – other denominations, such as the Congregationalists and Baptists, had less flexible consciences and far fewer of their number were to be found in civic office. Their opposition was not unfounded, for it is clear that many of those who were reabsorbed into the established church had found their passage eased by the practice of occasional conformity; once elected to office it involved but a simple transition for occasional conformity to become permanent. In 1715, estimates put the number of adult Dissenters in Exeter at around 4,500. By 1744, the returns of the Anglican clergy indicate that numbers had fallen to 1,610, the loss having been sustained chiefly from among the ranks of the merchant elite.[134] Those who refused to conform might find themselves subjected to fines for refusal to take up office, since it was argued that if a Dissenter could conform in order to take up office, he should not therefore be able to escape all civic obligations simply by refusing to practise occasional conformity. Some corporations, of which London was the most notorious example, used this as a strategy for raising money – reputedly raising well over £15,000 between 1689–1754, from £400 fines inflicted on those who refused

132. Basil Short, *A Respectable Society. Bridport, 1593–1835* (Bradford on Avon, 1976), p. 32.
133. Watts, *The Dissenters*, i, p. 483.   134. Newton, *Eighteenth-Century Exeter*, p. 76.

to serve the office of sheriff. It should also be born in mind that it was always possible for Dissenters to assume an active role in local affairs, without the need to practice occasional conformity at all. Parochial offices did not require the swearing of any oaths, and it was quite usual for a Dissenter to hold the offices of churchwarden and overseer of the poor. Martin Dunsford of Tiverton, a Dissenter, was churchwarden four times and portreeve of the manor of Tiverton three times, and also served as overseer of the poor. We have already seen that many of the improvement commissions, societies, and philanthropic organizations were often dominated by Dissenters, who found an opportunity to exercise leadership in the public sphere unencumbered by religious restrictions.[135]

We should always be wary of over-emphasising the extent to which religious differences polarized urban society. Dissent and anglicanism were far from being incompatible, and the dividing line which could on occasion be insuperable, could equally be very permeable. Anglicans in Poole often attended the evening service at the Presbyterian chapel because there was none in their own church. Methodism is conventionally portrayed as drawing many away from the established church, but in fact it exercised a complementary ministry in many areas – as indeed Wesley had intended. The vitality of the hymn singing and the immediacy of the sermons offered a counterbalance to the more formalised ritual of the Anglican service. There were many who, like the merchant William Dyer of Bristol, took advantage of the religious pluralism of urban society to experiment with a variety of spiritual experiences. In his diary he records attending Anglican services, Methodist meetings, visiting Quakers in Liverpool and listening to a Baptist preacher from America.[136] The vicar of St Alphege, Canterbury commented upon a similar ecumenical spirit in 1784, 'Many persons in all parishes in this town go to the Cathedral in the morning, to the Presbyterian meeting in the afternoon, and to the Methodist meeting at night'.[137] The eighteenth-century emphasis on toleration, and horror of enthusiasm, allowed a more conciliatory attitude to prevail between Anglicans and Dissenters. Ideally, the common good of the town came before the

---

135. See, for example, the Taunton Market House Trust discussed above, p. 50.
136. Derek Frank Beamish, 'The Parliamentary and Municipal History of the Borough of Poole, Dorset, c. 1740–1840', Univ. of Southampton M.Phil. thesis (1982), 34; BCL Mss B20095–7, Diary of William Dyer.
137. Quoted in Jeremy Gregory, 'Canterbury and the *Ancien Régime*: the Dean and Chapter, 1660–1828', in P. Collinson, M. Sparkes and N. Ramsay (eds), *A History of Canterbury Cathedral* (1995), p. 234.

pursuit of narrow interests, of which sectarianism was one, and the day-to-day management of local affairs was not to be undermined by religious feuds or party strife.[138]

Apparent sectarianism could be misleading – it is important not to confuse cause and effect when identifying religious exclusivity. Families and business partners often shared the same religious persuasion, and a similarity in religious outlook often led to the same political stance. As the town clerk of Bridport judiciously commented to the Royal Commissioners, on the alleged religious exclusivity of the dissenting corporation, 'It is probable that consanguinity and similarity of sentiment on Religious and Political matters may have had their influence in Elections – Small bodies would naturally wish to add to their number those who are least likely to produce disunion among them'.[139] Religion was just one of a variety of factors which must be taken into account when trying to unravel the groupings and affiliations of local politics. Indeed, civic interest could overcome religious rifts. Interdenominational activity, particularly in the area of philanthropy, became increasingly common in the later eighteenth and nineteenth centuries. Dissenters and Anglicans from the middling sort united in promoting schemes for the moral and physical improvement of their towns, and joined together in preaching Christian values and encouraging obedience and morality among the labouring sort, and upholding the social order. Sunday schools, for example, were often established on an interdenominational basis, even in traditionally high church Tory centres, such as Oxford. In Manchester, famous for its deeply divided churchmanship, the sunday school set up in 1784 brought together Anglicans, Nonconformists and Roman Catholics in collaboration.[140] Political and religious differences could be subsumed when faced with a common social problem, such as rising poverty and immorality among the labouring sort. However, in times of heightened religious tension, such as the debates over repeal of the Test and Corporation Acts in the run up to 1828, this ecumenism was always liable to break down.

In this chapter we have focused upon the lines along which urban society could be divided. Socio-economic status and occupation,

138. Peter Clark, 'The civic leaders of Gloucester, 1580–1800', in Clark (ed.), *Transformation of English Provincial Towns*, pp. 327–8; Perry Gauci, *Politics and Society in Great Yarmouth, 1660–1722* (Oxford, 1996), pp. 236–8.

139. *Report of the Royal Commission on Municipal Corporations*, PP (1835), xxiv, p. 1141.

140. James Wheeler, *Manchester: its Political, Social and Commercial History, Ancient and Modern* (Manchester, 1843), pp. 384–9.

gender, and religio-political affiliations combined and interacted to form a highly mutable and complex society. Having established some basic outlines for the sociological diversity within urban society, we will now move on to consider how contemporaries perceived this complex social organism, and the kinds of cultural activity which it manifested.

CHAPTER SEVEN

Urban Culture and the Urban Renaissance

Here humanity attains its most complete development and its most brutish; here civilization makes its miracles, and civilised man is turned back almost into a savage.[1]

The contrast drawn here by de Tocqueville, between the extremes of brutality and civilization to be found within the town, was one which fascinated the eighteenth-century mind, and in this chapter we will be looking more closely at how and why towns aroused such strong reactions, and the place of urban society in the development of eighteenth-century culture. We will begin by considering how the town was perceived in the contemporary imagination, and we shall see that this became an increasingly problematic issue in the latter part of our period. This raises the question of why it was that the nature and influence of urban society were so much debated in contemporary discussions, on issues ranging from political liberty to the nation's morality. We will then look more closely at some of the attractions, which were the occasion for much of the allure and appeal of the town in the eighteenth century, but which did not always meet with unqualified approval. Finally we will consider the timing and incidence of this 'urban renaissance', which will raise the question of to what extent these cultural developments were dominated by the influence of London, or whether there is a case for asserting a greater degree of provincial autonomy.

1. Alexis de Tocqueville, *Journeys to England and America,* (ed.) J. P. Mayer (New York, 1968), p. 96.

Perceptions of the Town

The eighteenth century was an age which was confident in the potential of human society for improvement and the advancement of learning, and for many, these hopes were best realized within the context of the town, and the importance of urban society, as the agent of liberty, prosperity and civilization, was upheld in a vigorous branch of literature.[2] The reading public were well aware that momentous historical events, which had shaped the nation's past, had, as often as not, taken place in towns. The King's seat of government could not be divorced from its urban setting; the important affairs of state, from royal marriages, diplomatic negotiations or the holding of parliaments, had always taken place in towns. Histories of Britain, invariably among the most favoured items in local libraries, accredited towns with a crucial role in breaking the bonds of feudalism, and ending the 'Norman Yoke' which had been imposed upon freeborn Englishmen. Towns were the first havens of liberty, in a society labouring under feudal oppression. The wealth which they generated had always endeared them to kings, who granted them liberties and freedom in return for additional revenue; liberties which were gradually extended to the rest of society. In the eighteenth century, their contribution to national greatness was becoming ever more obvious, as the income from commerce and manufacture rose steadily. Even though land might still retain its primacy as the basis of wealth and financial stability, it was argued that it was the wealth generated by the commerce of towns which underpinned the value of land and which supported the nation's rise to great power status.[3] The rapid growth of towns was in itself an object of wonder and admiration. Visitors commented endlessly upon the industry to be seen in towns, such as Birmingham or Norwich, 'all are in a hurry, running up and down with cloudy looks, and busy faces, loading, carrying and unloading goods and merchandizes of all sorts, from place to place'.[4] Or they reflected upon the obvious signs of opulence and magnificence to be seen in the public buildings or merchant houses of towns such

2. The importance of ideas of progress and improvement are discussed in David Spadafora, *The Idea of Progress in Eighteenth-Century Britain* (New Haven, 1990).

3. A. Anderson, *An Historical and Chronological Deduction of the Origin of Commerce*, 2 vols (1764), i, p. xii.

4. *A Complete History of Somerset* (1742), pp. 27–8. Quoted in Peter T. Marcy, 'Eighteenth-century views of Bristol and Bristollians', in Patrick McGrath (ed.), *Bristol in the Eighteenth Century* (Newton Abbot, 1972), p. 27.

as Bristol or Liverpool. The range of goods to be bought and sold exercised a perpetual fascination. Defoe's *Tour* waxed lyrical over the markets and the variety of the merchandise, catering for highly specialized and sophisticated tastes. The quickened pace of activity, the concentration of people, the wealth and variety of consumer goods and luxuries available, were novelties in a society unaccustomed to urban growth. Trade directories made their first appearance outside London in Bristol and Liverpool in the 1760s, and their example was rapidly followed all over the country. They bear witness to the rapid expansion of towns, which necessitated putting some order into the maelstrom of urban society. The lists of shopkeepers, suppliers, urban officials, information on public transport and other services encapsulated the essence of urban society. This proliferation engendered a burgeoning confidence and pride – a fact acknowledged in a Worcester guide book of 1808, 'In a well governed City, nothing tends so much to increase the number of its inhabitants, and the general wealth of the place as the industry of the people and the multiplicity of its manufactures.'[5]

While moralists might inveigh against the laxity of urban morals and the danger to the nation's strength, there were plenty of others who were prepared to counter such allegations with a defence of urban life, demonstrating its contribution, not just to the nation's economic prosperity, but to the progress of civilization, the spread of polite society and the encouragement of the arts, for 'a barbarous and commercial people is a contradiction'.[6] There was a long tradition of writing, which espoused the cause of urban civilization – the sixteenth-century antiquary John Stow had argued in the *Survey of London* that cities bred love and goodwill and promoted the stability of society, that they allowed the liberal arts and sciences to flourish and that they were a bridle against tyranny.[7] This kind of rhetoric exerted a far greater influence, given a fashionable eighteenth-century gloss, as it was more fully developed in the philosophy of the Scottish Enlightenment. David Hume's essays on 'Commerce', 'Money' and the 'Rise and Progress of the Arts and Sciences', demonstrated that the possession of property and

5. P. J. Corfield with Serena Kelly, 'Giving directions to the town: the early town directories', *Urban History Yearbook*, xi (1984), pp. 22–34; *A Concise History of Worcester* (Worcester, 1808), p. 41.

6. William Hutton, *An History of Birmingham* (1781), p. 62. For a survey of the problematic issue of 'luxury' in this period see John Sekora, *Luxury: the Concept in Western Thought. Eden to Smollet* (Baltimore, 1977).

7. John Stow, *The Survey of London containing the Original, Antiquity, Increase and Modern Estate of that City*, 2nd edn (1603), pp. 483–4.

exchange of goods, which arose from urban commerce, refined the passions and led to the emergence of civilized society.[8] Social virtues could only be fully developed in an urban environment. This positive tradition was continued in the nineteenth century by liberal spokesmen for the manufacturing towns, such as Edward Baines of Leeds or the Unitarian Robert Vaughan, who lauded the increase to national wealth brought about by the growth of industry and commerce, and held up the factory as the means for moral regulation and improvement. Cities, it was argued, encouraged a zeal for religion and charity and gave further encouragement to the progress of the arts and sciences.[9]

As a physical structure, the town was viewed in positive, if rather blinkered, terms for most of the eighteenth century. Observers congratulated themselves on the improved appearance of the thoroughfares, the array of goods in shop windows, the newly paved and lighted streets and the fine public buildings, which, it was claimed, would dazzle foreigners with their magnificence. 'Nothing seems more capable of affording satisfaction to a liberal mind than the many public improvements of elegance and convenience which have lately been made in the metropolis. Every inhabitant participates of their advantages, and every man of generous feelings shares in the reputation which his country acquires from them.'[10] Engravings of town scenes, which illustrated urban histories, guide books and travel literature, all depicted wide, clean streets, with ample lighting, impressive buildings, with classical facades, and human figures fashionably dressed or seated in a sedan chair.

However, such pictorial conventions were no truer to the reality of urban life than are the glossy pictures of holiday resorts in the brochures of modern-day tour operators. Both are designed to convey a desirable image, rather than to give an accurate portrayal. Beyond the main public arenas, such as the chief thoroughfares and fashionable residential areas, housing was unregulated and streets were unpaved. There were no drains, no cleansing took place, and overcrowding and squalor was the norm. The extent of urban sprawl was still limited, in comparison with the nineteenth and twentieth centuries, but the essential elements of slum life and grinding poverty were well established and steadily growing. Yet such matters

8. David Hume, *Essays Moral, Political and Literary* (Indianapolis, 1987).
9. Andrew Lees, *Cities Perceived. Urban Society in European and American Thought, 1820–1940* (Columbia, 1985), pp. 1–40; Robert Vaughan, *The Age of Great Cities: or, Modern Society viewed in Relation to Intelligence, Morals and Religion* (1843).
10. *Critical Observations of the Buildings and Improvements of London* (1771), p. 1.

were seldom commented upon. A critique, which focused on the structural problems of urban living, as opposed to simply blaming the immorality of the poor and their feckless dependence upon gin, was slow to develop. As late as 1842, Edwin Chadwick, the pioneer of sanitary and welfare reform, commented that his inquiries had been met with surprise by the members of the wealthier classes 'to whom the facts were as strange as if they related to foreigners or the natives of an unknown country'.[11] That is not to say that the filth and dirt, and the deprivation of the lower classes in towns, went entirely unnoticed; Hogarth's engravings, such as *Gin Lane* or the *Harlot's Progress*, captured the seediness and squalor of London life vividly enough. Poets and writers alike deplored the habits of the poor and expressed revulsion at urban immorality and crime with predictable frequency, as in book four of William Cowper's 'The Task'.

> The town has ting'd the country; and the stain
> Appears a spot upon a vestal's robe,
> The worse for what it soils. The fashion runs
> Down into scenes still rural; but, alas,
> Scenes rarely grac'd with rural manners now! (553–7)

But this was part of the traditional opposition of urban and rural values, which had fascinated writers since antiquity; poverty and squalor were considered to be the product of a corrupt and luxurious society. The writers and moralists of the eighteenth century were the heirs to a long literary tradition which had always presented towns as centres of evil and vice, going back to the cities of Sodom and Gomorrah or Babylon in the Old Testament, and to the classical satires of Juvenal and Horace.[12] This genre of urban criticism, concentrated on the physical and moral corruption of the town, as compared with the idealised purity and simplicity of the countryside, blaming the evils of urban living upon the impact of commerce and luxury. The dirt, filth and physical corruption of urban streets were repeatedly employed as a metaphor for the immorality and spiritual corruption which urban living engendered among its inhabitants. Towns were regarded with suspicion because the fluidity and potential anonymity of urban life challenged the ordered and hierarchical notions of society, as it existed in the

11. Edwin Chadwick, *Report on the Sanitary Condition of the Labouring Population of Great Britain*, (ed.) M. W. Flinn (Edinburgh, 1965), p. 397.

12. A general overview is to be found in Keith Thomas, *Man and the Natural World. Changing Attitudes in England 1500–1800* (1984), pp. 242–53.

context of village and rural society. Gradations of status became harder to maintain, and traditional forms of social control became strained, and broke down, until there was no distinction or subordination left. London naturally attracted the most comment, both critical and complementary, but the burgeoning growth of the towns of provincial England began to rival the metropolis's role as the urban paradigm.

Just as there was a stock theme in literature which compared the evils of the town to the virtuous simplicity of the countryside, there was another which ridiculed the cultural pretensions of the merchant and the tradesman and derided the town for being bare of the cultural refinements of polite society. One writer on Liverpool dismissed its cultural life as 'but a wild and barren waste', and complained at the lack of civilized amenities, such as walks and amusements, concluding that 'Commerce alone appears to engage the attention of its inhabitants'.[13] Those involved in commerce were too taken up with making money to devote themselves to more elevated pursuits, and too fond of maximizing their profits to risk the levels of expenditure necessary in the cultivation of true taste. The most notorious examples come from those who were outsiders, or who had reason to feel aggrieved towards the town. The poet Richard Savage, who was thrown into Bristol Bridewell, composed some of the most savage indictments directed against any town, and Thomas Chatterton, who was similarly spurned by the people of Bristol, vented his anger in *Kew Gardens*:

> A mean assembly room, absurdly built,
> Boasted one gorgeous lamp of copper gilt;
> With farthing candles, chandeliers of tin,
> And services of water, rum and gin.
> There in the dull solemnity of wigs,
> The dancing bears of commerce murder jigs.[14]

Other examples abound, especially in the pages of popular literature. In the second half of the century, the animus of anti-urban satire was increasingly directed against manufacturers rather than merchants (who were now more often portrayed as reconciling civilized culture with trade).[15] Manufacturers were parvenus, vulgar, uneducated and lacked the attributes of 'taste' which defined a

---

13. James Wallace, *A General and Descriptive History of the Ancient and Present State of the Town of Liverpool*, 2nd edn (Liverpool, 1797), p. 2.

14. Quoted in Marcy, 'Eighteenth-century views of Bristol and Bristollians', p. 34.

15. James Raven, *Judging New Wealth: Popular Publishing and Responses to Commerce in England, 1750–1800* (Oxford, 1992).

gentleman. It was assumed that people who were involved in business could have no time for literature, and that it could not flourish in a manufacturing town. As Mrs Elton memorably commented in *Emma*, 'They came from Birmingham, which is not a place to promise much, you know, Mr Weston. One has no great hopes from Birmingham. I always say there is something direful in the sound'.[16] Such criticism was almost always penned by those who did *not* belong to urban society, who feared the threat which urban wealth, credit networks and commercial practices posed to traditional landed values, or who were simply repeating the stereotypes fed to them in the travel literature of the time.

The most hostile criticism of urban society was targeted upon London. Samuel Johnson famously once declared to Boswell that, 'Sir, when a man is tired of London, he is tired of life; for there is in London all that Life can afford'.[17] However, there were many who believed that London posed a threat not just to life but to the very fabric of society itself. London's high mortality rates were well known. Thanks to the bills of mortality (the records of burials and baptisms kept by parish clerks), it was obvious that deaths greatly exceeded births. Yet at the same time, London was growing daily, with a visibly swollen population upon its streets. This could only be achieved by constant immigration from the surrounding countryside, draining the country's population and sapping the national strength. The seriousness of this 'fatal attraction' can only be understood if we remember that for much of the century there was a widespread belief that the nation's population was actually in decline. In a period when national strength, in terms of productive capacity and fighting potential, was held to rest squarely upon the size of the population, the lure of the great city had very serious implications.[18] The inexorable expansion of the metropolis had a distorting effect on the economy – provisions and coinage alike were relentlessly drawn to the capital city to meet its insatiable appetite, raising prices elsewhere and hampering trade through a shortage of coinage.[19] 'The capital is become an overgrown monster which,

16. Quoted in Eric Hopkins, *The Rise of the Manufacturing Town. Birmingham and the Industrial Revolution* (Stroud, 1998), p. 135.

17. James Boswell, *The Life of Samuel Johnson*, Everyman edn, 2 vols (1906), ii, p. 131.

18. For a fuller discussion of this debate see D. V. Glass, *Numbering the People* (Farnborough, 1973).

19. A good example of this kind of critique of London is Henry Home, Lord Kames, 'A great city considered in physical, moral and political views' in *Sketches of the History of Man,* 3rd edn, 2 vols (Dublin, 1779), i, pp. 69–79.

like a dropsical head, will in time leave the body and extremities without nourishment and support.'[20] Not only was the death rate higher, but people born in a great city were more likely to be weak and effeminate. Unhealthy living conditions sapped their labouring and reproductive strength. The sallow complexions and enfeebled gait of the pigeon-chested tailors who worked cross-legged all day, hunched over their sewing in a close and noxious atmosphere, epitomised the contrast between the urban worker and his lusty rural counterpart. Effeminacy was encouraged by the easy availability of luxury and the pervasive immorality of the town. Vice and corruption flourished in London, as the endless variations upon the tale of the *Rake's Progress* and the *Harlot's Progress* warned those who had not yet succumbed. Provincial moralists expressed alarm at the prospect of servants and other migrants bringing back vicious habits from the city, and predicted gloomily that it was 'draining the Country of the most useful class of people, who if they return at all, always come home worse than they went out'.[21] Sexual immorality and licentiousness carried its own danger of venereal disease, but it also undermined the family and the stability of the social order with its implied loss of self-control. The close proximity to each other in which people lived meant that the contagion of vice spread as easily as disease in the contaminated air. The analogy between the corruption of morals and the filth of the town was frequently made. Matthew Bramble in *Humphry Clinker*, described with horror the pollution, filth and decay which he saw all around him, compounding it with the luxury, deception and vice of the inhabitants, 'Nay, as there is not sense enough left among them, to be discomposed by the nuisance I have mentioned, they may for aught I care, wallow in the mire of their own pollution'.[22] The vast concourse of people bred a society where contacts were brief and impersonal. True worth could not be known, virtue could not be recognised. Deception in all its forms flourished amidst anonymity. Shopkeepers adulterated the flour and milk, servants dressed up in their masters' finery, stockjobbers deluded the public with paper money and promises of wealth. The ultimate expression of the fear, suspicion and fascination that London exerted over the eighteenth-century imagination came in its representation of

20. Tobias Smollett, *The Expedition of Humphry Clinker*, (ed.) Angus Ross, Penguin edn (1988), p. 118.

21. George Hadley, *A New and Complete History of the Town and County of the Town of Kingston upon Hull* (Hull, 1788), p. 378.

22. Smollet, *Humphry Clinker*, pp. 149–55.

Bedlam, as an institution which symoblized the perversion of all normal forms of behaviour and social values, but was nevertheless a favoured destination for an afternoon's entertainment.

As urban growth in the manufacturing areas accelerated to unprecedented peaks in the early nineteenth century, due to increasing fertility and declining mortality, we may begin to identify a change in tone and attitude. In literature, the change in attitude was heralded by Blake's 'London', whose opening lines are already suggestive of the despair of urban life, which was to become associated not just with London, but with large cities all over the country:

> I wander thro' each charter'd street,
> Near where the charter'd Thames does flow.
> And mark in every face I meet
> Marks of weakness, marks of woe

London was no longer the disproportionately outsized head of the body politic. While it still crowned the urban hierarchy, other towns were growing much more rapidly, and challenging not just the capital's political and cultural hegemony, but its capacity to shape society's perception of the town. Urban growth peaked in the years 1821–31, whereas for most of the eighteenth century, political economists had feared a depletion of the nation's population due to the pernicious influence of the towns, by this time it was clear to all that the population was rapidly increasing, irrespective of urban immigration. Many espoused the theories of the clerical statistician, Thomas Malthus, who warned that the population would increase beyond the capacity of the nation to feet it and feared that a Malthusian crisis of subsistence threatened both town and country, when Manchester and Salford grew by over 47 per cent, and Bradford by 78 per cent, spawning the factory work-force and an acute crisis in the living conditions and housing of the poor. Economic recessions and high levels of unemployment exacerbated the problems of poverty and public order. Destitution and social protest had become uncomfortably obvious features of urban life, and when combined with political protest, as at Peterloo or the riots of 1831, gave the authorities serious cause for alarm. They began to see the labouring classes as a menacing threat which could at any time pull the whole edifice of society down into ruins. The threat of disease, highlighted by the cholera epidemic of 1832, and the rising tide of endemic typhus and TB, shocked the nation into an awareness of the realities of urban mortality. Both government and the public became receptive to the necessity of urban reform.

In the 1820s and 30s, district visitors for the evangelical missions compiled extensive evidence on the condition of the working classes, discovering huge areas of deprivation, where the existing parochial system had proved inadequate in adapting to the religious needs or administrative demands of urbanizing society. During the 1830s, statistical societies in the largest towns began to investigate subjects of political and social economy, often including detailed house-to-house investigations into the conditions of the working classes.[23] By 1840, there had been a decade or more of informed empirical observation, the findings of which were brought together by Edwin Chadwick in his *Report on the Sanitary Condition of the Working-classes* (1842). It was increasingly recognized that the large towns, at least, posed problems of health, housing, education and employment, which existing resources were unable to deal with, whereas in the eighteenth century it had generally been assumed that there were no problems which could not be resolved by a more thorough implementation of the 'police' of the town.[24] The scale of the problem was such that it could not be ignored. Writers, such as Smollett, had attacked the luxury and vanity which dominated urban values, and the poor had been criticized for profligacy and idleness. The immorality of the poor was still a major concern of the reformers, but now it was targeted as immorality arising from a life of destitution, ignorance and deprivation. Pride in urban achievement and its contribution to national greatness was still expressed, but it was tinged with deepening shades of pessimism and horror at the condition of the labouring sort in towns. The tenor of debate on urban society had irrevocably changed. The 'large' town, as a problem and a phenomenon, with its own distinctive characteristics, had come into being, epitomised in the bleakness of Dickens' Coketown.[25]

The Emergence of a Distinctive Urban Culture

Urban society in the eighteenth century became more sharply differentiated from that of the rural hinterland. Historians have often

23. Michael J. Cullen, *The Statistical Movement in Early Victorian Britain. The Foundations of Empirical Social Research* (1975).

24. I am very grateful to Joanna Innes for letting me see an unpublished paper, 'Large Towns' to which this paragraph is heavily indebted.

25. For an introduction to some of the attitudes to Victorian towns, see Asa Briggs, *Victorian Cities* (repr. 1990), esp. pp. 59–87.

emphasised the strength of the interrelationships between town and country in the early modern town. As Fernand Braudel commented, 'town and countryside never separate like oil and water'.[26] 'Agrarian' activities were always to be found in the town, and industrial or manufacturing enterprises were often located in the countryside. It is very difficult to distinguish specifically urban and agricultural occupations at the start of our period, not least because contemporary commentators never did so. Agriculture was arguably the prime mover, if not employer, of the economy, and almost all the nation's industry was based upon processing some form of agricultural harvest, or providing for agricultural needs. Even in the nineteenth century, employers were complaining that industrial workers, in towns such as Norwich, were deserting the workshops for the fields during the harvest period.[27] The early modern urban calendar was essentially dictated by rural festivals, the towns themselves were full of gardens, orchards, and pigs, and were at their busiest when filled with the population of the countryside at markets or fairs. However, in the course of the eighteenth century the increasing specialization of urban manufacturing, the inbuilding of town centres and the sheer growth in size and population, steadily eroded the influence of rural society in many areas. The Braudelian emulsion of society began to separate out into oil and water. Concurrently, the impact of the agricultural revolution was to create a more highly specialized agricultural system which no longer made such demands upon urban populations for assistance. But how different was urban culture from rural? Although contrasts clearly became far more widespread and extreme, historians should always beware of assuming a polarity. The pastoral ideal of the countryside, for example, was a prominent theme in town planning; the square was supposed to create a *rus in urbe*, and sheep were to be found wandering around some London squares. Suburban developments were informed by ideas of the rustic and the picturesque. At the level of consumerism, so often taken as one of the defining features of the urban lifestyle, it has been found that household inventories do not show particularly marked divisions between town and country; other factors, such as the evolution of the distribution network and the regional economy had rather more bearing on

26. Fernand Braudel, *Capitalism and Material Life, 1400–1800* (1967), pp. 376–7.
27. Peter Mathias, 'The social structure in the eighteenth century: a calculation by Joseph Massie', *EcHR*, x (1957), pp. 30–45; John Patten, *English Towns 1500–1700* (Folkestone, 1978), p. 198.

what kind of consumer goods were purchased.[28] Town and country had always been interdependent, and remained so. The town existed not only for itself, but for its hinterland – its custom came from the surrounding area; shops, professional services, cultural events, hospitals, gaols, were all intended to serve as county or regional institutions rather than being exclusively urban.

The provision of these cultural and administrative services became an increasingly marked part of urban life, and provided the foundations for the 'urban renaissance'. This is the term which was first used by Peter Borsay in his highly original study of the cultural development of towns, in the period following the Restoration. Borsay argues that from the 1660s, after a period of stagnation and comparative decline in the earlier seventeenth century, there was a revitalization and renewal in many towns, preceding the impact of industrialization. This was based largely upon the provision of leisure and luxury, creating a social and intellectual environment which was distinctively urban. The emphasis in recent eighteenth-century historiography upon the concepts of public and private spheres, the experience of women within society and the emergence of class identities, much of which has been based upon urban cultural studies, has endowed the concept of the urban renaissance with far-reaching implications.[29] However, there has been some debate as to how widely applicable the term is to towns as a whole, or whether it should be limited to specific towns. Angus McInnes has made the case that in many smaller towns the real extent of any 'renaissance' was extremely limited, involving only a small proportion of the population, and effecting little change within the town as a whole. He prefers to talk about the emergence of a restricted number of 'leisure towns', which provided a range of cultural services and amenities, and whose economies were, to a large extent, dependent upon attracting the custom of visitors. The debate, however, is over the finer details, not over the wider issue. Historians can agree that urban culture did change very significantly; new cultural forms were developed, new kinds of entertainment were popularized, and the provision of 'leisure facilities' became a substantial part of the urban economy of almost all towns, to a greater or lesser extent.

28. Lorna Weatherill, *Consumer Behaviour and Material Culture in Britain, 1660–1760*, 2nd edn (1996), pp. 75–9, 89–90.
29. See for example, Margaret Hunt, *The Middling Sort. Commerce, Gender and the Family in England, 1680–1780* (Berkeley, CA, 1996); John Smail, *The Origins of Middle Class Culture: Halifax, Yorkshire, 1660–1780* (Ithaca, NY, 1994).

Inns and Alehouses

In many ways, the foundations of the urban renaissance may be said to have been laid in the inns 'or alehouses, which were as essential a feature of urban life as was the parish church. It is hard for us to comprehend the ubiquity of the inn and the alehouse, not least because we no longer depend upon beer and ale as our major source of liquid refreshment.[30] A small town, such as Loughborough, with a population of only 4,000 or so, could support 43 inns in 1770, and an additional seven by 1783.[31] The inn was the superior establishment, patronised by the gentry, selling food and wine as well as beer, and providing accommodation for visitors. Taverns were smaller and unlikely to provide accommodation, and alehouses were more generally frequented by the less wealthy and the labouring sort. The inn, or rather inns, for it was a very small community which could not support more than one, performed an enormous range of functions.[32] In fact, there was little in the cultural, administrative, economic and political life of the town which did not have some connection with the inn. Initially, almost all activities were based upon an inn, but gradually alternative institutions were created, as the social and cultural life diversified and became more specialized, and the inn lost some of the centrality of its role in urban life.

The inn was the focal point of the community and the centre of communications. The ever increasing number of travellers arrived at and departed from inns, and the latest news, not to mention newspapers, were always to be found there. The inn was the natural gathering place for any meeting or committee, whether it was providing the venue or acting as the location of the more informal, relaxed proceedings afterwards. The meetings of the corporation, the vestry, the improvement commission, the land tax or the militia would generally be held at the local inn, or would at least retire there. Most inns had a number of rooms which could be set aside for such purposes. At the Star Inn at Maidstone, for example, there was a room called the Justice Chamber where the magistrates conventionally met.[33] Many towns lacked a formal county hall until the

30. Gregory King calculated that about 28% per capita annual expenditure went on ale and beer. Peter Clark, *The English Alehouse. A Social History, 1220–1830* (1983), p. 209.

31. Alan Everitt, 'The English urban inn, 1560–1760', in Everitt ed., *Perspectives in English Urban History* (1973), p. 94.

32. Clark, *The English Alehouse*, p. 5.   33. Everitt, 'English urban inn', p. 110.

end of the eighteenth century or even later, and for want of any-
where else county meetings would be held at the inn, where there
might be a room specifically set aside as the 'County Chamber',
as at the New London Inn at Exeter. The urban inn was the location for political as well as administrative business. Petitions and
addresses, on issues of local importance, were left to be signed at
inns. In the days before structured party organization, politics was
conducted in a much more informal manner, in which conviviality and social intercourse, based around the inn, were a crucial
element; many of the dining clubs were essentially political clubs, for
example. At elections, inns were conventionally used as campaign
headquarters where the candidates would install themselves and
offer hospitality to woo their voters, and, if necessary, accommodate them and ply them with drink until the poll should take place.
Following the election, the celebratory feast would, of course, take
place at the inn. The capacity of some of the eighteenth-century
inns was enormous; it is not uncommon to find references to dinner being given for several hundred guests. Every feast and celebratory dinner, which punctuated the urban year, would take place
in an inn. It is not surprising that innkeepers, who had a monopoly on such large-scale entertaining, often numbered amongst the
wealthiest elite in the town.

Inns were also the centre for other forms of entertainment. Assemblies and balls were held at the local inn, and the innkeeper
often constructed a large room especially for dancing. Until regular theatres were built, plays were generally held in the yard of an
inn. Even the presence of a purpose-built theatre could not seriously undermine the role of the inn as the chief purveyor of entertainment and for the consumption of culture. The inn was the first
reception point for all the cultural imports; the travelling players,
musicians, circuses, exhibitions, salesmen, and lecturers inevitably
arrived at the urban inn, and based themselves from the premises.
The diary of Stephen Witton, an umbrella maker in Kendal, records
that between 1812–17, in a number of the 21 Kendal inns, he saw a
man spinning glass, a Hottentot woman, a display of 'Mnenomicks',
transparent painting, a 'shew', waxworks, a 'horse of knowledge
slight of hand tumbling slack &c.' [sic], a peep show, a collection of wild beasts, a boxing demonstration, and he attended a
ball.[34] Even a cursory examination of contemporary newspaper

34. J. D. Marshall, 'The rise and fall of the Cumbrian market town, 1660–1900',
Northern History, xix (1983), p. 176.

advertisements, gives an idea of the extraordinary range of entertainments being offered at inns all over the country; innkeepers
were cultural entrepreneurs by default, if not by design.

The alehouse attracted rather lower class personnel; it was chiefly
the resort of the artisan and the workman, although not exclusively
so. The alehouses were even more numerous than the inns, especially in the centre of the town around the market-place. Their
pervasiveness made them an essential part of the fabric of urban
life, and they constituted an important element in the formation of
social networks among the urban community. Not only did they
provide food and drink and accommodation, but they also operated as informal labour exchanges and pawnbrokers. They might
sell a selection of basic goods, and labourers were often paid their
weekly wages there. The friendly societies, box clubs and debating
societies almost always met at an alehouse, a practice which the
alehouse keepers naturally encouraged, as their business inevitably
benefitted from the increased consumption. The virtuous philanthropists of the latter part of the eighteenth century, however, looked
rather askance upon this, as the funds which were supposed to
support the poor in times of need were being dissipated in drink
and idleness. The alehouse was also suspect as the location of
popular recreations, such as cockfighting or pugilism; occasions
which could lead to disorderly behaviour and other vices, such as
gambling. JPs had the authority to licence alehouses, and in the
mood of moral reform, which swept the country from the late eighteenth century onwards, many tried to undermine the ubiquity of
the alehouse in working class culture by limiting the number of
licenses granted – but to little effect; the alehouse and its variants
of pub and ginshop continued at the centre of working class urban
culture.

By the nineteenth century, both inn and alehouse had lost some
of their multifunctionality and become more exclusively associated
with the provision of food and drink and accommodation. In London and the larger provincial towns, inns had begun to call themselves hotels and were primarily places of accommodation and
refreshment. William Hutton's history of Birmingham, published
in 1781, referred to several hotels which had been recently established – which, unlike the French hotels, from which the name
came, offered accommodation to travellers, rather than being the
urban residence of a nobleman. Many of the services which had
been provided by the inn and the alehouse were now offered by
alternative establishments. We must consider now what these were.

The Assembly Rooms

In most towns, the first addition to the 'social space' was the assembly room.[35] Assemblies or balls had been held in some towns since the mid-seventeenth century or earlier, and they appear to have provided one of the main opportunities for the social mixing of both sexes. Even very small towns, with less than 1,000 inhabitants, could support an assembly, although there might have been a shortage of couples to stand up to dance on occasion. Daniel Defoe believed them to encourage scandalous behaviour and sexual intrigue, and warned his readers that they attracted women with dubious reputations.[36] In spite of these dangers, the assembly flourished as one of the staples of urban society throughout the century. It was only in the nineteenth century that private gatherings came to be favoured among the circles of the social elite. Assemblies attracted visitors in from outside the town, and not just the wealthy county gentry. Families living further afield, who would normally only rarely visit the neighbouring town, might sink their resources upon one season, in a make or break bid to marry off their daughters, with a round of social activity based upon the assembly. It was not for nothing that it had the reputation for being a marriage market – one traveller remarked of Winchester that 'formerly the Country Ladies were stewed up in their Fathers' old Mansion Houses and seldom saw Company. . . . but by the Means of these Assemblies, Matches are struck up'.[37] This functional aspect of bringing together eligible young men and women, brought out in so many novels, rendered it even more important as a social institution than its provision of diversion and entertainment. It is not to be wondered at that the assembly rooms were often among the first public buildings to be erected in any town. One of the most famous examples, which still survives today, is also one of the most splendid: the Egyptian Hall, designed by the palladian architect, the Earl of Burlington, in 1731, for the city of York. Few other towns, however, with the exception of Bath, could hope to match the elegant grandeur of the metropolis of the north, and most made do with rather less resplendent accommodation. In the larger towns, it was often found necessary to build more than one assembly room to

35. The best description of assemblies and assembly rooms is Mark Girouard, *The English Town* (Yale, 1990), pp. 127–44.

36. Daniel Defoe, *A Tour through the whole Island of Great Britain*, (ed.) P. Rogers, Penguin edn (repr. 1986), p. 76.

37. John Macky, *A Journey through England*, 2 vols (1724), ii, p. 38.

accommodate the company, and Bath had three sets of purpose-built rooms by 1770.[38] In other towns, there was often a distinction made between the tradesmen and the gentlemen's assembly, and either separate rooms would be built, or respective balls would be held on different nights. The divisions of partisan conflict spilled over into even the easy sociability of the assembly room; excluding one's political opponents was an effective way of making a political statement. In Manchester, a town deeply divided along political and religious lines in the first half of the century, not only were there rival assemblies, but even the choice of dances was rendered politically partisan by names such as 'Down with the Rump' and 'Sir Watkin's Jig', and Jacobite sympathisers regularly indulged in 'dancing down' the Hanoverian regime.[39]

Assemblies were generally held regularly on a weekly or fort-nightly basis throughout the winter, and in spa towns during their summer seasons, and those attending would pay a subscription for the entire series. Additional assemblies or balls were held to mark important occasions in the civic calendar, such as the election of the mayor, or to celebrate royal anniversaries. The cost of annual subscription to the Newcastle assembly rooms, in the 1770s, was one guinea, and tickets for the assembly during the races and assize week were 5s 6d. Assembly rooms were generally leased to an inn-keeper or hotelier, who would provide the musicians, the tea, or supper and other amenities, and they were free to make what money they could from the sale of tickets. Balls were always advertised with posters and in the local press. Social propriety depended upon certain conventions being observed, and most assemblies drew up their own regulations to govern the behaviour of those participating. This was generally based upon the code developed in the early eighteenth century at Bath by Beau Nash, and a master of ceremonies was generally employed to enforce the rules and keep order. As one French visitor commented, 'Such an official is very useful in a public hall since he prevents the possibility of any dispute'.[40] The various dances were performed in a strict order (proceedings usually opened with a minuet, but might finish with a more boisterous country dance), and the protocol of taking partners was regulated

38. Borsay, *Urban Renaissance*, p. 336.
39. Paul Langford, *Public Life and the Propertied Englishman* (Oxford, 1990), p. 120. The 'Rump' referred to the supposed connection between the Whigs and the Rump Parliament of the Protectorate, and Sir Watkin was Sir Watkins Williams Wynn, one of the leading Jacobites.
40. F. La Rochefoucauld, *A Frenchman in England in 1784* (1995), p. 59.

to avoid embarrassment. In Newcastle, rule number four stipulated that:

> 'Persons of Rank shall take precedency according to their Rank in Minuets and Country Dances. Gentlemen who afterwards dance Minuets, are requested to ask those Ladies who sit at the Head of each Side of the Room, and then proceed to the others in Order in which they shall happen to sit; and such Ladies as do not to dance Minuets, are requested to sit on the Back Seats.'

Rule thirteen required that in country dances 'no Lady will offer to sit down until every Couple have danced to the bottom unless she is indisposed'.[41] In Sheffield, no country dances were to be called for after twelve o'clock, but minuets could be 'danced promiscuously until one', after which the music stopped.[42] The extremes of regulated dancing were reached in Bath where the high turnover of the clientele and the very mixed social backgrounds necessitated a very strict dress code to be drawn up. Space was also at a premium in the densely crowded rooms, and ladies who were unaware of the rule forbidding the wearing of hooped petticoats were informed that those 'that chuse to pull their Hoops off, will always find a servant maid ready to assist them, and a proper Place to retire for that purpose.'[43] In Jane Austen's novel, *Pride and Prejudice,* Elizabeth Bennett's comments about talking by rule to Mr Darcy at the Netherfield dance were pointedly ironic, but also parodied the minute conventions of the etiquette to be observed on such occasions. In another novel, *Emma,* Mr Elton created ripples of horror when he broke with the rules of polite behaviour in his refusal to dance with Harriet Smith.[44]

Theatres

The theatre, taken together with balls and assemblies might be considered to constitute the bare necessities of eighteenth-century urban culture. Early theatres were almost always based at the inn, and even when regular playhouses had been built, inns often

41. TWAS ZBL/228, Sir Walter Blackett Correspondence on Civic Affairs: Rules of the Newcastle Assembly Room.
42. R. Leader, *Sheffield in the Eighteenth Century* (Sheffield, 1901), p. 114.
43. Brigitte Mitchell and Hubert Penrose (eds), *Letters from Bath 1766–7 by the Rev. John Penrose* (1983), p. 136.
44. Jane Austen, *Pride and Prejudice* (Oxford, 1982), p. 91; and *Emma* (Oxford, 1982), pp. 326–8.

continued to offer rather less decorous forms of theatrical entertainment. Despite the Stage Licensing Act of 1737, which made
provincial theatres illegal without parliamentary licensing, their
spread continued more or less unabated. By 1770, established theatres were to be found in at least 26 towns outside London.[45] The
Enabling Act of 1788, which allowed JPs to licence plays, helped to
accelerate the spread of theatres, and coincided with a second wave
of urban improvement. There were few towns which lacked a venue
for plays; the university authorities in Oxford resisted the presence
of a theatre, but nearby Abingdon provided an alternative, if less
convenient solution, for theatrically deprived undergraduates and
townsmen. The theatre was accessible to an extremely broad swathe
of society; the cheapest tickets could be as low as 3d or 6d each,
which, although possibly beyond the means of a manual labourer,
were not too much for the smaller artisans and shopkeepers. Although theatres were subjected to something of a moral backlash
from the 1770s by some urban authorities under the influence of
John Wesley and the evangelical revival, among the population at
large their popularity was uninterrupted. Anxiety was expressed
about the corrupting influence of the plays, and the moral laxity
which the culture of the theatre encouraged. The very comprehens-
iveness of its appeal was in itself a cause for upper class hostility;
not least because they resented sharing their entertainment with
their social inferiors.[46] Advocates of the theatre were quick to
enlarge on its morally improving qualities, however, on the grounds
that well written plays could only reinforce excellent precepts.
The most popular kinds of plays were the comedies by playwrights
such as Congreve, Cibber, Foote, Farquhar and Vanbrugh. Tragedy,
of greater moral and didactic value, was almost entirely confined
to Shakespeare, whose supremacy in the canon of English literature
was indubitably confirmed in this period. Almost all plays were
performed by companies of travelling players; some larger towns,
such as Norwich or Liverpool, had their own companies, but these
too went on tour around the neighbouring towns of the region.
Famous names from the metropolis, such as David Garrick or
Mrs Siddons, regularly toured the provincial towns, but it is possible to exaggerate the influence exerted by the metropolis upon
provincial dramatic culture. For most provincial theatre-goers, their
experience was one of locally based theatre companies whose annual

45. Peter Borsay, *The English Urban Renaissance* (Oxford, 1989), pp. 329–31.
46. Paul Langford, *A Polite and Commercial People. England, 1727–1783* (Oxford, 1989), p. 612.

season was a familiar part of the urban calendar. The arrival of a London based company was greeted with suspicion and some hostility, even in as cosmopolitan a city as York.[47]

Other forms of entertainment were generally offered with plays, as '*entreactes*' or simply to get around the licensing laws. Charles Macklin and Theophilus Cibber attempted to exploit the loophole in the licensing laws, whereby musical performances went unrestricted, by charging for a musical entertainment while offering a dramatic rehearsal or demonstration to the public for free.[48] The ruse was short-lived, but it reminds us that the entertainment offered in theatres was never restricted to plays. In London, opera was very popular, acrobatics, tumbling, and dancing were likewise provided as entertainment. From the 1760s, another kind of entertainment took to touring the provinces. The circus, epitomised in the eighteenth century by the company formed by Joseph Astley, became one of the most popular forms of 'mass' entertainment. It had evolved originally from displays of equestrian virtuosity given by military officers on half-pay in peacetime, as a means of earning additional income. Astley introduced an ever broadening range of tricks and entertainments, such as tight-rope walking and acrobatics, as well as a greater dramatic element to the performance. Such was his success that he was soon facing competition from other companies.[49] By the time that he died, the circus had acquired a rather more upmarket image, reflected in the prices of the tickets. But, as with the theatre, the lower priced tickets were well within the range of the lower middling sort and below, and the circus audience also embodied considerable social diversity.

Musical Entertainments

The kind of musical experience to be had in most theatres was generally on the raucous and populist side. Musical pursuits of a more decorous variety were, however, an important part of urban cultural life. Music, in the form of City Waits, had always been an

47. Sybil Rosenfeld, *Strolling Players and Drama in the Provinces, 1660–1775* (Cambridge, 1939), p. 159.

48. John Brewer, *The Pleasures of the Imagination. English Culture in the Eighteenth Century* (1997), p. 386.

49. Marius Kwint, 'Astley's Amphitheatre and the early circus in England, 1768–1830', Oxford Univ. D. Phil. thesis (1994).

integral part of the civic pageantry of towns, and they were often disbanded only in the wake of the Municipal Corporations Act of 1835. These were small bands of musicians who provided music on all occasions of public festivity, often retained by the corporation, as they formed an important part of civic ceremonial. In Bath, they occupied a distinctive role, welcoming new arrivals to the city by performing outside their lodgings. Some visitors were more appreciative of this gesture (for which they were expected to offer some pecuniary emolument) than others. More 'superior' music was provided by concerts and musical festivals.[50] Concerts arose from informal origins; groups of music loving individuals gathered together to perform chamber music, and admitted the 'public' on certain evenings to listen. Claver Morris, a physician in the cathedral town of Wells, was one such enthusiast. His diary, which he kept from the 1680s until his death in 1726, regularly recorded occasions when there was 'a very great Company of Strangers' at the music meetings, especially when the town was full of company for gatherings such as the Quarter Sessions.[51] Music of this kind was an expensive pastime for its practitioners – the cost of the instruments being prohibitive, but concerts were more accessible and were generally organized like assemblies, on the basis of subscribing for a series. The public were charged 2s 6d for Claver Morris's 'musical gatherings'. In most towns, they were performed in the parish church, at the assembly rooms, or even the inn. At Oxford, as if to compensate for the lack of a theatre, the Holywell Music Rooms were built by subscription between 1742–8, and were the setting for regular series of concerts. Subscriptions for the concerts there cost two guineas for a season in 1790.[52] The music hall built in Liverpool in 1785 had a rather greater capacity, seating 1,300, and held twelve subscription concerts a year.[53] The kind of music performed tended not to be the more orchestrally complex symphonies of Haydn and Mozart, but the simpler compositions of the baroque period; composers such as Purcell, Handel, Vivaldi and Albinoni were particularly popular.[54] Subscription concerts were not always

50. Trevor Fawcett, *Musical Life in Eighteenth-Century Norwich* (1979); William Weber, *The Rise of Musical Classics in Eighteenth-Century England* (Oxford, 1992) is particularly good on London concert life.

51. Edmund Hobhouse (ed.), *The Diary of a West Country Physician, 1684–1726* (Rochester, 1934), p. 84.

52. *Jackson's Oxford Journal*, 23 Jan. 1790.   53. *History of Liverpool* (1810), p. 326.

54. Claver Morris recorded playing Purcell, Byrd, Croft, Clark, Scarlatti, Albinoni, Handel, Visconti, Vivaldi, Maria Fiore, Fetz, Alberti Bonparti, Fiocco, Polanski, Tibaldi, Geminiani, Bassanit, Corelli and Valentini. *Diary of a West Country Physician*, p. 39.

well attended; in Oxford, the Stewards of Holywell Music Rooms were sometimes forced to abandon plans for want of support, but the musical festivals and oratorios generally attracted much more interest. The oratorio was essentially the invention of Handel, although such was its success that he had numerous imitators. At a time when there was considerable anxiety about the moral rectitude of Italian opera, the oratorio, based on Biblical texts and without any of the associations with the theatrical world, was a welcome solution for those who wanted to enjoy a vocal performance without compromising their moral principles. In keeping with their religious subject matter, they were generally performed in the local church. The first oratorios were composed to raise money for charity, and their performance remained closely identified with charitable enterprise throughout the eighteenth century. Music festivals, such as the Three Choirs Festival based around the cathedral cities of Hereford, Worcester and Gloucester, embodied both the philanthropy and the cultural aspirations of polite society.[55] Smaller festivals were regularly staged in other towns all over the country with profits similarly being directed towards some charitable end.

The timing of concerts, oratorios, plays, and assemblies had to be carefully calculated. It would be wrong to imagine that all provincial towns offered an endless round of titillation for the cultural palate. For all that there was so much apparent enthusiasm for culture, its proponents were also very prone to complain about the lack of interest shown by their fellow citizens. Most of these events were concentrated during a particular period, such as the Assize Week, when the gentry and other visitors were drawn to the town for administrative and political purposes. Otherwise there was not enough indigenous enthusiasm to support a wide range of activities. Similarly, other important occasions, such as elections or a royal visit, created their own round of balls, assemblies and entertainments. Music festivals, which were heavily dependent upon the patronage of the gentry and nobility, had to be staggered across the summer season, so that towns were not competing against each other for custom. A violent quarrel broke out between Chester and Worcester in the early nineteenth century, when both towns planned to hold their music festivals in the same week.[56]

---

55. Daniel Lysons, *History of the Origin and Progress of the Meeting of the Three Choirs of Gloucester, Worcester and Hereford, and of the Charity connected to it* (1812); Anthony Boden, *Three Choirs: a History of the Festival* (1992).

56. Mrs Edwin Gray (ed.), *Papers and Diaries of a York Family* (1927), p. 167.

Race Meetings

Music festivals and theatrical performances were frequently timed to coincide with race meetings which, along with the Assizes, attracted more outsiders to the town than any other event. Racecourses were established at numerous towns across the country, and meetings were staged throughout the summer from July to September.[57] So numerous were they, that legislation had to be introduced in 1740 to put a check to their proliferation. All prizes had to carry a minimum value of £50; this automatically excluded all but ten per cent of the races then being run. This had the effect of weeding out the smaller events, and those which persisted were almost always based upon a town, generally a county capital. By the 1770s, 90 per cent of races were being held under urban auspices. Corporations were well aware of the importance of such occasions in establishing the town's relationship with the surrounding community – the notion of a corporate hospitality tent would not be entirely anachronistic. The county elite and nobility attended them with great regularity, and made the most of such an extensive gathering of people. The political potential was always exploited to the full, in building up connections and cementing the interest of a political patron in a constituency, with a display of affability and munificence. However, as with theatres, the elite could not command the races for their exclusive entertainment (indeed their political value would have been greatly diminished if they had). The grandstand was their preserve, but beyond that the races were accessible to all, from duke to peasant, and were an important part of the urban calendar, bringing excitement and valuable business to the town.

Walks, Gardens and Promenades

The race-course and the grandstand have brought us out into the open air; it should not be forgotten that although much social activity took place within doors, the opportunities for public display were far greater when venturing abroad. The provision of public places for recreation and in which to walk, assumed a high priority in most schemes of urban improvement.[58] Walking around the town

57. Borsay, *Urban Renaissance*, esp. pp. 185–96.
58. Urban walks are described in more detail in Girouard, *The English Town*, pp. 145–53. See also Peter Borsay, 'The Rise of the promenade: the social and cultural use of space in the English provincial town, c. 1660–1800', *BJECS*, 9 (1986), pp. 125–40.

was an important part of the daily ritual for those with no particular occupation to follow; it filled the time between breakfast and dinner (which outside the circles of the aristocracy took place in the early afternoon). Those who were employed by day, flocked to the public walks in the evenings and on Sundays. The Reverend John Trusler warned his readers that the walks in St James Park were always crowded with the trading part of the people during summer, and recommended Kensington Gardens or riding in Hyde Park as a more fashionable alternative.[59] 'Taking the air' offered the paramount opportunity to be seen and to see other people. The benefits of physical exercise and fresh air offered an additional incentive, and urban guides listed the possibilities for 'ambulatory exercitation' among the attractions of the town. Most towns had some kind of open space where public festivities had traditionally been held, such as the Rood Eye in Chester or the Kingsland in Shrewsbury, where the annual guild processions had been held, but eighteenth-century taste demanded something more formal. Specific walks were laid out with trees to provide shade, gravel paths for more inclement weather and seats and even follies. They took the pedestrian along the river, or in view of the sea, and through the more attractive parts of the town. In cities like Exeter, Chester or York, where the town fortifications were still intact, the circuit of the city walls became a popular promenade. The corporation of York found itself saddled with the considerable burden of expense for the upkeep of the walls, long after they had become redundant from the point of view of defence, not least because of their importance in attracting visitors to the town.[60] Squares, avenues, and the newly laid out streets, provided similar opportunities for public promenading. These walks often evolved into shopping arcades – such as the Pantiles in Tunbridge Wells, as shopkeepers recognised the potential purchasing power of ambulatory custom, thereby bringing together the distinctly urban pleasures of consumption and conspicuous display in one experience. Public gardens and pleasure grounds offered another variant. London had led the way in developing the pleasure ground as a social venue, with its famous Vauxhall and Ranelagh Gardens. The fashion was to attend in the evening when the grounds were illuminated, and music, concerts and refreshments were provided,

59. John Trusler, *The London Adviser and Guide* (1786), pp. 163–4.

60. E. J. Dawson, 'Finance and the Unreformed Borough: a critical appraisal of corporate finance, 1660–1835, with special reference to the boroughs of Nottingham, York and Boston', Univ. of Hull Ph.D. thesis (1978), p. 584.

'Its [Ranelagh's] sole aim is to bring together an enormous crowd of people to take tea there, or ices'.[61] Promenading seldom began before midnight and continued until the early hours of the morning. In the early eighteenth century, these gardens had acquired the reputation for sexual intrigue and assignations – as Sir Roger de Coverley, the country squire of Addison and Steele's *Spectator*, indignantly informed the mistress of the house at Spring Gardens, he 'should be a better Customer to her Garden, if there were more Nightingales, and fewer Strumpets'.[62] After 1730, the rather dissolute character of pleasure gardens was tempered by a more rigorous enforcement of propriety, and they became distinctly genteel, although Vauxhall always retained a slightly more risqué element than Ranelagh. Bath, Birmingham, Norwich and other provincial towns had their own Ranelaghs and Vauxhalls, and visiting the gardens became an indispensable part of the summer social scene.

Literary Tastes and Literary Societies

It has often been said that one of the characteristics of urban rather than rural society in this period was that the literacy rates in towns were generally much higher. The question of what constituted literacy and how we can assess it is not what concerns us here – but it is likely that at least two-thirds of the male population in a large town, such as London, would have been able to read, if not write, although that figure may have declined in certain areas during the first phase of the industrial revolution.[63] With respect to the middling sort and the urban elite, literacy among men, and many women, would have been almost universal. Be that as it may, it is indisputable that the medium of the printed word was an essential constituent of urban culture. An important date for the development of print culture was 1695, when the Licensing Act which had

61. Trusler, *London Adviser*, p. 165; Borsay, *Urban Renaissance*, pp. 162–72; Norman Scarfe (ed.), *Innocent Espionage. The La Rochefoucauld Brothers' Tour of England in 1785* (Woodbridge, 1995), p. 207.

62. Joseph Addison and Richard Steele, *Selections from the Tatler and Spectator*, (ed.) Angus Ross, Penguin edn (1988), p. 247.

63. On literacy see David Cressy, *Literacy and the Social Order. Reading and Writing in Tudor and Stuart England* (Cambridge, 1980). He estimates that in 1650 30% of the male and 15% of the female population were literate, rising to 70% and 55% respectively by 1850 (p. 177). See also R. S. Schofield, 'Dimensions of illiteracy, 1750–1850', *Explorations in Economic History*, 10 (1972–3), pp. 437–54.

restricted printing to London, Oxford, Cambridge and York lapsed, leaving the way open for printing presses to be established throughout the nation. Provincial newspapers had been established in Bristol and Norwich by 1701, and by 1770 there were over 40 provincial titles, a figure which had doubled by the end of the century. London was even better provided, having a number of weeklies, tri-weeklies and, by 1770, nine dailies in circulation. By the end of the century, there were no towns of any significance in which there was not at least some provision for printing.[64]

The expansion of the provincial press has been of considerable interest to historians for its contribution to the growth of political culture outside the metropolis, and as an expression of provincial identity. Newspapers could and did reflect local consciousness and articulate local concerns and grievances. This element became increasingly marked towards the end of the period, as the amount of space devoted to editorial comment and local issues became more substantial. Donald Read has explored the growth of provincial opinion through debates on slavery and parliamentary reform, and the reporting of Luddite disturbances and incidents such as Peterloo, in the pages of the press in the Midlands and the north of England.[65] He concentrates on the nineteenth century, since for much of the eighteenth century overt partisan comment was avoided by many editors for fear of alienating readers.[66] It was therefore thought safer to keep news coverage to affairs of more general import, rather than reflect on local events. Yet, the provincial press could build up a sense of local community by more implicit means. From the very onset of provincial printing, the pages of local newspapers had operated in the manner of local notice-boards, advertising not just consumer goods, but events such as assemblies, plays, concerts, appeals for subscriptions, announcements of meetings, and lists of charitable donors. Articles lost and found, situations vacant and bankruptcies were also brought to public attention through the local press. It is true that this was not a specifically urban development –

64. G. Cranfield, 'Handlist of English provincial newspapers and periodicals', *Cambridge Bibliographical Society Monograph*, no. 2 (1952); R. M. Wiles, *Freshest Advices: early Provincial Newspapers in England* (Ohio, 1965); John Feather, *The Provincial Booktrade in Eighteenth-Century England* (Cambridge, 1985); C. Mitchell, 'Provincial printing in eighteenth-century Britain', *Publishing History*, 21 (1987), pp. 5–24.

65. Donald Read, *The English Provinces c. 1760–1960. A Study in Influence* (1964).

66. Although see Hannah Barker, 'Catering for provincial tastes: newspapers, readership and profit in late eighteenth-century England', *Historical Research* (1996), pp. 44–61, who argues for a greater degree of editorial independence, even partisanship, than has traditionally been allowed.

indeed, arguably these pages were even more important for those living in rural communities, who had far less contact with the urban centres, but the cultural world which was embodied was one which was firmly grounded in the local town.

Newspapers illustrate the extent to which eighteenth-century culture was dependent upon printed and literary sources, but they represent only a small fraction of the amount of published material which became available for the urban readership. One of the most successful genres was the periodical or magazine, offering a combination of essays, reviews, letters and news. These were originally a product of the pamphlet debate of the Civil War.[67] The first example of a paper with no element of news, appears to have been a periodical called *The Athenian Mercury*, chiefly made up answers to readers' questions (real or fictional) and correspondence, published by John Dunton from 1691–7. The success of the format was assured in the first decades of the eighteenth century with the publication of *The Tatler*, a thrice weekly periodical which ran from 1709–11, published by Richard Steele and *The Spectator*, which Steele published in partnership with Joseph Addison on a daily basis for 22 months from 1711. *The Spectator* was an enormous success especially amongst its urban readership. Addison boasted that over 3,000 copies were being published every day in 1711; the actual readership would, of course, have been much higher.[68] Its essays ranged over issues of taste, social values and the conventions of civilized behaviour, providing urbane and entertaining guidance on negotiating life in a polite and commercial society. It became, in effect, a conduct book of the middling sort. It was frequently republished throughout the century and spawned numerous imitations (both in England and throughout the rest of Europe), providing a touchstone for literary journalism and framing expectations of polite behaviour for years to come. Of equal fame but greater longevity was the *Gentleman's Magazine*, a highly successful combination of news of current events and political reportage, essays, obituaries, book reviews and readers' letters, on a broad range of subjects. Founded by Edward Cave, a journeyman printer, in 1731, it survived until after the end of the First World War, spawning many imitators.

The rapid spread of coffee houses, initially in seventeenth-century London, but in provincial towns such as Oxford from 1650,

67. Walter Graham, *The Beginnings of the English Literary Periodicals: A Study of Periodical Literature, 1665–1715* (Oxford, 1926).
68. Addison and Steele, *Selections from the Tatler and the Spectator*, p. 210.

was due not just to the alacrity with which the English took to the caffeine habit, but the opportunities which these places offered for the consumption of the printed word and discussion. The format of many of the essays in the *Tatler* and *Spectator* was based upon conversations of an imaginary group of friends meeting in a coffee house. Not all establishments which aspired to style themselves coffee houses, could really justify the claim, as John Macky commented rather caustically on Shrewsbury, 'There is a good Town House, and the most Coffee Houses round it that I ever saw in any Town; but when you come into them, they are but Ale-houses, only they think that the Name of Coffee House gives them a better Air'.[69] There were said to be over 2,000 in London in the eighteenth century, but the accuracy of such figures is impossible to establish. In London and a number of other towns, the coffee house was gradually superseded by taverns and inns, and lost out to the competition from tea drinking, but the principle of a comfortable location for reading news, periodicals and other matters, combined with an element of conviviality, was transferred to other institutions.[70] Many towns had purpose-built 'newsrooms', open to subscribers and the public upon payment of a fee. Inns frequently offered the provision of newspapers as one of their attractions, and libraries, such as the Athenaeum in Liverpool, took on an element of the full-blown club.

The Athenaeum was primarily a library and, as such, was one of the more grandiose examples of its kind.[71] Libraries, book clubs and literary institutions owed their raison d'être to the eighteenth-century enthusiasm for reading and discussion. At least 160 parish libraries were endowed in towns and villages across England between 1680–1800, for religious and educational purposes, and in addition to these there were around 130 'Bray Libraries', which were intended specifically for the education of the clergy. However, few of these libraries allowed books to be borrowed, and their selection was generally limited to theological works. In a few towns, the parish library was of wider public access, or became transformed into a lending library. The Castle Book Club at Colchester, for example, was originally based upon Bishop Harsnett's private library, which he had left to the parish of All Souls in the seventeenth century.[72]

---

69. Macky, *Tour through England*, ii, p. 154.
70. Aytoun Ellis, *The Penny Universities. A History of the Coffee House* (1956).
71. Thomas Kelly, *Early Public Libraries. A History of Public Libraries in Great Britain before 1850* (1966).
72. Thomas Cromwell, *The History and Description of the Ancient Town and Borough of Colchester in Essex* (1825), p. 344.

Of more importance to the public at large were the subscription or proprietary libraries, book clubs and circulating libraries. These were very much an eighteenth-century phenomenon. Subscription or proprietary libraries were based upon members paying a membership fee and annual subscription, out of which funds books would be purchased, rooms would be hired, and possibly a librarian employed. These libraries generally comprised several thousand volumes, many of which would have been weighty tomes published by subscription, costing several guineas a piece. Borrowing records have not generally survived, but where they have, as in Bristol for example, they provide fascinating insights into reading habits. History and travel literature were the most widely read; Hume's *History of England* and Sir John Hawkesworth's *Voyages* proved particularly popular among the Bristolian reading public.[73] Entrance fees were normally of the order of one guinea, rising to four or five guineas by the 1790s, and the annual fee was usually an additional ten shillings. By the 1820s, some libraries had become extremely exclusive, charging £20 or more. Subscription libraries were, therefore, effectively restricted to the wealthier elite, and often drew on many county gentry who joined as 'corresponding' members. The earliest provincial subscription library appears to have been that in Liverpool, founded in 1758, but the format was quickly adopted elsewhere in over 30 other towns by 1800. Joseph Priestley, the dissenting scientist and man of letters, was involved in establishing libraries in three centres: Warrington (1760), Leeds (1768) and Birmingham (1779). Book clubs tended to be smaller bodies, with around 25 members. The club's books were generally sold off after a number of years, thereby generating income, and cutting costs, as there was no need to rent special accommodation or to pay a librarian. They could therefore be supported by much smaller communities, and even villages, and the existence of over 100 such book clubs has been traced between 1700–1800.[74]

Cheaper alternatives were available for the less wealthy; the circulating libraries and the public libraries were within the range of a much wider income bracket. Circulating libraries seem to have evolved out of bookshops, originating in the tendency of customers to browse. The first recorded circulating library was that belonging to Francis Kirkman of London in 1661. Many were run as a profitable sideline by booksellers who charged a small fee for the loan

73. Paul Kaufman, *Borrowings from the Bristol Library, 1773–84. A Unique Record of Reading Vogues* (Charlottesville, 1960).
74. Kelly, *Early Public Libraries*, pp. 136–40.

of individual volumes from their stock. Readers in Stamford were charged 2d for volumes worth more than 18d, and 1d for those worth 1s, for a week's loan. Customers were also able to buy a variety of patent medicines and other products stocked by the bookseller.[75] They generally offered lighter reading material, predominantly duodecimos (the smallest, least expensive kind of book) in cheap bindings, which could be laid aside without too much loss after they ceased to be fashionable. Circulating libraries were extremely popular in 'resort' towns, providing an essential service to visitors, not only in terms of reading matter, but as a meeting place. Smollett's heroine Lydia Melford, writing to her school friend Miss Willis, explained that young women were not permitted to frequent the coffee houses in Bath, where 'the conversation turns upon politics, scandal, philosophy and other topics above our capacity', whereas she was free to visit the booksellers' shops 'which are charming places of resort; where we read novels, plays, pamphlets, and newspapers, for so small a fee as a crown a quarter; and in these offices of intelligence . . . all the reports of the day, and all the private transactions of the Bath, are first entered and discussed'.[76] There were at least nine in Bath as early as 1780, of which the establishment in Cheap Street offered its readers not only a choice of over 7,000 volumes, but over 30 daily and weekly London and provincial papers.[77]

Traditionally, they were regarded as the haunt solely of young impressionable girls, such as Lydia Melford, seeking romantic novels and possibly romantic excitement. Research has, however, demonstrated a more prosaic truth; that they were in fact frequented by a much broader mix of age and gender.[78] Nevertheless, moralists frequently expressed concern at both the social informality encouraged in such settings, and also the effect which such frivolous and lightweight reading might have upon the reader's mind – corrupting the morals of the young, leading on to habits of luxury, and stifling all original thought. Conversely, there were those who believed that encouraging reading habits was the best means of countering the threat of alcohol and gambling. Extravagant claims were made of men who had been cured of these vices simply by subscribing to

75. R. J. Goulden and M. J. Crump, 'Four library catalogues of note', *Factotum*, 3 (1978), pp. 11–13.

76. Smollett, *Humphry Clinker*, pp. 69–70.

77. *Bath Chronicle*, 1 Jan. 1784. Quoted in Trevor Fawcett (ed.), *Voices of Eighteenth-Century Bath* (Ruton, 1995), p. 118.

78. Jan Fergus, 'Eighteenth-century readers in provincial England. The customers of Samuel Clay's circulating library and bookshop in Warwick, 1770–2', *Bibliographical Society of America Papers*, 78 (1984).

circulating libraries. These literary converts, it was argued, would gradually acquire a love for reading, and the money, which was formerly spent on alcohol, would be spent on books and the hours spent in wasteful gambling would be profitably employed in reading and self-improvement.[79] By the early nineteenth century there was much more reading provision for the less wealthy classes, reflecting the importance attached to encouraging literacy among the labouring sort, as a means of moral improvement, and creating a more highly skilled work-force. Artisans' book clubs were set up in a number of towns, such as Birmingham (where they acquired the reputation of being centres of radical activity), and working class subscription libraries, which cost only a few shillings per year, were established in Liverpool and Sheffield in 1823. Mechanics Institutions, which spread rapidly following the end of the Napoleonic Wars, were similarly aimed at encouraging literacy, reading habits and self-improvement among the labouring classes. Controversial books on theology and politics were often forbidden – literacy had dangerous potential as well, of which the establishment was well aware.

Libraries were often affiliated to other institutions, most notably literary and philosophical or scientific societies. The prototype for these societies was the Royal Society of London, founded in 1660, and the Society of Antiquaries which was refounded in 1707.[80] The Gentleman's Society of Spalding, founded by Maurice Johnson in 1712, was obviously modelled on these institutions, and in turn it inspired followers in several other towns in the area including, Peterborough, Stamford and Grantham.[81] The latter was very short-lived and, indeed, this was not untypical of such provincial associations. It was difficult to maintain attendance and interest over a number of years, especially in these smaller towns. In the later eighteenth and early nineteenth centuries, there was a marked up-surge in the number of literary and scientific institutions, many of which were of rather longer duration and drew on a more 'urban' constituency. Large towns, such as Manchester (1781), Newcastle (1793) and Exeter (1796), established such societies before the end of the eighteenth century, but they only became widespread following the end of the war in 1815. Inter-town rivalry was clearly an important stimulus, as in 1822 Hull, Whitby, Sheffield and York each

79. *The Use of Circulating Libraries Considered* (1797).

80. Michael Hunter, *Science and Society in Restoration England* (Cambridge, 1981); Joan Evans, *A History of the Society of Antiquaries* (Oxford, 1956).

81. D. M. Owen (ed.), 'The minute book of the Spalding Gentlemen's Society, 1712–55', *Lincoln Record Society*, lxxiii (1981).

acquired one of these institutions, and their respective rules and constitutions were closely modelled upon each other. Societies cor-
responded with each other, exchanging papers and information, a
practice which became increasingly relevant as they became more
deeply involved in the discussion of matters of public welfare in the
nineteenth century.

The earlier Spalding Society is best seen as a society for gentlemen from the surrounding area meeting in the town, for convenience rather than a specifically urban meeting. The later 'lit and
phil' societies tended to have a closer connection with the town
itself, both in terms of membership and the subjects discussed.
Some societies sponsored important research; the first local census
in Hull in 1792 was supported by the Society for the Purpose of
Literary Information. Many of the results of Thomas Percival's
investigations into population and public health in Manchester
were presented in papers for the Literary and Philosophical Society.
It would, however, be wrong to suppose that these societies were
restricted to industrializing areas, or had a special utilitarian relationship with science and the development of industry. Professor Porter
has persuasively argued that the importance of such societies was as
an expression of cultural status, and that they offered little in the
way of a utilitarian bent. Although scientific papers were read at a
number of societies, the literary element was also strong and often
predominated – in Newcastle this occasioned some conflict between
those who wanted to see the Literary and Philosophical Society take
on a more scientific orientation, and those who held that its main
importance was to provide library facilities.[82] The society in Hull
was founded on the belief that the cultivation of the arts (rather
than the sciences) was indispensable to the happiness and prosperity of any town.[83] William Roscoe, merchant, reformer and leader
of Liverpool's intellectual circle, lived out this principle in his own
life and achieved fame for his biography of Lorenzo de' Medici. However, even if these societies did little in real terms to push back the
frontiers of knowledge, they certainly encouraged a culture of self-
improvement and education, through their libraries and meetings,

82. Roy Porter, 'Science, provincial culture and public opinion in enlightenment
England', in Borsay (ed.), *The Eighteenth-Century Town*, pp. 243–67; compare Michael
Neve, 'Science in a commercial city. Bristol, 1820–60', in I. Inkster and J. Morrell
(eds), *Metropolis and Province. Science in British Culture, 1780–1850* (1985), pp. 179–
204; A. Thackray, 'Natural knowledge in cultural context: the Manchester model',
AmHR, lxxix (1974), pp. 672–709.

83. Charles Frost, *Address Delivered to the Literary and Philosophical Society at Hull,
5 Nov. 1830* (Hull, 1831), p. 59.

and also by sponsoring other projects such as lectures and demonstrations, or establishing Botanic Gardens. The decision of Hull subscription library to allocate £50 of its funds to lectures on mechanics, chemistry, natural history, and subjects related to commerce, was typical of the kind of public spirited patronage of the arts upon which such societies prided themselves.[84]

The public lecture with scientific experiment, like that depicted in Joseph Wright's painting *An Experiment on a Bird in the Air Pump* (1768), became a popular form of urban entertainment. Lecture courses are to be found regularly advertised in the pages of the local press all over England. As a form of instruction, these lectures can be traced back (yet again) to the coffee houses of eighteenth-century London, where scientists, such as John Theophilus Desaguliers and William Whiston, earned a living by demonstrating the new science to the public.[85] Provincial lecturers have been identified enlightening the people of Leeds in the 1730s, and by the 1770s courses were being held in resorts and smaller towns, as well as the provincial centres. The 1766 guide to Tunbridge Wells referred to 'Lectures upon the arts and sciences superficial enough to entertain the imagination without fatiguing the understanding'.[86] Birmingham had received over seventeen different lecturers by the 1790s, including the famous Prussian lecturer, Dr Katterfelto.[87] Lectures were enlivened with models and demonstrations – electrical experiments appear to have been particularly popular on account of the sparks produced. Further entertainment was provided with musical interludes. These occasions often cost as little as 6d to attend, and were therefore accessible to the skilled artisan as well as the more prosperous middling sort. Their value as a medium of education is not easily established, but they would at least have increased the familiarity of the audience with the advances being made in science.

Timing and Incidence of the Urban Renaissance

Inns, assemblies, theatres, literary societies and print culture, represented some of the principal expressions of cultural life in English

---

84. Ibid., p. 7.   85. Larry Stewart, *The Rise of Public Science* (Cambridge, 1992).
86. T. Burr, *The History of Tunbridge Wells* (1766), p. 124.
87. John Money, *Experience and Identity. Birmingham and the West Midlands, 1760–1800* (Manchester, 1977), pp. 140–1.

towns. The incidence of these innovations and improvements varied greatly from town to town, and was highly contingent on other factors, notably communications and finance. Prior to the eighteenth century, the most heavily urbanized areas were in the south east, but by the end of our period the balance had shifted towards the Midlands and the north, where the industrial towns had long outpaced their southern counterparts. However, the regional centres and market towns of the south characteristically had much longer urban traditions and a stronger sense of civic identity, and it was often these smaller centres which led the way in establishing new forms of cultural activity. There was a strong input of local pride in the establishment and patronage of these cultural forms, and the older urban communities were far richer in this respect than the newly established towns, which had had little chance to build up a sense of tradition or inherited identity. The pattern of publication of urban histories, a typical product of the 'urban renaissance', also suggests a greater propensity for cultural investment among the older centres of the south during the eighteenth century, whereas by the nineteenth century the self-confidence of the manufacturing towns was being expressed in a rash of historical publications in the Midlands and the north.[88] Clearly, far more wealth would eventually be generated in the large manufacturing and commercial towns, but the growth of internal and domestic trade, accompanied by an increase in handling efficiency from the late seventeenth century onwards, benefitted the market towns, and created greater profits which could be channelled into civic improvement and cultural development. Enterprises, such as public building and improvements to the urban environment through lighting and paving acts, offered an attractive investment in towns where there was capital to spare.[89] In manufacturing towns, however, such investment was slower to take off because spare capital tended to be ploughed back into business concerns. This trend is corroborated by research which indicates that retail shops took longer to become established in the north than in the south of

88. Sweet, *Writing of Urban Histories*, pp. 9–12, 286–7.
89. C. W. Chalkin, *The Provincial Towns of Georgian England: A Study of the Building Process, 1740–1820* (1974); Malcolm Falkus, 'Lighting in the dark ages of English economic history: town streets before the industrial revolution', in D. C. Coleman and A. H. John (eds), *Trade, Government and Economy in Pre-Industrial England* (1976), pp. 248–73; E. L. Jones and M. E. Falkus, 'Urban improvement and the English economy in the seventeenth and eighteenth centuries', in Borsay (ed.), *The Eighteenth-Century Town*, pp. 116–58.

England.[90] By the early nineteenth century, the tremendous wealth at the disposal of the merchant and manufacturing plutocracies of Liverpool or Manchester meant that they were beginning to lead the way in grandiose schemes of public expenditure.[91] The people of Liverpool raised £28,000 in 1801 from voluntary subscriptions, for the building of the Athenaeum, the Union News Room and the Botanic Gardens – and these were far from being the only schemes underway. In 1803, £80,000 in £100 shares was raised in just a few hours towards the £100,000 cost of rebuilding the Exchange.[92]

Urban improvement required what is often known as 'lumpy' investment, that is, large sums of capital. Credit facilities were still very primitive; improvement commissions could raise money by mortgaging the paving rates or the tolls allowed under the terms of the improvement, while the capital was generally raised among local investors rather than from a bank. Annuities were another popular form of finance, although they could turn out to be a very expensive solution if the annuitants lived longer than expected. The Cheltenham improvement commissioners, presumably banking on the fact that people who chose to live in a spa must be in bad health and therefore likely to be short-lived, raised money by issuing annuities at 9.5 per cent. Unfortunately, the annuitants were clearly living proof of the efficacy of the spa's curative properties and were extremely long–lived, helping to precipitate the commissioners into financial crisis in 1810.[93] Single or widowed women, who tended to congregate in towns, often invested their capital in this way, as it provided them with an assured income. The high risks involved in promoting such schemes meant that matters were often left to private initiatives, by selling shares, forming a tontine (a scheme of life annuity) or simply by public subscription. The pages of any provincial newspaper, after 1770, regularly carried advertisements appealing for subscribers for public undertakings, such as an infirmary, a new theatre or assembly rooms. Even mundane enterprises such as repaving streets or taking down obstructions might be financed by an appeal to private charity, as in Scarborough in 1810, when it was found necessary to seek voluntary subscriptions to pay for lighting

90. H. C. and L. Mui, *Shops and Shopkeeping in Eighteenth-Century England* (1989).

91. C. W. Chalkin, 'Capital expenditure on building for cultural purposes in provincial England, 1730–1830', *Business History*, 20 (1980), pp. 51–70.

92. Henry Smithers, *Liverpool: its Commerce, Statistics and Institutions with a History of the Town* (Liverpool, 1825), pp. 342–61.

93. Gwen Hart, *A History of Cheltenham* (Leicester, 1965), p. 269.

the street lamps, despite having the power to levy rates of up to two shillings in the pound under an improvement act of 1805.[94] Once the money was secured, it was not always easy to keep up the improving momentum, especially when the costs of the original plans began rapidly to exceed the money available. Time and again improvement commissioners reached the limit of the sums they were allowed to borrow under the terms of the act, while the generosity of subscribers had an alarming tendency to dry up after the first flush of enthusiasm. Financial planning was handicapped by inexperience; in the seventeenth century there had been almost no investment in public building and there was little precedent for assessing how much large-scale projects would cost. Most problematic of all, the rate-paying public were not accustomed to being called upon to fund such capital-heavy investments, and had a low tolerance threshold for what they were prepared to contribute. Later, statutory bodies were given more latitude with respect to the funds which they were permitted to raise, but the expectations of the public always outstripped their willingness to spend.

Peter Borsay's study focused on a number of towns which were more obviously influenced by the custom of the gentry. In towns such as Warwick, Bury St Edmunds and York, there was considerable improvement in the 1690s, and again in the 1730s (when the cathedral town of Salisbury acquired the first non-metropolitan improvement commission). However, for most towns, the real impact of urban improvement was not felt until rather later in the century, after the end of the Seven Years War in 1763. More towns were experiencing greater prosperity and the spending power of the middling sort was increasing proportionately. Contemporaries were very conscious of the dramatic changes which were taking place, and looked back on an era of pre-improvement, before the ascendancy of civilized manners and polite society. Alexander Jenkins, historian of Exeter, singled out 1768 as the year when the 'spirit of improvement' began to manifest itself, when the houses on the high street were rebuilt, a hotel was erected for holding assemblies, and the tower of St Mary's, the Northgate and the Conduit at Carfax were all taken down.[95] By the nineteenth century, improvement had left its mark in almost all towns; it was only the most decayed market town where no kind of investment in the urban fabric had been made. Although historians now tend to think

94. Phyllis Hembry, *The English Spa, 1560–1815: A Social History* (1990), p. 214.
95. Alexander Jenkins, *The History and Antiquities of the City of Exeter and its Environs, ancient and modern, civil and ecclesiastical* (Exeter, 1806), pp. 212–14.

in terms of the availability of capital and credit, in determining the extent and pace of change, these factors were less immediately obvious to the eighteenth-century observer, who tended simply to look upon improvement as the tangible proof of progress towards a more perfect society. As communications throughout the country were opened up, with turnpikes and better travel facilities, few areas were left untouched by the beneficial influence of urban civilization.

CHAPTER EIGHT

Conclusion: Metropolitan Influence or Provincial Identity?

Following the improvement of the roads leading to Taunton, its historian, Joshua Toulmin noted 'a general civilization and refinement of manners, the spread of the same modes of dress and living, of the same taste and amusements, through the kingdom; in consequence of the frequent and easy communications which turnpike roads have opened between the capital and other towns, to the remotest extremities of the isle'.[1] There were many others who shared Toulmin's assumption that all cultural progress could be traced back to London; 'the central point where arts originate and from whence they ramify', as another local historian described it.[2] Observers were quick to draw attention to the influence of the metropolis upon architectural styles, pastimes, fashions and all matters of taste. Provincial towns were assumed to be striving to become 'little Londons'. Historians have tended to follow this assumption and have written in terms of the growth of homogeneity and uniformity in urban culture, as a result of the metropolitan influence, arguing that 'the provincials' prime aim was to assimilate metropolitan cultures and values'.[3] It is indeed highly plausible that provincial towns should have avidly adopted the latest fashions from London, and that the ease with which these could be communicated greatly enhanced this tendency. The boom in publishing – newspapers, books, pamphlets and novels – created not only a greater sense of national consciousness, but common cultural values. Vernacular architecture was abandoned in favour of the neo-classical facade, disseminated through architectural pattern books; civic rituals gave way to

1. Joshua Toulmin, *The History of the Town of Taunton* (Taunton, 1791), pp. 175–6.
2. Richard Warner, *The History of Bath* (1801), p. 224.
3. Roy Porter, 'Science, provincial culture and public opinion in enlightenment England', in Peter Borsay (ed.), *The Eighteenth-Century Town, 1688–1820* (1990), p. 251.

the rituals of the assembly, and local identity was arguably subsumed in the pursuit of urbane refinement. The remarkable progress made in transport was breaking down regional particularities. Thanks to the turnpikes, road travel costs had been dramatically cut, in terms of both time and money. The canals linked together the nation's regional economies, and highly complex webs of economic inter-dependence were being constructed, while the postal service ensured that no part of the country could remain unacquainted with affairs in London for long.

London had a symbolic importance as the embodiment of urban depravity and crime, and as the arbiter of taste and fashion.[4] As we have already seen, there were plenty of examples of London's role as a cultural innovator, whether it was in building regulations, pleasure gardens or charity oratorios. It is also clear that among the landed elite a 'uniquely metropolitan identity' emerged in this period, which was based upon their social and cultural exper-ience of London during the Season.[5] But to suggest that every innovation and fashion of the metropolitan elite was slavishly and uncritically adopted is, to say the least, an unflattering assumption to make on the part of the provinces, denying them any sense of their own traditions and cultural integrity, or the possibility of altern-ative patterns of cultural transmission. The model of cultural as-similation as being a 'trickle-down' effect from London, which has been so frequently set up, is too simplistic and focuses too narrowly on an unrepresentative view of the urban elite. Historians of urban culture have perhaps been overly influenced in the past by the comments of contemporary *metropolitan* observers, who judged towns according to their own experience of London, and found them accordingly satisfactory or wanting. Hence, there is a need to reas-sess provincial urban culture on its own terms, in the same way that political historians have been trying to move away from an under-standing of politics, which has viewed the rest of the country from the perspective of Westminster. As Dror Wahrman has suggested, there are two ways of viewing eighteenth-century society, one is from the national perspective, and the other is from the 'communal-local', which was typically espoused by the urban middling sort.[6]

4. John Brewer, *The Pleasures of the Imagination. English Culture in the Eighteenth Cen-tury* (1997), provides a good introduction to contemporary perceptions of London, esp. chs 1 and 2.

5. J. M. Rosenheim, *The Emergence of a Ruling Order. English Landed Society, 1650–1750* (1998), pp. 215–52.

6. Dror Wahrman, 'National society, communal culture: an argument about the recent historiography of eighteenth-century Britain', *Social History*, xvii (1992), pp. 43–72.

Unfortunately, many of our sources for descriptions of provincial life are inherently more prone to support a 'national' perspective, being derived from the diaries of the visiting gentry, or the observations of travellers (generally from the metropolis), who concentrated on precisely those aspects of urban culture which were most obviously derivative of the metropolis, comparing them always to those to be found in London. Similarly, descriptions of urban society were penned by moralists, who, as we noted above, were disturbed by any evidence of vice, extravagance and immorality, and immediately associated it with middling society in any town. The 'communal-local' perspective on urban culture needs to be brought into focus. Stana Nenadic has shown, for example, that for most of our period middle class consumers in Glasgow and Edinburgh were much more likely to purchase locally made goods, and participate in the second–hand market, rather than chase after London fashions. However, the kind of consumerism driven by social emulation which elite commentators were eager to pin upon the middling sort, as proof of their 'mindless hedonism and luxury', is a gross oversimplification – but shows us how little the elite understood the culture of the middling ranks, and the meanings which they attached to these objects.[7] It would not seem unreasonable to suggest that the elite were similarly unreceptive to other expressions of local cultural values and identity. It is important to bear in mind that the gentry, for whom much of the more exclusive entertainment and facilities were provided, and who were the most likely to have had experience of London's lifestyle, represented only a very small, albeit a high profile, proportion of the urban population, and in many cases were only transitory residents. Even in Hanoverian London, the 'genteel' constituted a maximum of three per cent of the population.[8] The extent to which the social elite could form a separate community, with little contact with the rest of the town, is highlighted in the case of Lincoln, where a sharp division existed between society 'below hill', comprising the labourers and poorer middling sort, and society 'above hill', where the county gentry gathered with the families of the cathedral close, in a round of social activities in which there was almost no contact with the people below the hill at all, to the extent that they had separate assemblies and playhouses.[9]

7. Stana Nenadic, 'Middle-rank consumers and domestic culture in Edinburgh and Glasgow, 1720–1840', *P&P*, 145 (1994), p. 154.

8. George Rudé, *Hanoverian London* (1971), p. 58.

9. Francis Hill, *Georgian Lincoln* (Cambridge, 1966), esp. pp. 1–75.

If we take a more inclusive view of what constituted urban culture, we find that the persistence of traditional cultural forms challenges any assumptions about the effortless ascendancy of metropolitan fashions and values. Cultural identities, whether local or national, have always depended on a sense of historical tradition, and towns in the eighteenth century were no exception. Civic identity, based upon a sense of the past, especially as expressed through rituals, histories, architecture and in politics, was extremely strong in many towns. This historical awareness was a defining feature of the way in which urban communities perceived themselves and their place in the broader national context.

Considerable importance was placed upon preserving the emblems of former greatness, as well as current prosperity, and the antiquity of the town was an essential element in its cultural standing. As William Somner, historian of Canterbury, had declared in 1640, 'So great and Universal is the Respect that is worthily given to venerable Antiquity, that not any one Ornament sets off any place, whether City or other, with greater lustre ... than the time and known Antiquity, and long duration of the place.'[10] Even William Hutton, the historian of Birmingham, who revelled in its modern vibrancy and dynamism, still felt it incumbent upon himself to give the town some historical credentials by arguing that the depth of the sunken roads leading into the town betokened a settlement of very great antiquity, as it would have taken a great length of time to wear the roads down to such an extent.[11] Corporations vied with each other to prove the higher antiquity of their foundation, and even those with no foundation charter to prove their origins were loath to relinquish all claims to historical standing. Urban improvement involved the destruction of much of the medieval fabric of many towns, but not all gothic buildings were pulled down heedlessly, in the pursuit of regularity and straight lines; market crosses, city gates and churches were often preserved (or even relocated) because of their historical associations for the town. Bristol High Cross, whose carvings represented key points in the city's history, enjoyed a chequered history in the eighteenth century, admired and revered by some and disregarded by others. However, when improvers wanted to dismantle it in 1763, in order to widen the walks on College Green where it stood, a subscription was opened to rebuild the cross in an alternative location.[12] Civic rituals declined in the wake

10. William Somner, *The Antiquities of Canterbury*, 2nd edn (1701), p. 1.
11. William Hutton, *An History of Birmingham* (Birmingham, 1781), p. 17.
12. William Barrett, *The History and Antiquities of Bristol* (Bristol, 1789), pp. 274–5.

of refined taste and politeness, but their memory lived on as part of the distinctive culture of the town. The Stamford Bull Running, regarded by the polite as a barbaric outrage, was jealously upheld as the town's 'supreme glory', and was not allowed to fall into abeyance, despite its barbaric origins.[13] The progress of civilization might have rendered such customs incompatible with polite society, but it did not mean that they should be surrendered to oblivion.[14]

The urban community still joined together in public celebrations, which conformed to a national calendar of anniversaries, such as 5 November, but these were also the occasions for the celebration of local achievement, solidarity and the reciprocal bonds of society, best represented by the philanthropic institutions. Processions of charity school children, freemasons, the companies and guilds and the civic elite, made a statement about the communal identity of the town, and gave tangible expression to the ideal of consensus, albeit one which was becoming increasingly hollow in a number of towns.[15] The corporation embodied authority and the legal standing of the town, the charities were a reflection of the strength of communal philanthropy and public spirit, and the guilds represented the commercial and manufacturing success of the local economy, even after they had otherwise fallen into abeyance. In Preston, although the guilds had been effectively disbanded in the early eighteenth century, they were nevertheless 'reconstituted' long afterwards, in order that they could process in the Guild Merchant every 20 years, in an important demonstration of communal spirit and pride.[16] The pseudo-gentry and the visiting elite may not have participated in events based around the church, the guild, or the friendly society, but for the middling sort they remained as an important element in the collective life of the town.

It is perhaps helpful here to take up the distinction drawn by Jonathan Barry between urban culture, which was 'urbane', and that which was 'civic'.[17] The two co-existed, and indeed could

---

13. W. Harrod, *The History and Antiquities of Stamford and St Martin's*, 2 vols (Stamford, 1785), i, p. 189.

14. Jonathan Barry, 'Provincial town culture, 1640–1760: urbane or civic?', in J. Pittock and A. Weir (eds), *Interpretation and Cultural History* (Basingstoke, 1991), 198–254; Rosemary Sweet, *The Writing of Urban Histories in Eighteenth-Century England* (Oxford, 1997), esp. ch. 6.

15. Mark Harrison, *Crowds and History: mass phenomena in English Towns, 1790–1835* (Cambridge, 1988), pp. 234–67.

16. R. D. Parker, 'The Changing Character of Preston Guild Merchant, 1762–1862', *Northern History*, xx (1984), pp. 108–26.

17. Barry, 'Provincial town culture'.

overlap, but it is the urbane element of assemblies and pleasure gardens which has tended to catch the historian's eye. Underneath the cultural innovations, we should not forget the continuity of older forms of civic culture among the middling sort, which were not necessarily displaced, or alternatively persisted under a contemporary eighteenth-century guise. Sermons and services in the parish church continued to provide a focal point to many civic occasions. Freemasons offered the same opportunities for conviviality and philanthropy as had the medieval guilds, and had a similar hierarchical structure and rites of initiation. The speed with which freemasonry spread in provincial towns was not due to the power of London to inspire a slavish emulation, but reflected the extent to which the freemasonic movement could be grafted onto existing traditions.[18] Fashions imported from the metropolis had their attraction, but a more practical model for emulation was often more easily found in a neighbouring town. Assembly rooms were generally modelled on those of leading spa towns, rather than London, where the scale of such buildings was far beyond the purposes of provincial towns. Literary societies were established after the example set by Manchester, rather than national bodies, such as the Royal or Antiquarian Societies. The intention of societies, such as the Newcastle 'Lit. and Phil.', was to concentrate on improvement in the local context, rather than pursue a programme of general scientific inquiry, as was done in London.[19] John Money's meticulous study of the cultural life of Birmingham and the West Midlands demonstrates how Birmingham developed a flourishing musical and theatrical life, in part derived from London models, in part following the lead set by the more 'genteel' town of Lichfield. The imported models, however, were considerably modified, not proving to be 'entirely amenable to paternalist control', in the face of the increasing articulacy of Birmingham's ordinary people. In turn, as he points out, the way in which music and theatre were promoted also had a highly significant impact upon the future development of the town's character and political culture.[20]

18. For a lengthier discussion of this issue, see Jonathan Barry, 'Bourgeois collectivism? Urban association and the middling sort', in Jonathan Barry and Christopher Brooks (eds), *The Middling Sort of People. Culture, Society and Politics in England, 1550–1800* (1994), pp. 84–112.

19. D. Orange, 'Rational Dissent and provincial science. William Turner and the Newcastle Literary and Philosophical Society', in I. Inkster and J. Morrell (eds), *Metropolis and Province. Science in the Provinces, 1780–1850* (1983), p. 211.

20. John Money, *Experience and Identity. Birmingham and the West Midlands 1760–1800* (Manchester, 1977), esp. pp. 80–97.

Assembly rooms, theatres, squares and terraces were built on the lines of pattern books published by London architects, and decorated by metropolitan craftsmen, bringing their skills to the provinces. But beneath the classical symmetry, we need not assume that this precluded their becoming objects of civic pride. We are accustomed to associate the building projects of Victorian towns, such as Leeds Town Hall, which at £122,000 exceeded the original estimated costs by 300%, with the expression of civic pride, but less has been made of the more restrained gestures of earlier generations. The end product might differ in architectural style, but the statement being made was ultimately the same. Buildings were the most tangible form of conspicuous consumption, and were proof of the success of the town's economy and the good taste of its inhabitants. It was this, rather than the London connection, which the locally authored guides and histories concentrated upon. Indeed, as a study of buildings in the West Riding of Yorkshire shows, London was seldom mentioned as a source of ideas.[21] Not all cultural innovation came from London, after all. The precedent for the movement in palladian and neo-classical architecture was, of course, that of the renaissance and classical antiquity, and as such, it was the common heritage of all towns, not just London. Provincial architects, such as Dean Aldrich of Oxford or John Wood of Bath, drew their inspiration direct from classical sources, unmediated by the influences of London architects, and, particularly in the case of Wood, re-interpreted the classical forms in a very idiosyncratic manner, determined by his understanding of Bath's history.[22] Not all towns adopted the classical forms, and nor were terraces and squares necessarily suited to the existing lay-out. Eighteenth-century Stamford consisted of many separate tenements, in what was already becoming an overcrowded environment, and there was neither the will nor the space for building an essentially collaborative project, such as a terrace or square.[23] One historian of Hull, while acknowledging the elegant architectural improvements to his town would attract and impress the visitors, insisted that nevertheless

21. K. Grady, *The Georgian Public Buildings of Leeds and the West Riding*, Thoresby Society Publications, lxii (1989); See also, Peter Borsay, 'The London connection: cultural diffusion and the eighteenth-century provincial town', *London Journal*, 19 (1994), pp. 21–35.

22. R. Wittkower, *Palladio and English Palladianism* (1983). On Wood's architecture see R. Neale, 'Bath: Ideology and Utopia, 1700–60', in Borsay (ed.), *The Eighteenth-Century Town*, pp. 223–42; and T. Mowl and B. Earnshaw, *John Wood: Architect of Obsession* (Bath, 1988).

23. A. Rogers, *The Book of Stamford* (Buckingham, 1983), p. 75.

such buildings were 'incongruous and inconsistent with the spirit of the place', preferring instead the traditional vernacular architecture of the merchants' houses.[24] Urban society was imbued with a strong sense of place and history, through which cultural innovations were mediated and modified.

York, as the other archiepiscopal see and metropolis of the north, had traditionally seen itself as a rival to London. In 1736, its historian Francis Drake argued, rather petulantly, that it was only the residence of the royal family which had led to London's phenomenal expansion. But provincial chauvinism was not the monopoly of the heirs to Ebrauk; Liverpool, an upstart in comparison with York, prided itself on the development of its docks – so successful were they, it was claimed, that the metropolis itself sought to emulate them.[25] When one concentrates upon local comments, as opposed to those of visitors, one is struck not by the deference to London, but the strength of local self-sufficiency, pride in achievement and independence. English towns were participating in an increase in prosperity and progression towards a more civilized society, which was affecting the *entire* nation; a progress in which each town had a contributory role to play. As one local historian claimed in rather grandiose terms, 'The history of a nation is inseparably connected with that of the component parts . . . cities, towns, and villages. Whatever may be its public pretensions, whatever splendour it may occasionally derive from military achievements and conquests, it is in these that we look for the true evidence of its strength or weakness, wealth or poverty, meanness or grandeur'.[26] London, as was readily acknowledged, was in a league of its own. Comparisons with London were made, it is true, but this was not just an exercise in measuring up to a metropolitan standard (and failing). More important, was to prove the superiority of the town in question over other similar towns, and London offered the common standard for such an exercise, 'It [Liverpool] now, as has been said, ranks next to the Metropolis: but not merely in political importance; it has also a claim to superiority over other provincial towns in the cultivation of the Fine Arts'.[27] Not infrequently, such

24. George Hadley, *A New and Complete History of the Town and County of the Town of Kingston upon Hull* (Hull, 1788), p. 702.

25. William Moss, *The Liverpool Guide*, 2nd edn (Liverpool, 1797), p. 69; *History of Liverpool* (1810), p. 100.

26. *The Stranger in Liverpool; or, an Historical and Descriptive View of Liverpool and its Environs* (Liverpool, 1807), p. 2.

27. *History of Liverpool*, pp. v–vi.

contrasts were made only to prove the superiority of the local product – for when London was invoked, it was to define what provincial culture was not. London was full of criminals, dissolute practices, corruption, luxury, disease. It was accused of 'communicating every species of moral taint and corruption to the provincial towns and the kingdom in general'.[28] It was best to maintain provincial values rather than to be lured into the seductive snares of the fashionable metropolis, where folly and vice reigned supreme. Moral decline, when it was identified, was attributed to the influx of London manners, and indigenous civic virtue was extolled in contrast; provincial towns were sober, industrious, law-abiding and philanthropic.

A sense of identity depends on a sense of difference, and this brings us back to our earlier chapters, where we discussed the immense difference which existed between towns, differences which arose from the economic base, the geographical location and from the institutions by which towns were governed. These variables contributed over the passage of time to the forging of a town's identity. Once created, however, the sense of identity, tradition, or independence became a variable in its own right – the rhetoric of civic tradition and urban independence constituted an important element in the political culture of a town, and could be crucial in determining the willingness of, for example, a corporation oligarchy, such as Bristol, to intervene in the urban economy. Steve Poole has convincingly argued that the success of measures to preserve stability in Bristol, in the face of a fluctuating market, was largely derived from 'the city's well-developed sense of self-respect and economic independence', which underpinned the paternalist strategies invoked by the magistrates.[29] Likewise, as research on local electoral politics and urban radicalism has shown, the success of the independence movement in many boroughs cannot be understood without comprehending the resonance which notions of local independence and local liberties continued to hold in the contemporary mind.[30]

It has long been realised that large cities are not simply 'insensate masses', as Lewis Mumford once described them, with little to

28. J. Corry, *The History of Macclesfield* (1817), p. 179.

29. Steve Poole, 'Scarcity and the civic tradition: market management in Bristol, 1709–1815', in Adrian Randall and Andrew Charlesworth (eds), *Markets, Market Culture and Popular Protest in Eighteenth-Century Britain and Ireland* (Liverpool, 1996), p. 112.

30. Frank O' Gorman, 'Campaign rituals and ceremonies: the social meaning of elections in England, 1780–1860', *P&P*, 135 (1992), pp. 79–115; Rosemary Sweet, 'Freemen and independence in English borough politics, c. 1770–1830', *P&P*, 161 (1998).

differentiate them except the building materials from which they were constructed.[31] Our survey has done something to show why towns were so varied in character, and how this in turn had far-reaching implications for social structure and political culture. However, important though it is to stress the diversity of towns and the distinctive character of each one, it is also crucial to remember that these towns, albeit unique in themselves, were not autonomous entities, hermetically sealed off from the rest of the nation; populations were mobile, communications were swift and economies were interdependent. The changes in administration we noted in chapters two and three, the movements of opposition and reform, described in chapters four and five, and the socio-cultural developments we saw in chapters six and seven, were never the prerogative of towns, but were prevalent in society as a whole. Thomas Hobbes, the seventeenth-century upholder of monarchical sovereignty, had railed against the 'immoderate greatness' of towns, which were like 'worms in the entrails of a natural man'.[32] We might modify the metaphor, towns were the vital organs of the body; each one unique, and each one performing a vital function, but at the same time interdependent and bound together by an arterial network of roads, rivers and canals. While it is important to study the organs in isolation, in order to come to a better understanding of the organism, we must not forget to put them back into the context of the body as a whole.

31. Quoted in Asa Briggs, *Victorian Cities* (repr. 1990), p. 24.
32. Thomas Hobbes, *Leviathan*, (ed.) C. Macpherson (1968), pp. 374–5, and see p. 62 above.

Select Bibliography

Place of publication is London unless otherwise stated.

CHAPTER ONE: INTRODUCTION

P. ABRAMS and A. E. WRIGLEY (eds), *Towns in Societies. Essays in History and Historical Sociology* (Cambridge, 1987).

C. W. CHALKLIN, *The Provincial Towns of Georgian England. A Study of the Building Process, 1740–1820* (1974).

PETER CLARK (ed.), *Small Towns in Early Modern Europe* (Cambridge, 1995).

——, *The Cambridge Urban History of Britain* (forthcoming) vol. 2,

P. J. CORFIELD, *The Rise of the New Urban Society* (Milton Keynes, 1977).

——, *The Impact of English Towns, 1700–1800* (Oxford, 1982).

M. J. DAUNTON, *Progress and Poverty. An Economic and Social History of Britain 1700–1850* (Oxford, 1995).

JACK LANGTON, 'Urban growth and economic change from the seventeenth century to 1841', in PETER CLARK (ed.), *Cambridge Urban History of Britain* (forthcoming).

C. M. LAW, The growth of urban population in England and Wales, 1801–1911', *Transactions of the Institute of British Geographers*, xli (1967), pp. 125–45.

——, 'Some notes on the urban population in the eighteenth century', *Local Historian*, x, (1972), pp. 13–26.

ANGUS McINNES, *The English Town, 1660–1760* (1986).

ROGER SCHOFIELD, 'British Population Change, 1700–1871', in R. FLOUD and D. McCLOSKEY (eds), *The Economic History of Britain since 1700*, 2nd edn (Cambridge, 1994).

A. E. WRIGLEY, *People, Cities and Wealth* (Cambridge, 1987).

CHAPTER TWO: STRUCTURES OF AUTHORITY

L. DAVISON et al. (eds), *Stilling the Grumbling Hive. The Response to Social and Economic Problems in England, 1689–1750* (Stroud, 1992).

M. E. FALKUS, 'The British gas industry before 1850', *EcHR*, 2nd ser., xx (1967), pp. 494–508.

M. E. FALKUS, 'Lighting in the dark ages of English economic history: town streets before the industrial revolution', in D. C. COLEMAN and A. H. JOHN (eds), *Trade, Government and Economy in Pre-Industrial England* (1976), pp. 248–73.

E. L. JONES and M. E. FALKUS, 'Urban improvement and the English economy in the seventeenth and eighteenth centuries', in PETER BORSAY (ed.), *The Eighteenth-Century Town, 1688–1800* (1990), pp. 116–58.

R. NEWTON, *Eighteenth-Century Exeter* (Newton Abbot, 1984).

ADRIAN RANDALL and ANDREW CHARLESWORTH, *Markets, Market Culture and Popular Protest in Eighteenth-Century Britain and Ireland* (1996).

A. REDFORD, *A History of Local Government in Manchester* (1939), vol. 1, 'Manor and Township'.

F. W. SHEPPARD, *Local Government in St Marylebone, 1688–835: a study of the Vestry and Turnpike Trust* (1958).

SIDNEY and BEATRICE WEBB, *Statutory Bodies for Special Purposes* (1922).

CHAPTER THREE: URBAN ADMINISTRATION

PETER CLARK, 'The civic leaders of Gloucester 1580–1800', in CLARK (ed.), *The Transformation of English Provincial Towns, 1600–1800* (1984).

PETER CLARK and PAUL SLACK, *English Towns in Transition, 1500–1700* (Oxford, 1976).

P. J. CORFIELD, *The Impact of English Towns, 1700–1800* (Oxford, 1982).

DAVID EASTWOOD, *Government and Community in the English Provinces, 1700–1870* (1997).

BRYAN KEITH LUCAS, *The Unreformed Local Government System* (1980).

PAUL LANGFORD, *Public Life and the Propertied Englishman* (Oxford, 1990).

JOHN PREST, *Liberty and Locality. Parliament, Permissive Legislation and Ratepayers' Democracies in the Nineteenth Century* (Oxford, 1990).

A. TEMPLE PATTERSON, *A History of Southampton, 1700–1914*, vol. 1, Southampton Record Society (1966).

SIDNEY and BEATRICE WEBB, *The Manor and the Borough* (1908).

CHAPTER FOUR: THE DIVIDED SOCIETY

H. T. DICKINSON, *The Politics of the People in Eighteenth-Century Britain* (1994).

T. R. KNOX, 'Popular politics and provincial radicalism in Newcastle upon Tyne, 1769', *Albion*, xi (1979), pp. 223–41.

JOHN MILLER, 'The Crown and the borough charters in the reign of Charles II', *EHR*, c (1985), pp. 53–83.

SYLVIA MCINTYRE, 'The Scarborough Corporation quarrel, 1730–60', *Northern History*, xiv (1978), pp. 208–26.

FRANK O'GORMAN, *Voters, Patrons and Parties: the Unreformed Electoral System of Hanoverian England* (Oxford, 1989).

NICHOLAS ROGERS, *Whigs and Cities. Popular Politics in the Age of Walpole and Pitt* (Oxford, 1987).

KATHLEEN WILSON, *The Sense of the People. Politics, Culture and Imperialism in England, 1715–85* (Cambridge, 1994).

CHAPTER FIVE: URBAN GOVERNMENT AND THE MOVEMENT FOR REFORM

DEREK FRASER, *Power and Authority in the Victorian City* (Oxford, 1979).

G. B. M. A. FINLAYSON, 'The Municipal Corporation Commission and Report, 1833–35', *BIHR*, xxxvi (1963), pp. 36–52.

——, 'The politics of municipal reform in 1835', *EHR*, lxxi (1966), pp. 673–92.

BRYAN KEITH LUCAS, *The Unreformed Local Government Franchise. A Short History* (Oxford, 1952).

A. TEMPLE PATTERSON, *Radical Leicester* (Leicester, 1954).

J. A. PHILLIPS, 'From municipal matters to parliamentary principles: eighteenth-century borough politics in Maidstone', *JBS*, 27 (1988).

C. E. WELCH, 'Municipal reform in Plymouth', *TDA*, xciv (1966), pp. 318–38.

CHAPTER SIX: SOCIAL STRUCTURE AND SOCIAL EXPERIENCE

JONATHAN BARRY and CHRISTOPHER BROOKS, *The Middling Sort of People. Culture, Society and Politics in England, 1550–1800* (1994).

P. J. CORFIELD, 'Class by name and class by number', *History*, 72 (1987), pp. 38–61.

PETER EARLE, *The Making of the English Middle Class. Business, Society and Family Life in London, 1660–1730* (1989).

JOYCE ELLIS, 'A dynamic society: social relations in Newcastle upon Tyne, 1660–1760', in PETER CLARK (ed.), *The Transformation of English Provincial Towns* (1984), pp. 190–227.

M. DOROTHY GEORGE, *London Life in the Eighteenth Century*, repr. (1992).

ERIC HOPKINS, *The Rise of the Manufacturing Town. Birmingham and the Industrial Revolution* (Stroud, 1998).

MARGARET HUNT, *The Middling Sort. Commerce, Gender and the Family in England* (Berkeley and Los Angeles, CA, 1996).

R. J. MORRIS, *Class, Sect and Party: The Making of the British Middle Class. Leeds, 1820–1850* (1990).

JOHN RULE, *The Labouring Classes in Early Industrial England, 1750–1850* (1986).

L. SCHWARZ, *London in the Age of Industrialisation* (Cambridge, 1992).

E. P. THOMPSON, *Customs in Common* (1991).

CHAPTER SEVEN: URBAN CULTURE AND THE URBAN RENAISSANCE

JONATHAN BARRY, 'Provincial town culture, 1640–1760: urbane or civic?', in J. PITTOCK and A. WEAR (eds), *Interpretation and Cultural History in Eighteenth-Century Britain* (Basingstoke, 1991), pp. 198–234.

PETER BORSAY, *The English Urban Renaissance. Culture and Society in the Provincial Town, 1660–1770* (Oxford, 1989).

JOHN BREWER, *The Pleasures of the Imagination. English Culture in the Eighteenth Century* (1997).

C. W. CHALKIN, 'Capital expenditure on building for cultural purposes in provincial England, 1730–1830', *Business History*, 20 (1980), pp. 51–70.

MARK GIROUARD, *The English Town* (Yale, 1990).

ANGUS MCINNES, 'The emergence of a leisure town: Shrewsbury, 1660–1760', *P&P*, 120 (1988), pp. 53–87.

NEIL MCKENDRICK, JOHN BREWER and J. H. PLUMB (eds), *The Birth of a Consumer Society. The Commercialization of Eighteenth-Century England* (1982).

JOHN MONEY, *Experience and Identity. Birmingham and the West Midlands, 1760–1800* (Manchester, 1977).

ROY PORTER, 'Science, provincial culture and public opinion in enlightenment England', in PETER BORSAY (ed.), *The Eighteenth-Century Town, 1688–1820* (1990), pp. 243–67.

MICHAEL REED, 'The cultural role of small towns', in PETER CLARK (ed.), *Small Towns in Early Modern Europe* (Cambridge, 1995), pp. 121–47.

CONCLUSION

PETER BORSAY, 'The London connection: cultural diffusion and the eighteenth-century provincial town', *London Journal*, 19 (1994), pp. 21–35.

ROSEMARY SWEET, *The Writing of Urban Histories in Eighteenth-Century England* (Oxford, 1997).

DROR WAHRMAN, 'National society, provincial culture: an argument about the recent historiography of eighteenth-century Britain', *Social History*, xvii (1992), pp. 43–72.

Maps

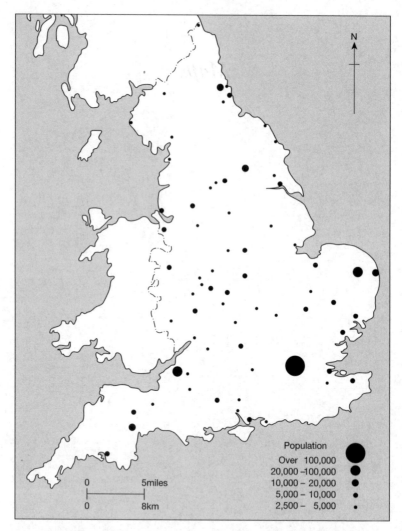

Map 1: Distribution of urban settlements with over 2,500 inhabitants in England and Wales in 1700. *Source*: P. J. Corfield, *The Impact of English Towns* (Oxford, 1982), figure 1, p. 12.

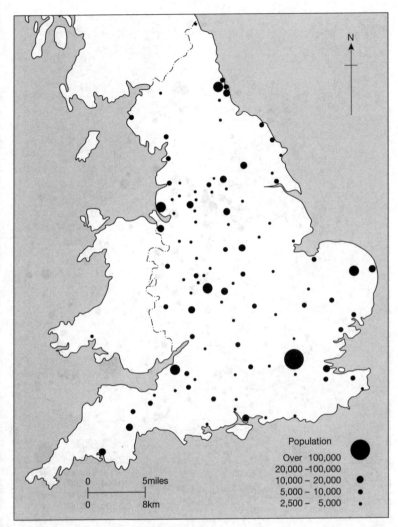

Map 2: Distribution of urban settlements with over 2,500 inhabitants in England and Wales in 1750. *Source*: P. J. Corfield, *The Impact of English Towns* (Oxford, 1982), figure 2, p. 13.

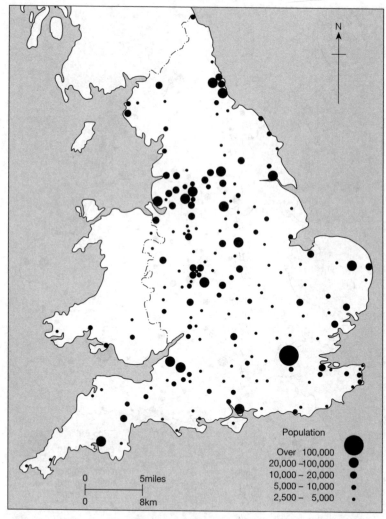

Map 3: Distribution of urban settlements with over 2,500 inhabitants in England and Wales in 1801. *Source*: P. J. Corfield, *The Impact of English Towns* (Oxford, 1982), figure 3, p. 14.

Index

Abingdon, 237
Abingdon, earl of, 60
accountability (in urban government), 51, 65, 125, 130, 135, 138, 142–3, 148, 188
Acland, James, 137–8, 143, 148, 153
Addison, Joseph, *see Spectator*
argicultural employment, 165, 167, 205, 229
agricultural revolution, 11, 175, 229
Aikin, John, 176, 193
aldermen, 36, 41, 48, 112, 121, 157, 161
Aldrich, Dean, 263
alehouses, 170, 200, 231–3
anglicanism, 207–12, *see also* religion
Anglo-Saxon constitution, 114, 127, 151, 220
animals (in towns), 77, 80, 229
apprenticeship, 37, 193
   decline of, 166–7
aristocracy, 56–7, 59–62, 129, 191–2
artisans, 164–5, 249, *see also* labouring sort
Arundel, 155
Ashford, 46
assemblies, 196–7, 199, 232, 234–6, 262
Assize of Bread, 71, 91, 98
assizes, 16–17, 67, 193, 240
Association Movement, 128, 135
Athenian Mercury, 245
Austen, Jane, 225, 236

back-to-back housing, 89, 175–7
Baines, Edward, 222
Baptists, 212, 213, 215, *see also* Dissent
Bath
   architecture, 84, 263
   city waits, 239
   corporation, 43, 51, 55
   freemen, 135
   leisure, 22, 181, 234–5, 248
   police, 47n
   population, 3, 24, 204
   town council, 161
Bath Journal, 77
Bedford, 63n
Benthamism, *see* utilitarianism
Berwick upon Tweed, 36, 63
Beverley, 17, 196
Bewdley, 66
Birmingham, 37, 171, 233
   Book Club, 189
   Chamber of Commerce, 164
   church and king riots, 93
   court leet, 29
   cultural life, 262
   improvement commission, 108, 113
   incorporation, 158
   police, 47n, 98
   population, 3, 12, 18, 19
   smoke abatement act, 89
   see also Hutton, William
Blackburn, 13, 19
Blackburne, John, 154
Blackstone, William, 123, 187n
Blake, William, 227

board of health (central), 159;
  (local), 176, 178, 208
Boase, Henry, 227
Bolton, 2, 13, 118
book clubs, *see* libraries
boroughs
  incorporated, *see* corporations
  parliamentary, 35, 61, 66,
    117–22
  rotten, 126–9
Boston, 145
Bourne, Henry, 200–1
bowling greens, 194
Bradford, 2, 12, 195, 227
Brand, John, 201
Bridgewater, 215
Bridport, 215, 217
Brighton, 3, 23–4, 30, 49
Bristol
  cathedral, 209
  charity, 103
  civic identity, 190, 195, 265
  corporation, 106, 112, 125, 137,
    149, 215
  corporation of the poor, 44, 102,
    125
  freemen, 54, 128
  high cross, 16, 260
  Hotwells, 43
  improvement, 101
  Library Society, 199, 247
  pollution, 20, 89
  population, 3, 19
  riots, 41, 93
  streets, 80
  water, 87
building regulations, 85–6
bullbaiting, 121, 171, 200, 202
bureaucracy, rise of, 14, 145–6
Burlington, earl of, 234
Burnley, 45
Burslem, 18
Bury (Lancs), 13
Bury St Edmunds, 3, 80, 144, 194
Butterworth, James, 177
Buxton, 22

Cambridge, 56–7
Campbell, Robert, 166, 181
canals, 11, 100, 258
Canterbury, 3, 13, 216
Carlisle, 16
catholics, 212, 217
cellar dwellings, 176–7
census, 14, 250
Chadwick, Edwin, 6, 79, 88, 178,
  223, 228
charity and philanthropy, 103–4,
  105, 131, 185, 205,
Charles II, King, 63, 90, 117, 119,
  122, 192
charters, 34, 42, 62–7, 117–19,
  122–3, 133–4, 148, 150–1,
  220
Chatham, 3
Chatterton, Thomas, 224
Cheltenham, 22, 24, 51, 86, 98,
  113, 153
Chester
  charters, 63, 134
  elections, 119–20
  music festival, 240
  population, 3–4
  trade, 21, 39
  walls, 242
Chichester, 52–3, 191
Chippenham, 143
cholera, 176, *see also* disease
church buildings, 210–12
circuses, 238
Cirenceseter, 16
city
  legal status, 7
  cathedral see, 17
  see also large town
City Elections Act, 65
city waits, 238–9
civic identity, 186–7, 252,
  260–6
civic ritual, 199–200, 261–2
Civil War, 62, 124, 192, 245
Civil Wars of Southampton, 144
Clarke, Joseph, 134

class, emergence of, 5, 179, 187–90, 197, *see also* social structure; middling sort
Clayton, John, 202
cockfighting, 121, 171, 199, 202, 233
coffee houses, 205, 245–6, 251
Coketown, 18, 228
Colchester, 2, 3, 13, 17, 118
    Castle Book Club, 246
Collier, John, 137
Colquhoun, Patrick, 96, 169n, 187
combinations, *see* strikes and collective action
commercial revolution, 11
commission for public accounts, 145
common council, 36, 41, *see also specific towns*
common land
    development of, 144
    disputes over, 134–5
competition, between towns, 23, 46, 249, 264–5
concerts, *see* music
conflict, 50, 115–39
Congleton, 160–1, 209
Congregationalists, 212, 213, 215, *see also* Dissent
constable, 30, 95–6, 125
consumerism, 183–5, 229, 259
Corfe Castle, 155
Corn Laws, 61, 190
corporations, 28, 33–7, 51–3, 70, 98–101, 208
    composition of, 36
    critique of, 130, 136–8, 141, 143–4, 149–52, 154–5, 189
    definition of, 34
    financial management of, 55–6, 59–62, 105–8, 134, 143–4
    judicial powers, 35
corporations of the poor, 44, 50, 102, 113, 125, *see also* poor relief
Corporation Mirror, 136, 150

cotton, 13, 19, 47
county towns, 16, 193–4, 197
Country Wife, The, 210
court leet, 28–30, 51, 78, 151–2
Courtney, John, 196
Coventry, 3, 4, 19, 39, 97, 131, 147, 158, 215
Cowper, William, 141, 223
crime, 81, 94–8, *see also* law and order
Cross, John, 112, 142
Croydon, 16
curfew, 81, 94
Currie, John, 176

Deal, 66, 104
Defoe, Daniel
    Essay on Friendly Societies, 194
    [Andrew Morton] *Parochial Tyranny*, 125
    Tour through the whole Island of Great Britain, 8, 17, 39, 98, 194, 221, 234
demography, *see* population
Derby, 4, 93, 97
Deserted Village, 14
Dickens, Charles, *see* Coketown
disease, 12, 78, 88–9, 127, 177–8, 226–7
Dissent, 211–18
    and middling sort, 189–90
    in local government, 49, 64, 124, 158, 160, 215–16
    in politics, 131–2
dockyards, 15, 21, *see also* port towns
domestic service, 168, 205–6
Doncaster, 17
Dorchester, 52
Dover, 43, 155
Downham Market, 45
Drake, Francis, 101, 264
Dudley, 4
Dunsford, Martin, 134, 216
Dunwich, 63
Durham, 48
Dyer, William, 216

East Anglia, 12, 21
East India Company, 150, 193
East Looe, 31
East Riding, 16
Eden, Sir Frederick, 15, 102, 165
Eld, George, 147
elections
  civic, 56, 116, 117–22
  parliamentary, 116, 117–22, 193,
    232
Ely, 8
Epsom, 23
Evelyn, John, *Fumifugium*, 8
Exeter
  chamber, 39, 43, 181
  civic elections, 121
  corporation of the poor, 125
  improvement commission, 48,
    142, 148, 254
  inns, 232
  literary and philosophical
    society, 249
  population, 3

factories, 18, 166, 170–1, 203
Farnham, 16
feasts, 107, 149, 199–200, 203, 232
Ferriar, John, 178
Fielding, Henry, 96, 204
fire, 84–5
Fisher, Jabez, 84
Fleming, Thomas, 58–9
Flower, Benjamin, 132
framework knitters, 172
franchise, 117–19, 127–9, 151–2,
  157
freedom, sale of, 107
freemasonry, 186–7, 202
freemen, 36, 54, 111, 157
  and economic regulation, 99–100
  participation in politics, 118–22,
    136
friendly societies, 38, 169–70

Gales, Joseph, 132
gas, provision of, 46–9

gas lighting, 82–3
gender, 203–7
Gentleman's Magazine, 245
gentrification, 193–7, *see also* social
  mobility
gentry, influence in towns, 192–7,
  259
Gilbert's Act, 71,
gin, consumption of, 93, 223
Glorious Revolution, 62, 64–5, 70,
  119
Gloucester, 3–4, 43, 101
godly cities, 101
Great Dunmow, 143
Great Reform Act, 61, 97, 127–8,
  153, 190
Great Yarmouth, 3–4, 21, 60, 68,
  80, 121, 151
Grosvenor family, 86, 119
guardians of the poor, 43, 52, 55,
  79, 102, 113, 121, 124, *see also*
  corporations of the poor; poor
  relief
guides and directories, 115, 181,
  221–2
guilds, 28, 37–9, 166–7, 186–7, 261
Gwynn, John, 85

Halifax, 4, 12, 16, 30
Hammet, Sir Benjamin, 50
Hanway, Joseph, 71, 168
Harrogate, 24
Hastings, 23
Hereford, 15
Hewson, Joseph, 132
high church politics, 50, 124–5,
  208, 210, 212
hinterlands, 20–1, 228–9
Hobbes, Thomas, 62, 266
Hobhouse's Act, 32
Hogarth William
  Four Stages of Cruelty, 174
  Gin Lane and Beer Street, 174,
    223
  Harlot's Progress, The, 174, 207,
    223, 226

Industry and Idleness, 166
Rake's Progress, 226
Holt, Daniel, 132
Home Office, 42, 69–72, 159
hospitals, 130–1, 185, 188
hotels, 233
Hull
  civic identity, 263
  corporation, 39, 43, 86, 101,
    106, 145–6, 155, 158
  population, 3
  society for the purpose of
    literary information, 250–1
  town council, 158
  trade, 20
Hull Portfolio, 138, 153
Hume, David, 221–2
Humphry Clinker, 198, 226, 248
Huntingdon, 151
Hutton, William, 27, 38, 54, 194,
    233, 260

improvement acts, 42–7, *see also*
    statutory bodies for special
    purposes
improvement commissions, 44–5,
    47–52, 56, 78, 100, 113, 185,
    195–6, 254
industrial towns, 11, 12, 15
industry, employment in, 11, 166–7
inns, *see* alehouses, 15, 231–3
Ipswich, 3–4, 13, 21, 36

Jacobinism, 127
Jacobites, 93, 120, 125, 235
James II, King, 63–4, 122
Jenkins, Alexander, 254
Johnson, Samuel, 225
Joseph Andrews, 204
justices of the peace, 35, 39–42,
    66–71, 91–2, 102, 111, 233,
    237

Keighley, 45
Kendal, 197, 212, 232
King, Gregory, 187

King's Bench, court of, 122–3,
    137–8, 148
Kings Lynn, 3, 101, 195
Knaresborough, 24

labouring sort, 164–79, 200–3,
    227–8, *see also* popular culture
Lancashire, 12, 13, 47, 63n, 213–14
large towns, 14, 227–8
Latimer, Richard, 142
law and order
  crime, 94–8
  riots, 70, 90–4, 202–3, 227
lectures, public, 251
Leeds, 16
  corporation, 52
  living conditions, 175
  partisan conflict, 132
  police, 47n
  population, 3, 18
  town council, 160–1, 263
  urban elite, 192, 197
  vestry, 32
  voluntary societies, 188
Leicester
  corporation, 39, 155
  improvement, 46, 54
  manufactures, 12, 19
  population, 3–4
  town clerk, 57
  town council, 158
leisure towns, 15, 22–5, 254
Lewes, 29, 193
liberty, ideas of, 110, 117–18, 219,
    220
libraries, 246–9
Lichfield, 155
Lincoln, 47n, 160, 259
Liskeard, 62
literacy, 243
Liverpool
  Athenaeum, 246, 253
  corporation, 39, 43, 52n, 63n,
    101, 106
  cultural life, 224, 264
  living conditions, 175–7

music hall, 239
police, 98
pollution, 89
population, 3, 12, 19
spa, 24
town council, 158
trade, 16, 221
vestry, 32, 76
livestock, *see* animals (in towns)
local legislation, 42–3, 59–60,
    100–7, 158, *see also*
    improvement acts
Lockhart, John Ingram, 61
London
  attitudes towards, 224, 225–7
  churches, 214
  coffee houses, 246
  corporation, 63–5, 106, 111,
    157, 215
  criminality, 47, 95–6
  cultural influence, 193–4, 195,
    219, 257–66
  employment, 166–7
  improvement acts, 45, 47
  mortality, 178
  planning, 84–5
  population, 2–3, 7–8
  riots, 90
  season, 172
  shops, 181–2
  street lighting, 82
  women, 205
London Tradesman, The, 166, 181
Lord Lieutenants, 69
Loughborough, 231
low church politics, 50, 124, 208,
    210, *see also* Dissent
Lowther, Sir John, 85–6
Luddites, 93, 190
Ludlow, 133
luxury, 181, 226, 265
Lyndhurst, Lord, 155–6

Macclesfield, 4, 17, 55
Mackenzie, James, 77–8
Macky, John, 246

magistrates, *see* justices of the
    peace
Maidstone, 55, 121–2, 133, 155,
    231
Maitland, F.W., 35, 150
Malmesbury, 112
Malthus, Thomas, 227
Malvern, 22
Manchester
  assembly rooms, 235
  court leet, 29, 58, 89, 112, 142
  cultural life, 197
  incorporation of, 158
  literary and philosophical
    society, 178, 256
  living conditions, 175–7, 227
  manorial structures, 8, 29
  manufactures and trade, 17, 19,
    39
  market tolls, 138
  partisan conflict, 123–4, 132
  police commissioners, 49, 51, 54,
    58–9, 82–3, 87, 97, 132
  population, 3, 12, 18
  Sunday schools, 217
mandamus, writs of, 122
manorial courts, *see* court leet
Mansfield, Lord, 123
manufacturing towns, 12, 17–19,
    175, 252
Margate, 23, 43
market buildings, 16, 98
market regulation, 98–101
market towns, 15, 91
Marlborough, duke of, 57, 60–1
Marsh, John, 191
Matthews, William, 103
Mayhew, Henry, 207
mayor, office of, 36, 104–5, 107,
    112
mechanics institutes, 249
Melcombe Regis, 23
Merceron, Joseph, 58–9
Merewether, H.A., 64, 151–2
methodism, 212, 216, *see also*
    Dissent

Metropolitan Police Act, 97
middle class, *see* middling sort;
    class, emergence of
middling sort, 179–91, 194–7
    associations, 185–90
    education, 182
    incomes, 180
    and lifestyle, 182–5
    occupations, 180–2
    values, 187–8
    see also class, emergence of
migration, 12, 163, 175, 177–8,
    225
mobs, *see* law and order, riots
monopolies, 47, 69, 83
moral economy, 91–2
morality, 104–5, 202, 218, 226, 237
Morris, Claver, 239
Mortlock, John, 56–7
Morton, Andrew, *see* Defoe, Daniel
Moseley family, 29
Moss, William, 24, 89, 177
MPs, 59–62, 117, 192
Municipal Corporation Act, 62, 67,
    72, 148, 152–61, 211, 239
music, 238–40

Nash, Beau, 23, 235
Newark, 66, 103
Newcastle
    assembly rooms, 235–6
    corporation, 43, 106
    court of guild, 37–8, 136
    freemen's hospital, 134
    hostmen, 21
    keelmen, 38, 91, 170
    literary and philosophical
        society, 249–50
    own moor, 135–6, 144
    population, 3
    radicalism, 130–1, 189
    trade, 20; water, 87
newspapers, *see* press
Nonconformity, *see* Dissent
Norfolk, 213
Northampton, 19, 77, 84

Norwich
    corporation, 36, 39, 154, 215
    elections, 120–2
    freemen, 128
    hinterland, 229
    improvement, 54
    population, 3, 8
    radicalism, 130–1
    water, 87
    workhouse, 173
Nottingham
    common land, 135
    corporation, 145
    dissent, 131, 215
    elections, 133
    gentry presence, 191–2
    living conditions, 175–7
    manufactures, 19
    population, 3–4, 12
    riots, 70, 93, 97

Oakes, James, 80
occasional conformity, 124, 215
Oldfield, Thomas, 129
Oldham, 3, 13, 18, 19, 30
oligarchy, 36, 41, 51–2, 56–9
    opposition to, 118
    see also corporations, critique
        of
opera, 238
overseers of the poor, 30, *see also*
    poor relief; corporations of
    the poor
Oxford
    architecture, 237
    churches, 211
    corporation, 60–1, 98–9, 181
    Holywell music rooms, 61, 239
    paving (improvement)
        commissioners, 54, 78–9,
        108–9
    population, 4, 204
    prostitutes, 207
    riots (bread), 70, 93, 98–9
    town clerk, 57–8
    town council, 158, 160

trading companies, 38, 57, 186
water, 86–7;

Paine, Thomas, 153
Palgrave, Francis, 152
parish, *see* vestry
parks, 242
Parkes, Joseph, 154
Parliament, 36, 42, 45, 53, 59,
    64–73, 155–9
  House of Lords, 155–7
Paul, Sir George Onesipherous,
    110
Peard, Oliver, 56
Peel, Sir Robert, 72, 155
Penzance, 98
Percival, Thomas, 178, 250
permissive legislation, 71–2
Peterloo, 93, 127, 190, 227
Phillips, Richard, 132
Place, Francis, 164, 170–1
playhouse, see theatre
Plymouth, corporation, 39, 100,
    107, 148, 210
  improvement commission, 113
  market, 99
  police, 47n
  population, 3, 20
  quarter sessions, 42
  riots, 70
  streets, 79
  town council, 158
  water, 86–8, 100
Pocoke, Bishop, 23, 191
police, 47, 95–8, 160, *see also* crime
    and law and order
politeness, 187–8, 198–203
politics, 50, 115–39, 160–1, 235,
    see also radicalism
poll books, 132–3
pollution, 88–9
population, 2–4, 7–14, 18–19, 24,
    225, 227–8
Poole, 21, 107, 133, 215, 216
Poor Law Amendment Act of 1834,
    72n, 102, 154, 159, 174

poor relief, 30, 44, 55, 101–4,
    172–4, 201
popular culture, 168–9, 200–3, 233
popular protest, *see* law and order
port towns, 11, 12, 15, 19–22, 91,
    100–1, 106, 136–8, *see also*
    under specific towns
Portsmouth, 3, 4, 20, 39
Powell Gabriel, 54, 147
press, 132–4, 148, 198, 244–5
Preston
  charter (1828), 67
  corporation, 100
  gas, 83
  gentry presence, 196
  guild merchant, 261
  living conditions, 175
  manufactures, 19
  population, 3, 13, 18, 67
Presyterians, 212, 215, *see also*
    Dissent
Priestley, Joseph, 247
Pritchard, Stephen, 104
privileges, 7, 34, 39, 53, 99, 116,
    117–18, 133–5, 150, 156–7
professions, 180–1, *see also*
    middling sort
promenades, 241–3
property qualifications, 30, 47–9,
    69, 157–8
prostitution, 206–7, 226, 243
provincial culture, 257–66
pseudo-gentry, 190–6
public health, 87–8
  boards of health (local),
public service, 101, 109–14

Quakers
Quarter sessions, 16, 28, 30, 40, 42,
    53, 69, 78, 90, 99, 100, 239,
    see also justices of the peace
quo warranto, writs of, 63–4, 172

race meetings, 199, 241
radicalism, 116, 127–38, 141–3,
    202

Ranelagh gardens, 242–3
rates, 53–5, 108–9, 160, 253–4
reform, 6, 116, 141–61
religion, 207–18
  and political divisions, 116,
    124–5, 131–2
*Report of the Royal Commission on
  Municipal Corporations*, 35,
    41, 52, 55, 57, 61, 96, 98,
    112, 137–8, 147, 154–7,
    217
resort towns, *see* leisure towns *and*
  spas
Richard, William, 195
Richmond, duke of, 52–3
Ridding, Thomas, 144
Ridley, Sir Matthew, 135–6
riots
  food, 91–2
  Gordon, 93, 202
  political, 93
  religious, 93, 202
Roberts, William, 36
Rochdale, 4n, 214
Rochester, 155
Romney Marsh, 7
Romsey, 155
Roscoe, William, 250
Royal Commissioners, *see Report of*
rural society, 193, 229
Russell, Lord John, 153, 179
Ryder Dudley, 56–7

Salford, 4, 227
Salisbury, 3–4, 13, 44, 254
Sandwich, 21
Sayer, Edward, 75
Scarborough, 23, 122, 160, 196,
    253
scavengers, 78–9
seaside resorts, 22, 23
sewers and waste disposal, 46,
    77–9, 86–8
Shaftesbury, 61
Sheffield, 3, 13, 18, 39, 127, 211,
    214, 236

Shrewsbury, 4, 102, 113, 174, 194,
    242, 246
slums, *see* back-to-back housing
small towns, 8–9
Smollett, Tobias, *see Humphry
  Clinker*
sociability, 184–6
social mobility, 198–9, 223–4
social structure, 5, 163–218
shops and shopkeepers, 181–2, 204
societies, 185–9
  Antiquarian, 249
  literary and philosophical,
    249–50
  Royal 249
Somner, William, 260
South Shields, 4
Southampton, corporation, 55,
    109, 144
  corporation of the poor, 159n
  improvement commission, 52–3
  spa, 23
  streets, 80
  trade, 21
spa towns, 15, 17, 22–5, 199
  see also specific towns
Spectator, 80, 243, 245–6
Speed, John, 153
Spranger, John, 88, 111
St Albans, 150
St Monday, 171
St Neots, 45
Stage licensing act, 237
Stamford, 15, 159n, 161, 248
  bull running 201, 263
standard of living, 12
state, growth of, 40, 73
  relation to towns, 28, 62–73
Statute of Artificers, 167
Statute of Winchester, 95
statutory bodies for special
    purposes, 28, 44–56, *see also*
    improvement commissions
Stephens, A.J., *see* Merewether,
    H.A.
Stockport, 3, 13, 47n

Stoke, 3
Stoney Stratford, 48
Stow, John, 221
streets, regulation of, 76–81
    lighting, 81–4
    paving, 79–80, 110
strikes and collective action,
        169–70
Sturges Bourne Act, 32, 72, 126
suburbs, growth of, 112, 200, 229
Sunday schools, 217
Sunderland, 3–4
surveyors, 145, 180
    of highways, 30
Swansea, 12, 54, 89, 147

Tatler, 245–6
Taunton, 17, 50, 52, 106, 128, 257
Taunton, William Elias, 57–8
taverns, 231, *see also* alehouses
Test and Corporation Act, 49, 124,
        131–2, 211, 217
textile towns, 13, 17–19, 92, 127,
        175
theatre, 199, 236–8
Thomas, Vaughan, 208
Throsby, John, 201
time discipline, 170–1
The Times, 153
Tiverton, 4, 13, 17, 56–7, 92, 134,
        151
Tocqueville, Alexis de, 18, 166, 219
Toleration Act, 124, 212
tolls, levying of, 107
    opposition to, 136–8
Tories, 50, 55, 63–5, 120–2, 124,
        151, 153, 156, 158, 159, 160,
        197
Toulmin, Joshua, 50, 257
town clerk, 56–8
town councils, 107, 157–61
towns, attitudes to, 219–28
    definitions of, 7–10
Townshend, Viscount, 60
trade combinations, 92–3, 169–70
trading companies, *see* guilds

traffic, 76–7, 81
Trusler, Rev. John, 198, 242
Tucker, Joseph, 210
Tunbridge Wells, 22, 85, 243, 251
turnpikes, 11, 45, 100
    trusts, 16, 193, 196, 258
Tynemouth, 3–4

Ulverston, 15
Unitarians, 131, 212, *see also*
    Dissent
urban histories, 252, 260
urban identity, *see* civic identity
urban planning, 84–6
urban typologies, 14–25
urban renaissance, 6, 194, 219–31
    financing of, 253–4
    timing of, 251–5
urbanization, 2, 9–10, 220–8,
    see also urban demography
utilitarianism, 154

Vaughan, Robert, 222
Vauxhall gardens, 242–3
vestry, 27, 30–3, 58, 106, 125–6,
        209–10
    select, 31, 125–6
    St George's, Hanover Square,
        32, 96
    St Martin in the Fields, 32
    St Marylebone, 32, 79
    Whitechapel, 32
Vestry clerk, 58
villages, 7, 14

Wakefield, 12, 17
walks, *see* promenades
walls and fortifications, 242
Walpole, Robert, 65, 93
war, impact of, 20–1
    American Independence, 21,
        131
    French Revolutionary and
        Napoleonic, 40, 35, 146
    Seven Years, 45, 254
    Spanish Succession, 92

Warwick, 84, 134, 151, 154, 193, 254
watching and ward, 95, *see also*
    lighting *and* police
water, provision of, 86–8, 100
Webb, Sidney and Beatrice, 6, 27,
    35, 44, 57, 68, 157
Wells, 239
Wesley, John, 212, 216, 237
West Looe, 151
Westminster, 13, 45, 71, 88, 128
    as centre of government, *see*
    Parliament
West Riding, 12, 13, 210–11, 263
Western Times, 142
Weymouth, 23
Whigs, 50, 63–5, 119–22, 124, 151,
    153, 154, 156, 158, 160, 197,
    212
Whitby, 51, 58
Whitehaven, 20, 21, 85–6, 101
Wigan, 4, 13
Wilkes, John, 127, 135
Williamson, Samuel, 208–9
Wilson, John, 161
Winchester, 17, 37, 234
Witton, Stephen, 232
Wolverhampton, 4, 45, 51, 109,
    112, 148n

women and domestic service,
    205–6
    and urban government, 31
    and urban lifestyle, 204–5, 248,
    253
    see also prostitution
Wood Beavis, 56–7
Wood, Isaac, 174
Wood, John, 263
Worcester, 3, 4, 13, 221, 240
workhouses, 44, 101–2, 173–4
working class, 190, *see also*
    labouring sort
workshop production, 166
Wright, Joseph, 251
Wyvill Christopher, 128

York
    assembly rooms, 234
    civic identity, 264
    corporation, 43, 52, 101,
        145
    police, 47n
    population, 2–4, 206
    trade, 21, 39, 264
    walls, 242
    water, 86–7
Young, Arthur, 79